Evangelism
after
Christendom

Evangelism after Christendom

The Theology and Practice of Christian Witness

Bryan P. Stone

BrazosPress

a division of Baker Publishing Group
Grand Rapids, Michigan

Published by Brazos Press
a division of Baker Publishing Group
P.O. Box 6287, Grand Rapids, MI 49516-6287
www.brazospress.com

Printed in the United States of America

Library of Congress Cataloging-in-Publication Data
Stone, Bryan P., 1959–
    Evangelism after christendom : the theology and practice of Christian witness /
Bryan P. Stone.
        p. cm.
    Includes bibliographical references and index.
    ISBN 10: 1-58743-194-7 (pbk.)
    ISBN 978-1-58743-194-4 (pbk.)
        1. Evangelistic work. 2. Evangelistic work—History. 3. Witness bearing (Christianity) 4. Missions. I. Title.
    BV3790.S85 2006
    269′.2—dc22   2006023654

In loving memory of my father, Henry,
a witness to the beauty of Christian holiness.

Contents

Introduction

Reclaiming the E-word

Shortly after I began teaching at Boston University School of Theology, a colleague placed in my hands a brochure introducing the Women's Interfaith Action Group. The brochure described the group as "a weekly gathering of women from all faiths, as well as those who feel drawn to the spiritual, but who do not claim a particular religion." The group plays an important role on campus in providing a forum for sharing and discussing religious and spiritual histories, commonalities, and differences. As my colleague pointed out, what was especially interesting about the brochure was the following sentence, in particular its use of the word *evangelization*:

> An environment of mutual respect is maintained in which members may freely share beliefs and differences without fear of disparagement or evangelization.

To *evangelize* means literally to offer "good news" or a "welcome message." Isaiah 52:7 celebrates the bringer of such good news:

> How beautiful upon the mountains
> > are the feet of the messenger who announces peace,
> who brings good news,
> > who announces salvation,
> > who says to Zion, "Your God reigns."

But clearly, today evangelism does not always mean good news, and the feet of the evangelist are not considered so beautiful. For many people in our world, both Christian and non-Christian, evangelism[1] is neither welcomed nor warranted. As the brochure made clear, this is especially true in the context of interfaith dialogue, where evangelism is perceived as something to be feared, as a barrier to mutual respect, careful listening, open sharing, and cooperation. But it is also the case in the wider context of an increasingly pluralistic culture, where the notion of evangelizing is automatically connected to an attitude of intolerance and superiority toward others—a belligerent and one-sided attempt to convert others to *our* way of seeing things, with the necessary implication that those who do not believe as we do are lost or in error. For some, the word calls to mind a shameful history of forced conversions, inquisitions, fraudulent television preachers, religious wars, crusades, genocide, colonization, and the ruthless expansion of Western power throughout the world. The E-word has become a dirty word—an embarrassment to the Christian and an affront to the non-Christian.

Is it possible nonetheless to reclaim the E-word as expressing something positive, vital, and beautiful about the Christian life? Might evangelism be a practice that calls forth the highest in the creative energies, intellect, and imagination of Christians rather than a crass exercise in marketing the church to consumers within a world of abundant and competing options? I think so. But given the weighty cultural, historical, and theological baggage attached to evangelism and given the church's temptation to acquiesce to the world's demand that the gospel be good news on the world's own terms, any such reconstruction of evangelism will not be simple or easy.

Rethinking and reconstructing evangelism is a task that must be taken up in every era and in every part of the world where the church takes seriously its calling to "announce peace" and to bear faithful, public, and embodied witness to God's reign in its own context. But evangelism is especially problematic today for those of us in societies where Christianity has historically been tied to the center of political, economic, and cultural power but in which the old "Christendom" model has for some time now been crumbling. The church that once was at the center of Western civilization and could presume for itself a privileged voice has increasingly found that center unraveling and itself in a sort of diaspora at the margins, though in a decentered and fragmented civilization, one might question the adequacy of the language of "center" and "margins" altogether (see Roxburgh 1997:5–12).The church can no longer assume as it once did that the surrounding culture will assist in the task of pro-

---

1. The words *evangelism* and *evangelization* are interchangeable. I have yet to find a compelling rationale for the use of one over the other, and the fact that I use *evangelism* throughout this book is simply due to its wider use in the circles in which I travel.

ducing Christians. The home base from which Christians thought to Christianize the rest of the world feels less and less like "home," despite the desperate attempts by some to keep it that way. A growing number of theological voices are helping us to ask whether Christians should have ever yielded to the temptation of making ourselves at home in the first place.

Ironically, it may be that it is precisely from a position of marginality that the church is best able to announce peace and to bear witness to God's peaceable reign in such a way as to invite others to take seriously the subversive implications of that reign. It may be that through humility, repentance, and disavowal of its former advantages, so that those things that were once "gains" to the church now come to be regarded as "loss" (Phil. 3:7), a church at the periphery *of* the world may yet be a church *for* the world. If so, then I take as fundamentally misguided the efforts by some to claw our way back as a church to the center of culture with renewed Constantinian vigor, whether through hostile takeover or whimpering accommodation. I likewise consider it folly to continue down one of the two now standard paths evangelism has taken within modernity. The first is preoccupied with establishing the intellectual respectability of the gospel in terms of purportedly wider or more universal criteria for what counts as truth and plausibility. The second busies itself with demonstrating the practical value and usefulness of Christian faith for persons in a society that determines *value* by the logic of the marketplace and measures *usefulness* by service to the nation, the economy, or the private well-being of individual egos. On the contrary, it is from the margins—epistemologically, culturally, politically, economically, and spiritually—that a fragmented, post-Christendom culture will have to be evangelized.

Evangelizers often fear the margins, because they worry that the church may go unnoticed. It is thought that only from the center can the entire world be reached, and it is at the center, or so we are tempted to believe, that firm foundations can be secured, the better to defend and propagate the gospel and to ensure the inevitability of faith. We are embarrassed by a gospel that isn't immediately "relevant" to prevailing needs and desires or that has no self-evident truths or irresistible power to convince and convert any and all whom it touches. The gospel needs our help, and the support of the center.

On one level, as John Howard Yoder has argued (1992b), the error here is in assuming that the center is actually the more universal and rational world (the "wider public") that we dream it to be, rather than just one more form of particularity like the margins, and frequently narrower than the margins in terms of the range of reality it takes into account. On another level, however, this evangelistic refusal of vulnerability, particularity, and marginality is finally a refusal of the way of the cross, a way that forgoes the privileges and security allied with winning and opts instead for costly obedience, incarnation, and gospel nonconformity. What the gospel needs most is not intellectual brokers or cultural diplomats but rather saints who have taken up the way of the cross and in whose lives the gospel is visible, palpable, and true. It needs disciples who follow Jesus with or without the support of their culture and for whom the power of the gospel is demonstrated not through winning but through obedience. Evangelism from the margins, then, requires no prior foundations in either human experience or reason that would somehow shore up the relevance, truth, power, or beauty of its gospel. It does, however, require a *people* that has been made into the temple of God in which the Spirit dwells, built upon the church's only secure foundation, Jesus Christ (1 Cor. 3:10–17).

Christian evangelism, as I will argue throughout this book, is *pacifist* in every way. The good news is, as Isaiah said, the good news of "peace." But this peace is not only the content and substance of evangelism; it is its very form. Christian evangelism refuses every violent means of converting others to that peace, whether that violence is cultural, military, political, spiritual, or intellectual. Evangelism requires only the peaceable simplicity of an offer and an invitation to "come and see" (John 1:46).

This does not mean that there is no *apologetic* dimension to evangelism—no room for making a case publicly, intellectually, or culturally for Christian faith. The character of Christian evangelism is not only invitation but also summons (cf. Webb 2004:27). It does mean, however, that a Christian apologetics must refuse to consider unbelievers as either barbarian or irrational. It also means that a Christian apologetics may very well rest on an aesthetics more than on an epistemology or a metaphysics, since, in declining every "secure" foundation for belief other than Jesus Christ, evangelism relies from first to last on the beauty of holiness made real in the church by the operation of the Holy Spirit. The very possibility of Christian evangelism, then, is premised wholly upon the faithfulness of the Spirit's witness in our lives rather than our own ability to calculate and predict how our obedience might translate into effectiveness.

Jesus talked about the reign of God as a radically new order that comes to put an end to the age-old patterns of wealth and poverty, domination and subordination, insider and outsider that are deeply ingrained in the way we relate to one another on this planet. But in order for that new order to become a serious option *for* the world, it must be visibly and imaginatively embodied *in* the world. And if Scripture is a faithful witness, the purpose of God throughout history is the creation and formation of a new people whose mission is to do just that. The fact that the old Christendom arrangements have been shattering therefore may prove to be liberating for the church and for the practice of evangelism. But then evangelism will have to be understood not as an adventure in "winning friends and influencing people"[2] but as a fundamentally subversive activity, born out of a posture of eccentricity (living "off center" or "outside the center," at the margins) and out of the cultivation of such deviant practices as sharing bread with the poor, loving enemies, refusing violence, forgiving sins, and telling the truth.

Creative reconstructions of evangelism are being attempted today, and they succeed in expanding the church by adapting it to new generations that are put off by boring liturgies, irrelevant preaching, and stuffy pipe-organ music. But while these reconstructions have triumphed in making the church more relevant to the tastes, expectations, preferences, and quest for self-fulfillment of both the unchurched and the dechurched, they have utterly failed to challenge the racism, individualism, violence, and affluence of Western culture. They in no way subvert an existing unjust order but rather mimic and sustain it. Our greatest challenge is to find ways of practicing evangelism in a post-Christendom culture without at the same time playing by the rules of that culture. But how to move forward is the question. One thing is certain; those who have long been marginalized, colonized, or made minorities by Christendom, and who therefore never had a stake in its survival in the first place, will have much to teach the rest of us.

This book attempts a reconstruction of evangelism for a post-Christendom, postmodern era. But it must begin with a caution. Christendom, like the Constantinian imagination that produced it, has proved to be "a hard habit to break" (Hauerwas 1991:18). One of the recurring claims in the popular literature on evangelism is that in order to practice a post-Christendom evangelism, the church must discard its "stained glass culture" so that it can better reach unchurched secular people in a pluralistic world. Christendom is thus identified with high-steepled church buildings, ancient liturgies, and stodgy hymns, and the elimination of these obstacles is presented as the way forward in becoming more post-Christendom and less "ecclesiocentric." Where evangelism in the past has been imposing, inflexible, and intolerant, contemporary evangelism must now become an exercise in reassuring the world that it has nothing to fear from us. Walt Kallestad, pastor of the large and fast-growing Community of Joy church in Arizona puts the matter this way in his book *Entertainment Evangelism*, "Effective churches are invitational,

2. I am here referencing the old self-help classic by Dale Carnegie, *How to Win Friends and Influence People* (1936), the philosophy of which surfaces as a goal toward which evangelizing Christians should aim in Hunter 1992:35.

not confrontational" (1996:82). In fact, "the Christian Church needs to be even friendlier than Disneyland" (81). Apparently, if the gospel is to reach our contemporaries, it must not offend. It cannot make—or at least it cannot begin with—demands. The strangeness of the church and its worship and the offensive nature of its gospel must be mitigated or abolished if evangelism is to be reconstructed and made effective in a post-Christendom world. "Tolerance," as R. R. Reno has suggested, "is the executive virtue of our time" (2002:100).

This habit of mind is, of course, not a uniquely twenty-first-century phenomenon. Almost two centuries ago, Søren Kierkegaard attacked it (rather than pipe organs) as the very heart of Christendom. He described the modern clergyperson thus:

> A nimble, adroit, lively man, who in pretty language, with the utmost ease, with graceful manners . . . knows how to introduce a little Christianity, but easily, as easily as possible. In the New Testament, Christianity is the profoundest wound that can be inflicted upon a man, calculated on the most dreadful scale to collide with everything—and now the clergyman has perfected himself in introducing Christianity in such a way as it signifies nothing, and when he is able to do this to perfection he is regarded as a paragon. But this is nauseating! Oh, if a barber has perfected himself in removing the beard so easily that one hardly notices it, that's well enough; but in relation to that which is precisely calculated to wound, to perfect oneself so as to introduce it in such a way that if possible it is not noticed at all—that is nauseating. (1956a:258)

Christian evangelism, while invitational, is a subversive practice. The church that is called to reach and engage the world should not be surprised to find itself also living in contradiction to that world. Contrary to prevailing opinions, I do not believe that our most daunting challenge as a church is *whether* we can reach unchurched secular people but rather *how* we reach them. We kid ourselves if we think we have moved beyond Christendom simply because we are able to reach more people by getting rid of our stained glass and stuffy sermons and providing a "product" that is more user-friendly. Neither large-scale revivals that boast thousands of converts nor fast-growing megachurches that have dropped from the sky into suburban parking lots as of late are in any way indications of the proximity of God's reign, nor is their winsomeness and friendliness to be equated with Isaiah's "peace." In fact, the failure of evangelism in our time is implied as much by the vigorous "success" of some churches in North America as by the steady decline of others.

On the contrary, our greatest challenge is that in reaching secular people we will fail to offer them anything specifiably Christian. And though we may end up recovering the E-word, the offensive and scandalous dimensions of the gospel will have been softened, disguised, forgotten, or placed on the back burner. We may reach more people, but the gospel with which we reach them will have become a version of "Christendom lite," a pale reflection of consumer preferences and a market-driven accommodation to felt needs. The subversive nature of the gospel will then have been itself subverted, and that which is unprecedented and radical about the church will have been compromised in favor of mere ratings.

What This Book Is About

The thesis of this book is that the most evangelistic thing the church can do today is to be the church—to be formed imaginatively by the Holy Spirit through core practices such as worship, forgiveness, hospitality, and economic sharing into a distinctive people in the world, a new social option, the body of Christ. It is the very shape and character of the church as the Spirit's "new creation" that is the witness to God's reign in the world and so both the source and aim of Christian evangelism. On this understanding, the *missio dei* is neither the individual, private, or interior salvation of individuals nor the Christianization of entire cultures and social orders. It is rather the creation of a people who in every culture are both "pulpit and paradigm" of a new humanity (Yoder 1997:41). Insofar as evangelism is the heart of this mission (cf. Robert 1997), this very people constitutes both the public invitation and that to which the invitation points. That is why all Christian evangelism is fundamentally rooted in ecclesiology. It can even be said that the church does not really need an evangelistic strategy. The church *is* the evangelistic strategy.[3]

Allow me to radicalize this a bit further. My point is not that the church, by behaving rightly in public, is capable of being truly evangelistic because to the extent it avoids hypocrisy it is able to attract the world to the gospel. While there may be some truth in this, it still tends to instrumentalize and externalize the church relative to the gospel and relative to Christian salvation. My point, rather, is that Christian salvation *is* ecclesial—that its very shape in the world *is* a participation in Christ through the worship, shared practices, disciplines, loyalties, and social patterns of his body, the church. To construe the message of the gospel in such a way as to hide or diminish the unique social creation of the

3. Here I am simply mimicking Stanley Hauerwas's dictum (hopefully putting it to good use) "The church doesn't *have* a social strategy, the church *is* a social strategy" (Hauerwas and Willimon 1989:43).

Spirit that the first Christians called *ecclesia* is to miss the point of what God is up to in history—the calling forth and creation of a people. The most evangelistic thing the church can do, therefore, is to be the church not merely in public but as a new and alternative public; not merely in society but as a new and distinct society, a new and unprecedented social existence. On this view, any evangelism for which the church is irrelevant, an afterthought, or instrumental cannot be Christian evangelism. "Social holiness," to use John Wesley's phrase, is both the aim and the intrinsic logic of evangelism. The practices of the church that embody this social holiness are the witness that becomes evangelism in the hands of the Spirit.

In contrast to this, the ecclesiology that currently underwrites the contemporary practice of evangelism—at least that which predominates in North America—is at best an ecclesiology in which the church is either instrumentalized in the service of "reaching" or "winning" non-Christians or reduced to an aggregate of autonomous believers, the group terminus of individual Christian converts. Such an ecclesiology derives in part from a social imagination made possible by Constantinian assumptions about the relationship of church and world. But that ecclesiology is most evidently derived from a social imagination made possible by modern, post-Enlightenment assumptions about history, society, and the nature of the self and its agency in the world. Within this imagination, the human person is an essentially free, autonomous individual self that exists over against other free, autonomous individual selves. The interrelationships possible among these selves, though essentially conflictual, can at best be contractual, and arising from this are modern conceptions of ownership, property, and rights as well as an understanding of "the common good" as fundamentally procedural and empty rather than participatory and substantive.

For the social imagination formed by the story of modernity, the church becomes a disembodied, mystical reality because there is no longer space for its communally and visibly embodied social patterns and relationships. The church becomes a whole that is actually less than the sum of its isolated, autonomous parts, each of which is busy pursuing its own private self-interests (including "getting saved"). All that is required is that the private subject not exercise its will in a way that violates the free exercise of other private wills. One may certainly (and ideally) yoke these wills together for united purpose and witness, but the subversively peaceful sociality named by the word *ecclesia* is inconceivable as constitutive of personhood, much less salvation.

It is within such a social imagination that salvation is able finally to be construed as a "personal relationship with Jesus" and thus something that takes place outside, alongside, or as a substitute for the church.

Under the conditions of modernity—and perhaps even more so under the conditions of what is sometimes labeled "postmodernity"—what has been referred to as "modernity coming of age" (Smart 1993:116)—the church is secondary, if it matters at all, because there is little or no imaginative room for a genuine social body in which what it means to be a person is to be *for* others (and so to have one's identity derived from and dependent upon those others). One of the enormous challenges of Christian evangelism today is that in order to learn once again to bear faithful and embodied witness to the Spirit's creative "social work," it may have to reject as heretical the pervasive characterization of salvation as "a personal relationship with Jesus."

This book, then, is an exercise in reimagining the practice of evangelism, and it offers a theology of evangelism that is nonfoundationalist in commending and defending the faith and instead grounded in confession, testimony, presence, and peaceful witness. It attempts to do this from within an ecclesial social imagination (and, thus, a soteriology) that runs counter to the social, political, and economic patterns narrated by modernity and enshrined in such "imaginaries" as the individual, the nation-state, and the market. Likewise, the ecclesial social imagination within which this book attempts to reimagine evangelism runs counter to the Constantinian narrative of church and world as fused. The challenge I propose to raise for the contemporary practice of evangelism is not, therefore, about how to be more effective or to get better results. It is a challenge at the more fundamental level of imagination.

Evangelism and Theology

Though the present volume concentrates on the practice of evangelism, its mode of concentration is unabashedly theological. Resistance to or avoidance of thinking theologically about evangelism is powerful. Those who think theologically rarely think about evangelism, and those who think about evangelism rarely take the discipline of theology very seriously. For one thing, very little in the present reward system of most churches supports thinking theologically about evangelism.[4] Excellence in

4. Edward Farley makes this point about theology in connection with ministerial preparation in general:

The typical product of three years of seminary study is not a *theologically* educated minister. The present ethos of the Protestant churches is such that a theologically oriented approach to the preparation of ministers is not only irrelevant but counterproductive. When we consider what appears to make ministers upwardly mobile, we suspect that the reward system for professional promotion and success is largely a matter of un- or anti-theological skills. Anticipating this, however

evangelism is almost wholly governed by numerical measures of success, and pastors are rewarded primarily insofar as they attain those measures. Those who produce the literature on evangelism—especially that which concentrates on the models that are widely touted as successful in the North American context—are particularly reluctant to think critically about the theology presupposed in their practice. Their focus instead is on finding new and creative ways to express Christian beliefs and practices—forms that are more indigenous, user-friendly, and "relevant" to the experience of contemporary human beings, or more successful in making converts in an already crowded market of competitors.

One result of this theological neglect is that little attention has been given to what sort of practice evangelism is or of the relationship between the practice itself and its proper *telos* or end. In one of the few serious theological treatments of evangelism now in print, *The Logic of Evangelism* (1989), William Abraham complains about the dearth of theological reflection about evangelism despite the numerous books that treat various aspects of its practice. Part of the problem, he notes, is that it is difficult to know what a scholarly theological contribution to evangelism would begin to amount to: "We do not know what precisely to define as evangelism, and therefore we are at a loss as to know what to designate as a contribution to a discussion about it" (7). Is evangelism a *productive* activity, governed by the aims of reaching, conversion, or initiation, and thus the *making* of converts? If so, the skilled evangelist might employ whatever creative means will "work" to achieve that end. The practice of evangelism is then evaluated by an instrumental logic whereby the means and the end of the practice are *external* to one another. If, however, the logic of evangelism is not primarily the logic of production but instead the logic of bearing witness, we find ourselves talking about evangelism differently. Now the "end" of evangelism is internal to its practice (as a quality of character and performance) rather than externalized in its "product." Martyrs rather than the pastors of megachurches might now become our evangelistic exemplars, and the "excellence" of evangelistic practice will be measurable not by numbers but rather by obedience to a crucified God. How we think about evangelism and how we judge it, the standards of excellence and the models we hold forth as exemplifying that excellence, the particular dispositions of character and the contexts of formation that prepare and enable us for its practice—the answers to all of these questions depend entirely on whether or not they are taken up as theological questions. Or, to put

---

vaguely, the theological student sees little point in "being a theologian." As students graduate into the reward system, they frequently discover the dispensability of their academic studies. (1983:4)

it another way, they depend entirely on whether or not they are taken up within a theological understanding of the church as the creation of the Holy Spirit rather than within nontheological understandings of the church that see it primarily in accordance with the alien logic of secular managerial or behavioral sciences.[5]

This book is written out of the conviction that there is no substitute for serious theological inquiry about evangelism as a practice. In fact, theological inquiry is itself an intrinsic part of that practice. We cannot proceed by merely trotting out a handful of "successful" pastors of fast-growing congregations to tell us what "works." For it is the very question of what we are working toward, what is deemed valuable and beautiful, what we are seeking, that in our time must be reexamined and that too often goes unchallenged altogether. Many current proposals for evangelism claim to offer a way of doing evangelism in a post-Christendom world. My sense, however, is that far too many of these proposals fail to reimagine evangelism in a way that responds to post-Christendom realities with something other than the very assumptions that gave birth to Christendom. Their failure, then, is not due to a miscalculation in tactic or strategy, to a misallocation of skill or energy, or to a missing level of commitment and creativity. To the extent that the problem with evangelism today is due to something other than our own frailty or sinfulness, it is at bottom a theological failure. When the church ceases to think critically and anew about its own existence before God, it remains stagnant and stale, or it reduces its criteria for success to mere relevance.

While the present volume intends itself as an exercise in what may be called practical theology, therefore, it is not a how-to manual for evangelism. The "practicality" of theology does not lie merely in its strategic movement toward concrete proposals for action. Practical theology is not a bag of tricks but a process of laying bare the assumptions that guide our practice and then drawing critically upon the practical wisdom of Scripture and the Christian tradition in order to rethink and reconstruct those assumptions. Karl Marx famously said, "The philosophers have only *interpreted* the world, in various ways; the point, however, is to *change* it" (1975:64). Marx makes a good point, but it is often true that to interpret the world is in fact to change it. In fact, few forces in human history have proved to be as powerful as interpretations (including, not incidentally, Marx's own interpretation of the world). How we view the world, the particular lenses through which we view it, the places where we stand in order to view it, that toward which our practice is aiming—all these are central to how the world gets changed.

---

5. This does not preclude managerial or behavioral sciences, when positioned theologically, from making an indispensable contribution to the life and ministry of the church.

I have already stated that I take as one of our most urgent challenges the recovery and reconstruction of the ecclesiological foundations of evangelism. It is symptomatic of the last half-century that discussions of evangelism stressed either its personal dimensions or its social dimensions, with an emphasis on one frequently excluding the other. Rarely, however, has this taken place in such a way as to escape the solipsism inherent in modern notions of the person, on the one hand, or Constantinian assumptions about the church's relation to society, on the other. Cracks in modernity and the progressive dismantling of Christendom afford us an opportunity to rethink evangelism in fresh, new ways—ways that take seriously the fundamental role of the church as the only theologically and sociologically prior reality out of which both personal transformation and social transformation make any Christian sense.

If the argument of this book is correct, reconstructing evangelism will not be an easy task. For the gospel to which evangelism invites persons is, by the standards of the Enlightenment, incredible; according to the logic of the market, it is cost-ineffective; measured by modern liberal notions of the social, it is uncivil; by the standards of an aesthetics formed by the capitalist discipline of desire, it is repulsive; and by the chaplaincy standards of Christendom, it may prove to be neither useful nor helpful. The conversion for which evangelism hopes may not necessarily make us better citizens, more productive workers, or more loyal family members; neither is it always likely to make us more well adjusted psychologically. As James McClendon says in response to the claim made by William James that in conversion "a disunited self is unified":

> That is doubtless so of many a conversion. But it is not a reliable index of conversion to Jesus Christ, a conversion which may set "a man against his father, a daughter against her mother" (Matt. 10:35), and so introduces antitheses between ego and internalized parental and social values. After conversion the convert to Christ may be not easier but harder to live with (see Acts 9:29), and may find it harder to live with himself or herself as well. This is not to deny that there is an interior aspect of evangelical conversion; it is only to warn that interiority must truthfully reflect actuality—which may bring peace with God and a share of the world's enmity. (1986:2:140)

The practice of evangelism, I believe, inescapably counters and disarms the world's powerful practices by unmasking the narratives that sustain them and by offering a story and a people that are peaceful and beautiful. The gospel can, therefore, be good news again in our world. But only if in Christ something new in the world has been made possible and by the Holy Spirit present—something both disturbing and inviting, a salvation in the form of a new story, a "new humanity," a new peoplehood.

Conversion, on this view, is not primarily a matter of deciding in favor of certain beliefs or having certain experiences. It is rather a change of worlds, participation in a new worship, and a journeying toward a new city. The practice of evangelism always hopes for such a conversion and seeks actively to nourish it. But where the evangelist is tempted to become impatient with the inefficiency of obedience and worship when more "efficient" means are readily available such as manipulation, accommodation, and imposition, we are reminded that evangelism is ultimately an activity of the Holy Spirit and is not subject to our own calculus of effectiveness and "return on investment." Evangelism, then, or so this book will argue, is not primarily a matter of translating our beliefs about the world into categories that others will find acceptable. It is a matter of being present in the world in a distinctive way such that the alluring and "useless" beauty of holiness can be touched, tasted, and tried.

John Howard Yoder

An additional word must be said about the influence of John Howard Yoder on the contents of this book. Since long ago reading *The Politics of Jesus* (1972), I have been convinced by Yoder's argument that the question is not whether the Christian should be political or not; the question is rather to what sort of politics the Christian is called. Yoder's ongoing project was to clarify the sense in which the church is itself a politics, albeit a peaceful one, and the way this politics is the Christian's witness in the world to God's salvation manifest in the victory of the Lamb. Witness, I have come to believe from studying Yoder, is the central and governing logic not only of Christian ethics but also of evangelism. In fact, there is no greater challenge for a church that would evangelize at the beginning of the twenty-first century than to relearn the practice of bearing faithful and embodied witness.

Insofar as the present book follows an approach to evangelism that seeks to move beyond Constantinianism and modern liberalism, I have found Yoder to be an extraordinarily important resource. His is a persuasive demonstration of the ways the church over the centuries has yielded to what he called the "Constantinian temptation" and the effect this has had on Christian worship, ethics, and mission. Any evangelism that seeks to be fully post-Constantinian rather than merely free of the embarrassing shackles of Christendom will, I believe, have to engage Yoder seriously. Likewise, like a number of others who have studied Yoder's thought, I consider him to be one of the best hopes in pointing us to a way beyond modern liberalism that is not antifoundationalist but rather nonfoundationalist, that does not reject reason and human experience but requires no criteria outside Scripture to justify the Christian's recourse to Scripture (cf. Carter 2001:23; see especially Park 2006).

It is tempting, then, to claim that the present book is little more than a gloss on Yoder's thought or, at points, an introduction to his theology of evangelism (to the extent he may be said to have had one). But that would be to lay too much blame on Yoder for what appears here, so I shall simply attest to my deep indebtedness to him and note that the present work is very much the result of following instincts formed by reading his work.

Part 1

The "Practice" of Evangelism

Christians *do* many things. They pray, worship, serve, forgive, love, eat, work, play, and, on occasion, sin. Not every activity that Christians perform, however, is distinctively Christian (especially sin!). Christians play, but so do non-Christians. Christians eat, but so do non-Christians. We would be hard pressed to make a compelling case for the way we put food into our mouths, chew, and swallow as embodying and exemplifying important Christian convictions. Yet one may nonetheless make a convincing argument that the activities involved in eating, when viewed as part of a wider and more comprehensive *practice*, do depend upon a larger context of religious conviction and meaning. It is possible, therefore, to specify Christian ways of eating, ways that are concerned for how our consumption affects others, including nonhuman others, or ways that are shaped by gratitude to God expressed in prayer before a meal or in habits of inviting others into our table fellowship who would otherwise be excluded.

Throughout this book, I will consider what it might mean to construe evangelism as an important, even constitutive, Christian *practice*. In so doing it will be important to show how the practice of evangelism is not just one activity but a context for multiple and varied activities that are performed as part of that practice. So, to use another example, worship includes a number of activities such as singing, praying, offering thanks, and celebrating. While each of these activities *is* worship, we may also speak of worship as a comprehensive, complex, and coherent context of activity—and hence, a *practice*. A practice is inconceivable apart from the activities that constitute it, and how we understand the nature, logic, and ends of a practice will shape what activities we take as constituting that practice and how these activities hold together within a wider context of faith.

Among the many practices performed by Christians, some naturally have a more internal and necessary relationship than others to the central purposes and convictions of the Christian faith and to the corporate forms of the church's life. These we may refer to as *constitutive, defining,* or *core* church practices. Worship, catechesis, forgiveness, and confession, for example, could arguably be considered *core* church practices. This does not mean that only Christians worship or forgive but rather that these practices are so central to what it means to be the body of Christ that it is impossible to talk about the church without also talking about these practices.

Reinhard Hütter's notion of "core church practices" is helpful here. For Hütter, core church practices are "grounded in a distinct *bios*; that is, they are activities of actualization inhering in a quite distinct comprehensive praxis" (2000:37). To understand the logic of such practices—a logic not to be confused with the theoretical logic of ideas that characterizes reflection—requires that we attend to what he refers to as the "comprehensive praxis" in which they inhere and the particular *bios*, or "form of life," in which they are grounded—something the first Christians called *ecclesia*. Nothing could be more important for evangelism, or so I will argue throughout this book, than situating it both imaginatively and practically within an ecclesial *bios*, or form of life; and while part 4 will look more closely at how *ecclesia* functions as this distinct *bios*, the whole of this book could be taken as an argument for a more ecclesially grounded evangelism. For now, however, it will be important to note that the logic of all core church practices is inseparable from the comprehensive praxis associated with a more or less distinct form of life that orients such practices and apart from which they are unintelligible, disordered, deformed, and, over time, likely to fall into disrepair or become wholly obsolete.

The notion of a form of life, so important in Ludwig Wittgenstein's work where it refers to the larger context of human activity in which language must be understood (cf. Wittgenstein 1953:§23), might usefully be compared to what Pierre Bourdieu describes as the *habitus* that organizes and situates human practices, structuring our actions in ways that remain largely unconscious to us.

> The *habitus*—embodied history, internalized as a second nature and so forgotten as history—is the active presence of the whole past of which it is the product. As such, it is what gives practices their relative autonomy with respect to external determinations of the immediate present. This

autonomy is that of the past, enacted and acting, which, functioning as accumulated capital, produces history on the basis of history and so ensures the permanence in change that makes the individual agent a world within the world. The *habitus* is a spontaneity without consciousness or will, opposed as much to the mechanical necessity of things without history in mechanistic theories as it is to the reflexive freedom of subjects "without inertia" in rationalist theories. (1990:56)

If Bourdieu is right, one cannot rightly understand the logic of a practice apart from taking cognizance of what we might describe as essentially a "group habit," a socially constructed way of living, knowing, and valuing received and internalized by the individuals within that group in a dynamic unity of "objectivity" and "subjectivity" (Haight 2004:129). A *habitus* provides the unconscious structures by which practices are generated and organized coherently and consistently in response to individual and unique situations but "without presupposing a conscious aiming at ends or an express mastery of the operations necessary in order to attain them" (Bourdieu 1990:53).

If, however, it is ultimately impossible, or at the very least distorting, to speak adequately about core church practices such as evangelism apart from the ecclesial form of life in which they inhere, it is likewise impossible to speak adequately about *ecclesia* apart from the practices that (partly) constitute it as a form of life. I add the word *partly* in parentheses here because the church is never constituted simply or wholly by its practices. This is true because the church is, in the first place, a people rather than a set of practices and, in the second place, because this people is constituted, vivified, and renewed by the Holy Spirit, who, as Martin Luther said, "sanctifies them daily" (1955–1976:41:143). Apart from the presence, activity, and fellowship of the Holy Spirit and the informing of our practices by the Spirit with the virtues of charity, faith, and hope, our practices are "nothing" (1 Cor. 13:3). To be sure, the Holy Spirit sanctifies and constitutes this people as a holy people precisely through practices, but the church is neither reducible to nor constituted as church by any one of these solely in and of itself.

Not all core church practices, it must be admitted, bear the same relationship to the comprehensive praxis of Christian faith. Among them Hütter distinguishes three types: (a) practices that are constitutive of this praxis—for example, proclamation of the gospel, commemoration of the law, celebration of the Lord's Supper, and baptism; (b) practices that are "inherently necessary without being constitutive"—for example, the practice of theology or the commemoration of saints and martyrs; and (c) practices that "can inhere within the praxis without being either necessary or constitutive"—for example, celebrating Christmas on December 25 or the tradition of the Christmas tree (2000:37, 211). While Hütter's distinctions are helpful, it is not always easy to distinguish between, for example, a "constitutive" core practice and a "necessary" core practice. Moreover, assigning practices to such categories, as he himself admits, is a matter of confessional dispute. Some Christian traditions will consider a practice constitutive that others do not.

Throughout this book, I will speak of and argue for evangelism as one among several *core church practices*, by which I mean something like Hütter's first category. Again, this does not mean that the Christian life is reducible to practices such as evangelism, but it does mean that by definition the Christian walk is impossible apart from them. In and through the operation of the Holy Spirit, these practices make the church what it is. They are not merely contingent activities that may or may not be performed by the church every now and then. They constitute the church as church and render it visible and recognizable in the world. Theologians have, from time to time, attempted to list or summarize the most important of these practices.[1] While I will not take up that task directly in this book, I hold that it is virtually impossible to discuss evangelism adequately without talking about other core practices in and through which Christian witness is embodied in the world. In this first part of the book, I will focus on the question of what it would mean to consider evangelism as itself a core church practice. This means asking about the movement and logic of that practice, its intentions, requisite dispositions, and aims, but also its relation to other core practices and to the larger context (or *habitus*) of Christian conviction, community, and formation.

Considerable recent attention has been given in Christian theology and ethics to the importance of practices in the Christian life, not simply as the way Christians "apply" what they believe but as the very embodiment of Christian identity and truth and the primary means by which we are enculturated into a way of life and formed into a people. So, for example, Hütter can describe the church as "a web of core practices which at the same time mark and constitute the church" (2001:35). Likewise, Stanley Hauerwas speaks of salvation as "being engrafted into practices that save us from those powers that would rule our lives making it impossible for us to truly worship God" (1995:8). This turn toward practices may be

1. Luther, for example, in his "On the Councils and the Churches," listed seven marks or "possessions" of the church, each of which might be considered a constitutive practice: (1) the word of God "preached, believed, professed, and lived"; (2) baptism; (3) the Lord's Supper; (4) the public exercise of "the office of the keys," or church discipline; (5) the consecration of individuals to ministerial offices; (6) "prayer, public praise, and thanksgiving to God"; and (7) the cross, by which Luther meant the suffering and persecution associated with discipleship (1955–1976:41:141–65).

seen as part of a more general turn toward ecclesiology in contemporary theology, and it may be interpreted as a growing dissatisfaction among contemporary theologians and ethicists with patterns of thinking over the last two centuries that located salvation and the meaning of history either outside the church in the broader cultural, economic, and political processes of society, on the one hand, or in the individual and solitary lives of Christian believers within the church, on the other. In both cases, the church turned out largely to be an afterthought.

I take this turn toward ecclesiology and toward the practices of the church as on the whole a positive development, especially in thinking about evangelism. But I do not think that the answer to the question of whether evangelism is to be considered a core Christian practice is simple, obvious, or to be presumed from the outset. For one thing, it may be that evangelism is not so much *a* practice as an intrinsic characteristic of *every* Christian practice and of the comprehensive praxis of Christian faith itself. If so, then all that we say or do is a public witness to God's peaceable reign and an embodied offer of new creation in Christ, whether that is our treatment of children, our management of money, our habits of prayer, our care of the ecosphere, our forgiveness of enemies, or the way we imagine and use time. To be made Christians is to be made witnesses. The fellowship, disciplines, practices, and social patterns by which we are made witnesses are themselves the very signs of God's mercy and judgment and a living invitation to a "watching world."[2]

But all of this means that we would do well, first, to be clear about what it would mean to speak of evangelism *as a practice*. For all the attention given to "success" and "effectiveness" in evangelism, very little consideration is given to just what sort of practice it is or how we are to understand its context, motivation, logic, and ends. Because of that, contemporary evangelism is frequently indistinguishable from activities such as marketing or public relations and is likewise subject precisely to their ends, criteria of excellence, and measurements of success. Moreover, if evangelism is not only a distinct practice but also a quality of all Christian praxis, something more will need to be said about the relationship of evangelism as a practice both to the story that "narrates" it and to the form of life, or *habitus*, in which that praxis inheres (that is to say, the Christian *ecclesia*). All of these considerations are important if Christians are to be able to give an account of evangelism that would commend it as a beautiful practice

---

2. I borrow this phrase from one of John Howard Yoder's book titles, *Body Politics: Five Practices of the Christian Community before the Watching World*. The question whether the world is, in fact, watching is certainly worth asking, and I will return to it later in the book.

and that would likewise provide us a framework for accountability regarding how we engage in it.

One recent thinker who has given considerable attention to the nature of practices and upon whose work I will draw throughout this first part of the book is Alasdair MacIntyre, a moral philosopher. MacIntyre offers a creative and complex account of practices that takes into account the relationship of practices to the social forms in which they arise, the narratives they embody, and the moral virtues they sustain. Though MacIntyre the philosopher makes room for a theological interpretation of practices in his analysis, he does not develop this interpretation, nor does he mention the practice of evangelism. But his work will set the stage for much of what follows in this book and for the book's organization around the narrative, community, and virtues that together constitute evangelism as a practice.

1

Is Evangelism a Practice?

Among Western moral philosophers at the turn of the century, few have had as profound and wide-ranging an impact as Alasdair MacIntyre. His *After Virtue* (1981, revised 1984) provided a major challenge to contemporary moral philosophy by arguing that the story of modernity is a story of fragmentation in which portions of the language of morality have survived from the past while the social context that would make such language intelligible has not. We are therefore at a critical juncture in the history of morality in which we are left with only "simulacra of morality" (1984:2). Apart from any shared social conception of what it means to be a human or of the good toward which a human life is to aim, value judgments are bound to be no more than arbitrary expressions of preference on the part of autonomous individuals, while morality is increasingly transformed into little more than an arena for the competition of individual wills. Lost along with a shared social conception of human nature and the human good are precisely the communal resources (the shared traditions, stories, communities, institutions, and practices) necessary for cultivating the kinds of habits, dispositions of character (virtues), and practical wisdom that would enable us to move toward the good.

In *After Virtue*, MacIntyre builds on and illustrates the strengths of the Aristotelian tradition while arguing for the virtues, practices, narratives, and tradition-bearing communities (in other words, the social and historical realities rejected by modernity) that render our moral judgments intelligible by embodying answers to the questions of what human life is for and what sort of persons we should be. Though my primary interest here is whether and how his notion of a practice can be helpful in thinking about evangelism,[1] so closely related are practices to virtues, narratives, and tradition-bearing communities that it is necessary to look at all four concepts together. MacIntyre's larger project is the recovery, defense, and recuperation of Aristotelian virtue theory, and so the notion of virtue itself is the central and driving force in his own moral philosophy. But that does not make his understanding of practice any less powerful for thinking about evangelism. Indeed, one of the central premises on which the argument of this book rests is the necessity and urgency of carrying out evangelism as a *virtuous* practice.

Practice

A practice is especially important in MacIntyre's overall argument, for it provides the context in which the identity of a tradition is constituted, the narrative meaning of human life is enacted, and the character, virtues, and skills for journeying toward that meaning are displayed and refined. MacIntyre defines a practice as

> any coherent and complex form of socially established cooperative human activity through which goods internal to that form of activity are realized in the course of trying to achieve those standards of excellence which are appropriate to, and partially definitive of, that form of activity, with the result that human powers to achieve excellence, and human conceptions of the ends and goods involved, are systematically extended. (1984:187)

As a way of unpacking this rather complex definition, we can identify four characteristics of what is here being called a practice.

(1) First, the goods that are realized in carrying out a practice are "internal" to that practice. So closely bound up together is participation in the practice with the goods realized through participation that those goods cannot be arrived at in any other way. As MacIntyre says, "I call a means internal to a given end when the end cannot be adequately char-

---

1. The significance of MacIntyre's work beyond the field of moral philosophy for how Christians might undertake theological reflection on a number of Christian practices is helpfully explored in Murphy, Kallenberg, and Nation 1997. MacIntyre's work, in fact, provides good reason to question any rigid distinction between moral theology and practical theology, since all morality is embodied in practices and all practices have a moral quality to them. See also Bass 1998, especially chapter 1, "Times of Yearning, Practices of Faith," by Craig Dykstra and Dorothy C. Bass, which builds on MacIntyre's work as a foundation for Christian reflection on practice.

acterized independently of a characterization of the means" (1984:184). Therefore, the internal goods of a practice can be specified only with reference to the practice in which they are realized. Consider, for example, four very different practices: baseball, painting, law, and medicine. Each of these practices requires a range of particular technical skills, many of which are regularly experimented with, sometimes improved upon, and therefore varied over time. Each practice itself, however, while complex and evolving, remains relatively coherent and distinct. No single technical skill (for example, the skill required for using a stethoscope properly) is itself a "practice"; rather, it is an activity that, along with other technical skills or activities, serves the practice in arriving at the goods internal to that practice. The practice of baseball may require that one is able to perform activities such as hitting and throwing a baseball properly. The practice of painting may require that one achieve a particular degree of naturalism. The practice of law may require that one be familiar with certain legal precedents. The practice of medicine may require that one be able to run a battery of tests on a patient's blood. But in each case, the practice itself may be distinguished from the activities employed by that practice. As MacIntyre says,

> Tic-tac-toe is not an example of a practice in this sense, nor is throwing a football with skill; but the game of football is, and so is chess. Bricklaying is not a practice; architecture is. Planting turnips is not a practice, farming is. So are the enquiries of physics, chemistry, and biology, and so is the work of the historian, and so are painting and music. (1984:187)

Is evangelism a practice? To the extent that it may be so understood, it likewise employs a number of varying skills, arts, techniques, and activities. But if evangelism is a practice, it is never reducible to any of these, and each of them must be judged by how well it serves the practice itself in arriving at the goods internal to it.

There are, of course, *external* goods generated by a practice: the celebrity that might come with playing baseball or the financial rewards that might come with the practice of medicine. There is nothing necessarily illegitimate about these external goods, but they do not define the practice, and they are likely realizable by other means. In fact, these external goods may even distort or subvert the practice and derail our movement toward the internal goods if they come to be that toward which we aim. To the extent that external goods become the ends sought in a practice, the practice will inevitably lose its integrity, and the virtues required for excellence in that practice will come to be replaced by (or end up subservient to) sheer effectiveness. This is especially true of evangelism, the practice of which is frequently associated with external goods such as the quantitative growth of the church along with its power, prestige, and influence. As should already be clear by now, in carrying out a practice with excellence, few tasks, if any, are more important than distinguishing its internal goods from its external goods.

As a way of clarifying and expanding upon MacIntyre's notion of a practice and applying it to Christian social life, James McClendon invites us to compare it with the concept of a "game."[2] McClendon is not implying that the Christian life is just a game or that its constitutive practices are merely recreational activities, but if we are willing to discard any prejudice we might hold against the word *game* as referring only to something frivolous or trivial, he believes we can learn something important about the structure of our practices from the logic of game playing.

Drawing upon Bernard Suits's *The Grasshopper: Games, Life, and Utopia*, McClendon identifies four necessary elements to a game: (a) an end or goal, (b) the means to that end, (c) the rules by which the game is played (these rules, in fact, can be said to "constitute" the game), and (d) the proper attitude in playing (what Suits calls a "lusory" attitude, from the Latin for "game": *ludus*). The end or goal is impossible apart from the means, rules, and lusory attitude; hence, as with MacIntyre, that end is "internal" to the game. On this understanding of a game, there are three sorts of "non-players": triflers, cheats, and spoilsports. McClendon explains:

> Consider Aunt Lucy, who doesn't really want to play checkers, but who to oblige bored nephew Billy sits down at the board and takes a turn moving the pieces on the squares. She is not playing, though, she is *trifling* with the red and black disks and her (definitional) failure to play is an exemplary though unattractive lack of the lusory attitude. Or consider burly Ben, dumb but eager to look athletic, who runs round and round with the ball after being tagged repeatedly; his *spoilsport* behavior breaks up a neighborhood touch football game whose procedures he simply ignores. Finally, naughty Nell doesn't count her strokes in the sandtrap until at last she chips to the green; she is, alas, a *cheat* whether anyone else knows it or not, though she appears to be playing golf by the rules. In Suits' neat summary, "triflers recognize rules but not goals, cheats recognize goals but not rules, players recognize both rules and goals and spoilsports recognize neither." (1986:1:164)

These illustrations help us to see that games, like practices, are inherently *social* activities that, even if played alone (for example, solitaire), require some sort of wider communal agreement about the nature of the

---

2. McClendon 1986:1:162–66. MacIntyre himself frequently uses games (such as chess) to illustrate and explain what he means by a practice.

game with respect to both its means and its ends (I will examine this social dimension more closely below). But they also help us to see that there is an *internal* relationship within a game between means and ends. On the one hand, the means are ordered to certain ends, and without playing "toward" those ends, the game has not properly been played—one is merely trifling. On the other hand, there is no game without the means (or rules). The rules constitute the game as a game, such that we cannot consider ourselves to have played simply because we achieved the end or goal (for example, we might have cheated). Simply walking across a finish line does not constitute having run a race. The model of a game helps us understand that, as McClendon notes, practices are "self-justifying or intrinsically valuable (rather than merely instrumental) human activities" (1986:1:165).

What might all of this mean for thinking about evangelism as a practice? A *trifling* approach to evangelism might be one in which our motions or actions are disconnected from the proper aims, motivation, or attitude associated with the practice. Perhaps evangelism has been imposed upon us or required of us by others. Maybe our church or denomination has mandated that this be the "Decade of Evangelism," so we carry out some obligatory set of recruitment programs or advertising campaigns. One could also associate the lack of a lusory attitude that characterizes trifling behavior with the absence of requisite dispositions, or virtues. Thus, a trifling approach to evangelism would be one that does not arise out of and is not motivated by the central Christian virtue of charity but is instead sheer busyness. Evangelistic *cheaters* would be those who, wholly preoccupied with ends (which frequently turn out to be external ends), disregard or trivialize the integrity of the practice itself and do "whatever it takes" to win. They point proudly to their results and successes, but fail to realize how hollow practice leads to hollow victories. A *spoilsport*'s approach to evangelism would, of course, be to give up on the practice altogether, perhaps out of frustration with the cheaters, or maybe out of discomfort with what appear to be the intrinsically public dimensions of a very old, strange, incredible, unenlightened, and downright embarrassing gospel. More likely than not, spoilsports simply do something else and then claim that whatever it is they are doing is, in fact, evangelism.

All of this, however, means that if evangelism is to be considered a practice, the task of determining the precise nature of the goods internal to its practice and distinguishing these from merely external goods is complex. Because these goods are internal to the practice, they are not self-evident and, as MacIntyre says, "can only be identified and recognized by the experience of participating in the practice in question" (1984:188–89). So, for example, those who practice jogging find in it a fulfillment internal to its practice, a fulfillment not always easy to explain to those who do not practice jogging. Jogging simply to lose weight or in order to get to work because I am late disqualifies my involvement in the activity *as a practice*. It is then not being performed as a practice but has been transformed into an instrument for some other remote or external purpose. The critical point here is that the goods internal to the practice are essential to its very nature as a practice. One cannot start with ends and work backward in order to derive the nature of the practice. In a very real sense, the practice *is* its ends. The task of determining the nature of the goods internal to a practice requires that we take into account (a) the living community, or tradition, in which the question about the proper aim of a practice is embodied and extended through time, (b) the narrative that renders our actions intelligible (while at the same time revealing some actions to be "cheating," "trifling," or "behaving like a spoilsport"), and (c) the acquired qualities of character (virtues) that are required for pursuit of those goods. To each of these I will return in a moment.

(2) Implied in the foregoing is a second feature of a practice, according to MacIntyre. Just as the goods realized in a practice are internal to that practice, so it is with the standards of excellence by which we judge a practice. In other words, the criteria for doing well in a practice are determined largely by the practice itself and, indeed, are "partially definitive" of a practice. MacIntyre takes as an example a child who is given candy to play chess and even more candy if the child wins: "So long as it is the candy alone which provides the child with a good reason for playing chess, the child has no reason not to cheat and every reason to cheat, provided he or she can do so successfully" (1984:188). The child will never learn to play chess *well*, even if the child is able to win consistently.

This principle partly explains why evangelism is so easily distorted as a practice. Once an external good (such as the quantitative growth, power, and influence of the church or the number of conversions one is able to produce) has come to be substituted for the internal good of the practice, and precisely to the extent that the church becomes skilled in achieving those external goods, the church ceases to have any good reason to practice evangelism *well* or virtuously. All Christian practices are, of course, subject to perversion, but as McClendon rightly points out, "the perversion associated with evangelism is potentially the more demonic, becomes demonic just to the degree that in a crass way it succeeds" (1986:2:439).

In MacIntyre's illustration, the candy is an external good that ends up subverting the practice by providing a substitute *telos* for playing the game (thereby turning the game into a mere means) that prompts the child to cheat and inevitably erodes the standards of excellence that define the practice of chess. In this instance we can immediately see the truth in the old cliché, "It isn't whether you win or lose, but how you play the game." That cliché is true in the case of a practice, because how well or poorly one participates is intrinsic to the very meaning of "winning or losing" (though this language is ultimately inadequate in the case of a practice). Naturally, one hopes that in the course of playing the game for candy the child will discover the goods specific to the practice of chess and begin to play chess for its own internal rewards and fulfillment, all the while seeking to excel at chess on the game's own terms. But this will not happen always, or even most of the time. The same is especially true, I think, with regard to evangelism. Thus, to talk about a practice in the MacIntyrean sense is to talk about what it means to practice it well according to standards of excellence (including the skills and virtues requisite to that excellence) that have been determined historically by a tradition of practitioners.

It is worth noting here that the word *excellence* denotes a far different way of evaluating or measuring a practice from ways denoted by words like *accomplishment, effectiveness, winning,* or *success,* all of which, when guiding our participation in a practice, tend to turn it into something instrumental relative to the *telos* of the practice. The very language we use has the power to sever the means from the end or to inadvertently redirect our attention to external goods that can be achieved without excellent, virtuous, or faithful practice. In fact, as MacIntyre points out, it is external goods rather than internal goods that characteristically become "objects of competition in which there must be losers as well as winners" (1984:190). When we hear people discussing a practice like evangelism in such terms, we may well ask whether a distortion is already present, whether external goods have begun to elbow out the goods internal to the practice. As MacIntyre goes on to note, external goods when realized are "always some individual's property and possession," while it is characteristic of internal goods that "their achievement is a good for the whole community who participate in the practice" (1984:190–91).

(3) We are thus brought directly to a third characteristic of a practice, its nature as a "socially established" and "cooperative" human activity. This does not mean that activities performed alone do not qualify as a practice (for example, painting) but rather that the goods internal to a practice are impossible apart from a community of other practitioners to whom we subordinate ourselves (every practice has a history that we do not simply invent), with whom we share and at times criticize standards of excellence and purposes internal to the practice, and in relationship to whom we transform ("systematically extend") the practice over time, making our unique contribution both to the standards of

excellence and to the purposes associated with the practice. To engage in a practice is to become a part of such a community, to be initiated into it, and to be formed by it, however much we may also end up forming others and initiating them into the same community. To engage in a practice is also, therefore, to enter into relationships of trust, and it is in this sense that a practice cannot be engaged in "alone," nor can the achieved internal goods of a practice ever be considered one's own property or possession.

(4) As has just been indicated, a fourth feature of a practice is that it may be "systematically extended." The standards of a practice are open to criticism by fellow practitioners. The practice itself (and the "excellence" that is sought in it) is not merely the quality of one individual's practice but a development of the practice with discipline and over time (hopefully practitioners learn something from each other that contributes to the betterment of the practice). Thus, a practice is never static or finished, and its standards and purposes may be enlarged and extended—though, of course, that is impossible if we have not first accepted "the authority of the best standards realized so far" and allowed our own performance to be judged by them (1984:190).

Here it is important to reinforce the previously mentioned contrast between a practice, on the one hand, and a technical skill required for participating in that practice, on the other hand. Dentistry is a practice; operating a drill on a tooth is a technical skill. While one hopes that technical skills will also advance and be refined over time within practices, MacIntyre has in mind the systematic extension not of skills but of practices. Sometimes an advance in the skills employed in a practice is confused with an advance in the practice itself. While that can be the case, it is not necessarily the case. So, for example, the advances in satellite technology and other forms of mass communication on our planet over the last century may have improved the church's ability to evangelize, but it may also be that they have deformed the practice of evangelism by substituting the remote for the incarnate, contrivance for authenticity, and image for substance. The latter would be true, for example, if we understand evangelistic "communication" not as the transmission of data to be decoded, adjudged, and decided by a "receptor" but rather as the embodied sharing of a form of life and thus as a type of communing oriented toward the offer of participation. In that case the character of the evangelist and the material nature of the communion she offers are intrinsic to the offer itself.

Not just any activity is a practice. While a practice may be complex and variegated in its performance, it is neither random nor haphazard. When carried out with excellence, a practice realizes internal goods that are at least partially definitive of that practice. Of course, both the standards of excellence and the goals of a practice may be transformed by its history, but this does not mean that the practice is merely provisional or instrumental. It is neither a mere preparation (as when a child is reminded, "Don't forget to practice your clarinet") nor a tool mechanically placed in the service of some external end.

Narrative, Tradition, and Virtues

Having examined the general contours of MacIntyre's notion of a practice, we are in a better position to ask more pointedly what it would mean to speak of evangelism as a practice. One of the conclusions we are bound to draw from the foregoing is that if evangelism is a practice we will do well to distinguish its internal goods from various external goods that, regardless of how legitimate, may distract us from faithfulness in our practice and in the long run subvert evangelism, transforming it into a mere utility for the achievement of those external goods. Christian evangelism has frequently been made to serve alien purposes. Sometimes this happens as a result of arrogance and idolatry, when evangelism is carried out through conquest in the name of the extension of imperial power. Sometimes this happens as a result of selfishness and pride, a preoccupation with flash, size, or sizzle, as in the case of Simon, a magician in Samaria who wanted to buy the power of the Holy Spirit from the apostles so that he too could attain the results associated with their evangelism (Acts 8:9 24). And sometimes this happens as a result of fear and anxiety, as when a church faced with numerical decline or diminishing cultural influence seeks to shore up that influence or restore its failing health by producing growth. In each case, evangelism is pressed into the service of external ends (power, influence, church growth) and is subverted from the outset. It loses even when it wins—indeed, it loses because it wins.

If, however, we would distinguish the internal goods of evangelism from various external goods, we know from MacIntyre's account that this cannot be done apart from specifying the proper *telos* of the practice of evangelism along with the standards of excellence, activities, and "rules" (the "grammar" or "logic") that constitute it as a practice. In order to do that we will need to look more closely at the other two concepts, narrative and tradition, that provide the background to MacIntyre's recovery of the virtue tradition, and then finally we must turn to the virtues themselves. For practices are finally unintelligible considered in the abstract apart from (a) a *narrative* or story that provides unity, meaning, and direction both for our lives and for our practices, (b) the *tradition* in which the question about the internal goods of a practice (and the relation of those goods to the practice itself) is embodied socially within a community and thereby extended through time, and (c) the dispositions or *virtues* that sustain our practices (and, indeed, our quest for the proper ends of life itself) "by enabling us to overcome the harms, dangers, temptations and distractions we encounter, and which will furnish us with increasing self-knowledge and increasing knowledge of the good" (1984:219).

Narrative

In thinking about the importance of the category of narrative for the practice of evangelism, MacIntyre would have us begin with the elementary observation that for any activity to be understood or explained, it must be considered within its appropriate context. That context can be significantly complex, of course, for it includes (a) our intentions in carrying out the activity, (b) the beliefs we hold that provide the background for our intentions, and (c) the setting in which the activity is carried out. If I see a woman writing a sentence and I ask her what she is doing, she might reply, "Writing a sentence," "Working on a research paper," "Finishing my course requirements," or "Trying to graduate." All four answers might be correct, and each of the answers would in some way reveal the woman's intentions. But in order to get an accurate picture of what she is doing, MacIntyre suggests that we must know how the shorter-term intentions relate to the longer-term intentions and how the longer-term intentions are built upon and presuppose the shorter-term intentions. In other words, we must know the "story" of how these intentions hang together. Clearly, the woman is not trying to graduate so that she can finish her research paper. It is the other way around. Once we know how her intentions are causally related to each other over time—how, that is, they are historically ordered—we are in a better position to understand what she is doing. What we require is a narrative that is able to characterize the practice from beginning to middle to end and from within which the practice comes to make sense.

No narrative will be complete, however, without indicating the beliefs, or convictions, that justify the way a person's intentions are ordered. From the example just given, it is relatively clear that the woman believes that by finishing her research paper she stands a good chance of completing her coursework and thereby graduating. In other contexts, one's beliefs may be more complicated and less apparent. Consider, for example, the interlocking and multilayered set of beliefs, however implicit, presupposed by one's participation in the various activities that make up a Christian service of worship.

In addition to specifying the intentions implicit in carrying out a practice and the beliefs that provide the background and motivation for those intentions, a narrative indicates the setting in which we are to make sense of actions. To return again to my example, we may assume that the woman is a student and that the setting is a school of some sort. But here MacIntyre uses the word *setting* in a broad sense that would include any institution, practice, or other milieu that possesses a history identifiable enough to make sense of the activity. The act of waving my hand in the air, for example, will be understood in very different ways depending on whether I am greeting a friend, hailing a cab, volunteering for a committee, or making a bid at an auction. It may well be, of course, that a single activity belongs to more than one historical setting (and so the history of the woman's life intersects with the history of the school she attends).

One of the primary reasons that narrative is an essential genre for characterizing our actions is its teleological character. Narrative is an intrinsically historical genre that embodies the unity of a life across time and points toward some good, end, or *telos*. Likewise, actions, if meaningful, are purposive and make sense only within lives lived (even if unpredictably) toward a future. No wonder that one of the central tasks involved in the process of learning to become a Christian is learning the stories that give the Christian life unity, focus, and direction and that help us to answer the question of who we are to be and what we are to do. To become a Christian is to join a story and to allow that story to begin to narrate our lives. As MacIntyre says, "I can only answer the question 'What am I to do?' if I can answer the prior question 'Of what story or stories do I find myself a part?'" (1984:216).

Talking about our actions within the context of stories is a natural feature of our daily existence. Consider how frequently we tell a story to get across a point or as a way of introducing ourselves to others. But critically reflecting on our actions or thinking theologically about them in terms of their narrative embodiment does not come so naturally. What I hope to show in the following chapters is that careful reflection on the practice of evangelism requires clarity about the narrative in which that practice is rendered intelligible and, within that narrative, about the *telos* that makes of evangelism a meaningful, purposeful context of action. In fact, it is entirely appropriate to consider the practice of evangelism (or any practice, for that matter) as an "enacted narrative" (MacIntyre 1984:211). In part 2 of this book, therefore, I will explore evangelism within the biblical stories of Israel, Jesus, and the apostles. These three stories can be read as forming a continuous, single narrative of God's election and formation of a people called to be an embodied witness and living invitation to God's peaceable reign in the world.

To identify the narrative that makes sense out of Christian evangelism, however, is also to challenge rival narratives from within which evangelism is often practiced (and thereby distorted). As Gabriel Fackre says,

> It is important for the Christian community to get the Story straight also because the world is aggressively telling its own tale. Assailed by its messages from every side, it is tempting to believe they are true. . . . To these half-truths and full fictions must be juxtaposed another scenario. It will be strange to the ears and eyes of modernity, a counter-word and a counter-vision. The task of Christian Storytelling is to keep alive the set of counter-perceptions so the Church may be what it is and see what it is called to see, rather than be made over in the image of the regnant culture. (1978:12)

This narrative challenge is hardly innocuous or innocently theoretical and abstract. A narrative not only renders certain practices intelligible but also legitimates power structures in which those practices are carried out. Jesus' subversion of authority came not from headlong attacks but from something much more threatening—a renarration of the tradition. In considering the relationship between evangelism and narrative, we must examine not only the way a particular story narrates the *telos* of evangelism but also the way it legitimates (or subverts) political and economic structures within which the practice is performed. Moreover, we must attend to the way a narrative has within it the resources not only for establishing identity but for self-criticism and transformation. While part 2 of this book asks what it would mean to narrate the practice of evangelism from within the story of the people of God and by construing God's peace as the end of that story, part 3 will take a more critical turn by examining two rival narratives—that of Constantinianism and that of modern liberalism—each of which is a story built on violence and therefore unable to narrate the shalom of God's reign. Each ends up narrating the practice of evangelism in ways that distort it by severing it from its proper *telos* and wresting it from the matrix of ecclesial holiness.

All of this is not meant to imply that a narrative *explains* the meaning of an action as if it were a theory that pretended to divine or distill from an action its "real" meaning. Rather, by narrating the story in which a practice is made intelligible, we discover the truth that meaning is inherently practical in the first place. It is the tragic legacy of the Enlightenment that the meaning of a practice was taken to lie behind that practice (and behind history) so that practices ceased to participate in a more substantive good and became merely instrumental. Philosophically, this is linked to the loss of a social or historical narrative for construing the self. Instead the self is segmented and partitioned in ways that prevent us from thinking about life as a whole or a unity: "So work is divided from leisure, private life from public, the corporate from the personal.

So both childhood and old age have been wrenched away from the rest of human life and made over into distinct realms" (MacIntyre 1984:204). Thus are we prevented from thinking of our lives and our selves as a unity embedded in a larger narrative or story. One of the most important functions of narrative in any practical theology is the cultivation of our skills in "seeing."

Tradition

The notion of the proper good or *telos* of a practice (and of life itself) raises the question of how it is that we come to know that good, and it is here that MacIntyre departs most radically from the individualist notion of the self canonized in the Enlightenment project. A narrative understanding of a practice coincides with a narrative understanding of the self, both of which imply that our lives and our practices are always part of a history, that is to say, a past, a present, and a future—or, to use MacIntyre's word, a tradition. A tradition that is alive and "in good order" is never a static, finished or once-for-all achievement but is a dynamic process that is responsive to ever-changing historical circumstances. It is "an historically extended, socially embodied argument, and an argument precisely in part about the goods which constitute that tradition" (MacIntyre 1984:222). It is therefore also possible to speak of a tradition as a community and of one's own life story as embedded in the story of a community. As MacIntyre says, "I find myself part of a history and that is generally to say, whether I like it or not, whether I recognize it or not, one of the bearers of a tradition" (1984:221).

Practices, too, are embedded within community-embodied traditions, and it is even possible to say that certain practices "constitute" a tradition and that through the historical extension of those practices the tradition itself is extended. Whether the practice of evangelism is such a practice is what I am here asking. In fact, it is the intent of this book to make a contribution to the ongoing argument about the goods that constitute the Christian tradition, that are embodied in the community called church, and that provide the *telos* for the practice of evangelism.

A tradition is not a dead deposit of truth or an infallible standard designed to put an end to debate. As MacIntyre further defines a tradition in *Whose Justice? Which Rationality?*

A tradition is an argument extended through time in which certain fundamental agreements are defined and redefined in terms of two kinds of conflict: those with critics and enemies external to the tradition who reject all or at least key parts of those fundamental agreements, and those internal interpretive debates through which the meaning and rationale of the fundamental agreements come to be expressed and by whose progress a tradition is constituted. (1988:12)

It should also be pointed out that the "traditioned" character of disputes about the goods of a human life or of a practice, or about the particular virtues required in order to arrive at those goods, need not be taken as restricting a tradition from making or implying universal claims. The Christian story, though it is but one tradition among others, necessarily makes a number of universal claims and cannot avoid the fact that it offers the world a "metanarrative." In fact, evangelism is one of the most outrageous and audacious of all Christian practices, for it understands the *telos* of human life to which it bears witness to be the *telos* of *every* human life (though one that may only be offered nonviolently, as we shall see). Further, the fact that a tradition is essentially a historical, socially embodied argument should not be understood as a sign of weakness or instability; nor should the fact that a tradition is constantly interacting with or receiving from other traditions be taken as a denial that the tradition has any specifiable identity. That a tradition is able to have an argument may very well be a sign of strength, coherence, and vitality. Traditions live insofar as they are able to take account of inevitable challenges from both inside and outside the tradition.[3]

As significant as a tradition is in shaping and guiding the practice of evangelism, perhaps most important is the community that both forms and is formed by that tradition—in the case of Christianity, the *ecclesia*—for it is precisely into this community that the practice of evangelism is an invitation. Evangelism stands as one of the most important and dinstinctive practices of the church in defining its relationship with the world and the relationship of the church as a tradition-formed community with other tradition-formed communities. Because the practice

3. Can MacIntyre's account be defended against charges that it has no way of deciding among rival traditions and narratives? In his later work—*Whose Justice? Which Rationality?* (1988) and *Three Rival Versions of Moral Enquiry* (1990)—he attempts to provide such a defense by showing that all traditions over time experience either internal contradictions or contradictions with other traditions with which their adherents come into contact. While in one respect traditions are incommensurable, they do engage other traditions and can even be challenged (and at times defeated or co-opted) by other traditions. A tradition may be able to resolve these contradictions and thus make some sort of "progress." MacIntyre therefore believes that rational argument is possible between traditions. Miroslav Volf agrees that no one stands "nowhere" and that all of us stand within a "tradition," but cautions against attempting to rid ourselves of all "hybridity" in the name of preserving or defending one coherent tradition. He thus argues for a "double vision" that means "not only creating space in ourselves for others, but in creating space for them making also space for their perspective on us and on them" (1996:215). See also McClendon and Smith 1994.

of evangelism always shows up at these boundary meetings with an invitation to a new world that requires conversion, it can frequently circumvent or thwart the listening, mutual respect, reciprocity, hospitality, and debate that make of Christianity a living tradition in good order. In other words, evangelism practiced poorly can prohibit the sort of argument that Christianity needs to have with other traditions. But then I take this as pointing all the more convincingly to the importance of an adequate ecclesiology to ground the practice of evangelism and to the significance of holy virtues in making the evangelistic offer. Part 4 of this book will explore the community called *ecclesia* as a distinctive context for offering the evangelistic invitation to conversion.

Virtues

In this narrative-shaped, tradition-formed quest for (and toward) the good of a human life, important dispositions surface as qualities of character that sustain the quest and assist us in achieving this good. These dispositions, or virtues, are not inherited but learned and cultivated over time (though we do inherit the "tradition" in which we learn them and through which we come to possess them). For the virtues find their place not just within an individual human life but within the particular historical and social context in which they arise. In fact, my use of the word *quest* here, following MacIntyre, already gives a narrative shape to the place of the virtues that will be more at home in some contexts than in others. In the early heroic societies of the Homeric poems, the social context of virtue was far more static and less historical than it is today, composed of kinship groups in which one's role was well defined, one's status was largely fixed and predetermined, and virtue referred to "any quality that is required for discharging one's role" (MacIntyre 1984:122). As we travel forward to the fifth and fourth centuries BCE, the social setting for the virtues becomes not the kinship group but the city-state along with the larger context of Athenian democracy, so that the virtues are now learned from and exercised within the context of the *polis*. To be a good person is to be a good citizen (MacIntyre 1984:135). It was in this context that Aristotle's virtue theory originally arose.

The ancient *polis*, however, no longer provides us with the context in which today we are to understand the unity and *telos* of our lives, nor does it provide the corporate good and highest ideals by which we could both recognize and cultivate a virtuous life. Here MacIntyre must move beyond Aristotle, and this he does by appealing to the medieval vision of human existence as a quest in which a person or a people have a particular historical task to be accomplished or journey to be completed, in which humans are understood to be essentially *in via*, in which they encounter obstacles or barriers on the way, and in which virtues are "those qualities which enable the evils to be overcome, the task to be accomplished, the journey to be completed" (1984:175). This vision has a narrative shape that resonates more adequately with the Hebrew and Christian Scriptures and thereby creates room for the full flowering of a Christian virtue theory such as that developed by Thomas Aquinas. Perhaps today we might incorporate other models of imagining the social context of the Christian life, for example, not only as a journey but also as a table fellowship (see Russell 1993), and so we might end up construing the virtues somewhat differently (generosity, egalitarianism, inclusiveness). In whatever context, however, "generally to adopt a stance on the virtues will be to adopt a stance on the narrative character of human life" (1984:144), so that the good toward which human life is to be lived can be achieved only by the actions and choices that spring from the virtues.[4] To lose one's sense of context and tradition is likewise to lose a space for the cultivation and exercise of virtue. For this reason, MacIntyre can insist that "all morality is always to some degree tied to the socially local and particular" and "the aspirations of the morality of modernity to a universality freed from all particularity is an illusion" (1984:126–27).

Within a tradition, practices are the field upon which the virtues are exhibited, defined, and formed. Apart from these excellences of character, we are unable to arrive at the goods internal to practices. Thus, virtues are not merely instrumental to the good life; they are constitutive of it. The virtuous life is both means and end. The separation is part of the problem in recovering virtue in a post-Enlightenment world. As we might well suspect from the distinction already encountered between internal goods and external goods, caution should be exercised in describing the exercise of the virtues as simply *a* means to the end of achieving the good of a practice or of a life.

> For what constitutes the good for [us] is a complete human life lived at its best, and the exercise of the virtues is a necessary and central part of such a life, not a mere preparatory exercise to secure such a life. We thus cannot characterize the good for [us] adequately without already having made reference to the virtues. And within an Aristotelian framework the suggestion therefore that there might be some means to achieve the good for [us] without the exercise of the virtues makes no sense. (MacIntyre 1984:149)

It is the very nature of a practice (evangelism is no exception) that there can never be an exhaustive prior knowledge as to how one should engage

---

4. In the *Eudemian Ethics*, Aristotle writes, "It is the correctness of the end of the purposive choice of which virtue is the cause" (quoted in MacIntyre 1984:149).

in that practice in any and every particular situation. The ability to make judgments in particular circumstances is not tied primarily to technical skill in the performance of a practice but to *perception*, and this, of course, requires the virtues. To practice well is to see well. But one can never come to see well merely by attending to the "how to" of a practice. That is why excellence in a practice like evangelism requires a virtuous formation and so an attention to and recovery of the social forms and institutions necessary for this formation. MacIntyre follows Aristotle in highlighting *phronesis*—"practical intelligence," or "practical wisdom"—as a central virtue in this regard. *Phronesis* is an *intellectual* virtue rather than a *moral* virtue, but without it we cannot exercise the moral virtues—courage, justice, temperance, liberality, etc.—in the right place at the right time in the right way. This intellectual excellence, however, is neither pure "theory" nor mere "know-how." Just as the moral virtues require the virtue of *phronesis*, so the latter cannot be exercised properly without the former, "otherwise it degenerates into or remains from the outset merely a certain cunning capacity for linking means to any end rather than to those ends which are genuine goods for [humans]" (MacIntyre 1984:154). Moreover, the cultivation of both types of virtue (moral and intellectual) requires the sorts of relationships (Aristotle talks about "friendship" as the fundamental form of these relationships) and communal agreements on the aim of the good life that we have already seen as constituting a community-formed tradition and as embodied in that tradition's practices.

What I hope to show in the following pages with regard to the practice of evangelism is that the prevailing emphasis in our time on technique and effectiveness must be subordinated to a greater emphasis on holy virtues, acquired and formed within the fellowship of the Holy Spirit, the possession and exercise of which enable us to move toward the goods internal to the practice of evangelism and, indeed, toward the peace that is the *telos* of every human life. In other words, the faithful practice of evangelism requires both "saints" and a social context (*ecclesia*) in which saintliness can be cultivated and recognized. For if, as we shall see, God's peace is the *telos* of human life, then holiness of life is internally related to that peace, as the author of Hebrews commands us: "Pursue peace with everyone, and the holiness without which no one will see the Lord" (12:14). The recovery of evangelism as a practice will necessarily include the recovery of evangelism as a virtuous activity.

Is Evangelism a Practice?

MacIntyre's notion of a practice is not the only one available to us, though it shares a number of important features with other definitions of practice that operate among practical theologians today and among the social scientists and moral philosophers who have influenced their work. MacIntyre relies heavily on an Aristotelian vision of practice, morality, and practical reasoning; yet, in keeping with his notion of tradition as historically extended, MacIntyre has himself moved beyond Aristotle in some rather un-Aristotelian ways, transforming the more conservative and ahistorical tendencies of Aristotle in creative, historical, and progressive directions. MacIntyre, for example, uses narrative and tradition to overcome the impossibility of conceiving the good from within a specific *polis* that no longer exists, instead resituating virtue in contexts that must now be understood to have a history. Likewise, MacIntyre recognizes that Aristotle's premodern metaphysical biology, in which a being's nature or essence is static and its *telos* immutable, is especially problematic for those of us who live in a post-Darwinian world and for whom what it means to be human is shaped not only by biological conditions but by culture, society, and history. Narrative, in MacIntyre's view, provides a more historical and socially teleological (rather than biologically teleological) framework for understanding the movement, continuity, and unity of a human life.

Still, while MacIntyre's work provides a useful frame of reference for thinking about Christian practices and while it creates the space for a tradition-informed, theological interpretation of practice, he does not provide that interpretation, nor does he develop a fully theological account of core church practices. In order to move beyond MacIntyre's relatively formal discussion of practices, we require a more substantive account of the particular narrative (parts 2 and 3), social context (part 4), and virtues (part 5) that constitute and sustain evangelism as a practice. Before turning to these, however, I will suggest one particular qualification to MacIntyre's notion of a practice that may be required for our thinking about the particular case of evangelism.

The qualification I have in mind relates to the question I raised in the introduction to part 1: whether it might be the case that evangelism is not so much a practice as an intrinsic characteristic of *every* Christian practice and of the comprehensive praxis of Christian faith itself, so that all that we say or do is a public witness, invitation, and offer of God's salvation to the world. Negatively, one might argue in response to such a possibility that "if everything is evangelism, nothing is evangelism" (Abraham 1989:44). Despite the fallacious logic of this response (when taken literally), its point is well taken: if all practices are to be considered evangelism, then there is no single, coherent, and distinct practice called evangelism. What is thus gained in rightly understanding the entirety of the Christian life as witness-bearing or as invitational is accompanied by a diminishment of the intentional practice of offering to others this life and, if accepted, nurturing and initiating them into discipleship, an activity consistently at the center of Jesus' ministry and that of his first followers. In fact, defining evangelism so broadly that it is an intrinsic characteristic of everything Christians do may turn out to be a mechanism for justifying our avoidance of this more intentional practice altogether.

Yet one can readily see how this tension is inescapably present in other core Christian practices. Catechesis, for example, is the practice of forming and educating persons in the faith, and surely the church could not be the church without the deliberate performance of this practice. But despite the importance of distinct and intentional forms of instruction and initiation, one could also argue that the most powerful way Christians teach and form each other is through a daily process of patterning that encompasses the whole of our lives as they are lived out in relation to one another.[5] Or consider the practice of worship. Is worship a discrete, intentional activity that Christians undertake only at certain times during the day, week, or year? Is it not also an intrinsic quality of our existence before God, so that to live as God's people is to perform life as an act of worship? Certainly the Hebrew prophets will not let us think about the practice of worship as self-contained apart from what we do with the rest of our lives. Practices that are intended as acts of worship, when unaccompanied by justice in our business dealings (Amos 8:4–7) or by the sharing of our bread with the poor and the fair treatment of workers (Isaiah 58:3–7), are not only discounted as worship but regarded as sinful. Amos warns, "Take away from me the noise of your songs; I will not listen to the melody of your harps. But let justice roll down like waters, and righteousness like an ever-flowing stream" (5:23–24).

If the practices of worship and catechesis, to take but two examples, may be considered both (a) distinct and intentional practices alongside other practices and (b) qualities of the comprehensive praxis of Christian faith itself, perhaps it is not too much of a stretch to make the same claim for evangelism. In that case, we need not commit ourselves to a trade-off in which the practice of evangelism understood in one of these two ways implies a rejection or diminishment of evangelism understood in the other way. On the contrary, this is precisely what it means to speak of evangelism as a *constitutive* Christian practice. If evangelism is intrinsic to the Christian faith, it would be surprising to find any Christian activity that was not in some respect evangelistic. By

5. See Webb-Mitchell 2003. Webb-Mitchell builds a solid case throughout this book that Christian education occurs through both moments of intentional instruction and a wider process of socialization into the life of the church.

holding worship, evangelism, and catechesis to be part and parcel of the Christian life itself, then, we need not detract from the intentional practice of any one of these.

Accordingly, the following chapters argue that evangelism is not one thing but many things. In the first place, we may speak of evangelism as an intrinsic quality of all Christian praxis, or simply as witness (*martyria*), precisely because to live faithfully as Christians in the world is to evangelize by sheer presence. In fact, I should like to argue that the logic of evangelism, whatever else we may want to say about it, is first and foremost the logic of witness. Literally everything Christians do—indeed, the very existence of the church along with its distinctive social patterns and processes—may properly be construed as evangelism. On the other hand, we may also understand evangelism as a distinct, identifiable, socially established, cooperative, and intentional practice along the lines developed by MacIntyre.

I can see no good reason that evangelism cannot have both this general meaning and this specific meaning as long as we insist on keeping the two bound together so that each completes and informs the other. Apart from the faithfulness of the church in all that it is and all that it does—its worship, its refusal of violence, its economic faithfulness, its confession and forgiveness of sins, its hospitality to strangers—the practice of evangelism is disengaged from the narrative that directs it and cut off from the community and virtues that sustain it. It then becomes a sham practice whose *telos* and standards of excellence are subject to the determinations of other stories and social bodies. Its successes are counterfeit victories. For it is only through the formation of a people and the practices that make such formation possible that we are made adequate to the practice of evangelism.[6] Stanley Hauerwas and William Willimon are right when they say, "The only way for the world to know that it is being redeemed is for the church to point to the Redeemer by being a redeemed people" (1989:94). When the practice of evangelism is not grounded firmly in the comprehensive life of witness, the church is inevitably instrumentalized, reduced to a mere tool in the service of heralding the gospel, rather than the social embodiment of God's new creation in Christ, the very news that is to be heralded as good. For, as always, the embodiment *is* the heralding; the medium *is* the message; incarnation *is* invitation. That is why, as I shall attempt to argue throughout the book, it is impossible for the church to evangelize the world and, at the same time, to serve as a chaplain to the state and allow itself to be disciplined by the logic of the market. This means that evangelism

---

6. McClendon rightly suggests that evangelism must be understood within the larger and more fundamental practice of "community formation" (1986:1:233).

and social ethics are ultimately not two different things. Nor is worship a third thing (Hauerwas 2000:155–61).

At the same time, the church cannot be understood to be faithful in all that it is and all that it does without engaging in the explicit practice of reaching the world, challenging sin, communicating the good news, offering Christ, sharing Christian worship, drawing persons into Christian friendship, inviting and welcoming persons to be a part of God's reign, and summoning persons to a new and living way. Fidelity to God's reign requires that what we have been given as a gift be offered in turn to the world. What we have been given is salvation in the form of a new peoplehood, and the task of evangelism is to graciously extend this peoplehood to the world. To conclude that one can bear witness to God's reign without ever explicitly offering others an invitation to be a part of that reign is not merely half right; it is wholly wrong. The practice of evangelism is intrinsic to the comprehensive *praxis* of an evangelistic faith. Evangelism is practiced implicitly whenever and wherever the church bears witness to the good news by its distinctively peaceful, cruciform, and subversive existence in the world. Indeed, evangelism is no less powerful a practice for that. But evangelism must also be practiced explicitly and intentionally as proclamation, hospitality, invitation, and initiation if the church is to be faithful in its witness.

Given this second and more specific, concrete, and explicit understanding of evangelism as a distinct practice, it is possible to misunderstand the practice of evangelism as an exercise in autonomous "production" (*poiesis*), the independent activity of *making* something, namely, converts. But against this misunderstanding, I would want to affirm that although evangelism hopes for much, it does not necessarily *produce* anything, it does not necessarily *accomplish* anything, it does not necessarily *result* in anything. It is not a means to some other end, for faithfulness in witnessing to and offering God's peaceable reign is its end, even if that witness is rejected. As MacIntyre concludes, one of the characteristics of a practice is that it is measured not by external standards of success or winning but rather by virtue (excellence or faithfulness) in performance.

Though it may seem counterintuitive, then, what is needed most in our time is not more attention to "effectiveness" and "success" in evangelism (at least as those words have come to be used in the context of production) but learning once again as a church how to bear faithful witness. While evangelism may be many things and while its practice may entail multiple logics, the central and foundational logic of evangelism is the logic of *martyria*, a logic of truthfulness, clarity, and incarnation, rather than the logic of production, accomplishment, or making. Ultimately, however, we need not force a trade-off between faithfulness and effectiveness. Rather, we could say that the effectiveness required of the practice of evangelism is effectiveness at being faithful rather than effectiveness at production. Evangelism is teleologically (or better, "eschatologically") ordered, but not measured by a product it might produce or the extent to which it might be successful in getting people to see things a certain way or to alter their behavior in certain ways. A *poietic* process, on the other hand, as Reinhard Hütter notes, "stands or falls with the quality of its result, a result which, quite in the sense of a product, can also exist in and for itself. By contrast, although practices do, under certain circumstances, generate by-products, their goal is never an end product as such. The goal and purpose of every practice is and remains to perform it as well as possible" (2000:211).

Admittedly, to advocate this model of practice is to swim against the currents of contemporary assumptions about excellence within our intensely pragmatic, competitive, and technocratic societies. Ours is a world in which excellence is typically configured within a means-end paradigm where (a) ends are external to means, (b) means are merely instrumental relative to those external ends (so that evangelism, rather than being construed as a practice requiring virtuous character, is reduced to a set of techniques), (c) a calculus of effectiveness can be employed whereby we hope to be able to control the achievement or production of those ends, and (d) this entire act of achievement, of production, and of relating means to ends stands independent and free of any community or tradition that would specify the substantive good, truth, or beauty upon which the unity, meaning, and purpose of practices might be premised or toward which it might be directed. The way we organize our work in capitalist economies contributes to this, as MacIntyre has noted, insofar as we are systematically alienated from the goods of our own activity (1984:227). Within such a paradigm, evangelism is understood as whatever set of intentional activities that will achieve a particular end (conversion, initiation, baptism, membership, church growth, etc.), so that the logic of the practice of evangelism becomes wholly governed by that aim. Evangelism then becomes not a virtuous practice but an autonomous, creative act of "making" on the part of the evangelist, for whom the church as the fellowship of the Holy Spirit is an afterthought, a by-product. The aim of evangelism is then the production of "converts." Jesus offers a critique of this practical logic when he lashes out at some of the evangelists of his own day: "Woe to you, scribes and Pharisees, hypocrites! For you cross sea and land to make a single convert, and you make the new convert twice as much a child of hell as yourselves" (Matt. 23:15).

If MacIntyre's model holds water, excellence in the practice of evangelism may not, then, coincide necessarily with winning, effectiveness, production, or success, however much we should seek to excel in achieving the goods internal to evangelism. Let us recall McClendon's comparison of a practice to a game. The comparison has obvious limitations, but if only for a moment we were to think of the practice of evangelism as something like a game of chess, we might say that we have been called to play chess, not to win at chess. Of course, there is a sense in which it is not possible to truly play chess without trying to win (that would be trifling). But winning, in and of itself, is not the measure of chess well played, because even if we were to win we might have cheated. In fact, winning by cheating is not really winning. The judgment that winning is "all that matters" is a judgment inappropriate to a practice, and no less so in the case of evangelism.

As a way of further clarifying this point, consider the following words from Paul's first letter to the Corinthians, portions of which have frequently been used to defend an evangelism that seeks success, winning, and results at all costs:

> For though I am free with respect to all, I have made myself a slave to all, so that I might win more of them. To the Jews I became as a Jew, in order to win Jews. To those under the law I became as one under the law (though I myself am not under the law) so that I might win those under the law. To those outside the law I became as one outside the law (though I am not free from God's law but am under Christ's law) so that I might win those outside the law. To the weak I became weak, so that I might win the weak. I have become all things to all people, that I might by all means save some. I do it all for the sake of the gospel, so that I may share in its blessings.
>
> Do you not know that in a race the runners all compete, but only one receives the prize? Run in such a way that you may win it. Athletes exercise self-control in all things; they do it to receive a perishable wreath, but we an imperishable one. So I do not run aimlessly, nor do I box as though beating the air; but I punish my body and enslave it, so that after proclaiming to others I myself should not be disqualified. (9:19–27)

Clearly Paul is aimed at "winning" others to Christ. But notice that he is careful to specify the gospel itself as the *telos* of his practice, as that for the sake of which he is evangelizing. The faithful practice of evangelism is certainly not "aimless." But one must also be careful not to seek that *telos* in such a way that the disciplines associated with the practice are relativized or abandoned and the practice becomes wholly instrumentalized (one may become Greek to win the Greeks, but it would be another matter altogether to become a consumer to win consumers). How easily the aim of a practice, once detached from the practice to which it is internal, can cease to be a legitimate aim after all. That is why, while it is true that Christian evangelism is aimed at winning, it is just as true that, as the cross makes abundantly clear, Christians are not *called* to win. Paul makes a similar point in the thirteenth chapter of 1 Corinthians, declaring that even if we have gifted tongues, unbounded knowledge, or a powerful and effective faith, as long as we have not love, we gain nothing.

To put it plainly, then, there is only one criterion by which evangelism may be measured, and that is whether or not it is a faithful, virtuous witness to God's peace. As William Abraham says, "To say that we are to be all things to all people is a counsel of perfection; it is not a call to adjust the gospel to every wind of secular doctrine" (1989:203).

The problems involved in thinking about evangelism as a practice, therefore, are not only strategic but ultimately theological. The argument of this book is that the prevailing model of practical reasoning employed to a great extent by contemporary evangelism is inadequate to the Christian faith, ecclesiologically bankrupt, morally vacuous, and tyrannized by a means-end causality that is eschatologically hopeless insofar as it externalizes the means from the end. The way this usually works is that once the aim of evangelism is asserted in terms of converting, initiating, recruiting, or persuading, strategies are developed and implemented, typically on the basis of their strictly utilitarian value in reaching that end. Both the "end" and the "means" then tyrannize the church as it is forced to forget itself and the One whom it follows in the name of both the end and the means. In the process, the church's fundamental calling to bear faithful witness is edged out in favor of what "works." Moreover, we who have been made witnesses by the Holy Spirit fail to be guided in our practice by Spirit-formed virtues such as love, hope, faith, presence, patience, humility, and courage, for "witness" has now been hijacked by an evangelism that turns it into a tool employed as a means to something else—namely, the converting or initiating of other persons. Evangelism finds it all too easy to jump ahead to some imagined result and then to adjust the meaning of witness in accordance with what will "work" to achieve that result. It forgets that Christian witnesses engage in the practice of evangelism for no other reason than that they have been made witnesses.

This reduction of evangelism to production, its accompanying logic of effectiveness and success, and its inevitable instrumentalization of the church in the service of whatever "works" may be termed "the tyranny of the practical." In fact, however, it is not the practical per se that is tyrannizing but rather the way we construct the practical and construe its logic. That construction is fine when we are engaged in assembling a television or fixing a toaster but not when we are engaged in bearing faithful witness to God's peaceable reign and inviting others into that reign. What is required in order to overcome this tyranny, as I hope to show, is a community created and formed by the Holy Spirit and a story vastly different from that which today prevails in modern Western cultures. As Albert Outler once said:

> Give us a church whose members believe and understand the gospel of God's healing love of Christ to hurting men and women. Give us a church that speaks and acts in consonance with its faith—not only to reconcile the world but to turn it upside down! Give us a church of spirit-filled people in whose fellowship life speaks to life, love to love, and faith and trust respond to God's grace. And we shall have a church whose witness in the world will not fail and whose service to the world will transform it. (1971:56)

Part 2

The Story of the People of God

The previous chapter's discussion of evangelism as a practice was largely formal. If something like MacIntyre's account of a practice is to be helpful, nothing less than a full account of the narrative, community, and virtues that guide and sustain the practice of evangelism is required in order to specify its nature, purpose, and logic. The following three chapters attempt to take a first step in that direction by narrating the practice of evangelism from within a particular story—the story of the people of God. This story, with its various characters, subplots, twists, turns, and surprises, literally "makes sense" out of the Christian life by depicting its beginning, way, and end and thereby orienting us on a journey. When inhabited faithfully, this story keeps us from being mere tourists on the journey; instead we become pilgrims who seek to live into the story. It is this story that evangelism inhabits, embodies, tells, and retells. If, as MacIntyre suggests, practices can be thought of as "enacted narratives," then it is this story that evangelism enacts.

To begin thinking about the practice of evangelism from within a story is not to begin with a theory or a set of beliefs or doctrines that will later be applied to practice. It is instead, from the beginning, to situate our practice within a particular account of the purpose and ends of the Christian life, apart from which evangelism easily becomes a technology in the service of rival stories and competing ends. That is why the very capacity for evangelizing requires that our lives are formed by remembering—not the sort of remembering that is only a mastery of information or a memorization of creeds (the path of the tourist), but the saturation of our lives by a story such that its beginning is our beginning, its journey our journey, its end our end. Christians become Christians not merely by hearing a story but by being formed bodily into one. Only as this happens can we become faithful tellers and enactors of that story in a world that is watching and listening, even when we are tempted to think it is not.

As the discussion in the previous chapter has shown, an especially significant function of narrative for the practices it renders intelligible is its depiction of the story's end, thereby providing the *telos* of those practices. Urgent attention to the *telos* of evangelism is needed today. Evangelism lives by hope and is essentially a restless activity, called forward by the promise of the end of our journey together as a church and, ultimately, by the confidence that the *telos* of the church is the *telos* of the world itself. Hope punctuates the practice of evangelism in much the same way that a final punctuation mark gives meaning to an entire sentence. Hope is, of course, oriented toward the future—where things are headed and how they shall turn out, toward God's love as not only the source and ground of our lives but their ultimate aim and end. Yet hope utterly transforms the present and reinterprets the past, ultimately making of our lives a journey. While hope is future oriented, it may never be reduced to a menu of beliefs about the future. We live from hope, create out of hope, and love in hope. Moreover, as Christians, we are called to a way of life that is an embodied testament to hope (1 Peter 3:8–17). Jürgen Moltmann expresses this splendidly when he says,

> Does this hope cheat [us] of the happiness of the present? How could it do so! For it is itself the happiness of the present. . . . Expectation makes life good, for in expectation [we] can accept [our] whole present and find joy not only in its joy but also in its pain. Thus hope goes on its way through the midst of happiness and pain, because in the promises of God it can see a future also for the transient, the dying, and the dead. That is why it can be said that living without hope is like no longer living. Hell is hopelessness, and it is not for nothing that at the entrance to Dante's hell there stand the words: "Abandon hope, all ye who enter here." (1967:32)

If Christians are called to live out of hope, they are also called to share that hope with others, to offer it to others, and even to inspire it and call it forth in others. While evangelism is frequently referred to as "faith sharing," it might just as appropriately be termed "hope sharing." Sharing hope, though, is a matter not merely of talking about it or testifying to it but of quite literally *sharing* it.

But sharing the experience of hope is problematic today on several counts. We live in a world that is increasingly cynical, pessimistic, and calloused—a world that has learned not to trust, expect, or hope. Perhaps the wars, holocausts, terrorism, and scandals of our time have wearied us of hoping for too much out of ourselves or our social arrangements. Or maybe the comprehensive formation of our consumer identity is so overwhelming that we have numbed ourselves to the possibility of a freedom that is more than the emptiness of sheer choice. But this is not the first time in history that Christians have found themselves in a context of despair. The Greco-Roman world into which Christianity was born was likewise characterized by fatalism, cynicism, and apathy. As Robert Jewett notes, hope was considered to be "a weakling's resort, a refusal to face the difficult fate that life inevitably imposes" (1993:162). In such a climate, characterized by despair and weighed down by the heavy sense that human lives are predetermined, perhaps even written in the stars, it was tempting to construe hope in terms of escape and release. It is not difficult to understand how the Greek notion of an immortal soul that upon one's death returns to the realm of the divine whence it originated would have enormous appeal in such a context. Perhaps it is also not too difficult to understand the particular attraction today of that narration of hope within a story of the final removal of a righteous remnant from this planet while the rest of humanity is simply "left behind." But it is worth asking whether the hope that Christian evangelism aims to share can be anything more than a distraction when narrated as escape and release.

Very much is at stake for evangelism, then, with regard to the story with which we begin and the meaning and end of human life that is narrated by that story. For it is this story that makes possible some ways of thinking and acting while other ways remain quite impossible—or, rather, *unimaginable*. Within this story some questions are conceivable while other questions simply do not come to mind. In our time, of course, it is "reality" we crave—and we are offered a steady diet of something called "reality" on television. But perhaps we may put in a good word for the imaginary. For virtually every aspect of evangelistic practice (and, indeed, of our lives) depends upon and is ordered from within a social and practical imaginary.

By *imaginary* here I do not mean an abstract set of ideas or flight of fancy. I borrow the term from persons such as Charles Taylor (2004), John Milbank (1990), Benedict Anderson (1996), and William Cavanaugh (1998, 2002), for whom *social imaginary* refers to that whole complex of practices, habits, relations, and stories that has the "power to discipline bodies, to habituate them and script them into a drama of its own making" (Cavanaugh 1998:31). A social imaginary is an all-embracing set of practical, moral, and ontic norms that are largely unconscious and pretheoretical, through which we interpret and prescribe our social existence, relationships, and expectations relative to power and agency. In Taylor's discussion of modern social imaginaries, he has in mind broad sets of common assumptions about the way things are and the way things ought to be (as well as, of course, the way things "ought not" to be), sets that change over time and yield political systems, states, economies, and societies. But one might also think of societies or economic markets themselves as imaginaries. Cities, counties, and states—in fact, all of our political arrangements—function very much as social imaginaries. The argument of this book is that core church practices such as evangelism require that we understand the church as itself a social, political, and economic imaginary.

Nation-states such as the one called "the United States of America" are very impressive examples of imaginaries. As Cavanaugh points out in his *Theopolitical Imagination*,

> The state as such does not exist. What exists are buildings and aeroplanes and tax forms and border patrols. What mobilizes them into a project called "nation-state" is a disciplined imagination of a community occupying a particular space with a common conception of time, a common history and a common destiny of salvation from peril. (2002:2)

To be sure, there really is a huge land mass bordered on each side by large bodies of water. But like all political entities, the United States of America is a construction of political imagination.

> We are often fooled by the seeming solidity of the materials of politics, its armies and offices, into forgetting that these materials are marshaled by acts of the imagination. How does a provincial farm boy become persuaded that he must travel as a soldier to another part of the world and kill people he knows nothing about? He must be convinced of the reality of borders, and imagine himself deeply, mystically, united to a wider national community that stops abruptly at those borders. (Cavanaugh 2002:1)

These words ought to take our breath away. What sort of imaginary could possibly motivate and mobilize a Christian in this way? How powerful must be the politics sustained by such an imaginary that it could ask an eighteen-year-old Christian to kill other people (including, quite often, other Christians) and not only would he agree to do so, but he (and his family) would hold in contempt fellow Christians who refuse so to kill. It is true, of course, that most of the time we do not choose the social imaginations in which we live; they choose us. But it is also true that not everything about our lives has to be the way it is. Things could be different if our lives were lived from within other social imaginaries.

Once again we are driven back to the importance of stories. If the United States of America is a formidable social imaginary, it is one created and sustained by a story. To be sure, it is a story founded on violence. It is, moreover, a story that is constantly being retold in ways that will make us and others believe that because the world is founded on violence, it can be saved only through violence. Christians, however, have a rival story—one that claims the world is founded on peace and can be saved from its violence only by peace.

Social imaginaries—whether the state, the market, the university, or the church—are nurtured and passed along in fundamentally story form, complete with beginnings and ends. It is true, of course, that we embody stories in largely unconscious ways. But these stories are no less powerful in forming the way we act or the way we think of ourselves, our neighbors, the church, and the world. It makes a very great difference, therefore, whether the practice of evangelism is grounded in the biblical narrative of the people of Israel, the life and work of Jesus, and the acts of the apostles, or whether it is instead grounded in the story of patriarchy, the story of capitalism, the story of the Enlightenment, or any in a long line of imperial stories, including that relatively recent story called the United States of America. In thinking about evangelistic practice, we do well always to ask ourselves, "How *evangel-like* is evangelism?" (Klaiber 1997:11).

The church's story turns out to be doubly important for evangelism. Evangelism not only enacts that story but, in doing so, offers it to others. In fact, the Christian offer of salvation is, as Walter Brueggemann puts it, "an invitation and summons to 'switch stories,' and therefore to change our lives" (1993:11). The power of the Christian story, however, is in part its ability to embrace rather than exclude other stories. In fact, Paul makes it clear that the practice of baptism forms us into a new story in which our previous stories are united to Christ through inclusion and reconciliation rather than negation, evaporation, or homogenization (in Christ, Jew and Greek, male and female, do not disappear but are instead reconciled). To emphasize Christian narrative then is not a way of discounting the importance of our other narratives. Indeed, as Stanley Hauerwas has pointed out, the Christian story helps us to tell our other stories more honestly. Our individual or group stories are reoriented rather than removed in baptism. They are no longer *determinative* for our relationships. Thus, while I may be gay or straight, American or Korean, hearing or nonhearing, it is my membership in a new people, the people of God, that is now the decisive factor for my patterns of relating to others.[1] Another way of saying this is that conversion is not a matter of

---

1. So Matthew records:

While he was still speaking to the crowds, his mother and his brothers were standing outside, wanting to speak to him. Someone told him, "Look, your mother and

fitting another new story into *my* story; it is a matter of allowing myself to be narrated by a new story, one authored by God rather than me.

Identifying the church's story is always a complex and unfinished task. Part of what unites Christians is an attempt better to understand that story together and to learn how to shape our lives according to it. This also means that Christianity as a living tradition is, in the words of MacIntyre, an "extended argument" about the most important features of that story and, importantly, that story's *end*. In fact, being a Christian means being "a community of argument concerning the meaning of true discipleship" (Tanner 1997:156). We must, of course, still make choices, and the truth of the matter is that the Christian story cannot embrace every story. On the contrary, it actively resists and rejects other stories that require our allegiance to and worship of powers that would either fragment us into individuals or form us into travelers on another journey altogether. So, for example, if the state asks us to kill for it or if the market asks us to shop for it, the narrative that sustains these twin powers cannot be embraced by Christians and must be "counternarrated."

It is in the very nature of a story like the church's, which has lasted for almost two thousand years, that some of its features have at times been given more prominence than others and have also been integrated with, placed in opposition to, or challenged by other stories. Thus, identifying the church's story is an undertaking not without controversy. The way the story is told depends greatly on the circumstances of its telling, the audience to whom it is told, and, most notably, who is doing the telling. The story may be distinguished but never separated from the storytellers themselves, the community of tradition and traditioning that both is constituted by the story and shapes it across the years. One of the greatest challenges of Christian evangelism is faithfully remembering and creatively retelling the story while always listening to new voices, especially those who have been silenced or marginalized by previous tellings. For often they help us to see how those previous tellings have not taken important parts of the story into account and unduly privileged other parts of the story.

For this reason, two resources—*memory* and *suspicion*—turn out to be extraordinarily important for evangelism. On the one hand, we tend toward amnesia, and so we need persons who can help us remember the story and tell it faithfully. On the other hand, we need persons who raise suspicions about our storytelling, ask new questions, and are even able to tell the story *against* tradition. Apart from the latter, the story

---

your brothers are standing outside, wanting to speak to you." But to the one who had told him this, Jesus replied, "Who is my mother, and who are my brothers?" And pointing to his disciples, he said, "Here are my mother and my brothers! For whoever does the will of my Father in heaven is my brother and sister and mother." (12:46–50)

would remain lifeless, depositlike, oppressive, self-justifying, and less than fully catholic.[2] Frequently, the sources of this suspicious creativity in the telling of the church's story are the persons and communities that have been marginalized by or locked out of the church. As Letty Russell puts it,

> Like other central biblical and church traditions, the interpretation of salvation is situation-variable. It not only has evolved over time but also continues to take on different meanings in the face of concrete struggles and hopes for wholeness and life. Its gospel meaning is often illuminated most clearly by those whose struggles with death and hopes for life help us understand what good news is all about. This is because salvation is a story and not an idea, a word that describes God's mending and reconciling action in our lives and in the whole of creation. As we respond in faith to God's saving action, we are drawn into the story and God's gift of justice and love is revealed in our lives. (1993:115)

If suspicion plays a creatively subversive role in evangelism, it is also true that memory itself can be creatively subversive. Mortimer Arias suggests that the Scriptures and the Holy Spirit are "the two great subverters of history and the church," insofar as the Scriptures provide a "subversive memory of Jesus" and the Holy Spirit has an "antiamnesic ministry" (1984:67). All of this makes the telling and retelling of the Christian story a joyous but messy enterprise with no finished product. "In the end," says Kathryn Tanner, "how the identity of Christianity should be summed up is an unanswerable question in that Christianity has its identity as a task; it has its identity in the form of a task of looking for one" (1997:155).

As important as narrative memory is for Christian existence and for evangelism, multiple factors work against memory. Historical-critical tools that challenge the accuracy of our storytelling, perspectives gained from the social sciences that demonstrate the particularity and bias that come with our social locations and histories, the irreducible plurality of voices and versions of the story present within the Christian tradition itself (even and especially within Scripture), and the presence of other stories beyond our own: all of these may tempt us into believing we have no story. In both word and deed, we become "unscripted anxious stutterers," a phrase MacIntyre uses to describe children who have been deprived of stories (1984:216). We cannot even begin to evangelize, for we have no story to tell.

2. Yoder makes this very point when he says, "There is no time when there is not a contemporary issue demanding critical scrutiny and structural change. The challenges addressed today by feminism to patriarchal visions of ministry, or by the base communities to ritualistic notions of sacrament, or to absentee notions of episcopacy, are contributions to, not criticisms of, catholicity properly conceived" (1998:315).

My conviction is that plurality, historicity, and difference, while naturally producing feelings of insecurity, are nonetheless central to the task of telling the story of the people of God. For that story is itself the story of an encounter with difference (including God's difference!) and a record of how that encounter makes a people distinctive in the world. The story of the people of God is the story of a people who encounter other stories in a variety of ways, sometimes in the form of a gift and an offer while at other times in the form of a confrontation and a scandal. We need not be paralyzed in making decisions about our story or frightened about allowing it to interact with other stories, provided we do so with appropriate discipline, suspicion, self-criticism, and humility. After all, our story is not entirely rosy. It is a story of detours and dead ends, reversals and failure. It is a record of faithlessness, stubbornness, and rebellion as much as it is a story of obedience and hope. We need the whole of the Bible, because as a whole it does not shrink from narrating both sides of the story.

The emphasis here on narrative does not permit us to ignore or discount nonnarrative texts such as wisdom, law, instruction, poetry, or exhortation. Yet narratives have an existential depth that renders them *habitable* and that invites others not only to be persuaded of the truth of the Christian story but "to share imaginatively" in it (cf. Doak 2004:197). For more often than not, it is stories rather than isolated ideas, principles, or propositions into which we find ourselves formed. In the following three chapters, therefore, I will make a case for the possibility of an evangelism practiced from within the story of the people of God. But there can be nothing triumphalistic about this story or the peoplehood and practices that arise from it. In fact, any evangelistic confidence must lie ultimately in the fact that it is God's faithfulness, not our own, that is being narrated (cf. Lindbeck 2002:157). At the same time, God's love and election is always offered as a gift and never creates a people unilaterally. Rather, peoplehood must always be freely accepted as *vocation*. Likewise, if Christian evangelism is the activity of proclaiming a story, it is also the activity of inviting others to make that story their own. This activity is performed by telling the story and also by living out that story imaginatively and openly in the world. But then evangelism can never be only proclamation or invitation, for it begins logically (even if not always chronologically) in allowing ourselves to be narrated by that story. Apart from our own formation into that story through baptism, worship, and the various practices and patterns of ecclesial life, we do not have the capacity to be faithful "rememberers" of the story, much less narrators or "counternarrators" of the story to others.

2

Israel and the Calling Forth of a People

Of the many things to be said about the story that narrates the Christian practice of evangelism, among the first is that it is Jewish (no small embarrassment, by the way, for those who would convert Jews to Christianity). The dozens of books that are bound together in the single volume that Christians call the Bible address multiple topics, but what is frequently hidden to Christians—perhaps because of its prominence—is the sheer bulk of pages devoted to a particular people whose story takes place in Asia and Africa around the eastern end of the Mediterranean. Ask any Christian what subject the Bible talks about more than anything else, and it is unlikely that he or she will answer "Israel." On the contrary, we have been trained to think of the Bible as handing over information about important *beliefs* (sin, death, salvation, faith, God, etc.). Yet it is through the story of this particular people that we first come to know how God acts in the world and what sort of salvation God has in mind for us. In contrast to other religions of the ancient world, the story contained within the pages of the Bible is not the story of a god or the gods as such, but rather the story of a people and their having been chosen, called, liberated, and led by God from among the nations as a new and holy nation, a new race of human beings from among all the races.

That is not to say that this unique people is the sole or primary concern of God. For the God of Israel is the creator of the entire world, of all the creatures in the world, and of all the peoples of the world. This God is likewise the ruler of all history (though this will need some clarification, given our customary use of the word *ruler* to mean "despot"). The choosing of this people is on behalf of and for the sake of the entire world, as the initial and paradigmatic story of God's love for and election of Abraham attests. God promises to bless Abraham and his people and, through them, to extend that blessing to all humanity. Abraham is thus commanded by God to "go forth" from his own country and family.

But the story of Abraham is preceded by a narrative of how humans were first created in unity and community and of the subsequent destruction of both by a "fall" into rivalry, shame, arrogance, and mistrust (told through the stories of Cain's murder of Abel and the corruption and violence that lead to the flood), with the net result that our human attempts at building a society, or a city, end in frustration, confusion, and alienation (Gen. 11:1–9). The story of Abraham's trust in God's promise, therefore, is a contrast story. It provides an alternative to the fall, a way that is the realization in history of the possibility of community for which all humans were created.

In much the same way, the story of Moses is narrated as the story of a new beginning, the formation of an alternative community that is both a radical break with and an embodied criticism of virtually every aspect of the social, political, and economic reality of its time. As Walter Brueggemann puts it,

> The program of Moses is not the freeing of a little band of slaves as an escape from the empire, though that is important enough, especially if you happen to be in that little band. Rather, his work is nothing less than an assault on the consciousness of the empire, aimed at nothing less than the dismantling of the empire both in its social practices and in its mythic pretensions. (1978:18–19)

What we find throughout the biblical narrative of Israel, then, is that while the story of the people of God may be situated within a larger narrative of creation or empire, it is never told in such a way as to diminish the crucial importance of that people's particularity *for* creation or empire. God's activity in history is directed toward all of the nations and, indeed, all of creation. Yet the particular, historical relationship between God and a distinctive people, spoken of as "the people of God,"[1] is the central clue for understanding God's purpose for all, God's rule over all. In his valuable study *Does God Need the Church?* Gerhard Lohfink remarks, "God begins with very small things, not by setting masses in

---

1. Though audacious, the label is deeply rooted in Hebrew Scripture. Several New Testament texts use similar terminology—for example, Romans 9:25–26; Hebrews 4:9 and 8:10; 1 Peter 2:9.

motion. To change the whole world God has at first no one but Abraham" (1999:29).

Because of the improbable and unpredictable particularity of God's election of a people, the relationship between this people and the salvation of the world remains a scandal. Our temptation theologically, apologetically, and evangelistically is to play down the particularity of this people, to existentialize their story so that it becomes symbolic of a universal quest or a metaphor for the salvation of each individual.[2] But the Bible refuses to lend itself to our fondness for configuring particularity and universality over against each other as a null-sum proposition. Rather, particularity is the instrument of universality; it is its beginning and point of departure. The few are given for the many, and as Lesslie Newbigin has pointed out, throughout the Bible there is a "repeated narrowing" of focus that reveals the inner logic of election within God's mission (1995:34). The particularity of Israel is related to the universality of God's reign as the place, the time, and the people through whom God chooses to unfold God's purpose in the world. This does not mean that at some point Israel gets cast off or forsaken in favor of a wider universality. Even the gates through which one enters the heavenly city envisioned by John as the ultimate future of the entire world have written upon them the names of the twelve tribes of Israel (Rev. 21:10–14):

> John makes it clear that the city is nothing other than the restored people of the twelve tribes, the people of God in its eschatological perfection. But then in turn it is clear that no matter how universal the eschatological city, God's new society, its arrival is not something that happens at just any time and everywhere; it is bound to a concrete place and time; to the people of the twelve tribes and its history. This connection is for many today a stumbling-block that can scarcely be overcome. (Lohfink 1999:26)

On the one hand, then, the salvation intended by God for the entire world has a history, a place, a concrete social form, and an embodiment in a people while, on the other hand, the particularity of this people and its history is not for itself but for the entire world. The story of the people of Israel arises out of and is defined by a double relationship—its relationship to God and its relationship to the nations. The former is, of course, determinative for the latter, since the peculiarity of this people among and for the nations is but a reflection of its having been created, freed, and formed by a peculiar God.

2. Since at least Friedrich Schleiermacher, the modern ecclesiological project has been to flatten out the particularity of the people of God so that "church" is but a way of talking about religious association in general or human sociality as such. See, for example, Schleiermacher 1958, especially the fourth speech on "Association in Religion."

This double relationship is frequently expressed in the Bible with words like *election, promise,* and *covenant.* Indeed, it is impossible to tell the story of Israel without considering what it means to be elected by God—and elected precisely as a missionary people who are called to trust God and to be led by God. Within the story of Israel, one discovers that to be elected is to be saved: to be freed from slavery but also to be provided the social structures, economic patterns,[3] laws, worship, leadership, and practices that together form a people into "the people of God." But one also finds the temptation to turn this election (and the salvation it makes possible) into exclusion, nationalism, ethnocentrism, and self-trust. Now the social and material salvation by which God has made "a people out of no people" turns in on itself. The story of Jonah is a cautionary tale in this regard, and so are the repeated warnings of the prophets, who call the people of Israel and its leaders to faithfulness, who remind them that God has chosen them not because of their worthiness or genealogical inheritance but because of God's sheer love and mercy (Deut. 7:6–9). So, for example, God has given the people a worship; but when feasts, holy days, and practices such as prayer and fasting are unaccompanied by justice, compassion, and a righteous life, that worship can be rejected. Election, it seems, can just as well bring God's judgment as blessing,[4] and throughout the story of the people of God the "outsider" may appear as the one who is the bearer of God's judgment and purpose (Cyrus, for example, cf. Isa. 41:1–4).

Election is a precarious theological notion and plays out ambiguously in the story of the people of God (this will prove to be just as true in the case of the church as of Israel). This people is elected for mission and service, but there is a tendency to turn that into "election for security and superiority" (Russell 1993:164).[5] The alternative and countercultural community formed under Moses will eventually be subverted by the temptation of building a theocratic kingdom (first under David, but then dramatically under Solomon), such that God's election comes to be equated with military might, geographical expansion, economic affluence, and an imperial mindset, or as Brueggemann puts it, a "royal consciousness." Though the Davidic king can be narrated as an advocate of the oppressed and marginalized and as one who trusts in God (thereby

3. For example, the provisions for the poor and the stranger in the form of tithes, jubilee debt cancellation, and gleaning access.

4. "You only have I known of all the families of the earth; therefore I will punish you for all your iniquities" (Amos 3:2).

5. As Russell goes on to say, "Election provides a source of identity in a particular social-historical reality, but it becomes contradictory when abstracted as a doctrine that is applicable in all realities. Without grounding in a reality of oppression, election quickly moves from a gift of grace to a justification of privilege" (1993:170–71).

providing the foundation for the emergence of messianism), the royal politics of Israel is largely narrated as the abandonment of the gift of freedom under Moses and the institutionalization of social hierarchies, self-trust, and a "politics of oppression" (Brueggemann 1978:28–43). Election for mission can now appear as something like a proprietary ownership of God.

Because of this ambiguity in the meaning of election, the prophets of Israel gravitate to Israel's double relationship to God and the nations, calling the people to remember whose people they are (at times with such intimate terms as God's *beloved* and *firstborn*) and also chastening them lest they drift into idolatry or forget their missionary existence (now with a very different set of terms such as *adulterer* and *prostitute*). Remembering turns out to be one of the central and defining activities of the people of Israel. It is the basis for both their cultic and their moral life. It funds prophetic reform and liberative praxis and is never to be simply equated with a "conservative" as over against a "progressive" outlook. Remembering likewise gives this people's existence its narrative quality—God's dealings with them in the past are decisive for making sense out of the present and guiding them into the future.

This prophetic call to remember, however, is not aimed at merely recalling the past mentally but takes the form of a summons both to worship and to obedience. In Israel's story, worship and obedience are each discovered to be impossible without the other, and the two together constitute its witness to the nations (here we find our first clue that evangelism is inseparable from worship and ethics). God's ways are to become Israel's ways, so that in order to know what God is up to, one need only look at Israel. The story of Israel, therefore, is a story in which these three postures—worship, obedience, and witness—are bound up with and integrally related to one another. The consistent prophetic message in all this is that election rests entirely on God's free grace, a grace that rules out all claims to entitlement and all pretensions to worthiness.

The story of Israel, then, may be understood as a journey through which a people is called and formed "for the nations" (Isa. 11:12). Moreover, this journey will result in "foreigners who join themselves to the Lord" through Israel's witness by joining themselves to Israel's ways of worship and obedience. Nor will these foreigners be second-rank citizens. As Isaiah promises,

> The foreigners who join themselves to the LORD,
>   to minister to him, to love the name of the LORD,
>   and to be his servants,
> all who keep the sabbath, and do not profane it,
>   and hold fast my covenant—

> these I will bring to my holy mountain,
> > and make them joyful in my house of prayer;
> their burnt offerings and their sacrifices
> > will be accepted on my altar;
> for my house shall be called a house of prayer
> > for all peoples.
> Thus says the LORD God,
> > who gathers the outcasts of Israel,
> I will gather others to them
> > besides those already gathered. (56:6–8)

In these words we again discover that there can be no trade-off between God's calling of and love for Israel, on the one hand, and God's purpose and love for the world, on the other. Central to the narrative of Israel's formation as a people is, of course, its liberation from Egypt. Israel is a people formed in freedom, for freedom, and against any subordination, accommodation, and privatization of freedom to structures of oppression (cf. Lohfink 1999:71–73). But this election for freedom is inseparable from Israel's eschatological purpose in extending that election to the rest of the world. Israel has thus been chosen by God to be a nation with a priestly role among the other nations—not merely a nation *with* priests but a nation *of* priests:

> You have seen what I did to the Egyptians, and how I bore you on eagles' wings and brought you to myself. Now therefore, if you obey my voice and keep my covenant, you shall be my treasured possession out of all the peoples. Indeed, the whole earth is mine, but you shall be for me a priestly kingdom and a holy nation. (Exod. 19:4–6)

The series of events, therefore, that become decisive for Israel's self-understanding (the exodus, the sojourn in the wilderness, the law giving at Sinai, the crossing of Jordan, the building of the temple) is to be understood as the fulfillment of God's purpose in creation and as the preparation and formation of a people who will bear witness to God's sovereignty in the world, who will serve as "a light for peoples, a lamp for nations" (Isa. 42:6 REB).[6]

So central is this priestly and witness-bearing purpose in the relationship between God and Israel that in Isaiah 60:1–11, the end of time can be imagined in terms of an ultimate pilgrimage of all the nations to Jerusalem, drawn by its light:

---

6. Rodney Clapp offers the helpful observation that this priestly witness to the "nations" must not be interpreted individualistically. The purpose of Israel as a nation is to exemplify a common life that is to be the model for other nations and communities (2000:154).

> Arise, shine; for your light has come,
>   and the glory of the LORD has risen upon you.
> For darkness shall cover the earth,
>   and thick darkness the peoples;
> but the LORD will arise upon you,
>   and his glory will appear over you.
> Nations shall come to your light,
>   and kings to the brightness of your dawn.
>
> Lift up your eyes and look around;
>   they all gather together, they come to you. . . .
> Your gates shall always be open;
>   day and night they shall not be shut,
> so that nations shall bring you their wealth,
>   with their kings led in procession.

This vision is echoed by Micah, who foresees the nations streaming into Jerusalem to learn God's ways:

> In days to come
>   the mountain of the LORD's house
> shall be established as the highest of the mountains,
>   and shall be raised up above the hills.
> Peoples shall stream to it,
>   and many nations shall come and say:
> "Come, let us go up to the mountain of the LORD,
>   to the house of the God of Jacob;
> that he may teach us his ways
>   and that we may walk in his paths."
> For out of Zion shall go forth instruction,
>   and the word of the LORD from Jerusalem.
> He shall judge between many peoples,
>   and shall arbitrate between strong nations far away;
> they shall beat their swords into plowshares,
>   and their spears into pruning hooks;
> nation shall not lift up sword against nation,
>   neither shall they learn war any more;
> but they shall all sit under their own vines and under their own fig
>   trees,
>   and no one shall make them afraid;
> for the mouth of the LORD of hosts has spoken. (4:1–4)

Shalom as Social Imagination

As Micah's vision makes clear, the "ways" of God embodied in this particular people (for the nations) are ways of justice and peace, the

very substance of what Israel will come to understand as holiness. The
prophets critique any understanding of holiness that is purely formal,
ceremonial, and positional, and that does not include the transformation of human hearts (Jer. 31:27–34) along with social and economic
arrangements. But here again is the scandal in God's election of Israel:
holiness has a particular form. It is exemplified in its institutions, practices, rituals, and in each of the three major offices that are to be visible
demonstrations of God's ways before the people: the prophet, the priest,
and the king (cf. Hauerwas 1983:78). God's purpose in history is not
just the creation of holy individuals but the creation of a holy people,
a people whose very existence in the world is a living testimony to the
rule of God. Holiness, therefore, is unreservedly social, political, and
economic. Every aspect of Israel's existence is to reflect the character of
the God it serves; Zechariah, for example, can imagine a day in which
"there shall be inscribed on the bells of the horses, 'Holy to the LORD.'
. . . And every cooking pot in Jerusalem and Judah shall be sacred to the
LORD of hosts" (Zech. 14:20–21). This holiness, however, is not because
of any intrinsic quality possessed by Israel but because of its priestly
constitution vis-à-vis the world, because of its missionary existence for
the world.

Given the character of God's ways as described in Micah 4, it should
not be surprising that when the prophets of God's people reach for a
word to describe God's rule, they inevitably fasten upon *shalom*, a term
that weaves together peace and justice in the context of a Spirit-created
community where human flourishing, blessedness, and wholeness is
accompanied by the well-being of animals and even plant life (cf. Isa.
11:1–9). Shalom thus imagined is not a merely spiritual, interior, or
private reality, nor is it an idealistic utopia about which Israel was allowed to sit around and dream longingly. Rather, shalom as both the
foundation of the universe and a coming state of affairs is a material
"commonwealth" that is to guide human activity and aspirations here
and now.

The prophetic vision of shalom may, I think, be helpfully thought of as
a form of what I earlier identified as a "social imaginary." But, again, an
imaginary does not here point to something abstract or fanciful. It is a
way of "seeing" that is embodied in a present and material constellation
of practices, rituals, memories, disciplines, and social arrangements that
forms us into a new world, or as Cavanaugh puts it, "scripts" us into a
"drama of its own making." If shalom, therefore, is a social imaginary, it
is not so in the way we normally use that word (as referring to something
unreal) but is instead premised upon what the prophets took to be most
real: God's unfailing presence, activity, and sovereignty in history. What
we learn from the Hebrew prophets, therefore, is that to live both toward

and out of shalom, as the beginning and the end of the story of the people of God, is to be eminently realistic. It is not shalom but the present order that lacks legitimacy. It is not hope but complacency that has no firm basis in reality. Moltmann grasps this when he says, "Hope alone is to be called 'realistic,' because it alone takes seriously the possibilities with which all reality is fraught. . . . The despair which imagines it has reached the end of its tether proves to be illusory, as long as nothing has yet come to an end but everything is still full of possibilities" (1967:25). However much God's rule of shalom may still be coming, it is no less "real."

Because of this hope and this realistic confidence in God's presence and activity in history, the people of God are released from the burden of needing to control history, "to make things come out right" (Hauerwas 1983:87). To be the people of God is not a matter of presuming that our plans coincide with God's; it is a matter of trusting, being open, and being guided and led into an uncontrollable future. Karl Rahner can even describe hope as "the enduring attitude of 'outwards from self' into the uncontrollability of God" (1981:231).

And so it is that to live within the social imaginary of shalom—to worship God and thus to be able to see anew, to obey God and thus to be led down new paths—is to live in such a way that the resort to violence is no longer an option.[7] As Zechariah affirms, we are called to live "not by might, nor by power, but by [God's] spirit" (4:6). At the same time, to live out of and toward shalom is to live responsibly as instruments of God's care for the world and especially for those who would otherwise be trampled on or forgotten—specifically, widows, orphans, the poor, and the stranger in the land. Shalom as a social imaginary implies an economics of abundance (narrated, for example, in the story of manna in the wilderness) in which there is enough for everyone and in which, moreover, human well-being is interconnected with the well-being of all God's creation. While in Israel's story nature is never divinized (and thus magic is ruled out as a tool for realizing shalom), it is no mere foil against which the salvation of humans is accomplished. From Adam and Eve in the garden to Noah and the flood, to Israel crossing the Sea of Reeds to Jonah and the whale, destruction and redemption, sin and salvation are never free-floating "spiritual" realities but knit-together

7. In his discussion of Jesus' wilderness temptation to accept dominion over the nations, Hauerwas gets this just right by showing how violence is ultimately linked with a refusal to worship God: "Jesus thus decisively rejects Israel's temptation to an idolatry that necessarily results in violence between peoples and nations. For our violence is correlative to the falseness of the objects we worship, and the more false they are, the greater our stake in maintaining loyalty to them and protecting them through coercion. Only the one true God can take the risk of ruling by relying entirely on the power of humility and love" (1983:79).

humans and nature into a seamless story of God's peaceable reign that is nothing short of cosmic.

A life lived in shalom may be described as both peaceful and content, but by no means is it tedious or tiresome. Coupled with the prophetic hope for the future is a dissatisfaction with the present—a dissatisfaction not to be confused with either pessimism or mania. Though shalom was clearly to be announced as "good news" (Isa. 52:7), the prophets understood that it is impossible to announce shalom without also denouncing the injustice and exposing the idolatry that block the realization of shalom. Thus, even though the prophetic message was attractive and captured the public imagination, it was perceived as subversive of existing social arrangements—as indeed it was. Long before the apostle Paul spoke of "the principalities and powers" that systematically attempt to thwart God's reign, the prophets of Israel took aim at "the powers that be," whether those be the king, the courts, the priesthood, or the market.

Witness to God's shalom (what Christians will eventually come to call "evangelism"), therefore, is born out of the prophetic intersection between hope and dissatisfaction, invitation and confrontation, attraction and subversion. It is to the great detriment of evangelism in our time that it has largely lost its moorings in this Jewish prophetic social imagination and in a hopeful vision that is utterly social, this-worldly, historical, material, and peaceable. While Christian evangelization is anchored in and points to the person of Jesus, it must learn to drink deeply from the wells of the prophetic tradition apart from which the life, ministry, and message of Jesus make no sense.

The reference to Jesus at this point is not entirely premature, for no narration of Israel's hope, and indeed no account of shalom as the imaginative substance of that hope, can be adequate that fails to highlight its distinctively messianic form. Israel's messianic hope is but a further exemplification of the repeated narrowing of focus earlier noted as revealing the inner logic of election within God's mission to the world. It is also an exemplification of God's intention to save Israel not by any action on Israel's part or in response to Israel's merit but strictly because God's own character is merciful and redemptive. There can be no more scandalous particularity in God's election of a people than that which is summed up in the promise of a coming Messiah who will initiate a realm of shalom and who will therefore be called the "prince of shalom" (Isa. 9:6–7). Moreover, this messianic prince reveals the kingship of God to be radically different from earthly kingships founded on violence and located in male privilege and hereditary social roles. For this king is a shepherd, a servant, and a suffering lamb (cf. McClendon 1986:2:65–66). No wonder the early Christians had no problem seeing God's election of Israel as both continuous with and paradigmatically expressed in Jesus of Nazareth.

If Israel's story is a clue to understanding God's rule in history, then it is a very odd sort of rule when measured by our customary use of such terms as *sovereignty*, *lordship*, and *rule*. For shalom is not only the aim of God's rule; it is also God's way of ruling—and of extending that rule. Rather than imposing this rule by coercion or fiat (either would be a contradiction of shalom), God offers it to the world through its social embodiment in a distinct and visible people. Already in the people of Israel, then, we discover what we shall later find to be the case in the story of Jesus and the story of the church. The people of God is called into existence to bear witness to God's reign, to "say among the nations, 'The LORD is king!'" (Psalm 96:10). But there can be no witness to God's reign where there is no people who, through worship and obedience, reject triumphalism, nationalism, and militarism and live instead according to the politics of shalom. Lohfink drives home this point in exemplary fashion:

God, like all revolutionaries, desires the overturning, the radical alteration of the whole society—for in this the revolutionaries are right: what is at stake is the whole world, and the change must be radical, for the misery of the world cries to heaven and it begins deep within the human heart. But how can anyone change the world and society at its roots without taking away freedom?

It can only be that God begins in a small way, at one single place in the world. There must be a place, visible, tangible, where the salvation of the world can begin: that is, where the world becomes what it is supposed to be according to God's plan. Beginning at that place, the new thing can spread abroad, but not through persuasion, not through indoctrination, not through violence. Everyone must have the opportunity to come and see. All must have the chance to behold and test this new thing. Then, if they want to, they can allow themselves to be drawn into the history of salvation that God is creating. Only in that way can their freedom be preserved. What drives them to the new thing cannot be force, not even moral pressure, but only the fascination of a world that is changed. (1999:27)

3

The Evangelistic Significance of Jesus

That Jesus is of paramount significance for Christian evangelism should go without saying. Yet that significance has frequently been abstracted from its historical and narrative context and emptied of its ethical content, so that what Jesus actually said and did is obscured by or subordinated to the church's later interest in the saving implications of his death and resurrection or with his status as a divine being, as God incarnate. It would be a mistake to reverse this process so that Jesus is reduced merely to an ethical teacher or sage, an eschatological prophet, or as Leonardo Boff puts it, "a person of extraordinary creative imagination," an individual with "courage," "a person of extraordinary good sense and sound reason," and "an extraordinary believer" (1978:113). It is not Jesus' own valiant faith that serves as the basis for our faith or that constitutes his significance for evangelism.[1] The church's relationship to him, as Kierkegaard said, is not that of admirers.[2] Rather, Jesus is the church's Lord, or, as Paul says, its "head" (Col. 1:18).

---

1. I have elsewhere discussed this problem as it appears in liberation Christologies generally and, specifically, in the Christology of Juan Luis Segundo (cf. Stone 1994). Segundo says his multivolume Christology "can be described as a methodical acceptance of the challenge embodied in Guerrero's apt and profound observation: 'We would save ourselves much wasted effort to gain believers *in* Jesus if instead we tried to interest human beings in what was truly original in Jesus' life—his faith, i.e., the faith *of* Jesus'" (1988:10). I believe that this dichotomy is ultimately untenable in light of the New Testament witness to Christ.

2. As Kierkegaard prays, "Arouse us therefore if we have dozed away into this delusion, save us from the error of wishing to admire Thee instead of being willing to follow Thee and to resemble Thee" (1956b:96).

This, however, raises a number of important questions about the nature of Christian evangelism and the identity of the Christian gospel. If Jesus is not merely an exemplar of faith (however unique or extraordinary), if he is not merely a witness who transmits faith to us as one link in a chain of witnesses, but rather the "primal source" of our faith (Ogden 1982:78–79), then the relationship of our evangelism to his must be something other than merely imitative. In some sense, Jesus becomes the very content of evangelism, and we are invited to make his story ours. In this chapter, I will begin by considering how Jesus was understood by his earliest witnesses to have practiced evangelism and how they understood the substance of his "good news." I will then turn to the question whether (and if so, to what extent) we are to continue with that originating practice or whether some sort of shift is instead required as the gospel becomes Christ himself and evangelism the practice of offering Christ.

To begin with, let us remind ourselves that we have no nontheological version of the story of Jesus. His entire life is told in such a way as to highlight the common thread that connects its various events—the activity of God the Spirit. This is especially the case in the first of Luke's two-volume narrative, where Jesus is conceived by the Spirit, anointed by the Spirit at his baptism, led by the Spirit into the wilderness to be tempted, and empowered by the Spirit to begin his evangelism. In John's Gospel, the risen Jesus breathes on his disciples so that they also are empowered by the Holy Spirit and enabled to forgive sins. The story of Jesus *is* the story of the Spirit. Indeed, the Spirit's operation connects the story of Jesus with the story of Israel and with the story of the church, thereby making of all three a single story.

From beginning to end, the story of Jesus is the story of God's offer of life to the world. The interpretive statement found in John's Gospel—"I came that they may have life and have it abundantly"—is but a gloss on the entire course of that life. Where Elizabeth is barren, where Mary is a virgin, where Herod puts up opposition, and where Bethlehem affords no room, God brings about new life and new birth anyway. Everything in Jesus' story places him on the side of the poor and marginalized and as a living critique of the "royal consciousness" mentioned in the previous chapter.

In reconstructing the story of Jesus, it is virtually indisputable among New Testament scholars today that within the earliest layers of apostolic witness the content of Jesus' evangelism was understood to be "the reign of God."[3] Jesus did not invent this message; for, as we have already seen,

3. The Greek word *basileia*, most often translated "kingdom," could also be translated "rule," "government," "dominion," or even "commonwealth." I choose *reign* rather

Israel's very identity as a people and its orientation toward shalom was premised upon the reality of God's reign in all of the world and in all of history. Likewise, John the Baptist, as with the prophets before him, came proclaiming the reign of God. Yet Jesus' entire life, ministry, and teaching were fixed on the message of God's reign in ways that were both continuous and discontinuous with what came before him. It was God's reign that Jesus announced as having arrived, it was God's reign for which he both prayed and worked, and it was God's reign to which he invited persons to give themselves over. It was also God's reign—and his faithfulness to it—that ultimately got him into trouble. Any theology of evangelism that fails to take seriously the reign of God, therefore, forsakes a claim to have any firm mooring in the narrative of the person and work of Jesus. As William Abraham rightly concludes, "Whatever evangelism may be, it is at least intimately related to the gospel of the reign of God that was inaugurated in the life, death, and resurrection of Jesus of Nazareth. Any vision of evangelism that ignores the kingdom of God, or relegates it to a position of secondary importance, or fails to wrestle thoroughly with its content is destined at the outset to fail" (1989:17).

Though Jesus taught extensively about the reign of God, his earliest witnesses do not present him as holding up the reign of God as simply a doctrine or an ideal. Rather, Jesus appeared announcing the reign of God as an actual state of affairs that was now breaking into history. For Jesus, God's reign does not merely show up at the end of history. Rather, the end of history is itself now irrupting into the present, and Jesus' evangelism both heralds and embodies the signs of that irruption. Jesus

---

than *kingdom*, first, because it conveys a more dynamic sense of God's ongoing activity and presence in the world rather than the more static sense of the already-achieved end product of that activity and, second, because *reign* is better able to eliminate (though not entirely) the patriarchal overtones of the word *kingdom*. I admit to being attracted by the proposal of Mujerista theologians Ada María Isasi-Díaz and Yolanda Tarango, who suggest "kin-dom" rather than *kingdom*:

> There are two reasons for not using the regular word employed by the English Bible, *kingdom*. First, it is obviously a sexist word that presumes that God is male. Second, the concept of kingdom in our world today is both hierarchical and elitist—which is also why we do not use *reign*. The word *kin-dom* makes it clearer that when the fullness of God becomes a day-to-day reality in the world at large, we will all be sisters and brothers—kin to each other. (1992:116)

However attractive, this suggestion fails to take into account that the phrase "reign of God" intends to say something not only about our relations to one another within that reign but about ultimately the relationship of God to the world (a relationship that, if not hierarchical, is surely asymmetrical) and God's activity in the world. I do believe, however, that *kin-dom* is as deeply political a term as *kingdom* or *government*, albeit in a direction that points to a radically new politics of mutuality and social leveling that is central to Jesus' vision.

is, therefore, an eschatological evangelist, but not one who is wholly preoccupied with the future. He appeals to a world that is surprising and unfamiliar but that is nonetheless making itself present in and through events that are transpiring here and now. As with the prophets before him, the genius and allure of his evangelism is that he offers an imaginative vision that has very present and material consequences, but one that is radically unlike what we already know and experience. He announces something that is genuinely "new." What is more, it is not just his words that do the announcing. His announcement is accompanied by deeds such as healings, association with sinners, and exorcisms (all sometimes referred to as "sign-actions") and by an authoritative engagement with power (especially around matters pertaining to Torah observance and interpretation), so that the whole of his life and ministry may be considered "gospel" (*evangel*).

As we reconstruct the earliest layers of witness to Jesus' evangelism, a number of things can be said about his gospel and about the reign of God to which that gospel points. In the first place, Jesus does not conceive of God's reign as primarily individual and only indirectly social, or as fundamentally private and interior and only derivatively visible and public (in eschewing the individual, privatized approach, he would be very much in line with the prophets who preceded him). To be sure, God's reign is both announced and offered to persons. But to speak of God's reign breaking into history is to speak also of a people called into being by that reign and in whom that reign is embodied in habits, practices, disciplines, and patterns that are intrinsically social, practical, and public. Moreover, it is through this people that God's reign, by being displayed, is offered to the world.

The reign of God, therefore, was nothing abstract or ethereal for Jesus and for those who heard him. The inbreaking of God's reign both demanded and made possible an altered set of allegiances in which obedience to God relativizes one's family and national identities while calling into question customary patterns with regard to the status of women, children, the poor, and those otherwise ostracized or considered strange (tax collectors, prostitutes, lepers, Samaritans). These new patterns of kinship and social relation are not merely an *implication* of one's prior acceptance of salvation. Rather, they are precisely that which is offered *as* salvation. To be called to discipleship, therefore, is to be called into a company of disciples that is both sign and foretaste of a new social order as well as a participation in and agent of that new order. According to Lohfink,

> For Jesus the coming of the *basileia*, that is, the acquisition of a space
> for the reign of God in the world, was the center of his existence. Jesus

announces the reign of God; better still, he calls it forth. But never did it remain at the level of mere words. It had to take on flesh. It requires not only the ear, but the eye and the taste buds. (1999:131)

This "space" for God's reign is not a simple geographic location, but it does have its own "geography." It is characterized by tangible practices of eating, sharing, meeting, and service. Jesus' evangelism is not just the preaching of a message but the gathering together of a new family, a new household.

The story of Jesus' table fellowship may be singled out as especially important in this regard, for it exemplifies not only the abundance, sharing, and communion into which persons are invited when God's reign breaks in (so that the great eschatological banquet has already begun) but also the "table manners" that create the conditions under which such communion is possible.[4] At this table, tax collectors, Pharisees, Zealots, and prostitutes eat together—a commonality made possible only by the dismantling of social hierarchies and oppositions. There is an equality around the table: each is called to care for the other person's plate over one's own, and greatness is defined by serving at table and washing dirty feet.

It should be clear from even this much that for Jesus the visible and social dimensions of God's inbreaking reign were manifested in the ways that power was to be used and distributed. We can therefore begin to speak of a distinctive and radical "table politics" that lies at the heart of his evangelism. Jesus' table fellowship was not just an offer of hospitality but was, at the same time, an overturning of tables (cf. Russell 1993:58–59). Apparently, Christian evangelization cannot take place where there is limited seating or where the table has been fashioned in such a way as to reinforce social privilege and hierarchy (and this means that at times evangelists must of necessity be "troublemakers"). Jesus instructed his disciples that while the rulers of the Gentiles "lord it over them" and while their great ones "are tyrants over them," this was not to be the case among them; instead, "whoever wishes to become great among you must be your servant, and whoever wishes to be first among you must be slave of all" (Mark 10:42–44). In this politics, the first become last while the last become first (Matt. 20:16), rulers are brought down from their thrones while the humble are exalted (Luke 1:52–53), the poor and the hungry are satisfied while the rich and the well-fed are sent away hungry and empty-handed (Luke 6:20–25), and those who suffer now find comfort and healing while those who have

4. For Lohfink, "the whole ethos that Jesus presents to his disciples" may be described as "table manners in the reign of God" (1999:182).

been excluded now are included (Matt. 21:31; Luke 4:25–27). In essence, the arrival of God's reign means that those who have been treated as objects now become subjects. This implies a new world not only for victims but for those who victimize and for those who silently benefit from the victimization of others.

It would be wrong, then, to conclude that God's reign is otherworldly in the customary sense of that term—a reality deferred to some time or place beyond this world. Standing before Pilate, Jesus does answer, "My kingdom is not from this world. If my kingdom were from this world, my followers would be fighting to keep me from being handed over to the Jews. But as it is, my kingdom is not from here" (John 18:36). Clearly, the kingdom Jesus is talking about does not derive from this world's order and runs counter to it. Perhaps the most startling proof of that is the fact that this reign produces a people who are not "fighting," because God's reign makes retaliation and retribution unnecessary (Matt. 5:38–48). But while it may not be a kingdom *from* this world, it is certainly a kingdom *for* this world—that is precisely why Jesus is standing before Pilate.

Central to the pattern prayer Jesus offers his followers is the petition to God, "Your kingdom come. Your will be done, on earth as it is in heaven" (Matt. 6:10). However otherworldly the reign of God may be ("counterworldly" would be a better way of putting it), it is no less political, public, or material for that. In fact, as Juan Luis Segundo suggests, in using the term *basileia*, "Jesus could not have been unaware of the *political* content it *already* had in the minds of the people" (1985:88). Nor does Jesus always appear interested in dispelling the ambiguity of the term. That he was ultimately either uninterested in or incapable of dispelling that ambiguity is testified to by the fact that he was eventually crucified on charges of sedition: all four Gospels agree on the charges against him, summed up in the inscription placed by Pilate on the cross: "Jesus of Nazareth, the King of the Jews."

If the first thing to be said about Jesus' evangelism, then, is that it announces and invites persons into a new government called the reign of God, a second observation is that because the new social order made possible by God's reign runs counter to the present order, Jesus' proclamation of God's reign requires a radical critique of the present order. It is in this connection that we should understand his eventual torture and execution by the powers of his day. The truth of the matter is that the reign of God is downright subversive—politically, economically, religiously, and culturally. Jesus' announcement of that reign, his calling together a community that would bear embodied witness to it, and his own incarnation of its values and allegiances undermined longstanding patterns of domination and subordination. It subverted prevailing structures of authority and control, overturned commonsense wisdom about enemies, violence, and the possibility of forgiveness, and collapsed familiar dichotomies about insiders and outsiders, saints and sinners, the sacred and the profane. However much Jesus' execution may be interpreted later by the church as redemption or as an atonement for sin, it was, in the first place, the price of subversive evangelism.

A third observation is that the announcement of God's reign was, for Jesus, the announcement of peace. The kind of government that Jesus understood now to be breaking in was unlike any other government, for its substance, form, and *telos* was peace. The disciples were sent out as emissaries of peace, and their first assignment when entering a house was to say "Peace to this house!" (Luke 10:5). Jesus asked his disciples not to fight, and he instructed them to turn the other cheek instead of resisting evil. He himself refused the path of coercion or resistance relative to those who would be his enemies. Thus, however subversive, confrontational, and conflict-laden was Jesus' gospel (so much so that he can even say of the new kinship loyalties demanded by God's reign, "Do not think that I have come to bring peace to the earth; I have not come to bring peace, but a sword" (Matt. 10:34), it is also clear that for Jesus any reliance upon the sword (now understood literally) can only be self-defeating. Radical loyalty to the gospel of peace is a loyalty that divides.

Peace, moreover, is not simply a topic or theme in Jesus' evangelism. Peace permeates his witness, for it is the inner logic of a life that is yielded to God's sovereignty. Peace is a pattern in which domination is exchanged for servanthood, punishment for forgiveness, and ethnocentrism for enemy-love (cf. Yoder 1997:46–49). It is therefore true that

> what Jesus renounced is not first of all violence, but rather the compulsiveness of purpose that leads [people] to violate the dignity of others. The point is not that one can attain all of one's legitimate ends without using violent means. It is rather that our readiness to renounce our legitimate ends whenever they cannot be attained by legitimate means itself constitutes our participation in the triumphant suffering of the Lamb. (Yoder 1972:243–44)

No wonder that the writer of the Epistle to the Ephesians could describe Jesus as One who came proclaiming peace (Eph. 2:17) and in preparing Christian followers for the ministry of evangelism could likewise advise, "As shoes for your feet put on whatever will make you ready to proclaim the gospel of peace" (Eph 6:15).

A fourth and distinctive characteristic of Jesus' evangelism has to do with the *proximity* of God's reign in his preaching and ministry. All three of the foregoing observations about the social, subversive, and peace-

able nature of God's reign in the witness of Jesus could also characterize
Israel's own witness. There is a sense in which the content of Jesus' gospel
is not something new or unknown to Israel. What is new, however, is
that for Jesus the day of the Lord has dawned. The promises have been
fulfilled. The hope of Israel has found its object. The reign of God "has
come near." The concrete inbreaking and impending presence of that
reign, however, is offensive and shocking:

> Although the eschatological action of God has been prayed for and dreamed
> of by all, at the hour when it happens the people discover that they had
> imagined it would be different. Not like this. Not so concrete. Not so
> fixed in space. Not, of all places, in Nazareth, and above all not at this
> moment. . . . Apparently it makes people uncomfortable to have God ap-
> pear concretely in their lives. It puts all their desires and favorite ideas in
> danger, and their ideas about time as well. It cannot be today, because in
> that case we would have to change our lives *today*. So we prefer to delay
> God's salvation to some future time. There it can rest, securely packed,
> hygienic, and harmless. (Lohfink 1999:136)

The proximity of God's reign does not change the fact that we are
required to pray for its coming (Matt. 6:10). But that is not because God
is holding something back. That the reign of God is both "already" and
"not yet" is not because it is only partially present or provisionally given,
but rather because while it is given concretely and in the present, it may
always be rejected and refused. Jesus' evangelism, as Lohfink reminds
us, violates Israel's "distant expectations" (by being immediate) just as
it also violates Israel's "imminent expectations" (by appearing in unexpected form). The twelve disciples represent the twelve tribes of Israel
"gathered" and "re-created," but under new conditions and in a new
form. God's reign in the world is not the progressive result of our hard
work, nor is it a natural consequence of either genealogical inheritance
or social engineering. It is an unexpected interruption, a new beginning,
a new creation. It may be sought and found, invited and received, but
never calculated, conjured, built, or predicted.

   In characterizing Jesus' evangelism, we may say, fifth, that the reign
of God is offered as both a *gift* and a *demand*. In the first place, we are
reminded that the reign of God is *God's* reign and therefore a gift. We
are to receive it as little children (Mark 10:13–16), and we are not able
to predict it, control it, or know how, like scattered seed, it sprouts and
grows (Mark 4:26–27). Within God's rule, we can be confident in leaving
all care about tomorrow until tomorrow (Matt. 6:24–34). Yet the sheer
gratuity of God's reign can serve as a pretext neither for resignation nor
disobedience. Receptivity is no warrant for passivity. Rather, for those
who accept God's reign, life can be lived creatively and in freedom, since

we now have been freed from the tyranny of needing to impose our will onto others and from the fear and burden of trying to scrape and claw our way into God's favor. The reign of God means for us existence as a *project* rather than existence as a *test* (Segundo 1987:90–91).

Jesus is not just a preacher of moral obligation and command. The reign of God is offered as a gift, and so he can compare its discovery to the joy one might experience at stumbling across a great treasure or a valuable pearl. At every point in the story of Jesus, the Gospels, when speaking of the reign of God, picture "overflowing abundance, of profligacy and superfluity" (Lohfink 1999:143). Five thousand persons feast on bread and fish that have been multiplied by Jesus so that there are baskets of leftovers; fish nets are filled to the point of breaking; a fatted calf is served up for the returned prodigal; and in Bethany, Jesus is anointed by Mary with a jar full of expensive perfume—a seemingly irrational waste of the community's resources. When the reign of God breaks in, there is not merely enough for everyone. There is *more than enough*. New hopes and imagination are made possible as old rationalities and old patterns of calculating effectiveness and greatness are supplanted by a new logic—the logic of God's reign.

If, however, Jesus' proclamation of God's reign takes the form of an invitation, offer, or gift, it also shows up in the form of a summons or demand. Like the shalom that provides both the beginning and the end of Israel's story, the reign of God proclaimed by Jesus is an alternative and deviant state of affairs that undermines existing patterns of relating to one another and of relating to God. It is, indeed, a "social imagination" in which, as we have seen, present social orderings are turned upside down and inside out. Because of this, the reign of God is something urgent that human beings need to take with utter seriousness. The proximity and immediacy of God's reign requires change. It requires looking for God's reign in different places and in different directions from those in which one had grown accustomed to looking. The short summary of Jesus' ministry found in Mark 1:14–15 says simply that "Jesus came to Galilee, proclaiming the good news of God, and saying, 'Time is up! The reign of God is at hand; turn around and exercise faith in the good news.'"[5] Here we see the unmistakable connection between what Jesus took to be the proximity of God's inbreaking reign and the corresponding call to "conversion" (*metanoia*), a radical change of the direction in which one looked and a radical change of patterns by which one lived. That is not to say that Jesus' call for conversion always took the same form in every situation. Given the very content of Jesus' reign-of-God witness, it is understandable that not everyone would hear the summons to convert

5. Translation mine.

to God's reign in the same way; neither was it the case that everyone who heard that summons would naturally or immediately consider it a piece of good news.

In much of the popular literature on evangelism, it is now common to advocate different evangelistic approaches or styles based on the evangelist's or prospective convert's personality type, theories of multiple intelligence, or whatever strategy will be most effective in appealing to the "felt needs" of the prospective convert.[6] Without denying the critical importance of using contextualized methods of communication, in the story of Jesus narrated by the Synoptic Gospels, the most relevant criteria for the contextualization of Jesus' evangelistic practice are considerations of wealth, comfort, and power, on the one hand, and poverty, suffering, marginality, and powerlessness, on the other hand. Jesus directs his evangelistic activity to persons from both groups, that much is plain. But if the reign of God spells an end to a social order in which the wealth, comfort, and power of some comes at the expense of the poverty, suffering, marginality, and powerlessness of others, then it should not be surprising that Jesus does not direct his evangelism to all persons in the same way, nor is his offer perceived by all persons in the same way.

On the one hand, those who benefit from the present social order and who have a vested interest in things remaining the way they are will not likely perceive conversion to a community where that order is challenged and subverted by God's reign as a piece of good news. They must be converted not only to this community and this reign but also to the realization that such a conversion is good news (cf. Segundo 1985:120). Jesus concludes, "Truly I tell you, it will be hard for a rich person to enter the kingdom of heaven" (Matt. 19:23). Those, on the other hand, who have no vested interest in the status quo and who see in the arrival of God's reign the reversal of an economic and social condition that entails their own poverty, suffering, and exclusion naturally find God's reign to be good news and a cause for rejoicing. They do not need to be converted to that fact. Jesus insists therefore that those who are poor, hungry, and suffering are already blessed (Luke 6:20). The rule of God is a gift that is already theirs. And so Jesus accepts as fulfilled in his own person and ministry the prophecy of Isaiah that the poor are offered the gospel, prisoners are released, the blind see, the oppressed are liberated, and the year of jubilee can no longer be delayed (Luke 4:18–21; Isa. 61:1–2).

6. See for example, Hybels and Mittelberg 1994, where we learn that Peter took a confrontational approach to evangelism, Paul took an intellectual approach, the blind man took a testimonial approach, Matthew took an interpersonal approach, the Samaritan woman took an invitational approach, and Dorcas took a service approach. The important thing in evangelism is "to be yourself" (132).

Jesus' evangelization of the poor, suffering, and powerless is nonetheless a call to conversion. Poverty and oppression can breed a hardened fatalism, resignation, and time-worn skepticism about the possibility of lasting good news. Moreover, the "sinned against" begin to believe that their situation is a result of their own sin. As Paulo Freire has shown, it is frequently the case that the oppressor is internalized within the oppressed (1983:30); this internalization can take a variety of forms ranging from self-loathing to imitation of the oppressor. Jesus' call to conversion, therefore, is a summons to the poor and the marginalized to understand themselves as inheritors of God's reign, as children of God, as blessed. They have been invited to a banquet in which all are welcome at the table. They are invited onto a journey in which something new is now possible because the end of that journey has already made its appearance in the present and by so doing has opened up a new road. All Christian evangelism, therefore, whether directed to the rich or to the poor, is ultimately eschatological from beginning to end. It is not an exercise in getting persons ready for "the end" but rather the practice of inviting persons to be transformed by the end that has already made itself present, and on that basis to see differently and live differently.

Despite the contextualization of Jesus' proclamation, there is a consistent focus: the reign of God and the new social patterns and relationships that are both demanded and made possible by that reign. Both the poor and the rich are invited to the same banquet. The task of inviting the poor who have otherwise been excluded, forgotten, or tossed a few crumbs from the tables of the rich will clearly be very different from the task of inviting the rich who will have to reorder their values, leave behind the security of possessions, and alter their eating habits—not merely making room at the table but moving to a table of entirely new construction. But both are invited to the same banquet, and remarkably, in the humanization of the dehumanized, the ones who have practiced dehumanization are likewise humanized (Freire 1983:38). The contextualization of Jesus' evangelism, then, while it is premised on a consistent focus, is an invitation to all of us, as Brueggemann says, to allow our lives to be "redescribed."[7]

Again, the very fact that God's reign spells an end to business as usual means that Jesus' evangelism necessarily had a dimension of conflict and confrontation with the powers—legal, economic, political, and religious. Precisely because God's reign is not from this world, it smashes headlong into prevailing power structures and so brings a politics of its

---

7 For some, says Brueggemann, this means a "new possibility"; for others it will mean "a departure"; and for still others it will mean "entitlement" (1993:60). But in every case, the lure of the gospel story is its "narrative power" to imagine ourselves differently (ibid. 62).

own. The call for realignment of loyalties, including the subordination or abandonment of other values and loyalties, is radical. Jesus uses the word *hate* to describe the posture toward other loyalties that character-izes those who say yes to him (Luke 14:26). Those invited to God's reign are invited to leave family and possessions, to let the dead bury the dead, and not to look back (Luke 9:57–62; 14:26–33). His evangelistic offer can even be expressed in terms of taking up a cross.

To speak of Jesus' own way of evangelizing, therefore, is impossible apart from its reference to the reign of God. It serves not just as a single or important doctrine that he held but rather as "the orienting concern" that guides his thought and activity.[8] His invitation to followers was an in-vitation to accept this reign as reality, to order their lives together around it, and to serve as a sign and foretaste of it together in the world.

But something happened.

Jesus the proclaimer became Jesus the proclaimed. As Segundo says, "The message *of* Jesus became a message *about* Jesus" (1987:19). The announcement of God's reign so prominent in the evangelism of Jesus is virtually absent from the postresurrection evangelism of those who became followers of Jesus. As Mortimer Arias laments, "The kingdom-of-God theme has practically disappeared from evangelistic preaching and has been ignored by traditional 'evangelism.' . . . We have tried many definitions of our own regarding mission or evangelism. Why not try Jesus' own definition of his mission—and of ours? For Jesus, evange-lization was no more and no less than *announcing the reign of God!*" (1984:xvii).

Arias's plea is compelling. However, it is not at all clear that this is what the apostles themselves did. While the phrase "reign of God" ap-pears eighty-three times in the Synoptic Gospels, it shows up only twice in John and in fewer than ten other New Testament passages. Where Jesus summoned people to life in God's reign and invited them to con-vert to a distinctive way of living with each other, the apostles invited people to convert to Jesus. So, for example, Jesus says, "Not everyone

8. I borrow the phrase "orienting concern" from Randy Maddox, who himself has adapted the phrase from Gerhard Sauter's notion of an "orienting concept": "the integra-tive thematic perspective in light of which all other theological concepts are understood and given their relative meaning or value" (Maddox 1984:10). According to Maddox, an orienting concern is "not simply one theological concept or metaphor among others. It is a perspective within which one construes (or a 'worry' which one brings to) all of the various types of theological concepts." It is "not an architectonic Idea from which all other theo-logical affirmations would be deduced, or under which they must be subsumed," but rather, "the abiding interest which influences the selection, interpretation, relative emphasis, and interweaving of theological affirmations and practices" (ibid. 18).

who says to me, 'Lord, Lord,' will enter the kingdom of heaven, but only the one who does the will of my Father in heaven" (Matt. 7:21). Paul, however, teaches that "if you confess with your lips that Jesus is Lord and believe in your heart that God raised him from the dead, you will be saved" (Rom. 10:9).

One can clearly see the effects of this shift in the case of the historic creeds of Christianity, which typically have to do with how we are to understand Jesus' dual nature and his relationship to God and in which nothing at all is mentioned about servanthood, enemy-love, forgiveness, prayer, simplicity, and radical discipleship. We likewise look in vain for any reference to Jesus' attitudes toward power, wealth, and hypocritical religiosity. In other words, the creeds mention nothing at all about the actual content of Jesus' reign-of-God preaching. Consider, for example, the second article of the Apostles' Creed:

> I believe in Jesus Christ his only son, our Lord, who was conceived by the Holy Spirit, born of the virgin Mary, suffered under Pontius Pilate, was crucified, died, and was buried; he descended to the dead. On the third day he rose again; he ascended into heaven, is seated at the right hand of the Father, and will come again to judge the living and the dead.

As Robert Funk points out, the Apostles' Creed (the same could be said for the Nicene Creed) has an "empty center" in that its second article leaps without explanation from Jesus' birth to his suffering under Pontius Pilate. Says Funk,

> It scarcely requires notice that this creed calls on the believer to affirm nothing about the historical Jesus other than his virgin birth at the beginning of his life and his suffering, execution, and resurrection at the end. . . . The ethical dimensions of the gospels of both Jesus and Paul have been lost in the creedal formulation: believers only have to believe; they are not required to modify their behavior in any other respect. (1996:43)

It was not the later creedal formulations of the church in the third and fourth centuries, however, that produced this shift from Jesus the proclaimer to Jesus the proclaimed. We can detect it already in Luke's account of Peter's sermon on the day of Pentecost, the very first post-Easter sermon recorded in the New Testament. The striking thing about this sermon is that no reference to Jesus' own message, ministry, or values is offered—his table fellowship with sinners and prostitutes, his preferential option for the poor, his message of nonviolence, the importance of extending forgiveness to enemies, the liberation of captives, the rejection of wealth and material objects as indicators of one's well-being. The reign-of-God content of Jesus' message has now been replaced by an exclusive preoccupation with Jesus himself—who he was, the purpose of his death and resurrection, his fulfillment of messianic prophecy, and his status as Son of God. Where Jesus himself had been preoccupied with the historical question of the reign of God, the apostles now appear to be preoccupied with the theological question of the status of Jesus as Messiah, Lord, and Savior.

Peter's sermon, for example, interprets Jesus' death on the cross not as the consequence of a radical obedience to God that upsets the status quo and gets one into trouble but as the result of a prior design by God. Jesus' own language about the reign of God completely disappears, as does any reference to his own historical project of bearing witness to its arrival. Instead of Jesus' typical emphasis on the practice of forgiving *one another's* sins (a distinctively reign-of-God practice with immediate and revolutionary implications for our social order), what is now emphasized is Jesus as the One who forgives *our* sins.

Segundo points out the striking fact that the post-Easter preaching of the apostles was also far more successful, numerically speaking, than that of Jesus. Though Jesus was able to attract crowds from time to time, his radical invitation to follow him by taking up the cross yielded only a handful of serious converts. On the heels of Peter's sermon, however, three thousand are reportedly converted, with additional conversions occurring on a daily basis (Acts 2:41, 46). Was this because the apostolic message was easier to convert to? Segundo says of Peter's preaching:

> There is no longer any need to know whether people's values fit in with those of the kingdom, however primitively and gradually. The only question now is whether they do or do not recognize Jesus as the Messiah of Israel. The former question could take a matter of months or years to answer, and it could entail concrete manifestations. The latter question is answered in a matter of seconds or minutes. (1987:21)

What are we then to conclude about the church's post-Easter proclamation of Jesus? Does it represent a distortion of Jesus' proclamation of God' reign—perhaps even a betrayal? How should we take account of this shift, and of what relevance is it for our own evangelism today? Has anything important been lost in the transition from Jesus' evangelism to our own? If, on the one hand, the proclamation of Jesus focuses on the reign of God and the altered pattern of living both offered and demanded by that reign, and if, on the other hand, the postresurrection proclamation of the church is centrally a call to confess Jesus as Messiah and Lord, where does that leave us? With two evangels? Or is the call to confess Jesus as Lord perhaps now to be construed as the essence of evangelism, so that Jesus' own concerns can be relegated to the sphere of "ethical implications" after one is converted to him as Lord? It would certainly appear that something very much like this is the case with many forms of contemporary evangelism, but perhaps we ought to be disturbed by that fact. Perhaps something has gone strangely wrong when we can speak of conversion to Christianity in such a way that talk about how we are actually to live would constitute a second step.

How then should we understand the apostolic preaching that is centrally a call to confess Jesus as Savior and Lord? Is it the case that virtually from the beginning of the church's story, the gospel *about* Christ began to overshadow and eventually edge out the gospel that was announced *by* Christ? With such questions in mind, let us turn to the story of the apostles themselves.

4

Apostolic Evangelism
and the Genesis of the Church

Perhaps the shift from Jesus the proclaimer to Jesus the proclaimed was
bound to happen, for while Jesus was yet alive his followers began to
understand that in and through him something new and powerful had
begun to break in on the world. This, along with the various currents of
messianic expectation already present in Israel, naturally raised questions
about who Jesus was. John the Baptist, for example, sent disciples to Jesus
to question him about his possible messianic identity (Luke 7:19). Yet as
is characteristic of Jesus in the Synoptic tradition, he avoids the question
of his own divine status or messianic identity (making, at the most, only
cryptic remarks in reference to it) and instead steers their attention to
the characteristics of God's reign—liberation, healing, resurrection, and
good news for the poor. Jesus offered no explicit teaching about his own
person and refused to lend himself to any interpretation of his healings
as evidence of his divinity, proof of his messiahship, or legitimation of
his word (Mark 8:11-12). Rather, miracles were to be construed as signs
of the impending force of God's reign, and he explicitly rejected the approach of those who wished to establish his divinity first before deciding
whether or not they should follow him. The evangelism of Jesus was not
an invitation to accept himself as savior or Lord, but a call to Israel to
accept the reign of God as having come near and to take seriously its
subversive implications for life together in the world.

If, then, Jesus appeared proclaiming the reign of God and calling
together a community of disciples as witnesses to its arrival, the answer
to our question about the shift from Jesus the proclaimer to Jesus the
proclaimed requires that we turn to the story of these very disciples.[1]
New Testament scholars are generally agreed that while the question of
Jesus' messianic identity may well have been raised during his earthly
ministry, it is in the postresurrection preaching of the church that the
shift from proclaimer to proclaimed took place.

Bultmann's Proposal

One of the prominent paradigms of the last century for interpreting
the postresurrection evangelism of the apostles, and one that continues
to exert influence even today, comes from German New Testament theologian Rudolf Bultmann (1884–1976). Bultmann was skeptical about
the historical reliability of the Gospel narratives for reconstructing the
actual life and message of Jesus. Much of these narratives consist of early
Christian legends and ideas, often polemical, projected backward and
placed on the lips of Jesus. We have nothing from Jesus himself. If the
historical-critical study of the New Testament has taught us anything,
it is that even our earliest sources are all secondary and are evangelistic
treatises and testimonies to faith rather than objective historical reporting
(Ogden 1985:44). Over against the liberal theology that flourished after
Schleiermacher in the nineteenth and early twentieth centuries and the
quest for the historical Jesus that such theology occasioned, Bultmann
rightly insisted that what we discover in the New Testament reports is
not the faith of Jesus but the faith of his followers.

But then this means that to talk about a transition from Jesus' evangelism to that of the apostles, from the proclaimer to the proclaimed, is an
inadequate way of putting the matter, at least on the basis of what we find
in the New Testament materials. The story of Jesus and his announcement of God's reign presented in the Synoptic Gospels and discussed in
the previous chapter is *already* the apostolic message proclaiming Jesus,
only now in story form rather than in the form of individual, isolated

1. This is not the place to provide a full treatment of the distinction between *disciple*
and *apostle*. The former refers to all those called to follow Jesus and, in the book of Acts,
to any who are members of the Christian community, while the Gospels equate the latter term with "the Twelve" who symbolized Israel and whom Jesus set aside both "to be
with him" as traveling companions and "to be sent out to proclaim the message" (Mark
3:14) to Israel. Theirs is a particular eschatological function or office that will persist in
the church. Paul also uses the word *apostle* to refer to himself as well as others such as
Andronicus and Junia.

propositions. The Gospel accounts of Jesus' life and message are from beginning to end: *Christology*. That this Christology is presented in narrative form may incline us to think that we have more impartial historical reporting in the Synoptics, whereas when we move to John or Paul we think we have now encountered the Christ of apostolic preaching (kerygma). But telling the story of Jesus is itself a way of announcing the kerygma.

By peeling back the layers of tradition and mythology, the historical-critical research of liberal theologians prior to Bultmann confidently believed it could comprehend the *real* figure of Jesus on which faith must be based. It thus became preoccupied with reconstructing the actual "life" of Jesus and of recovering his authentic message, which it expressed in such formulas as "the fatherhood of God and the brotherhood of man." By shucking away the historically conditioned husks in which "the essence of Christianity" was expressed, liberal scholars would retrieve a reliable kernel that could serve as a basis of faith. As Bultmann says, "This confidence soon proved to be delusional" (1969:30). For all these "lives of Jesus" (each one different from the others) were but a reflection of the values, concerns, and projects of the researchers who "scientifically" produced them. Liberalism's historical method became its own worst critic, exposing its pretension to liberate us from a servile dependence upon the past as little more than a servile dependence upon the present and upon contemporary worldviews.

If recovery of the historical Jesus through the materials of the New Testament was for Bultmann largely a historical impossibility, it was not in any case a theological necessity. For Christian faith is not a faith in what the historical Jesus said or did. Christian faith is not handed on from Jesus to his followers or learned by them from him in such a way that the connection between Jesus' evangelism and the apostles' evangelism is repetitive, imitative, or contagious. Still, though we can know little with certainty about the historical Jesus, we *can* know with relative certainty, according to Bultmann, that "the dominant concept of Jesus' message is the *Reign of God*" (1951:4).

As we have already seen, Jesus' message did not merely impart information about God's reign but summoned his hearers to decision on the basis of what he took to be the truly urgent nature of the present situation in which that reign was breaking in. Thus, Jesus understood the reign of God as a factual, future, and coming, but also impending, reality. The reign of God is

the regime of God which will destroy the present course of the world, wipe out all the contra-divine, Satanic power under which the present world groans—and thereby, terminating all pain and sorrow, bring in salvation for the People of God which awaits the fulfillment of the prophets' promises. The coming of God's reign is a miraculous event, which will be brought about by God alone without the help of [humans]. (Bultmann 1951:4)

However radical it might be at several points, the basic content of this sort of preaching is nothing new, claims Bultmann; it stands firmly within Jewish expectations about the end of the world and the future coming of the "day of the Lord." Jesus does not, however, appeal to Jewish national hopes, nor is the inbreaking of God's reign to be understood as a restoration of the ancient kingdom of David. But if Jesus' proclamation of God's reign was taken to be liberating and decisive, that is not because God's reign was something Israel did not already know. As Bultmann says, "His teaching is not a new teaching because of its conceptual content, for in its content it does not differ from pure Judaism, from the pure prophetic teaching" (1969:283). For Bultmann, however, Jesus, like the prophets who came before him, was wrong: "The proclamation of the irruption of God's Reign was not fulfilled," and "Jesus' expectation of the near end of the world turned out to be an illusion" (1951:22).

This, of course, raises the question of what we are to do with Jesus' proclamation of the reign of God, and here Bultmann's existentialism provides a way forward for him. "The essential thing about the eschatological message," says Bultmann, "is the idea of God that operates in it and the idea of human existence that it contains—not the belief that the end of the world is just ahead" (1951:23). Christian faith, then, is faith in the Christ-event itself and in the action of God in Christ that now makes possible for us a new self-understanding, a "consciousness of standing in a new world in which [we move], free from law and sin, in obedience under God and in love for [our] neighbor" (1969:275–76).

For Bultmann, accordingly, proclaiming the Word of God today requires the sort of thoroughgoing criticism of traditional theological formulations (including the "demythologizing" of those formulations) made possible by historical-critical research,[2] simultaneous with ever new interpretations of the Christian message that correspond to the modern picture of ourselves and our world and that arise out of an analysis of our existence. These two movements together (the one more critical and the other more constructive) constitute what Bultmann refers to as the "existential interpretation" of the Christian kerygma. Lest Bultmann be misunderstood here, this existential interpretation is not meant to determine the content of the kerygma, nor does it presuppose that the worldview of the New Testament has no value or that contemporary

2. Whatever criticisms of liberalism Bultmann may make, he is still very much standing on the shoulders of liberal scholarship.

worldviews are to be accepted uncritically. Rather, "the only criticism of the New Testament which is theologically relevant is that which arises *necessarily* out of the situation of modern [humans]" (1961:7). In the modern situation, claims Bultmann, humans understand themselves and their world in accordance with a modern scientific worldview, and the human being is "a self-subsistent unity immune from the interference of supernatural powers" (ibid.).

Bultmann's point is neither to eliminate nor to privilege parts of the gospel, nor is it to accommodate the gospel to the tastes and preferences of contemporary persons or to diminish the scandal of Christianity, namely, the "word of the cross" (1969:29). Rather, such criticism and interpretation are meant to enable human beings today to understand that scandal all the more deeply and radically in terms of their own experience and so to be able to exercise faith authentically, rather than to obscure the scandal with myth and legend. Thus as Schubert Ogden, one of Bultmann's ablest interpreters, says:

> Until we translate this gospel into a language that enlightened [persons] today can understand, we are depriving ourselves of the very resources on which the continued success of our witness most certainly depends. . . . If the price for becoming a faithful follower of Jesus Christ is some form of self-destruction, whether of the body or of the mind—*sacrificium corporis, sacrificium intellectus*—then there is no alternative but that the price remain unpaid. (1961:130)

In Bultmann's proposal, the very structure of the disciples' encounter with Jesus required that they could not persist with his own announcement of God's reign, for that was not of primary importance. While Jesus himself did not likely offer any explicit teaching about his own messianic status or divine nature, from the very beginning his hearers understood themselves as being summoned to a decision not only about God's reign but about the decisive nature of Jesus' own person as the bearer of God's word. Whereas the content of Jesus' preaching was nothing new, "the unheard of thing is that he is speaking *now*, in the final, decisive hour. What is decisive is not *what* he proclaims but *that* he is proclaiming it" (Bultmann 1969:283). Bultmann therefore sees the shift from the *what* of Jesus' message (its actual content) to the *that* of his message (his hearers' having been decisively addressed by him as the Messiah of God) as a necessary shift and one that is already implicit in Jesus' own proclamation:

> The proclaimer must become the proclaimed, because it is the fact *that* he proclaimed which is decisive. The decisive thing is his person (not his personality), *here* and *now*, the event, the commission, the summons.

> When the primitive community called him Messiah, they were confessing
> that he was the decisive event, the act of God, the inaugurator of the new
> world. (1969:284)

Jesus' proclamation of God's reign, then, already entails a Christology—at first only implicit in the fact that his hearers do not merely understand him to be teaching about God's reign but summoning them to a
decision about that reign through his word and person. But Jesus himself
does not develop this Christology. Rather it becomes explicit as the first
Christians come to confess that by the resurrection God has made Jesus
the Messiah. What is crucial in the concept of Messiah is not so much
the message proclaimed by the Messiah but rather that the Messiah is
"he who in the final hour brings salvation, God's salvation" (ibid.).

Later apostolic preaching would go on to explicate the decisiveness
of Jesus' person, and thus the cross of Jesus became a central part of
the church's proclamation about Jesus along with the resurrection. For
while the cross could not call into question the content of Jesus' message, "it could and did render questionable his legitimation, his claim
to be God's messenger bringing the last, decisive word. The church had
to surmount the scandal of the cross and did it in the Easter faith"
(Bultmann 1951:44–45).

For Bultmann, then, the christological shift from *what* to *that* is inevitable and existentially necessary, for it is what makes possible our
being both confronted by Jesus' message as decisive for our existence
and also called to decision on that basis:

> Jesus' word—not any timeless ideas it may contain, but the fact that it is
> spoken by him and that the community is addressed by it—is understood
> as the decisive act of God. This in turn means that the further transmission
> of Jesus' proclamation could not be a simple reproduction of his ideas.
> Christ the proclaimer had to become the proclaimed. It is the *fact that he
> proclaimed* which is decisive. (1969:237–38)

Bultmann goes on to say:

> The great enigma of New Testament theology, *how the proclaimer became
> the proclaimed*, why the community proclaimed not only the content of his
> preaching, but also and primarily Christ himself, why Paul and John almost
> wholly ignore the content of his preaching—that enigma is solved by the
> realization that it is the fact, "*that* he proclaimed," which is decisive.
>
> There appeared to be an "enigma" only because attention was focused
> on "religio-ethical" concepts and on the worldview instead of on the event
> itself. Then the existence of a double gospel was claimed, two proclama-
> tions with different ideas were alleged, and a development which was

determined by the history of ideas or by other external causal relations, was postulated. This concept of development was correct in so far as it was applied to the *forms* of presentation. But the really essential and decisive element was ignored. (1969:283–84)

For Bultmann, to exercise faith in Christ is, in the first place, neither doctrinal nor ethical; it is not primarily a matter of holding certain beliefs about his nature or following him in an imitative fashion. "Faith is certainly following Christ," says Bultmann, "but by accepting his cross, not at all in the sense of imitation, but as grasping the forgiveness and the possibility of life created by the cross" (1969:277). No wonder Bultmann frequently quotes with approval Melancthon's famous dictum "To know Christ is to know his benefits." In Bultmann, the actual course of Jesus' life and the ethical content of the reign of God (the "way of the cross") are relativized, if not evacuated altogether, in favor of a new self-understanding of being forgiven and no longer under the law, which is an acceptance of the salvation made possible in Christ.

There is no question that Bultmann's own Lutheran emphasis on justification by faith and not by works contributes to this relativization, as he is clearly distanced by his own theological commitments from any understanding of the gospel in which ethical obedience would be central to salvation. In fact, Bultmann is consistently drawn to Jesus' rejection of legalism and to what Bultmann sees as a general trajectory within the prophetic literature of relativizing the Jewish ethic and delegalizing it. One might also conclude that there is more than a hint of anti-Semitism involved here. For Bultmann, what is most important about Jesus is how he is least Jewish and most Protestant. Bultmann's method of existential interpretation so dehistoricizes (and de-Judaizes) the gospel, and in the process so individualizes it, that it is disconnected from any direct social, ecclesial, or ethical significance. In other words, Bultmann solves our problem of how the proclaimer became the proclaimed by insisting that it should never have been a problem for us in the first place. It is the apostolic gospel that is primary, not the gospel of Jesus. It is the apostolic faith that is to be imitated, not the faith of Jesus.

Another way of saying this is that, for Bultmann, a shift from Jesus to the apostles has indeed taken place, but this shift is necessary so that we can move beyond Jesus' particular "religio-moral ideals" in order to be confronted decisively by God in the *person* of Jesus. For Bultmann, it is not the Jesus of history but the Christ of faith that is existentially significant for human beings today. Bultmann is a good example of what happens when the decisiveness of the person or the "event" of Jesus so relativizes the content of his proclamation that the latter (Jesus' set of "religio-moral" ideas) comes to be muffled if not silenced altogether (contemporary Bultmannians are, ironically, just as likely to look like conservative evangelicals as demythologizing liberals). It is for this reason that Bultmann cannot imagine Jesus to be directly relevant to contemporary questions of Christian ethics—or at least Christian ethics cannot simply be the ethics of Jesus.

Bultmann may well be right that the content of Jesus' reign-of-God proclamation is not "new" or "distinctive," being firmly anchored in the law and the prophets as well as in the story of Israel. But it is worth asking whether that serves as a warrant for its substitution by the person of Christ such that the proclaimer is now "replaced" (as Bultmann puts it) by the proclaimed.

Bultmann's position is partially echoed by Walter Klaiber, who in his important study of evangelism *Call and Response* argues that "the postresurrection church took up Jesus' proclamation and yet did not simply continue it. In so doing the church made clear that the rule of God does not come from simply persisting with Jesus' ministry" (1997:47). While on the surface Klaiber's statement appears to be consistent with Bultmann,[3] it turns out to hold possibilities that go beyond Bultmann as a way of holding together the message and the messenger. Klaiber's statement "The post-resurrection church took up Jesus' proclamation and yet did not simply continue it" points to the fact that Jesus' proclamation was not allowed to be lost or diminished in the disciples' proclamation of Jesus, nor was the latter allowed simply to "replace" the former. It is true that the disciples could not see it as their task "to adopt Jesus' messianic practice and then to continue it." But what they could do and had to do was "to imagine it indirectly through the mediation of Jesus' person and to see this image grounded in God's activity in him alone" (Klaiber 1997:46).

For Klaiber, therefore, the "permanent content of the gospel" is nonetheless that the reign of God has come near. All disciples must "take up Jesus' call and carry on with it" (1997:48). Rather than simply mimicking Jesus, however (for example, by asking Charles Sheldon's classic question "What would Jesus do?"), we are called to live out imaginatively the kind of discipleship that will faithfully re-present God's reign before others in daily life. The reign of God proclaimed by Jesus is central to apostolic evangelism, though it takes a different shape for us from what we see in the evangelism of Jesus, precisely because of what for us have become inescapable christological dimensions of that reign in the shadow of the cross and in the light of the resurrection.

3. Klaiber elsewhere criticizes Bultmann for "reducing the contents of the message of salvation to the bare 'fact' of Jesus' having come and died on the cross" (1997:89).

Evangelism befitting the gospel is evangelism in service of this invitation. It relieves those of whom too much is demanded. It liberates the captive. It heals the sick and worn down and gives new courage to those who have failed. But it does that not on its own authority, but rather in the name of Jesus. "Naming the name" is the most important function of evangelism in the context of the integral mission of the church. (Klaiber 1997:48)

Where Bultmann's existentialist interpretation of the significance of Jesus has the unfortunate consequence of spiritualizing, interiorizing, and privatizing Christian faith by loosing it from its moorings in the content of his proclamation and deeds and in the particularity of its Jewish origins, Klaiber points to the possibility that we have not so much a shift from message to messenger as the continuation of Jesus' message, only now qualified decisively by the messenger.

Klaiber's view is not without it own problems, since it is all too easy for an evangelism focused on "naming the name" to find itself over time with a name that has become emptied of any reign-of-God content. "Naming the name" can also translate into a disembodied evangelism that waves words around as if they were magic talismans. The name of Jesus has a history and is open to a number of ideological distortions apart from the cruciform life to which it points. To forget this is to risk not mere ineffectiveness but an essentially Gnostic distortion of the gospel.

Bultmann's existentialist approach to our question too easily grants Gotthold Lessing's "ugly, broad ditch" between faith and history expressed in his famous dictum "Accidental truths of history can never become the proof of necessary truths of reason" (1956:53). In believing the latter to be the only secure foundation for faith, Bultmann is attracted to the apostolic preaching about Jesus as a necessary shift away from the particular, historical, and contingent (or Jewish or ecclesial) to that which is deemed to be more universal and therefore existentially decisive.

Another Way Forward?

Perhaps there is another way forward—a way that refuses to assume that the universality or intelligibility of the gospel is sacrificed if we hold to the historical and Jewish particularity of Jesus' gospel and the embarrassing eschatology from within which it calls for a new social order. For this way of answering our question, the journey to which Jesus called his listeners was, to be sure, a journey already begun by Israel and already entailed in its understanding of who God is and of the peculiar and unexpected way that God rules—namely, shalom. Moreover, there was indeed a transformation that took place between Jesus' evangelism and that of the apostles. But that transformation was neither the abandonment of Jesus' gospel nor its subordination to a more credible, universal, and existential gospel. To understand the transformation, we must first ask how it is that the death of Jesus at the hands of the powers in Jerusalem, rather than serving as the end of his movement, occasioned its transformation into something called the church. And this requires that we recall the story of the birth of the church.

Let us begin by remembering that the followers of Jesus were a band of countryside Galileans who, upon his death in Jerusalem, fled back north to Galilee, almost certainly devastated, scared, and uncertain about the future. Jesus had been arrested during the highest holy season, publicly exposed as a blasphemer and deceiver before the crowd of pilgrims who had gathered in Jerusalem for the Passover festival, and executed by the Romans for sedition. The events between Jesus' death and the next festival in Jerusalem, the Feast of Weeks (Pentecost), are unclear, but undoubtedly a belief in Jesus' resurrection began to spread and to gather steam, so much so that this group of followers who might otherwise have simply gone back to their former walks of life instead reconstituted themselves in Jerusalem, despite the danger posed both to themselves and to the friends and relatives on whose hospitality they would have had to depend. Jesus had been condemned as a heretic, executed as a criminal, and debased as one cursed by God by being hanged on a cross. But now his followers were back in the city (120 of them, both men and women, according to Luke), gathering together to pray and to discern their future together. Lohfink makes the following observation about this remarkable turn of events:

> The fact that after Good Friday Jesus' disciples assemble as the eschatological people of God is in itself a testimony to the resurrection. As important as the testimony to Jesus' resurrection in the word of proclamation is—and it is as fundamental as Israel's confession of its rescue from Egypt—equally important is the testimony that lies in the very existence of an Easter people of God. In fact one really cannot speak of the resurrection of Jesus without at the same time speaking of the *consequences* of his resurrection in the Church. (1999:206–7)

If Lohfink is right, to find the earliest testimony to the resurrection we must look not only to the public proclamation of the church but to the church's very existence—so much so that the resurrection may be taken as standing in the same relationship to the formation of the church as the exodus stands to the formation of Israel. Richard Lischer is right, then, in claiming, "When Jesus came out of the tomb, the church came out with him, and it came out talking, singing, praying, and suffering" (1999:22). The resurrection is not only the raising of Jesus from the dead but the improbable raising to life of a new people—thereby producing a community of "witnesses." The resurrection is, as McClendon puts it, "the reestablishment of the community of the Israel of God (Gal. 6:16) on a new basis, vindicating the justice of God in the older establishment, and promising that very justice, through Christ, to all the world" (1986:1:249). By his resurrection, then, Jesus ceases to be merely an eschatological prophet; he becomes the eschaton itself. And through incorporation into his resurrected body, we likewise become "an eschatological people" (McClendon 1986:2:100).

In addition to its ecclesiological significance, therefore, the resurrection must also be understood in its eschatological context relative to Jesus' preaching of God's reign and the salvation of Israel—and, indeed, the salvation of the entire world. Jesus had come preaching that the end of time was breaking into history in the form of God's reign, turning things upside down and both offering and requiring a new way of living together. The crucifixion of Jesus silenced that message and halted any expectations that might have developed regarding Jesus' own person in relation to this cataclysmic event. The resurrection of Jesus not only revived the message but confirmed it by situating it firmly within a host of expectations in Israel about the end of time, two of which were the resurrection of the dead and the pouring out of God's Spirit (Lohfink 1999:205). The disciples believed that the resurrection of Jesus had vindicated his proclamation about the inbreaking of God's rule and that through it God had actually taken dramatic action in initiating the events of the end of time. He must now be proclaimed as the One through whom this new age had actually begun to dawn. Wolfhart Pannenberg's claim that "with the resurrection of Jesus, the end of history has already occurred" (1968:142) is not entirely an overstatement, then, as long as this is not taken as denigrating all subsequent history that, because of the resurrection, has been made possible. The resurrection is a reversal of history's judgment on Jesus and an identification of Jesus' life with the life of God, so that from now on "the history of this man, Jesus of Nazareth, was to be counted identical with God's inner history, in such a way that in the knowing of Jesus Christ God could be truly known" (McClendon 1986:2:247).

This association between the death and resurrection of Jesus, on the one hand, and Jewish eschatological expectation about "the day of the Lord," on the other hand, began to percolate among the followers of Jesus, and as it did they began to resurface and add to their number in Jerusalem. Almost two months after Jesus' death, on the day of Pentecost, the assembly of 120 took to the streets, with the apostles boldly proclaiming that God had raised him from the dead, exalted him as Lord and Messiah, and through him offered salvation to Israel. Moreover,

they referred all of this, including their own boldness, to the gift of the
Holy Spirit, which they took as having been poured out upon them and
now available to any and all who would repent and be baptized in the
name of Jesus for the forgiveness of their sins. If the resurrection was
the first decisive evidence that God's reign was being ushered in, here
was the second: the gift of the Spirit. Peter makes explicit the connection between the pouring out of the Spirit and the now-present end of
time in his Pentecost sermon:

> These are not drunk, as you suppose, for it is only nine o'clock in the morn-
> ing. No, this is what was spoken through the prophet Joel:
>
> > "In the last days it will be, God declares,
> > that I will pour out my Spirit upon all flesh,
> >   and your sons and your daughters shall prophesy,
> > and your young men shall see visions,
> >   and your old men shall dream dreams.
> > Even upon my slaves, both men and women,
> >   in those days I will pour out my Spirit;
> >   and they shall prophesy.
> > And I will show portents in the heaven above
> >   and signs on the earth below,
> >   blood, and fire, and smoky mist.
> > The sun shall be turned to darkness
> >   and the moon to blood,
> >   before the coming of the Lord's great and glorious day.
> > Then everyone who calls on the name of the Lord shall be saved."
> >   (Acts 2:15–21)

Jesus had believed that the end of time was breaking in. The disciples
had, in turn, believed him and had followed him. But his death had
called all that into question. Now the disciples were believing again,
only in such a way that the twin events of Jesus' resurrection and the
outpouring of the Spirit both framed and confirmed that belief. That is
why we are able to read Easter-Pentecost as a single unified narrative
about the birth of a new form of apostolic evangelism, the church. A
new age had dawned and a new social option was now necessary and,
through baptism, possible.

As with the prophetic understanding of shalom and Jesus' proclamation of God's reign, apostolic faith was neither private nor merely intellectual or interior. It was, in fact, a faith that had to do with the destiny
of all Israel and ultimately the cosmos. If Jesus had not been wrong and
if his resurrection was the confirmation that the end of time had in fact
occurred, then the salvation of Israel had arrived and, through Israel,

the salvation of the world. Jesus the resurrected Messiah had therefore been exalted as Savior and Lord. The two most important items now on the apostles' agenda were to spread this news to anyone in Israel who would listen and to live together as a new community constituted by this stunning turn of events—both of which constitute the essence of early apostolic evangelism. For the apostles, to serve a resurrected Messiah and to be filled with the Spirit was to be "sent forth,"[4] and sent forth together as a body. Indeed, the very meaning of the word *apostle* is "one who is sent."

What were the characteristics of this new eschatological and evangelistic society? At its very heart was the experience of joy and gladness, as evidenced by the repeated use of these words and their derivatives. Joy is hardly a piece of nontheological or amoral trivia in the story of the early church; it not only fuels the witness of the disciples in the world but serves as one of the central and manifest expressions of their life together and of the presence of the Holy Spirit. Joy is the church's response not only to daily healings and conversions but also to being accorded worthy to suffer shame for Christ's name. According to Luke, the church's response to rejection and persecution was that "the disciples were filled with joy and with the Holy Spirit" (Acts 13:52). We can affirm just as confidently today that a church that confesses itself to be "apostolic" but lives without joy has failed to live up to its confession and is unable to evangelize. For joy is both the experiential prerequisite for Christian evangelism and its content. As Orthodox theologian Alexander Schmemann says,

> Without the proclamation of this joy Christianity is incomprehensible. It is only as joy that the Church was victorious in the world, and it lost the world when it lost that joy, and ceased to be a credible witness to it. Of all accusations against Christians, the most terrible one was uttered by Nietzsche when he said that Christians had no joy. . . . To enter into that joy, so as to be a witness to it in the world, is the very calling of the Church, its essential *leitourgia*, the sacrament by which it "becomes what it is." (1997:24–26)

If joy was a central characteristic of the first apostolic communities and intrinsic to their evangelistic witness, we know that unity was as well—not only in faith and worship but also in ethical conduct, allegiances, and commitments. As the story of the early church unfolds, we read:

> Now the whole group of those who believed were of one heart and soul, and no one claimed private ownership of any possessions, but everything

4. Matthew 28:19–20; Mark 16:15; Luke 24:47; John 20:21; Acts 1:8.

they owned was held in common. With great power the apostles gave their testimony to the resurrection of the Lord Jesus, and great grace was upon them all. There was not a needy person among them, for as many as owned land or houses sold them and brought the proceeds of what was sold. They laid it at the apostles' feet, and it was distributed to each as any had need. (Acts 4:32–34)

Here again we see that for the people of God, worship, ethics, and evangelism are indistinguishable. Worship took place within a new social form that included a common life, a common purse, common meals, daily prayer and meeting, decision making through discerning the Spirit rather than through democracy or dictatorship, economic leveling, joy and gladness, ethnic and gender inclusiveness, and apostolic obedience. Such behavior was, as Yoder says, "a kind of life strikingly, offensively different from the rest of the world; it dared to claim that Christ himself was its norm and to believe in the active enabling presence of the Holy Spirit" (1998:228).

Moreover, this social form, by its very existence, was the witness to the world that God's rule had arrived. Baptism was far more than a symbolic nod to tradition or a quick initiatory rite, but rather one's commissioning into a missionary existence. In baptism one transferred one's allegiances to God and accepted God's rule in the form of a new household meant to de-idolize every other household and indeed every other competing social body, whether that was the nation, the *polis*, the military, the market, or the *ethnos*.

Needless to say, the evangelistic implications of Easter-Pentecost are considerable. The church, far from being one more social organization within civil society (and little more than a religious version of the Rotary Club), is instead the eschatological sign, the living demonstration that the end of time has come. Its very existence is a witness to the resurrection of Jesus, and this means that believers are now to live together before the world *as if* the end has come. Salvation is not, therefore, received by believers upon death; rather, those who are children of God have already passed from death to life (1 John 3:14). The apostles' sense of urgency was generated not by the need to get people ready for some imagined end that was yet to come but by the need to live within a new creation that had already arrived in the life, death, and resurrection of Jesus. There could no longer, therefore, be any poor among them. Former lines of gender, ethnicity, and family structure would need to be subordinated to or relativized in favor of a new family structure. Property would be sold if that was needed and the proceeds distributed among this new family. Houses were made available to the community for meeting, for eating, and quite likely for housing the band of Galileans who were now headquartered in Jerusalem.

Last, if Jesus is Lord, then resistance was due to any power that would attempt to exercise rival lordship in the life of the believer, either by determining that person's identity or by requiring the believer to do things contrary to the reality of God's reign. As the movement spread among the Gentiles throughout the first century and on into the second and third centuries, this would inevitably translate into nonparticipation in imperial festivals, pagan rituals, gladiatorial contests, and military service, along with, in many cases, the abandonment of former occupations.[5] All of this was not a withdrawal from or renunciation of the world. It was rather obedience to God for the sake of the world and for the sake of being a foretaste of the change that God desires in the world.

This latter point about resisting the powers is central to the apostolic narrative of the birth of the church but is frequently overlooked in the present church's retelling, probably because we do not represent anything like a threat to the status quo (whether that be the state, the military, the market, or civil society). Jesus, as we know, was executed on charges of crimes against both the temple and the state. But even before his birth, he was already perceived as an enemy of the state (Matt. 2:1–16). His resurrection was likewise against the law, the tomb having been sealed by the state and guarded by its military. According to the book of Acts, the apostles soon discovered for themselves that to be followers of Jesus was no less politically subversive. Already in the first verses of Acts 4, the story is told of Peter and John's being hauled off to jail for preaching the resurrection of Jesus and for their involvement in the healing of a man more than forty years old who had been unable to walk from birth. After being threatened, they were then released, whereupon the church gathered to discern their course of action by hearing what the Spirit was saying to them through prayer and by listening to the Scriptures (4:23–31). By the end of chapter 5, we find that, having determined they must obey God rather than people, the apostles were again arrested, thrown in jail, and forbidden to preach. Yet again they continued to offer public resistance—"they did not cease to proclaim Jesus as the Messiah" (5:42).

In all that the apostles said and did, we find again the common thread that runs through the narrative of Jesus' life and that connects the story of Jesus with the story of the apostles: the activity of God the Spirit. The Spirit constitutes the church, initiates its mission, and constantly reforms it. At virtually every turn in the story of the apostles narrated in Luke's Acts, it is the Spirit who is guiding the apostles, preparing the ground for their evangelism, instigating meetings, breaking down barri

5. See, for example, Hippolytus, *The Apostolic Tradition* (third century), especially part 2.

ers, transgressing borders, and challenging ethnic and racial stereotypes (most notably in the case of Peter and Cornelius, Acts 10). Ministry, mission, and evangelism, it appears, are not in the first place what the church does but what it has been given by God the Spirit. Moreover, as Newbigin notes, "that mission changes not only the world but also the church" (1995:59).

While the church evangelizes by exemplifying the good news in its worship and obedience, the church can never wait until it "gets its own house in order" before beginning to reach out with its evangelistic offer. Insofar as the disorder of the church is directly related to its narcissism, the very process of being sent, of reaching out, is central to how the church's house gets puts in order in the first place.

> Mission is not just church extension. It is something more costly and more revolutionary. It is the action of the Holy Spirit, who in his sovereign freedom both convicts the world (John 16:18–11) and leads the church toward the fullness of the truth that it has not yet grasped (John 16:12–15). Mission is not essentially an action by which the church puts forth its own power and wisdom to conquer the world around it; it is, rather, an action of God, putting forth the power of his Spirit to bring the universal work of Christ for the salvation of the world nearer to its completion. (Newbigin 1995:59–60)

Whether openly in public or in private fellowship together, the marks of the early church are concrete and visible: jubilation, unity, consensus built on spiritual discernment, material sharing, inclusive table fellowship, bold proclamation, and public defiance of the powers. This visible shape was, moreover, a way of being narrated by the story of Jesus and of narrating it to others. As the church spread throughout the first century and on into the second, we see a progressive obliteration of social and ethnic boundaries as determining the shape of God's reign and thus delimiting the scope of the church's evangelism. Within this spread, there is no denying that the church's composition, ministries, organizational structures, patterns of governance, and forms of ritual activity and assembling all went through numerous changes as the church interacted with its many new environments, borrowing from, adapting to, and transforming the various structures it encountered. Yet as Roger Haight concludes in his extensive study of the formation of the church, it had "a predominant, centering mission, namely, to extend forward in history the ministry and message of Jesus, to keep his mission alive" (2004:95, cf. 67–198).

An alteration had indeed taken place in the transition from Jesus' evangelism to the apostles' evangelism, but it was not an abandonment by the latter of that which came before it. Nor was it merely a recontextualizing of Jesus' Jewish evangelism into a Gentile world. The church now announced the good news of God's reign within the framework of its belief in the resurrection of Jesus and out of its experience of the Holy Spirit. A new social body had been created in history that was a messianic extension of Israel to the Gentiles (Israel's story was not superseded but could now become the story of others; cf. Lindbeck 2002:149–50). Through the visible patterns, allegiances, and relationships of that body in which Jew and Gentile were now reconciled in Christ, the church's story was visibly embodied within the world and for the world.

The answer to our question about the shift from proclaimer to proclaimed is complex, for it is certainly the case that the church has at times betrayed Jesus by abandoning his proclamation of the reign of God and abstracting the significance of Jesus from his life and practice and from the story of Israel in which his life and practice make sense. Peter's sermon on Pentecost can then be lifted out of its narrative context[6] and detached from the actual worship, practices, and habits of the early church that provide the *Gestalt*, the recognizable pattern of embodied witness that renders Peter's preaching intelligible and bound up with the reign of God as lived and proclaimed by the One he followed. If the story of the apostles shows anything, it shows that the shift in their understanding of God's salvation history occasioned by the death and resurrection of Jesus and interpreted as the fulfillment of messianic prophecy and the triumph of God over the powers is not at all a shift away from Jesus' focus on God's reign (though it does not always persist with that explicit verbiage). Rather, it involves an insistence that since it is in the person of Jesus that God's reign has come near, the world can never again be the same, and a whole new way of living is now necessary and possible.

The evangelistic question with which I began this chapter, then—how it is that the proclaimer became the proclaimed—must receive an answer that is narrativist in its logic and ecclesial in its exemplification. First, the answer is narrativist in its logic. Part of the difficulty for us in understanding how it is that the early Christians were able to keep together that which we are prone to separate—the message and the messenger—is that we have been trained not to think of messages as embodied in persons or social bodies, embedded in narratives, and enmeshed in practices. Messages instead come to us in the form of propositions, treatises, and syllogisms—in Lessing's words, "the necessary truths of reason." No wonder the good news so frequently turns from bread into stone. That the postresurrection church should focus on Jesus in its proclamation where Jesus himself was apparently reticent to do so need not indicate

6. Again, it is worth remembering that Luke-Acts is a single narrative.

a betrayal or a loss. It is, rather, an insistence that in light of the resurrection, the story of Jesus and the story of God's reign proclaimed by Jesus are not finally two stories but one. The reign of God, as Newbigin puts it, "was no longer a distant hope or a faceless concept. It had now a name and a face—the name and face of the man from Nazareth. In the New Testament we are dealing not just with the proclamation of the kingdom but also with the presence of the kingdom" (1995:40).

The unity of message and messenger, however, cannot be established quantitatively by demonstrating the extent to which they either agree or disagree. Nor is it established qualitatively by showing how they say the same thing at different logical levels or in different contexts or "keys."[7] Instead the unity of message and messenger is the same as that exhibited by the Bible as a whole—"a unity of narrative that 'goes somewhere' as opposed to a flat unity in which every text in every part of the Bible is to be read in exactly the same way as every other text" (Carter 2001:64).[8] If Jesus' good news of God's reign is to be communicated to the world, that will now need to be done precisely in and through telling his story and thereby offering him to the world.[9] Thus, the transition from Jesus the proclaimer to Jesus the proclaimed must be read directionally, as a story of promise and fulfillment (cf. Yoder 1984:9).[10]

But while the unity of message and messenger has a narrativist logic, it also has an ecclesial exemplification. The reign of God proclaimed by Jesus and embodied in his person becomes a concrete possibility in the world when a space is created for it through the Spirit's formation of persons into the life, death, and resurrection of Christ (and thus into his "body"). By being joined to Jesus, a new community is created that stands not as a *different* people of God from Israel but as a messianic enlargement of Israel and as a formation through whom Gentiles would now become citizens of its commonwealth.

Whatever else the early Christians understood to be the significance of Jesus for their lives, that significance was understood as not just

7. This is the strategy employed by Juan Luis Segundo, who sees later reflections on the significance of Jesus as a "meta-message" about the message. See his five-volume *Jesus of Nazareth: Yesterday and Today*.

8. Craig Carter, in this statement, is discussing the views of John Howard Yoder on the narrative unity of the Bible.

9. "This new thing does not enter the world as pure instruction, a mere idea, a brain wave, a bolt from the blue. It appears in a concrete person. That person is Jesus Christ. . . . He is the fulfillment of the long history that began with Abraham. He is the definitive appearance, the full clarification of everything that has heretofore happened to Israel" (Lohfink 1999:133).

10. This also implies that the relationship between Jesus and Israel is not that of love to law, inwardness to outwardness, the individual to the social (Lohfink 1999:121–24), but rather promise to fulfillment.

a story to be told but a story into which they themselves were being incorporated. So, for example, the ordering of the Christian calendar after the life of Jesus that has come to be known as the "church year" was more than a nice way to use color in the sanctuary or to keep things from getting boring across fifty-two Sundays. It was—and is—the way our lives are patterned together into the narrative of his life. It is a way of scripting our minds and bodies through worship and ministry into a new timeliness, a timeliness that transcends (and frequently subverts) biological time (days, years, birthdays) or social time (national holidays, superbowls, anniversaries) and is, instead, "gospel" time, resurrection time. Learning to be Christian, then, is not just learning *about* a story; it is learning to live *into* a story.[11] That is why Christian ritual, as strange as it sometimes may appear, far from being an obstacle to Christian evangelism and catechesis, is its backbone. For it is in "learning to perform the gestures that embody the narrative of God's people" that the character of membership in Christ's body is cultivated (Webb-Mitchell 2003:37).

Let us not forget that verbally telling the story of Jesus and the story of his proclamation of God's reign remained central to apostolic evangelism. That is why we continue to call the four tellings of that story that begin the New Testament "Gospels." The telling of the story *is* evangelism; the narrative *is* the evangel. It is impossible, moreover, to read the book of Acts or the New Testament epistolary literature without being struck by the centrality of preaching in the early church's evangelism.

The point I have been trying to make here, however, is that it would be wrong to look only in the words of later apostolic witness for the continued presence of Jesus' gospel of God's reign. Just as important as verbal witness for the first Christian communities (if not more so) was the character of their life together before a watching world. The reign of God does not disappear or get "replaced"; it is instead impressed upon their worship, their economic practices, their fellowship, their crossing of social boundaries, and their joy and boldness; it shows up daily in the patterns and practices of their new life together.

Because soteriology, Christology, and eschatology were for the apostles also and at the same time ecclesiology (rather than the church's being

11. When the apostles bore witness to Jesus' understanding of God's reign, they found it impossible to do this meaningfully without telling the story of his life and then connecting that story to the story of the people of God. As Hauerwas says,

The kingdom is not simply some cipher that we can fill in with our ideas about what a good society ought to look like. Nor is it merely a way of reemphasizing the eternal sovereignty of God, though this is certainly part of what the proclamation of the kingdom entails. Rather the proclamation of the coming kingdom of God, its presence, and future coming is a claim about *how* God rules and the establishment of that rule through the life, death, and resurrection of Jesus. (1983:83)

an afterthought to what one believed about salvation, Christ, and the meaning of history), the early Christians bore witness both to the message and to the messenger, not as two messages but as one. Perhaps the greatest challenge of the church today is to demonstrate this unity in its own evangelism, to offer Jesus as Lord precisely by bearing embodied witness to the reign of God he proclaimed. For as Lohfink rightly suggests, "The reign of God requires a space in which to exercise its sovereignty; it needs a people" (1999:133). To offer Christ to the world is also to offer to the world a people, a body that may truly be spoken of as "Christ's," created and formed by the Holy Spirit as that space.

What looks like a shift, then, from the gospel *of* Jesus to the gospel *about* Jesus is instead the apostolic way of connecting the dots. The reign of God is not something vague, abstract, or general. It has a Messiah and so is embodied in a person who is God's way of engrafting the entire world into God's reign and into the history of Israel. As Origen said, Jesus is the *autobasileia*—the reign of God in person. On the one hand, then, salvation is very much about acceptance of Jesus as the presence of God's reign—and as the story of Jesus in the various Gospels make clear, this focus on Jesus is inescapably a cause for offense and stumbling. On the other hand, Christian salvation is distorted (along with the evangelistic practice that follows from it) when it is reduced to "getting right with Jesus" as a private spiritual affair with, at best, reign-of-God consequences. Because of the new order present in Jesus and because of the social, political, and subversive dimensions of that new order, "believing in Jesus" is not a private mental assent to a set of propositions about his nature, an individual experience of his person, or a legalistic performance of his teachings. Apostolic evangelism is an invitation to be formed socially by the Holy Spirit into the life, death, and resurrection of Jesus through incorporation into his body. Anything less can never be a full "offer" of Christ.

Part 3

Rival Narratives, Subverted Evangelism

In part 1 of this book, I drew upon the work of Alasdair MacIntyre in order to demonstrate that the intelligibility of a practice depends upon a narrative that, among other things, provides a directional unity across time and specifies the *telos* toward which that practice is aimed. In part 2, I argued for the story of the people of God and its journey toward the city of peace as the story in which the Christian practice of evangelism is properly situated, and I attempted to show the broad outline of that story as displayed in the calling and formation of Israel, the life, death, and resurrection of Jesus, and the transformation of the followers of Jesus into the church, the eschatological people of God. I noted that this narrative proves doubly important for the practice of evangelism, for it not only provides the *content* of Christian evangelism (the story into which persons are invited to become characters); it also forms the church's practical and evangelistic *imagination*. In other words, this narrative not only provides the *what* and the *what for* of evangelism; it also shapes the *how*.

To tell the story of the people of God, however, is at the same time necessarily to tell the story of all peoples and to narrate the meaning and end of all history—and to do so, moreover, in a way that stands as an alternative to other narrations of the meaning and end of history. In part 3, I now turn to two rival narratives that have shaped to varying degrees the social, political, and economic orders and religious life of Western cultures and, by extension, other cultures around the world.

111

The relevance of these narratives for our purposes is that they have proved themselves extraordinarily powerful at forming the evangelistic imagination—again, not only in the West but throughout the globe. From the standpoint of the narrative of the people of God, however, both narratives must be judged as having distorted it. Central to the argument of this book is that the conversion to which Christian evangelism invites persons takes place not *within* these rival narratives but rather *from* them to another narrative altogether. Evangelism is an invitation to join a new story and to allow that story to make sense of our past and orient us toward a new future.

In the following two chapters, I will argue that the situation in which the church finds itself today is characterized by the possibility of two important transitions: (1) from a Constantinian to a post-Constantinian narrative and (2) from the narrative of liberal modernity to a narrative that we might, for lack of better terms, speak of as "postmodern" or "postliberal."[1] I am not arguing that these transitions are complete, nor do I know where they will lead us. Though I will be critical of both the Constantinian narrative and the narrative of liberal modernity, I do not believe that every form of transitioning out of or beyond them is to be considered progress or an unequivocally positive development for the church. But these transitions (and the work of narrative criticism they occasion) do provide the church an opportunity for the constructive re-appropriation of its story, extricating the practice of evangelism from its colonialist and imperialist past and freeing it for a liberating and peaceful future. While this book arises out of and seeks to speak primarily to a North American context, moreover, these transitions have the potential to occasion shalom both in those Western cultures that have done the dominating and in those that have been dominated.

All this is not to say that attention to narrative alone is somehow "the solution" for evangelism. Narratives are always enacted and embodied in particular communities and in their practices and social patterns. Yet the narrative in which a practice is situated powerfully shapes (and sometimes distorts) that practice by providing its internal logic, motivation, and aim. Both the Constantinian narrative and the narrative of liberal modernity have the power to corrupt the practice of evangelism by situating it within a false *telos* (and therefore within a heretical eschatology), one that is ultimately violent.

Drawing attention to these rival narratives helps to clarify further the narrative of the people of God (by way of contrast) and to demonstrate

1. I understand the prefix *post-* not in solely temporal terms, as pointing to a state of affairs that simply supersedes that to which it is affixed, but rather as connoting a critical, discursive, and political relationship to that which it is affixed that attempts to take fully into account our "having gone through" the latter (cf. Pui-Lan 2005:2).

the sense in which evangelism is an essentially subversive activity insofar as it invites persons to abandon and defy these rival narratives. The practice of evangelism, then, is to some degree confrontational and is, in fact, the sort of practice McClendon calls a "powerful practice" (1986:1:173–77, 188). It challenges the violent, oppressive, and enslaving practices of the world (which are themselves also powerful) by forming us into a people capable of recognizing and resisting such powers and of recognizing and confessing our own sinful complicity with them.

That does not mean that evangelism is only or best carried out through strategies of irritation! Nor does it mean the universe or human life is founded on conflict. It is peace rather than violence that is the foundation of the universe, because God is the universe's source and end. But evangelism is inescapably a conflictual practice that counters and disarms the world's powerful practices, unmasks the narratives that sustain them, and ultimately subverts them by offering a story that is peaceful. Like other core practices of the church, evangelism is very much about power and inevitably involves a contest of power. For the Christian, however, the person and teachings of Christ reinscribe power (and so "politics") within the peaceful (Eph. 2:14–18), kenotic (Phil. 2:5–11), and cruciform (1 Cor. 1:18) matrix of God's commonwealth, which is the foundation, inner logic, and aim of Christian power.

Within the ecclesial reimagining of evangelism I am attempting in this book, to be saved by God is to be saved not only from sin but also from powers that make us incapable of recognizing and resisting sin—powers that form and discipline us into the kind of people who are incapable of being the church. The demonic power of various institutions such as the nation-state, the military, the university, the market, and even the church derives from their having been co-opted by these powers. The church, however, bears a unique relationship to the powers, because it is the public of the Holy Spirit and because its worship has been made possible by the resurrection of Jesus and by his patient and lamblike triumph over the powers. The church is a mode of participation in Christ and a fellowship that, though made up of sinners like the rest of the world, has discovered the capacity to publicly resist and redeem the powers through confession and forgiveness of sin around a common table.

Discussion of these two narratives as rivals to the story of the people of God is complicated by the fact that both of them are, in a crucial sense, part of that story. In one sense, then, it is not possible for the church simply to disown those stories by claiming they are "not ours." The story the church has been given, the story it is called to remember and to which it is called to be faithful, is always bound up with the actual journey the church has undertaken in history, complete with its dead ends, detours, and derailments. Remembering the church's story is not an exercise in primitivism by which we gleefully skip across two millennia of Christian history and baptize as infallible the practices and theological formulations of the past. But it is an exercise in confessing that in God's calling of the people of Israel, in the life and message of Jesus, and in the witness of the apostles, we have been given a true story that, by forming our practical imagination, renders us capable of living truthfully before the world and of resisting powers such as the state and the market that would have us believe that our identity is patriots and consumers and that our duty is to kill and shop on their behalf.

Because this story is true, it is capable of exercising a critical function with regard to the other narratives that have formed our imaginations throughout history but need not have. A church that lacks the ability to counter other narratives is a church adrift, a church that is hopelessly *civil*, a church that can never be the eschatological people of God for the world. If the church's story is subversive of other stories, that is true even of the other stories that we have made our own. So while in one sense we may not be able to disown such stories, in another crucial sense, insofar as we can discern their having proved to be dangerous departures from our journey, it is both possible and necessary to repent of them and disavow them.

5

The Constantinian Story

The story of the people of God is the story of a people that is always required to clarify its relationship to the nations, empires, communities, publics, cities, and cultures in which it finds itself. Whether that people is wandering in Mesopotamia, enslaved in Egypt, sojourning in the desert, exiled in Babylon, planted in Jerusalem, or following the Risen One to the ends of the earth, there is a "sent" and therefore intrinsically missionary quality to its existence. As Jonah was slow to figure out, to be the people of God is to be a people for the world.

But at the heart of a theology of evangelism is the question whether, called to be a people for the world, the people of God will yield to the temptation of making itself at home in that world, whether it will instead cloister itself off as a separatist enclave, or whether it will find some third way of imaginatively engaging the world with the peace of God through its worship and obedience as it journeys toward its true home, the city of shalom. What it means to be the people of God can never be something static, finished, fortresslike, or permanent. Indeed, exile and diaspora may very well be the "normal" existence, even the vocation, of the people of God (Yoder 1997:55–60). We are, of course, called to "seek the *shalom* of the city" where God has sent us into exile "and pray to the LORD on its behalf," for in its shalom we discover our shalom (Jer. 29:7). Yet no city can ever be "home" for the people of God (Heb. 13:14), and no love for, engagement with, or service to the world can diminish the truth that this people inevitably represents an alternative social arrangement wherever it is in the world. As the *Epistle to Diognetus* (c. 100–150 CE) describes the life of early Christians:

> But, inhabiting Greek as well as barbarian cities, according as the lot of each of them has determined, and following the customs of the natives in respect to clothing, food, and the rest of their ordinary conduct, they display to us their wonderful and confessedly striking method of life. They dwell in their own countries, but simply as sojourners. As citizens, they share in all things with others, and yet endure all things as if foreigners. Every foreign land is to them as their native country, and every land of their birth as a land of strangers. They marry, as do all [others]; they beget children, but they do not destroy their offspring. They have a common table, but not a common bed. They are in the flesh, but they do not live after the flesh. They pass their days on earth, but they are citizens of heaven. (5:4–8, in Roberts and Donaldson 1931:1:26–27)

Because the temptation of a people that is called to be for the world is to make itself at home in the world, one of the recurring and central issues for evangelism is what it means to be the pilgrim people of God and how, on that basis, we are to construct our relationships with the rest of the world so as to invite others to join us on the pilgrimage. That the people of God frequently discovers itself to have taken wrong turns or to have given up the journey and made itself at home demonstrates how important it is to be reminded of our journey and of its end.

The Constantinian story is the story of the church's forgetting its journey and making itself at home in the world. Though the word itself points to the emperor Constantine (c. 272–337 CE), it is not necessarily the man himself or his own intentions that are our primary focus when thinking about the set of assumptions and social arrangements referred to here as Constantinian, nor did the forgetfulness of the church happen in the span of one man's life. The Constantinian relationship of church to world has its origins in decisions, actions, and forces at work prior to Constantine and takes further and ongoing shape in the century after him up through at least Augustine. Emperor Theodosius I (379–95 CE) went beyond the mere toleration of Christianity imposed by Constantine, requiring instead that imperial subjects profess a trinitarian faith and relinquish all pagan worship and sacrifice.[1] It can be said that

1. From the Theodosian Code:

It is our desire that all the various nations which are subject to our Clemency and Moderation, should continue in the profession of that religion which was delivered to the Romans by the divine Apostle Peter, as it hath been preserved by faithful tradition; and which is now professed by the Pontiff Damasus and by Peter, Bishop of Alexandria, a man of apostolic holiness. According to the apostolic teaching and the doctrine of the Gospel, let us believe the one deity of the Father, the Son and

Constantinianism has its origins in what Yoder calls the "Solomonic temptation" of Israel—the temptation of sacralizing its power structures, hierarchy, military apparatus, and nationalistic aspirations, thereby turning YHWH into something like a state deity—a move for which it was roundly criticized by its judges and prophets (Yoder 1997:83; cf. Carter 2001:51, 147, 164–66).

Though Constantine is sometimes thought of as the first Christian emperor, questions may certainly be raised as to how thorough or sincere his conversion was (complicating what we mean by the very word *conversion*). Though he thought of himself as a Christian from the year 312 on, he also ordered the executions of his own wife, father-in-law, three brothers-in-law, and son (Comby 1982:68) and so is probably not to be considered a model Christian. But just this fact illustrates the ambiguity involved in applying the word *Christian* not only to persons but also to empires, countries, universities, wars, books, art, music, or television stations.

In 313, Constantine issued an edict mandating the toleration of Christians that would set the stage for the eventual "triumph" of Christianity in the West. Constantine saw in Christianity a force that could unite his fragmented empire, though Christians hardly proved to be a more united group than the other nations and tribes he sought to unite. He therefore began the practice of intervening in ecclesiastical affairs, including convening and presiding over the first ecumenical council at Nicaea in 325. Though the transformation was not immediate, so significant was the shift from Christians being a persecuted, deviant minority to Christians running the apparatus of the state and persecuting those who were now perceived as religious deviants that one might build a good case for the distinction between a pre-Constantinian church and a Constantinian church as in many ways more fundamental than more prominent distinctions within present-day Christianity such as Catholic, Orthodox, Protestant, liberal, conservative, evangelical, and mainline.[2] Whether it is possible

---

the Holy Spirit, in equal majesty and in a holy Trinity. We authorize the followers of this law to assume the title Catholic Christians; but as for the others, since, in our judgment, they are foolish madmen, we decree that they shall be branded with the ignominious name of heretics, and shall not presume to give their conventicles the name of churches. They will suffer in the first place the chastisement of the divine condemnation, and in the second the punishment which our authority, in accordance with the will of heaven, shall decide to inflict. (Theodosian Code 16.1.2, in Bettenson 1963:22)

Naturally, it may be debated how well enforced or broad in scope were the edicts of Theodosius.

2. Cf. Yoder 1984:82–85, 135–47; 1997:8, 103–8; 1998:143–67. At the same time, Yoder would argue that there is an even more fundamental distinction to be found in Christian

to imagine a post-Constantinian church and, so, a post-Constantinian evangelism is the question we are concerned with here.

The term *Christendom* is frequently applied to this Constantinian state of affairs, and it is possible to conflate the terms *Constantinianism* and *Christendom* so that they are, for all practical purposes, synonymous. Indeed, they are synonymous insofar as *Christendom* refers to a framework for construing the relationship between church and state in which the two are fused together for the sake of governance in such a way that Christianity becomes a project of the state or an appendage to the state, subject to its violent ends. But in our time we should be careful not to assume that merely because Christians have been forced to give up on the Christendom project, they have, at the same time, rejected the Constantinian assumptions that both gave rise to that project and sustained it.[3] In the Constantinian synthesis of church and world, princes became bishops, church discipline was applied by civil courts and enforced by its police, and the empire guaranteed the meaning of people's lives (and so was to be maintained and defended at all cost). Though many of the legal structures created in the service of this synthesis either have been dismantled or are retained as merely symbolic vestiges of the past, it is not necessary to think of the Constantinian arrangement or of the Christendom it produced only as a legal or cultural establishment of Christianity. We may also speak of Constantinianism as a set of deeper assumptions whereby Christians systematically confuse church and world, and as a conviction that lives on—and dies hard—in the ways we think of the church, practice evangelism, or attempt to convince unbelievers and expand Christian influence.

Though the Constantinian arrangement often worked to the advantage of the growth and stability of the church, there was a high price to pay. Indeed it is possible, with eighteenth-century Anglican reformer John Wesley, to see Constantinianism as the fall of the church:

> Persecution never did, never could give any lasting wound to genuine Christianity. But the greatest it ever received, the grand blow which was struck at the very root of that humble, gentle, patient love, which is the fulfilling of the Christian law, the whole essence of true religion, was struck

---

history: between the early Christian church that included both Jews and Gentiles and the later church of the Jewish-Christian schism; see Yoder 2003.

3. Another possibility that likewise makes any easy conflation of Constantinianism and Christendom problematic is the possibility *in principle* (however unlikely in our own historical situation or within the context of the modern nation-state) of a "non-Constantinian Christendom" in which a nation and its rulers refuse to equate their own cultural, economic, and political order with the reign of God and in which that nation's rulers follow Jesus as Lord, even if that means the victory of their enemies over them (see Carter's helpful discussion of this very possibility, 2001:156).

in the fourth century by Constantine the Great, when he called himself a
Christian, and poured in a flood of riches, honours, and power upon the
Christians, more especially upon the clergy. (1975:2:462–63)

Constantinianism made it easy for the world to be Christian—and the
church has been paying the price ever since. But the cost runs higher
than even Wesley could see.[4] As Yoder points out, what is most striking
about the transition from a pre-Constantinian church to a Constantinian church

> is not that Christians were no longer persecuted and began to be privi-
> leged, nor that emperors built churches and presided over ecumenical
> deliberations about the Trinity; what matters is that the two visible reali-
> ties, church and world, were fused. There is no longer anything to call
> "world"; state, economy, art, rhetoric, superstition, and war have all been
> baptized. (1998:57)

Prior to Constantine, Christians could assume that the church was
an identifiable body of believers in contrast to an unbelieving world;
persecution itself would have gone far toward insuring the voluntary
character of Christian conviction and the costly nature of Christian affiliation. But that contrast grew increasingly impossible once the entire
empire was officially Christian. It would now take more courage to refuse
Christianity than to embrace it.

Of course, not everyone thought that the empire was really Christian
just because the emperor declared it to be. As visible obedience to the
lordship of Jesus characterized by the politics and economics of God's
reign ceased to be a prerequisite for claiming a Christian identity, one
had to reach for new distinctions to ensure that faith and conviction
still mattered. By the fifth century, it could be suggested that the true
church is not the same as the visible church and thus it is more accurate
to speak of the true church as "invisible." The notion that the true church
is invisible or that faith is invisible would have been largely impossible
prior to Constantine, when the church's *visible* deviance and subversive
embodiment of something new and unparalleled in the world served both
as an invitation and that to which the invitation pointed. Here was a new
people, a new social option, where social lines were crossed, where the
poor were valued, where violence was rejected, and where patterns of
domination and subordination were turned upside down.

The visibility of the church was constitutive of its witness, as the life
and deaths of its martyrs attested; indeed, this visibility was constitu-

4. In many respects, Wesley was himself deeply Constantinian, as illustrated by his
views on God and king (cf. Grassow 1998).

tive of its very existence *as church*. The extent to which the distinction between a visible and invisible church is still with us illustrates how utterly Constantinian we still are. The task of Christian evangelism today is to recapture some of the church's pre-Constantinian deviance in a post-Constantinian world.

In what follows, I will explore three criticisms of the Constantinian synthesis found in the writings of John Howard Yoder, and I will then relate those to evangelism undertaken within the social imagination inherent in that synthesis. Yoder's criticisms of Constantinianism are focused primarily on Christian social ethics, but because the Constantinian story narrates a set of assumptions about obedience, witness, history, and the church, his criticisms are, I believe, of direct relevance to the practice of evangelism as well.

Constantinianism and the Lordship of Jesus

At the heart of the Constantinian story is a denial of the apostolic conviction that Jesus is Lord. That denial need not be verbally explicit; indeed, it usually is not. But when Christians serve the emperor, the king, the president, or the state *as Lord* (whether confessed verbally or not), then, as Yoder argues, worship has been rendered and the lordship of Jesus has been refused.

One of the most important ways this happens is when Christians give their obedience to a state that has asked or commanded them to kill on its behalf (and frequently to kill fellow Christians who have likewise been drafted by another state). According to Craig Carter, "Here is the point of testing, because here the state makes itself into an absolute value. When the concrete lordship of Jesus is modified, qualified, contradicted, or otherwise set aside by the state, then we have Constantinianism" (2001:157). Prior to Constantine, up until about 170 CE, Christians largely rejected military service both because it was part of the broader cult of empire and emperor and also because, quite simply, it was considered to violate the clear teachings of Christ. They found it difficult to love their enemies while killing them. This pacifism would not have been entirely unprecedented, since there was already a tradition of Jewish pacifism based on, among other reasons, the belief that it is the mission of the Messiah to establish a just social order and thus for Israel to assume that task would be to seize for itself God's rightful sovereignty.[5] For some

5. Yoder points out that what is often missing from debates about how uniform or widespread early Christian pacifism was is a recognition of this already present tradition of Jewish pacifism: "Jesus' impact in the first century added more and deeper authentically Jewish reasons, and reinforced and further validated the already expressed Jewish reasons,

of the Jews who understood Jesus to be the Messiah, that view would only have been intensified, given their perception of Jesus' way of being Messiah as suffering, cruciform, nonviolent, and nonnationalistic. As the Zealot attraction to Jesus demonstrates, however, not all Jews made this connection.

After about 170 CE, we find a gradual increase in those who joined the army—at first, most likely soldiers who had become Christians and simply remained in the military, but later those who joined the military after having become Christians (Driver 1988:14). By the late third century, we even have record of individuals who came to be considered military *martyrs*. At last the emperor himself became a Christian; subsequently Christianity became the official religion of the empire, and the emperor came to be described in functionally messianic terms as "pious," "God-honored," and "the servant of God and conqueror of nations."[6] Now state-sponsored violence could be considered "not only morally tolerable but a positive good and a Christian duty" (Yoder 1984:135). Christians would go forth to kill with the standard of the cross leading the way.

Of course, killing because Constantine commands it is not the only way that Christians betray Christ and deny his lordship. By modeling our social relations on kings, lords, and rulers (cf. Mark 9:35; Luke 22:25–27), we not only reject Jesus' explicit teaching that disciples are to be servants of one another but again reject his lordship, refusing his life and humility as authorizing for us a new way of living and a new set of social relations. The fundamental betrayal that stands behind all other betrayals of Christ by the church, argues Yoder, was "the reversal of Jesus' attitude toward kingship in favor of the 'Constantinian' glorification of imperial autocracy and wealth" (1992a:8). To follow Jesus as Lord is, on the contrary, to reject the identification of power with unilateral or coercive power and instead to embrace Paul's insight that God's power is made perfect in weakness (2 Cor. 12:9).

Perhaps, one might argue, Jesus may be served as Lord while we simultaneously render allegiance to the state or the emperor if and when the state is Christian. That condition, however, is highly unlikely due to the very nature of "statehood" or "empire" and the sort of power required to maintain the state or empire both from within and against those without.

Why then should there be anything wrong with Christianity's becoming an official ideology? It must be because that change itself calls into question something definitional about the faith. Perhaps this would not need

---

for the already well established ethos of not being in charge and not considering any local state structure to be the primary bearer of the movement of history" (1997:69).

6. See Eusebius's *The Life of Constantine*, in Schaff and Wace 1955:1:482–83.

to be absolutely true. It nonetheless tends to be the case, in the experience of the Christian community, that the only way in which the faith can
become the official ideology of a power elite in a given society is if Jesus
Christ ceases to be concretely Lord. Some other value: power, mammon,
fame, efficacy, tends to become . . . the new functional equivalent of deity.
(Yoder 1984:85–86)

The "Constantinian temptation" is the temptation to confuse obedience to Jesus as Lord with obedience to the state because the state or
the head of the state now bears the label "Christian." Needless to say,
this confusion, which is in effect a denial of Jesus as Lord, raises serious
questions for evangelism—not the least of which is whether it is even
possible to bear witness to the lordship of Jesus, much less offer that
lordship to others, while simultaneously rejecting it in practice, whether
by killing people on behalf of the empire or by mimicking and thereby
glorifying the power, wealth, and rule of another lord. What inevitably
takes place in the practice of evangelism within a Constantinian social
imagination is that the question of following Jesus as Lord is abstracted
from the concrete loyalties, habits, and patterns of conduct associated
with Jesus and the apostolic life. That question is instead transformed
into a question of one's nominal membership in a religious group. It
may also be transformed into a question of one's intellectual assent to
propositions about who Jesus is or, as we see increasingly within the
predominant consensus in modernity, into a private, inward, and dema-
terialized experience of Jesus' lordship. The common denominator in
all these transformations is that the sovereignty of Constantine remains
intact while Christian witness is disassociated from the intrinsically material and political dimensions of the lordship of Jesus. In other words,
the "practice" of evangelism is wrenched from the comprehensive praxis
in which it is rightly embedded.

The Constantinian Meaning of History

Jesus believed that the end of the world was breaking into history in
the form of God's reign, a reign that arrives unpredictably and in small
but concrete ways as a gift to be received but also as a demand that
requires a turnaround, a conversion, a new way of seeing. The apostles
understood themselves to have been made witnesses to Christ and to
have been formed together into his body as a foretaste of that reign here
and now. They therefore lived *between the times*, in the tension between
the already and the not yet. Under the conditions of Constantinianism,
however, this important eschatological tension is dissolved as the reign

of God comes to be identified with a particular human social construction, whether that is the empire, the church, or the two fused together. If Constantinianism is the church making itself at home in the world, it is centrally the church making itself at home in the world's *time* (cf. Cavanaugh 1998:222–23).

While this error is fundamentally eschatological, it is, as Yoder argues, intimately connected to a Christology that fails to recognize the relationship of the "old age" to the "new age" that has dawned in Jesus and his victory over the powers. In Paul's thought, the "principalities and powers" are invisible structures by which the world is ordered and held together. They are created by God (Col. 1:15–17) and, as with all creation, essentially good. But they are also, with all creation, fallen and rebellious. Rather than serving human well-being by mediating God's grace, these powers enslave humans and hold us hostage (Gal. 4:3; Col. 2:20; cf. Yoder 1972:143). Yet the powers are not "limitlessly evil," nor can they "fully escape the providential sovereignty of God" (Yoder 1972:144). We should be subject to them, as Paul urges in Romans 13, for God's purposes may still be realized through them.

The work of Christ, then, was not to destroy, ignore, or set aside the powers (since they are necessary for human existence and social organization) but rather to break their sovereignty over humans. This was accomplished by the course of Jesus' life, ministry, and disobedience to the powers, which "brought him, as any genuinely human existence will bring any [person], to the cross" (Yoder 1972:147). Paul asserts that Christ on the cross triumphed over the powers by disarming and unmasking them (Col. 2:13–15),[7] and this victory is manifested in the resurrection of Jesus, who has been exalted to the right hand of God the Father, whence he now "rules" (1 Cor. 15:20–28). Though the powers have been defeated and though we no longer need to live as slaves to them, they have not yet been subjected to Christ, as Paul affirms, yet we can be confident that this will be the case (Phil. 2:10–11).

In a world where the powers still have the capacity to destroy and enslave, there is no more important task of an evangelizing church than to live from a resurrection faith that Christ has defeated the powers and to demonstrate Christ's victory to a watching world by living and worshiping as persons who have been made free from those powers. Says Yoder, "The church does not attack the powers; this Christ has done. The church concentrates upon not being seduced by them. By her

7. On this important point, see also Walter Wink's trilogy: *Naming the Powers: The Language of Power in the New Testament* (Philadelphia: Fortress, 1994), *Unmasking the Powers: The Invisible Forces That Determine Human Existence* (Philadelphia: Fortress, 1986), and *Engaging the Powers: Discernment and Resistance in a World of Domination* (Minneapolis: Fortress, 1992).

existence she demonstrates that their rebellion has been vanquished" (Yoder 1972:153).

However, within a Constantinian social imagination, practitioners of evangelism are tempted to identify the victory of Christ with the expansion and growth of a church fused with the world in the form of a Christianized nation or empire. Insofar as eschatology is concerned with the meaning of the "end" of history for the present,[8] one can begin to see why Constantinianism is fundamentally an eschatological heresy—and one that is especially debilitating for the practice of evangelism. For the price of a Constantinian historical imagination is nothing less than the loss of Christian *witness*. A resurrection faith believes that God is sovereign rather than the powers, and this lived confidence is the form and substance of its witness. Under Constantine, however,

> Providence no longer needed to be an object of faith, for God's governance of history had become empirically evident in the person of the Christian ruler of the world. The concept of the millennium was pulled back from the future (whether distant or imminent) into the present. All that God can possibly have in store for a future victory is more of what has already been won. (Yoder 1984:136–37)

It is then a short distance from this eschatology to its manifestations in nationalism, empire building, conquests, crusades, and the synthesizing of "God and country" we find in varying Christendom constructions such as the Holy Roman Empire, the British Commonwealth of Nations, or the United States of America.

According to Yoder, while the basic fallacy here lies in a failure to understand that we live in an overlapping of the old age with the new age with the result that we "pull back" the millennium from the future to the present, the Constantinian heresy can also surface in something like a reversal of this "pullback"—the wholesale relegation of the new age *to* the future, so that since we are still living in the old age, we must be "realistic" about the possibilities of living faithfully as Christians in the present. Another variation of this same heresy is to relegate the new age either to a realm of inner piety (Christ reigns in my heart, but I can still kill other people if the state asks me to) or to a Neoplatonic and ultimately dualistic realm of the ideal, which leads to the distinction between a visible and an invisible church (Yoder 1998:140–41). The point here is that Christendom does not always take the form of an institutional church formally aligning itself with the state. It can take an individualistic, personalistic form in which what is construed as the

8. Eschatology, as Yoder says, is "a hope that, defying present frustration, defines a present position in terms of the yet unseen goal that gives it meaning" (1998:145).

true church has little or no empirical social reality and, to that degree, fails to bear witness to the Christ whose life, suffering, and death on the cross were nothing if not material, visible, and bodily.

What is at stake in all this for evangelism is the very meaning of history, whether and to what extent one believes that Jesus' life, death, and resurrection transformed history, and what then becomes the church's role or agency in history. For evangelism to resist the Constantinian temptation is, on the one hand, to take seriously the responsibility of embodied witness while at the same time, on the other hand, rejecting the utopian calculus of causality and effectiveness that holds providence no longer to be a matter of faith but rather an empirical matter of human control and construction. Says Yoder,

> The key to the obedience of God's people is not their effectiveness but their patience ([Rev.] 13:10). The triumph of the right is assured not by the might that comes to the aid of the right, which is of course the justification of the use of violence and other kinds of power in every human conflict; the triumph of the right, although it is assured, is sure because of the power of the resurrection and not because of any calculation of causes and effects, nor because of the inherently greater strength of the good guys. The relationship between the obedience of God's people and the triumph of God's cause is not a relationship of cause and effect but one of cross and resurrection. (1972:238)

To be the sort of church that is a company of disciples who follow the crucified and resurrected Jesus but who likewise reject the world's calculus of power will likely mean that the church will find itself operating in history as a minority (albeit a creative minority) and from a position of weakness and marginality rather than a position of power.[9] But then, as Yoder reminds us, Jesus "has always admitted that if we entrust our life to him and his cause, we will never be proven right until beyond the end of this story and cannot count on being positively reinforced along all of the way" (1998:112–13). An evangelistic church is called to patience, obedience, and martyrdom rather than effectiveness, control, or success. It will have to relinquish "winning" as a proper end, along with the logic of agency and causality that go with that end. It will have to relearn the truth that there is nothing we can do to bring about or extend God's reign, so that we are left with the singular task of bearing embodied witness to that reign. This does not mean that an evangelistic church is

9. As Yoder says, "To recognize that the church is a minority is not a statistical but a theological observation" (1998:175). Lindbeck puts it this way, "The Bible does not anticipate that the Church will ever be anything except a little flock until the end of time. From this point of view, majority rather than minority existence is anomalous for Christians" (2002:94).

unconcerned with the future or rejects all teleological reasoning. But it does reject any notion that the future is "a closed system" that can be manipulated or predicted in the service of God's reign (1998:138).

Still, if the church is "a chosen race, a royal priesthood, a holy nation, a people for God's own possession" (1 Peter 2:8), then Yoder is right in claiming that "the ultimate meaning of history is to be found in the work of the church" (1998:151). It is not the state that is the bearer of the meaning of history, nor is salvation to be identified with what the state will accomplish in terms of creating more or less just and peaceful social orderings (as valuable as those may be). On the contrary, the true meaning of history is "what the church achieves through evangelism and through the leavening process" (Yoder 1998:163). Yoder is not calling for the church to withdraw from or ignore the social order but to forsake a "responsibility" for the social order that is defined from within that order rather than from "the gospel as it infringes upon the situation" (1998:162).[10] The mistake of Constantinian Christianity is that it substitutes the state for the church eschatologically (Yoder 1998:176–77; cf. Carter 2001:162), so that the present social order rather than God's reign is seen as most real and permanent. Peace, justice, and the good are then defined in terms of what can reasonably be accomplished through the functions of the state by adopting behavior calculated to be a "lesser evil." The result is that "responsible" Christians are not only free to reject Christ's instructions about turning the other cheek but obliged to do so when violent resistance to injustice would better contribute to the maintenance of the social order. The loss to the church's evangelistic witness is enormous. What is secured in terms of a wider public acceptance of Christians by virtue of their social responsibility and civic duty is lost in terms of a faithful testimony to Jesus' life and work, death and resurrection, present reign and future coming.

Constantinian Church and Constantinian World

At their foundation, the ethical, soteriological, and eschatological distortions of evangelism come as consequences of its being narrated by a Constantinian account of history and of the loss of a proper distinction

10. This does not mean "in-group pride, nor does it mean quietism, nor does it mean clerical theocracy. . . . I am speaking neither of clericalism, whereby the institutional church claims a privileged handle on the social decision process, nor of quietism, whereby the fellowship patterns of the believing community are interested only in their own integrity or intensity." By contrast, Yoder is arguing for "the priority of the believing community" viewed "not as lordship but as servanthood, not as privilege but as pointer, not as achievement but as promise" (Yoder 1998:118).

between church and world, with a resulting loss of distinctive witness by the church in the world.

> Before Constantine, one knew as a fact of everyday experience that there was a believing Christian community but one had to "take it on faith" that God was governing history. After Constantine, one had to believe without seeing that there was a community of believers, within the larger nominally Christian mass, but one knew for a fact that God was in control of history. Ethics had to change because one must aim one's behavior at strengthening the regime, and because the ruler himself must have very soon some approbation and perhaps some guidance as he does things the earlier church would have disapproved of. The conception of a distinctive life-style befitting Christian confession had to be sweepingly redefined. It could no longer be identified with baptism and church membership, since many who are "Christian" in that sense have not themselves chosen to follow Christ. Its definition will tend to be transmuted in the definition of inwardness. Its outward expression will tend to be assigned to a minority of special "religious" people. "Mission" in the sense of calling one's hearers to faith in Jesus Christ as Lord must also be redefined. Beyond the limits of empire it had become identical with the expansion of Rome's sway. Within Christendom, since outward allegiance to Christ is universal, compulsory, the concern of the preacher will be "renewal," i.e., with adding inner authenticity to an outward profession which is already there, because obligatory. (Yoder 1984:137)

The Constantinian story is ultimately the story of the church's having arrived at a *chaplaincy* role within the empire. The church is welcomed or tolerated to the extent that it can improve social and economic stability, but having become fused with the world in this way, it is unable to exercise anything like an "evangelical nonconformity" in the world (Yoder 1998:217). The *telos* of the church now becomes its "usefulness" to the empire (or nation) and its "way of life." Now, instead of being able to be and to speak truth to power, the church becomes "a part of the power structure itself" (Yoder 1984:138). Rather than the teachings of Jesus providing the primary content of the church's witness and obedience, these are subordinated to more fundamental questions of efficacy and service to the wider social order.

But just to the extent that the church is "usefully" co-opted in its role as chaplain to the state, the market, the military, and other cultural institutions, it ceases to be able to bear faithful witness. As Michael Budde and Robert Brimlow write, the problem is that

> chaplains must themselves submit to the formative processes (physical, emotional, affective, and spiritual) of the institutions. Hence business chaplains must have corporate training or education, and must internal-

ize a capitalist worldview; military chaplains must experience military
formation ("basic training" and more advanced processes) and adopt the
worldview of peace through strength, service through death-dealing, and
national self-preservation as the ultimate goal. (2002:11)

The posture of chaplaincy puts a lid on the subversive nature of evangelism since the chaplain's attitude "by definition must therefore be 'positive' toward the rulers of the particular unit of society he serves, toward
its aims and toward its preservation" (Yoder 1997:119). The church of
Jesus Christ, on the contrary, seeks to form its members into a social
imagination embodied in a set of practices that may or may not be perceived as "civil," that may or may not be construed as "useful," that may
or may not serve the "good of society" as that is commonly understood
outside the church.

  Yoder distinguishes between two predominant forms of chaplaincy.
In its *puritan* form, the power of the chaplain, bestowed or confirmed by
the prince, is used "to impose upon all of society that vision of morality
prescribed by religion. . . . Those who do keep the rules are proud of it
because they can; those who do not wish to keep them or cannot because
of the way they are defined, are crushed or driven away" (1998:173). The
chaplain operating within a *priestly* form, by contrast, "renounces the
effort to use his or her position of power as a level to change society"
and instead calls down "sacramentally the blessing of God upon society,
sanctioning whatever means society (or rather the prince) needs to keep
society (or rather the prince's place in it) afloat. Then the moral standards that he or she preaches will be those that are feasible for everyone"
(ibid.). If, however, the church is not called to be chaplain either in its
puritan or priestly form, but rather a prophetic conscience and witness
in the world, then the usefulness of Christian action to the world is not
its feasibility relative to what can rationally be considered "possible" but
its obedience to Christ and its exemplification of a way of life "that is
impossible except by the miracles of the Holy Spirit" (ibid. 174).

  Within both of the models of chaplaincy made possible by a Constantinian social imagination, the church is now but one aspect of the larger
society, and so Christian behavior becomes the question of what sort of
behavior can be asked of everyone. At its heart, therefore, Constantinianism is the substitution of the general for the specific, the universal
for the particular. It represents the substitution of the embarrassingly
particular God of Jesus and of the Jews with a more transcendent and
"Godlike" God who better suits the logic of empire and who is better able
to underwrite the maintenance of the status quo. Even Jesus as God's
logos, utterance, or story now becomes reified into a universal metaphysical principle under the conditions of Christendom. The burning ethical

question that now justifies Christian nonobedience is "What would happen if everyone did it? If everyone gave their wealth away, what would we do for capital? If everyone loved their enemies, who would ward off the Communists?" Yoder's eloquent response is as follows: "More fitting than 'What if everybody did it' would be its inverse, 'What if nobody else acted like a Christian, but we did?'" (1984:139).

One of the persistent features of Constantinianism, following upon this "new universality" (which is a false catholicity) is that, by diminishing the distinction between church and world, the church refuses to allow the world to disbelieve. One way of accomplishing this refusal, of course, is the crusade, the conquest, or the imperial edict. A second way is the perpetuation of a cultural Christianity into which one is born, baptized, and thereby a member for life. In neither case is it necessary to evangelize—or, rather, evangelism is reduced to whatever mechanism will effectively transfer persons into the "in-group." In all its forms, Constantinianism refuses to allow that there could be any genuine obstacle to belief; and, again, what is lost thereby is the possibility of witness. Evangelism then has as its *telos* acceptance. Evangelistic practices are constructed and performed in such a way as to secure that acceptance. Against this Constantinianization of evangelism, however, Yoder argues for the freedom of the world to be the world as the necessary precondition, first, for hearing the good news and, second, for being able to repent and convert to it. The task of a post-Constantinian church, accordingly, is to disengage from a preoccupation with "results" and to seek to rediscover incarnation rather than effectiveness as the only adequate criterion for measuring Christian obedience (1997:108–11).

Of course, the church that offers the gospel to the world always *hopes for* an acceptance of the invitation. But there is a sense in which while evangelization in a post-Constantinian world hopes for such an acceptance, it cannot really "seek" it. What it does seek is to offer the invitation faithfully and in such a way that it can be understood clearly as good news and then either accepted or rejected responsibly. In our time, the church often feels that if it has not won, not convinced others, not secured Christianity's status and position in society, it must have failed. The impulse to win or succeed is overwhelming. Christians will sometimes stop at nothing—including sacrificing the integrity of their own witness—in the service of winning, in the service of respectability, in the service of having our truth be recognized by everybody as "the" truth. Then, says Yoder, we fail to respect "the integrity of disbelief."

But rejection can never be construed as failure on the part of Christian evangelism in a post-Constantinian context. In our world and given our times, it may be considered a success. In fact, with adequate clarification, one could well define evangelism in a post-Constantinian context as the practice of offering the gospel in such a way that it can be rejected responsibly. As Yoder puts it, "The challenge to the faith community should not be to dilute or filter or translate its witness, so that the 'public' community can handle it without believing, but so to purify and clarify and exemplify it that the world can perceive it to be good news without having to learn a foreign language" (1997:24).

At the end of the day, the only cure for a Constantinian church is the church's visible obedience and faithful witness, on the one hand, and a respect for the integrity of the world's disbelief, on the other hand:

> The most important error of the Christendom vision is not first of all its acceptance of an ethic of power, violence, and the crusade; not first of all its transference of eschatology into the present providence with God working through Constantine and all his successors in civil government, not its appropriation of pagan religiosity that will lead to sacerdotalism and sacramentalism, not its modeling church hierarchy after Roman administration, nor any other specific vice derived from what changed about the nature of the church with the epoch of Constantine. Those were all mistakes, but they were derived from the misdefinition of the place of the people of God in the world. The fundamental wrongness of the vision of Christendom is its illegitimate takeover of the world; its ascription of a Christian loyalty or duty to those who have made no confession, and thereby, its denying to the non-confessing creation the freedom of unbelief that the nonresistance of God in creation gave to a rebellious humanity. (Yoder 1998:109)

This respect for the world's disbelief does not mean that the church will leave the world alone or that it must hedge on its good news or shrink from the truth of the story it has been given. On the contrary, the church seeks faithfully to proclaim and embody that story in the world and for the world with the conviction that God has deemed the ultimate meaning of history to be borne not by the state or society, or by the emperor, but by the people of God. This is, of course, not a truth that can be confirmed by empirical observation, though it is scriptural, from Genesis to Revelation. On the contrary, the ends embodied in the church's witness frequently remain hidden within history so that, more often than not, we are reduced to the blessed poverty of hope. Yet this "hope does not disappoint us, because the love of God has been poured into our hearts through the Holy Spirit that has been given to us" (Rom. 5:5).

6

The Story of Modernity

The Constantinian story is the story of the pilgrim people of God forgetting its journey, including both its point of departure and its destination, and yielding instead to the temptation of making itself at home in the world. The reign of God is now equated with a particular human social construction called Christendom, and evangelism is now narrated as the expansion of Christendom outside the empire and the enforcement of a "Christianized" social order within the empire. The church thereby secures its public acceptance as chaplain of the empire but forfeits its subversive particularity and its capacity for obedient witness, radical discipleship, and prophetic critique. When church and world are effectively fused, the world is denied the gospel's invitation. But it is also denied the freedom of disbelief, whether through the violent imposition of Christendom upon it or the transformation of the empire or nation into a pseudo-church.

The story of modernity to which we now turn our attention stands in something of a contrast to the above insofar as it is motivated, though not unambiguously, by anti-Constantinian and anti-Christendom impulses. The story of modernity is the story of a world that believes itself to have "come of age," a world in which the chaplaincy function of the church is increasingly no longer necessary—or, rather, that function will now be relegated largely to the sphere of the private. In modernity, the world creates for itself an autonomous realm of the temporal, the "secular," as it pursues its own ends and asserts its freedom from the church's direct interference and involvement. The church no longer can expect the support and assistance of the state or of the surrounding culture in its task of making Christians, though the institutions of modernity will still expect the church's support or, at the very least, its submission. Evangelism will now be renarrated in terms of this modern story and its various subplots, two of which are the "self" and the "social," but the end result will still be an accommodation of the church and its story to modern structures of experience and plausibility such that difference—and therefore witness, and therefore conversion—becomes increasingly impossible. If the good news cannot be believed or is not viewed as valuable, it will be adjusted to what individuals do find believable and valuable.

The Modern "Self"

Of the many interesting genealogies of modernity, Alasdair MacIntyre's *After Virtue* provides one of the more compelling analyses of our characteristically modern way of thinking about the self and society—a way of thinking that has profoundly formed (and at points deformed) the way we understand the gospel, imagine the church, and practice evangelism. I introduced MacIntyre's work in chapter 1 when examining the nature of practices; we will now take a closer look at his narration of the story of modernity and the moral fragmentation that has resulted not only from the creation of the secular over against the religious but from the removal of the language of morality from any social context that would make such language intelligible.

MacIntyre begins by asking why it is that contemporary moral debates (about abortion, war, or homosexuality, for example) are characterized by their interminability and by their shrill tone. There never seems to be a resolution in such debates, the various positions within the debates appear to be incommensurable, and this leads to the widely held position in our culture that "all evaluative judgments and more specifically all moral judgments are *nothing but* expressions of preference, expressions of attitude or feeling" (1984:11–12)—a view MacIntyre calls "emotivism." Emotivists hold that there can be no rational or other grounds for making judgments among rival moral positions, so that all moral debate is essentially an exercise in rhetorical persuasion.[1] So pervasive is this position that "to a large degree people now think, talk and act *as if* emotivism were true, no matter what their avowed theoretical standpoint may be. Emotivism has become embodied in our culture" (ibid. 22).

1. MacIntyre rightly notes the circularity of such a claim, which is presented as itself a factual judgment and not merely an expression of preference.

MacIntyre's project in *After Virtue* is to undercut emotivism by demonstrating its historical genesis in the failure of "the Enlightenment project" of the eighteenth century, showing how prior to the Enlightenment things were quite otherwise, and arguing that they may yet be otherwise today. Two of the unique creations of the Enlightenment were "the individual" and "society." Of course there have always been individual persons and various forms of social order, but with the Enlightenment something new is created in each case (and with the two taken together) with significant implications for what it means to be moral and, as I shall attempt to argue, for what it means to be the church and to practice evangelism.

The modern notion of the self invented by the Enlightenment is essentially autonomous, abstract, empty of any "necessary social content," detached from its social context, and "entirely set over against the social world" (MacIntyre 1984:32). It is created by deliberately shedding the constraints of social bonds and the accompanying ordering of human life to a particular end or purpose (*telos*), which is now understood to be a merely superstitious and oppressive relic. The "state of nature" of all persons, says John Locke, is "a *state of perfect freedom* to order their actions, and dispose of their possessions and persons as they think fit, within the bounds of the law of nature, without asking leave, or depending upon the will of any other man" (1982:§4). This "state of nature" is also the source of Enlightenment equality and democracy. If human life is to be ordered toward an end, it will have to be an end that each individual creates or decides for himself or herself. Immanuel Kant's announcement is frequently quoted in this regard:

> Enlightenment is [one's] release from [a] self-incurred tutelage. Tutelage is [one's] inability to make use of [one's] own understanding without direction from another. Self-incurred is this tutelage when its cause lies not in lack of reason but in lack of resolution and courage to use it without direction from another. *Sapere aude!* [Dare to think!] "Have courage to use your own reason!"—that is the motto of enlightenment. (1993:263)

The emotivist self of the Enlightenment is expressed primarily in the acts of choosing and deciding "for one's own self." Accordingly, "everything may be criticized from whatever standpoint the self has adopted, including the self's choice of standpoint to adopt" (MacIntyre 1984:31), and in this "abstract and ghostly character" the Enlightenment project thinks to have discovered freedom. For this reason the name *liberal*, or *liberalism*, is frequently given to that project, so that "liberalism," in the sense that it is here being used, has very little to do with present debates in church and society between so-called liberals and conservatives, those two positions being in their own particular ways equally the product of Enlightenment liberalism. Far from a gain (or a genuine *liberation*), MacIntyre takes the invention of the modern self as a tragic loss:

> For one way of re-envisaging the emotivist self is as having suffered a deprivation, a stripping away of qualities that were once believed to belong to the self. The self is now thought of as lacking any necessary social identity, because the kind of social identity that it once enjoyed is no longer available: the self is now thought of as criterionless, because the kind of *telos* in terms of which it once judged and acted is no longer thought to be credible. (1984:33)

With the self's shedding the traditional boundaries that once provided social continuity and identity and by no longer accepting itself as ordered toward a given *telos*, the social world inhabited by the modern self is now bifurcated into a realm of the "organizational" in which ends are merely given and human life is handed over to the control and rationality of bureaucrats (both managerial and therapeutic) and a realm of the "personal," the realm of individual values without rational or other grounding, judged solely as a matter of personal preference. This is what is frequently referred to as the dichotomy of "fact" and "value" in Enlightenment thinking, a dichotomy that lurks behind other dichotomies such as that of science and faith. One can also begin to detect here the uniquely modern distinction between what is properly "public" (and thus universal and available for rational scrutiny) and what is properly "private" (and thus particular and irrational, arational, or suprarational). MacIntyre notes that in modern societies, this bifurcation also shows up in political debates between individualism and collectivism; but what both sides agree upon is that there are only these two options open to us, "one in which the free and arbitrary choices of individuals are sovereign and one in which the bureaucracy is sovereign, precisely so that it may limit the free and arbitrary choices of individuals." In the end, however, "bureaucracy and individualism are partners as well as antagonists," and so the emotivist self finds itself at home in a social climate we could call "bureaucratic individualism" (MacIntyre 1984:35).

One can readily see how this bifurcation will shape the Christian social imagination and inevitably affect our conception and practice of evangelism. For one thing, if Christian faith is to be practiced as a form of "public" witness, it will now have to be validated by "public" (and therefore what are alleged to be universal) criteria of rationality or usefulness. Otherwise, such witness can only be an intrusion of what is essentially "private" where it has no business. As the church in modernity is increasingly shaped by this bifurcated social imagination, it becomes, on the one hand, a bureaucratic institution directed by expert managers or therapists called "pastors"[2] and, on the other hand, a mere aggregate of individuals each of whom determines the character and *telos* of his or her own personal and essentially private relationship with God. Evangelism likewise becomes either a matter of rational technique, planning, and strategy aimed at promoting and defending the rationality, effectiveness, or usefulness of the gospel or a function of one's winsome personality and skills in rhetorical persuasion. It is, of course, always possible, as MacIntyre points out, to find the organizational and the personal partnered together, even if somewhat antagonistically, and certainly modern churches would be no exception. But in both cases, the means and end of the Christian life are severed from one another, and so also is the self from that Spirit-created social body from which Christians derive what it properly means to be a self in the first place—namely, the church.

It is unnecessary for our purposes to narrate in great detail MacIntyre's entire account of how the Enlightenment project was undertaken and failed. Enlightenment thinkers clearly believed that there were universal, objective moral imperatives, and they aspired to provide the sort of justification for moral judgments that any rational person (in other words, a person abstracted from her or his particular religion, tradition, culture, or society) would accept without having to appeal to authority or tradition.[3] It thus becomes a trademark of the Enlightenment distinction between the universal and the particular that to choose the latter is to forgo any claim on the former (again, with serious consequences for evangelism—one can only "go public" with the gospel by distancing oneself from the particularity of revelation in Israel, Christ, and the church). There is an irony here, in that the morally fragmented world of modernity yields a project that wants to provide a secure and universal foundation for morality "unfettered by the contingencies of our histories and communities" while at the same time stressing "freedom, autonomy, and choice as the essence of the moral life" (Hauerwas 1983:7).

The story of this failed project, according to MacIntyre, runs through Denis Diderot (1713–84) and David Hume (1711–76), who attempted to locate the basis of the ethical in the human passions or desires, to Immanuel Kant (1724–1804), who argued that the basis of the ethical

2. Management skills and therapeutic skills are, as MacIntyre notes, two ways of attaining given ends by similarly rational means. "The manager treats ends as given, as outside his scope; his concern is with technique, with effectiveness in transforming raw materials into final products, unskilled labor into skilled labor, investments into profits. The therapist also treats ends as given, as outside his scope; his concern also is with technique, with effectiveness in transforming neurotic symptoms into directed energy, maladjusted individuals into well-adjusted ones" (1984:30).

3. Cf. MacIntyre 1988:6–7 for a further development of the story of this aspiration.

is to be found in reason, to Søren Kierkegaard (1813–55), who claimed that the basis of the ethical is to be found in a choice or "leap" that lies beyond reason. In each case, the common project was to construct some argument from public and unassailable premises about human nature to conclusions about the content of the moral life. But while these thinkers share a more or less common conception of the content of morality (which is, quite interestingly, little different from the content they inherited) and a more or less common conception of human nature (despite the fact that they argue from different features of that human nature), they were unsuccessful in moving from their premises to their conclusion. In fact, the very existence of their numerous and rival positions, each a victory over the others, turns out to be—by the very criteria of Enlightenment universalism—the failure of them all.

According to MacIntyre, with the Aristotelian notion of an essential human nature and a corresponding *telos* that could answer the question of what human life is for, one had grounds for moving from what a person is to what a person ought to be. When human nature is understood to have a *telos*, value is implied in nature and *is* entails an *ought* (MacIntyre 1984:54–59).[4] In other words, for Aristotle, if we know what something *is*, we know what it is *for*. As Brad Kallenberg puts it, "In this way moral precepts weren't snatched out of thin air but got their 'punch' or their 'oughtness' from the concrete notion of what human life was for" (1997:11). Moreover, this *telos* is socially embedded. What is good for a person arises out of the character of one's community (or *polis*, for Aristotle), and though it is not thereby invariable or eternal, it is also not left to each individual.

Having refused both religion as providing a public, shared justification for morality and the Aristotelian notion of a *telos*, however, Enlightenment thinkers deprived themselves of any justification for moving from human nature as we find it to human nature as it ought to be. All that is left behind is an inherited (but now baseless) content for morality along with human nature as we find it. But one can hardly argue from human nature as we find it (without a *telos*) to that moral content. On the contrary, "the injunctions of morality, thus understood, are likely to be ones that human nature, thus understood, has strong tendencies to disobey" (MacIntyre 1984:55). The project of Enlightenment moral philosophers was doomed to failure.

As MacIntyre tells it, the story of the Enlightenment project is the story of what happens when human nature is deprived of its *telos* so that

4. The same could be said of the Jewish or Christian understanding of the human also, of course, and without Aristotelian language. Surely the doctrine of human creation in the *Imago Dei* points in this direction.

moral value judgments lose their factual character and can be taken as *"nothing but* expressions of preference."* Emotivism as a theory is now free to hold sway. With no conception of what a human is or of the good toward which a human life is to aim, we can likewise discard the communal cultivation of virtues, or "excellences of character," that would enable us to move toward the good. We may still find ourselves using the moral vocabulary of the past and even appealing to vaguely defined, ill-defined, or undefined notions such as "rights" (claimed especially within the sphere of individualism) and "utility" (claimed especially within the sphere of bureaucratic organization), but moral debate can be little more than the "indignant self-righteousness of protest"[5] and, inevitably, as Friedrich Nietzsche rightly understood, a mask for the arbitrary "will to power."[6] Morality becomes little more than an arena for the competition of wills, and it is simply the powerful, the clever, or those skilled at manipulation who win the day.

Building on and illustrating the strengths of the Aristotelian tradition (while arguing that that tradition should never have been rejected to begin with), MacIntyre challenges the emotivist conclusion of modernity and the Nietzschean position that preys upon it. This he does, as we have already seen, by arguing for the *virtues, practices, narratives,* and *tradition*-bearing communities (in other words, the social and historical realities rejected by the Enlightenment) that render intelligible our moral judgments by embodying an answer to the questions of what human life is for and what sort of persons we should be.

5. MacIntyre's analysis of how modern moral debate is unable to rise above mere "indignation" and "protest" is perceptive and worth being reminded of. Whereas "protest" was once "to bear witness *to* something and only as a consequence of that allegiance to bear witness *against* something else," it is now almost entirely that negative phenomenon that characteristically occurs as a reaction to the alleged invasion of someone's *rights* in the name of someone else's *utility.* The self-assertive shrillness of protest arises because the facts of incommensurability ensure that protestors can never win an *argument;* the indignant self-righteousness of protest arises because the facts of incommensurability ensure equally that the protestors can never lose an argument either. Hence the *utterance* of protest is characteristically addressed to those who already *share* the protestors' premises. The effects of incommensurability ensure that protestors rarely have anyone else to talk to but themselves (1984:71).

This does not mean that protest is not still very much a part of the Christian witness, but Christian protest is first of all rooted in witness to God's reign in Christ, which we perceive in and through the practices of the church that shape us into the kind of people who are capable of seeing differently and thus called to protest.

6. As MacIntyre says, "For it was Nietzsche's historic achievement to understand more clearly than any other philosopher—certainly more clearly than his counterparts in Anglo-Saxon emotivism and continental existentialism—not only that what purported to be appeals to objectivity were in fact expressions of subjective will, but also the nature of the problems that this posed for moral philosophy" (MacIntyre 1984:113).

Within the modern bifurcation of the self between the "organizational" and the "personal"—the realm of control and rationality in effectively achieving arbitrary goods and the realm of private individual values born out of nothing more than personal preference—faith is construed as belonging strictly to the latter, and so it is privatized, tucked away safely from any corporate or bodily discipline and formation except that for which the private self might "decide" (the will also goes through a reinvention in modernity). Selves may certainly "contract" together in private (the church) or in public (society)—and it is in this sense that the "private," the "public," and "society" are modern inventions. But neither the church nor the society of liberal modernity has any essential *telos*, having become merely the sites upon which private values compete and contract for "the greater good." The problem, of course, is that "the greater good" does not really exist but must always be invented, and it amounts primarily to safeguarding individual selves who are pursing their private ends from the undue influence or obstruction of other selves who are likewise pursuing their private ends. As Hauerwas says,

> Our society seems generally to think that to be moral, to act in a respon-
> sible way, is to pursue our desires fairly—that is, in a manner that does
> not impinge on anyone else's freedom. We assume we can do as we want
> so long as we do not harm or limit anyone else's choices. A good society is
> one that provides the greatest amount of freedom for the greatest number
> of people. Although such an ethic appears to be highly committed to the
> common good, in fact its supporting theory is individualistic, since the
> good turns out to be the sum of our individual desires. (1983:9)

Salvation in such a world is transformed into an essentially private, one-by-one affair, while evangelism becomes a practice based almost entirely on individual personality and persuasion, an attempt to lead individuals into a private decision to "have a personal relationship with Jesus" or to join the church, much as one might join any other club or as-sociation. The modern Western model of church and salvation, especially in its Protestant forms (which are considerably more "modernized" than Catholic or Orthodox forms), is largely predicated upon this narrative of the self. The church's evangelistic ministry becomes an expression of what MacIntyre refers to as "bureaucratic individualism"and entails the combination of rational technique and strategy, the creation of multiple programs to meet the needs of parishioners who will increasingly come to be viewed as customers or consumers, the tailoring of the gospel mes-sage to resonate with people's personal experience, and the alteration of the meaning and purpose of worship to what is existentially satisfying to the modern subject, all in the service of accomplishing the distinctively modern model of salvation. The authority of Christian leaders (and this will be especially true for their practice of evangelism) is now cast almost entirely in terms of effectiveness and is "nothing other than successful power" (MacIntyre 1984:26).

Because the bifurcation of the social world inhabited by the modern self affects the practice of evangelism (as with all practice) by reducing it to managerial or therapeutic technique, the ultimate and overriding question asked of evangelism is, will it work? As means of evangelistic practice are increasingly severed (or at least externalized) from the end to which they are properly related, both the content of salvation and the technique used to accomplish conversion can be adjusted in virtually limitless directions as long as the individual's "freedom" is not violated. The practical wisdom that would guide practice—what Aristotle called *phronesis*—is absent or neglected, as is the notion that faith is the cultivation of character through apprenticeship in a community of virtue, the communion of saints. For one thing, the modern liberal self could not abide the thought that such a "public" community might have something to say about what is done with its "private" life. If under Christendom the apostolic model of *ecclesia* is distorted or deformed by the visible and material fusion of the church with world, no less distorting and deforming is the Enlightenment reaction against Christendom, which seeks to eliminate anything visible, public, material, or corporate about the church altogether.

This shift from the public and corporate (albeit in a Christendom mode) to the private and individual parallels the shift in modern Western Christianity to a largely voluntaristic soteriology in which the possibility of salvation becomes a reality only by virtue of the decision and will of the individual self as agent. While such a shift has some roots in the Protestant Reformation, it is certainly not to be identified with it. In fact, in several crucial respects the Reformers stand opposed to it, especially as regards the priority of grace and the bondage of the will. Even more so is this Enlightenment shift to be contrasted with the notion of the will in someone like Augustine, for whom our will is not strictly speaking "ours," at least not in the abstract sense given to that word by Enlightenment thinkers such as René Descartes, for whom the will is wholly indeterminate, self-positing, and in command of its own choices. While for Augustine we are not mere puppets, our will is always defined relative to the objects that determine it—"by the company [it] keeps and the objects of [its] worship" (Hanby 1999:115). Thus our original condition is not indeterminacy but an intrinsic relationship to grace in which the will is free just so far as it is "intentionally directed toward its true *telos*: a *telos* which constantly re arrives as the gift of grace" (Milbank, Pickstock, and Ward 1999:9).[7]

---

7. I am indebted at this point and in what follows to Hanby 1999.

For Augustine, our will is not simply determined by God, but rather, existing in the form of the first Adam, we love the creation rather than the Creator, and thus our will is in bondage. To ask whether in the process of salvation God is active and we are passive would be to put the question wrongly (or at least it would be unintelligible to Augustine). The (to us) perplexing question of how our acts can be our own if our will is determined teleologically mistakenly presupposes an Enlightenment subject that is self-positing, self-possessed, and self-sufficient as its own end rather than a "doxological subject" that is created in "ecstatic openness" and "always receiving *itself* as a gift" (Hanby 1999:116). Moreover, when God is viewed as analogous to this Enlightenment subject, it is only possible to see God as a rival subject who stands over against us.[8] From the perspective of Augustine, we are perhaps able to see that one of the fundamental problems with modern notions of the self and of the will is that they have been constructed apart from any intrinsic relation to grace. Grace appears (if at all) as something exterior and extrinsic—an act of violence, an intrusion.

Under such conditions, the church's mediation must be seen as equally violent and intrusive. One of the greatest postmodern challenges for evangelism, therefore, is to imagine a church in which the truth about our own constitution as humans (and indeed the truth about the cosmos) is embodied and re-presented in the liturgical, political, and economic practices of the church that provide the mediations through which our essentially "doxological selves" are invited and enabled to participate in the incarnate love of God in Christ, which precedes us and through which our wills are both made free and yet rightly directed toward God. Perhaps then the church as the body of Christ will no longer be merely an afterthought to or implication of what is held to be prior and more fundamental—the private individual's relationship to God. Rather, the church can be understood as the christologically necessary habitation for communion with God and a school of formation in which our desire for God increasingly comes to shape our actions, behaviors, and relationships.

The Social

If modernity creates a new understanding of the "self" or the "individual"—with all the repercussions this will have for how we construe

8. This is paradoxical, says Hanby, "only if one has made a metaphysical decision in advance which fixes in opposition the ratio between our finitude and God's infinity and conceives the latter in terms of a perverted version of the former, as a subject over against its objects" (1999:118).

grace, the will, salvation, and conversion—it also creates a new understanding of sociality as cut off from any shared *telos* or substantive common good. Instead sociality is reconceived in keeping with this newly invented self along with its autonomy, freedom, and "rights." We should not therefore be tempted by "subtraction" accounts of modernity, as Charles Taylor argues, which only see communal ties and traditions as having been discarded or dissolved in favor of something called "individualism." Society is now to be construed as a contract between individuals whose freedom (or "right") to pursue their own private ends and maximize their own self-interest is restricted only by the freedom (or "right") of other individuals to do the same. The modern notion of the social, therefore, comes into existence hand in hand with the modern discourse of individual "rights."

The stripping away of the religious and the teleological that creates this new "secular" mode of sociality will come to be interpreted by the social sciences as "the removal of the superfluous and additional to leave a residue of the human, the natural and the self-sufficient" (Milbank 1990:9). One may argue, however (and this is the impressive achievement of John Milbank in his *Theology and Social Theory*), that the secular was not simply "uncovered" but rather "had to be invented" as a "sphere of autonomous, sheerly formal power" (ibid. 9). In fact, argues Milbank, the invention of the secular was, from the very beginning, a theological construction, just as the anthropology that undergirds it was theologically promoted.

While Milbank's argument has far richer complexities than I will attempt to summarize here, the theological construction of the "social" to which he refers begins, at least in part, with the creation of an inextricable link between the individual and private ownership of property as a divine endowment, a reflection of the *imago Dei* (ibid. 9–26). Though this connection to the divine will eventually come to be discarded, what will remain is the distinctively modern link between personhood, ownership, and property. Daniel Bell, in his *Liberation Theology after the End of History*, describes this modern shift in the narration of society as follows:

> The medieval vision that Aquinas articulated and the Cistercians embodied had construed rights in terms of the divine ordering of the human community as that order was spelled out in a series of divine, natural, and human laws. As such, right was fundamentally a matter of consent to or participation in the divine order and the individual was understood as possessed by Christ and a recipient of all the good that one is, has, and does. In the newer tradition, God's right established discrete rights possessed originally by individuals—by virtue of their creation in the image of God and endowment with a certain dignity—and then derivatively by communities. According to this conception, the individual occupies the

central position as right is associated with a human power to control and dispose of temporal things. Individuals, in other words, became essentially proprietors. (2001:105)

It is only as bearers of these inalienable property "rights" that persons (and that, of course, means "men") come to recognize one another in public, thereby giving rise to new forms of political, social, and economic order that will preserve these intrinsic and unrestricted property rights in relation to other persons or to secular society itself. Though society is now understood to stand over against the individual, it is still very much in and through society that one's freedom is exercised and one's desires and wishes are fulfilled. Society, however, can offer us no help in discerning what to do with our rights or even which rights are worth having. Constructed on the individualist model of freedom, rights, and private property, both the political order and the economic order must be kept free from any imputation of a common good or *telos* that could be anything more than the relatively thin good of "rationally" coordinating self-interest and protecting individual rights and entitlements.[9]

It is in this context that we also find the rise of the modern nation-state, whose purpose is the amalgamation, coordination, and preservation of individual rights and freedoms guaranteed by nature (Locke 1982:§135). This it does by "liberating" individuals (thereby also "creating" them) from communal ties, traditions, and social groups (such as the church), which are discredited as merely "tribal" or "sectarian," and instead positioning individuals in a direct relationship to it (Cavanaugh 1998:7). Indeed, the more the social order comes to be defined as an aggregate of self-centered individuals, the more authority is transferred to a highly centralized and absolutist state (Hobbes's Leviathan). In this way, nation-states become "fetishes" for which people will torture, kill, and die (ibid. 196).[10]

9. See Bell's discussion at this point, 2001:124–30. That the modern discourse of rights has its origins within the context of the acquisition of wealth and property is frequently lost on those who appeal to rights today in seeking economic justice. But if Bell is right (and much of his interesting book is a criticism of liberation theologians at precisely this point), the discourse of rights has no place to stand against capitalism because "the modern discourse of rights is an element of the capitalist discipline of desire; justice as the guarantor of rights is but one component in the capitalist deformation of desire" (ibid. 126).

10. As MacIntyre says, "The modern nation-state, in whatever guise, is a dangerous and unmanageable institution, presenting itself on the one hand as a bureaucratic supplier of goods and services, which is always about to, but never actually does, give its clients value for money, and on the other as a repository of sacred values, which from time to time invites one to lay down one's life on its behalf. As I have remarked elsewhere . . . it is like being asked to die for the telephone company" (1994:303).

Capitalism as an economic order is likewise fitted perfectly to this purely formal and contractual set of relationships in which the human as proprietor stands at the center. The acquisition and disposition of one's property and person neither serves nor is accountable to a substantive notion of the common good but is instead to be carried out as each individual sees fit, maximizing profit and minimizing risk, so long as other individuals are free to do likewise.

Evangelism and Modernity

Far from posing a challenge to the narrative of the self enshrined in modernity and to the forms of social relationship generated by that narrative, contemporary evangelism allows itself to be reinscribed within it. This occurs in a number of ways, all of which reflect the individualization and privatization of faith already noted. In this section, I will look at two contemporary directions in which evangelism has moved, first, in response to the secularization of late modernity and, second, in response to the religious pluralism of late modernity. The first is what George Hunter calls "apostolic" evangelism and is characteristic of a growing number of conservative evangelical congregations in the United States, while the second is what James Adams calls "progressive" evangelism and is more characteristic of various mainline Protestant congregations. Though each in its own way attempts to move beyond elements of the Enlightenment project and thereby to provide a "postmodern" option for evangelism, both remain liberal in the classically modern sense as narrated in this chapter. Their "postmodernity" is but modernity carried out to its logical conclusion.

The Challenge of Secularization

If the church narrated by modernity adopts, however unconsciously, the individualization and privatization of faith at the heart of the Enlightenment project, that church also comes to accept the now standard but one-sided and negative account of secularization described by Milbank as a process of "de-sacralizing" rather than as the process also of positively "inventing" (and, in its own way, "sacralizing") a new sphere of purely formal, contractual, and therefore purposeless social relationships (embodied especially in the modern institutions of civil society, the nation-state, and the market). To be sure, throughout the first centuries of modernity, when Christendom patterns of enculturation still held sway, one would be more likely to find a pervasive hostility to secularization on the part of most Christians. But over time, as Christendom begins to crumble and as the church increasingly adopts the story of modernity as its own, secularization comes to be perceived primarily as a benign "absence" of explicitly religious knowledge, affiliation, and encultura- tion. Evangelism will now be focused on finding new ways to *reach* secular people, introducing them to the "basics" of Christianity (which, under the conditions of modernity, amounts primarily to handing over information or "principles"), providing them *programs* that meet their needs, and persuading them of the intellectual credibility and practical utility of Christianity so that they will be favorably inclined to decide for the essentially private faith that Christianity has become.

This approach to secularization is especially visible in the evange- listic strategies of the largest and fastest growing evangelical churches in North America today (some of which are called "megachurches" or "seeker-sensitive churches") and in the literature that celebrates their achievements. While each of these churches has its own history, ethos, and set of evangelistic practices, I take as fairly accurate and represen- tative the identification of a consensus view of evangelism among these churches by George Hunter, who has studied these churches extensively and commends their successes in several books.[11]

Hunter argues that the "Great New Fact" facing the entire Western church is the "nearly complete secularization of the West" (1992:26). Most people now have no distinct Christian memory, background, or vocabu- lary, and so we find ourselves in a context where the pressing question is how to engage the West with the gospel all over again. For Hunter, secularization (in keeping with the standard account earlier mentioned) is "the withdrawal of whole areas of life, thought, and activity from the control or influence of the Church,"[12] such that the church no longer enjoys a "home court advantage" and we once again live in "a vast mis- sion field" (ibid. 25–26, 41, 37).[13] One of the common denominators of

11. See especially *How to Reach Secular People* (1992); *Church for the Unchurched* (1996); and *Radical Outreach* (2003). Hunter's nine paradigmatic churches (each of which has an average attendance of more than eight hundred) are Frazer Memorial United Methodist Church (Montgomery, Alabama), New Hope Community Church (Portland, Oregon), Wil- low Creek Community Church (suburbs of Chicago, Illinois), Community Church of Joy (Phoenix, Arizona), Saddleback Valley Community Church (Orange County, California), The Church on Brady (East Los Angeles), New Song Church (West Covina, California), Ginghamsburg United Methodist Church (Ginghamsburg, Ohio), and Vineyard Community Church (Cincinnati, Ohio).

12. While Hunter's work is oriented toward the loss of Christian influence in the West, his definition is similar to that of sociologist Peter Berger, who defines secularization more broadly as "the process by which sectors of society and culture are removed from the domination of religious institutions and symbols" (1969:107).

13. "The West was lost," says Hunter at one point, "when the 'Christendom' arrangement disintegrated" (1992:25). One could certainly argue against Hunter that the West was "lost" to Christianity not when the Christendom arrangement ended but when it began. Indeed,

the churches Hunter studies is their agreement with this diagnosis and their corresponding conviction that if the church is going to succeed in reaching "secular people," it will need to do a better job of understanding them and relating to them in new ways—ways that aren't as churchy, alienating, boring, and judgmental as the church has been in the past. Since persons are no longer as religious as they once were, we must engage them on their own turf. The problem with Christendom, from the standpoint of this consensus, is that it "spoiled" the church by teaching it the bad habit of setting the conditions under which people would become Christians. What is needed instead is a less "ecclesiocentric" and more "culturally relevant" evangelism.

Rather than despair over secularization, Hunter and the churches he is drawn to as successful celebrate the collapse of Christendom and see in it great similarities to the situation of the first apostles. Instead of viewing our new situation as "post-Christian," as some have called it, they prefer to see our culture optimistically as "pre-Christian." For this reason Hunter calls our context a new "apostolic era" in which what are most desperately needed are "apostolic churches" and "apostolic Christians" (1992:107–71).[14] "Apostolic Christianity," claims Hunter, is better able to relate to unchurched, secular people who know little or nothing about Christianity and who feel alienated from traditional congregations, which are perceived as boring, money-hungry, irrelevant, and judgmental. It finds ways of attracting secular people to the church by reducing (if not eliminating entirely) "churchy" music, architecture, and jargon and by focusing instead on relating the gospel to the "felt needs" of its target audience—for example, issues of self-esteem[15] or personal fulfillment[16]—in the context of a comfortable, safe, and friendly atmosphere. To the extent that these churches have been successful in reaching unchurched people, it is in no

---

the ability to interpret the demise of Christendom as a "loss" is possible only on the basis of Constantinian assumptions about the need for Christianity to have the sort of influence that it no longer has—assumptions that yield an identification of effective evangelism with monopolizing cultural influence. Hunter may well agree, however, for he admits that even where churchgoing remains constant in the United States, "much American church attendance is 'Christo-pagan'; that is, American civil religion in christian [sic] clothing" (ibid. 24). He likewise recognizes that secularization is far from an unambiguous reality and that just because "people are not substantially influenced by Christianity . . . does not mean they are 'irreligious'" (ibid. 20).

14. See also C. Peter Wagner, ed., *The New Apostolic Churches* (Ventura, CA: Regal, 1998).

15. See Robert H. Schuller, founder of the Crystal Cathedral. See *Self Esteem: The New Reformation* (Waco, TX. Word, 1982).

16. See Bill Hybels, pastor of the Willow Creek Community Church. See G. A. Pritchard, *Willow Creek Seeker Services: Evaluating a New Way of Doing Church* (Grand Rapids: Baker, 1996), especially 70–73, 138–144.

small measure due to their having removed the sorts of "culture barriers" that, as they see it, prevent people from encountering the gospel.

The most effective strategies for reaching secular people that surface in "apostolic" congregations focus on a heightened sensitivity to the secularity of secular people and on an invitational rather than confrontational posture toward them. It is likewise important to provide numerous "entry points" to the church, such as support groups for people with addictions, a variety of ministries and human services, Bible study groups, user-friendly "seeker services" that engage secular people with the gospel in a nonthreatening environment, and new off-site "daughter" churches. All these are ways of "multiplying units" of the church and offering ministries that scratch where people itch. As Rick Warren, pastor of Saddleback Valley Community Church, says, "The more hooks you use, the more fish you are going to catch" (quoted in Hunter 1992:69).

Because evangelism in these congregations is passionately committed to starting "where people are," its primary strategy focuses on demonstrating the *usefulness* of the gospel for "everyday living," a way of helping persons adjust to the ravages of modernity in their personal, family, and social lives. These churches have learned that if this is not done, secular people just won't be interested in the church. In fact, in visiting these congregations, studying their ministries, and reading their literature, one cannot help but conclude that the predominant strategy for convincing secular people of the truth of Christianity is a demonstration of its ability to *help*—to make us better persons, citizens, family members, or workers.

That is not to say, however, that the older strategy of demonstrating the rational credibility of Christian faith has disappeared in apostolic congregations. Says Mark Mittelberg of Willow Creek Community Church, "Seekers are more skeptical now. They have less knowledge of the Bible and of what it means to be a Christian. So you have to do more ground work, showing them this is not a blind leap of faith, that the Bible is a book with credentials and that it works in our lives. . . . People want to know, Is this a faith built on facts, or are you taking me toward a blind leap of faith? I see the need for apologetics going up, not down" (1998:24–25).

Evangelism in "apostolic" congregations depends, first, on its ability to reach secular people where they are and, second, on its ability to convince secular persons of the truth of the gospel by establishing either its factuality or its utility (or both). But of course both of these bases are foundationalist—that is, both represent an appeal to foundations outside the gospel to establish the meaning and truth of the gospel.

For Hunter, then, our situation is much like that of Christians in the first three centuries, and this means that we, like them, have to achieve four objectives in order to communicate Christianity:

> (1) Facing a population with no knowledge of the gospel, the christian [sic] movement had to *inform* people of the story of Jesus, the good news, its claims, and its offer. (2) Facing hostile populations and the persecution of the state, the Church had to "win friends and *influence* people" to a positive attitude toward the movement. (3) Facing an Empire with several entrenched religions, the Christians had to *convince* people of Christianity's truth, or at least its plausibility. (4) Since entry into faith is by an act of the will, Christians had to *invite* people to adopt this faith and join the messianic community and follow Jesus as Lord. (1992:35)

After Constantine and under the conditions of Christendom, argues Hunter, the church could expect the first three of these tasks to be accomplished through enculturation: "Most people were already informed in the faith's basics, were favorably disposed toward the faith, and already assumed its truth. So the Christian communicator could largely focus on inviting people, who were already informed, convinced, and favorably inclined, to adopt the faith" (ibid. 36). In the situation we are in now, however, we have to "begin farther back with people." Whereas under the conditions of Christendom the fields were "already plowed, seeded, and watered . . . today we must first plow, seed, and water the fields before we can reasonably expect to gather harvests" (ibid.).

From the perspective of the criticisms developed earlier in this and the previous chapter, Hunter's version of the story in which we find ourselves today contains a number of blind spots that generate forms of evangelistic practice likewise blinded to their domestication by the story of modernity. In the first place, if Yoder is right, Christendom did not so much prepare the world to be engaged by the gospel as it prevented the world from being engaged by it. Under the conditions of Constantinianism, the church's distinct witness embodied in its visible difference from the world is lost. At the same time Christianity (or what passes for it) is imposed violently or through cultural accommodation, so that "disbelief" is no longer an option.

In the second place, if MacIntyre and Milbank are right, while evangelism must today "begin farther back," the truth is that it must begin even farther back than Hunter and his exemplars of "apostolic" Christianity are aware. Modernity and the secularization invented by it represent not just the absence of Christian memory and vocabulary (and thus a sort of religious vacuum into which evangelism must step) but a pervasive and powerful (and in its own way "religious") transformation of self and society in directions that are antagonistic if not antithetical to Christian

faith. Viewed only as the rejection (or the "unlearning") of Constantinianism, perhaps the process of secularization may be viewed as not
only neutral to faith but as "continuous with the prophetic movement
in Israel and the gospel itself, crying out against all idolatry," or even
as "the cleansing wind of the Spirit of God" (McClendon 1986:2:446).[17]
But modernity has never been and can never be only this; it can never
produce only a religiously neutral iconoclasm. "Secularism," as Alexander
Schmemann says, "is above all a *negation of worship*" (1997:118).[18] This
is so not only because it removes God as the end of all life but because
it also creates traditionless, purposeless individuals who become their
own end. How we practice evangelism depends greatly on whether we
take the root issue to be a matter of information or idolatry.

To the extent that evangelism has adopted the modern story of the self
as its own, it is blinded to the individualism at the heart of secularity and
in this way proves to be more like a vehicle for extending the modern
story than an alternative to it. Again, Hunter's analysis of our situation
is an illuminating example. Hunter argues that "apostolic" evangelism
is "postmodern" in that it fills the void left by the breakdown of the
Enlightenment worldview. The Enlightenment taught us "that human
beings are basically rational, . . . that people are basically good," that
the universe is "orderly, predictable, machinelike, . . . that people could
base morality on reasoning alone, . . . that we could build and man-
age cities and societies on reason alone, . . . that science and education
would liberate humanity, . . . that all problems are solvable, and therefore
progress is inevitable," and "that all religions are essentially the same"
(1996:21–22). But as this worldview becomes increasingly unsatisfy-
ing and vulnerable, Hunter continues, "more and more people need,
and seek for, a satisfying worldview and spiritual fulfillment" (ibid. 23).
"Apostolic" evangelism is able to provide what is needed and sought by
offering a "culturally relevant" church. What is missing from Hunter's
list of things the Enlightenment taught us, however, is the very heart
and soul of the Enlightenment project: the self as abstract, autonomous,
inalienably "free," essentially purposeless and detached from its social

17. Borrowing from the work of Theodoor van Leeuwen, McClendon can even say that
"secularity, by destroying ontocracies East *and* West, serves as a kind of John the Baptist,
clearing obstacles and making a roadway along which eventually the gospel can travel"
(1986:2:447). McClendon goes on to say, however, that "secularity cannot itself be the
world-uniting force because its content is so largely negative; it can clear the way, but it
cannot constitute the required unity (cf. Matt. 12:43-45)" (ibid. 447). McClendon is here
saying something similar to Hauerwas, who suggests that "in some ways modernity is an
appropriate protest against Christian presumption" (2001b:32).

18. While some may want to distinguish between *secularization* as essentially neutral
and *secularism* as ideologically hostile to religious faith, I can see no grounds for making
such a distinction, given Milbank's convincing argument (1990).

context—indeed, the very notion that inevitably gives rise to each of the other features he lists. Because the church narrated by modernity has itself adopted this conception of the self, it cannot recognize that conception as a teaching of the Enlightenment, nor can it see that the contemporary dissatisfaction with Enlightenment "rationality" in the name of post-Enlightenment "freedom" and "personal experience" is every bit as much a product of modernity as that which it rejects.

One can appreciate the fact that "apostolic" congregations "are willing to be culturally flexible in order to reach people" (Hunter 1992:58). Hunter is undoubtedly right, moreover, that in more cases than not traditional congregations, rightly concerned for the integrity of the gospel, "perpetuate the cultural forms that God blessed in the past, often in a movement's European past, rather than adapting to the forms of today's target population" (ibid. 56). But it is not clear that Hunter and the churches he applauds grasp the full extent to which any attempt to meet "secular people" on their own turf (and here I am talking about far more than whether churches should use robed choirs and pipe organs) will inevitably be determined externally by the situation itself (leading the church to adopt that turf's negation of worship) unless the church's engagement with its context is governed logically by an end internal to the practice of evangelism, an end narrated by the story of the people of God rather than the story of the individual of modernity. That end is, of course, God's peaceable reign.

Unfortunately, the reign of God goes noticeably missing throughout Hunter's book-length descriptions of "what works" in contemporary evangelistic practice. Indeed, there is little or no indication of the nature and form of the salvation toward which evangelism is aimed—nor need there be, given the practical logic by which evangelism has been deformed under the conditions of late modernity. The evangelism of Jesus, as we have seen, is unintelligible apart from the announcement of a new government to which we are called to convert, embodied in such concrete practices as the rejection of violence, justice for the poor, love of enemies, economic sharing, and the relativizing of national and family allegiances. But not one of these reign-of-God characteristics shows up prominently in Hunter's summaries of "apostolic" evangelism, a fact that suggests, first, that the end of evangelism has been altered to fit the context of modernity and, second, that the means by which evangelism is practiced have become external to the practice itself. For if a practice can be described and understood apart from specifying its ends (in other words, if it can be described in solely pragmatic terms), then one must ask whether the ends have been made external to the means, thereby disqualifying the practice as a *practice*. Excellence is then determined by the efficacy of the activity in achieving or producing an assumed end rather than by the character of the practice itself as embodying an end to which it is internally related.

Effective evangelistic practice in the popular consensus documented by Hunter need not concern itself with the upside-down characteristics of God's reign, for those characteristics are only remotely and externally related to it. One gets the sense that the social transformations (indeed reversals) that accompany the reign of God are to be understood only as postconversion "implications" rather than the very politics to which we are invited to convert. They might therefore show up as the focus of a particular small group in the church that happens to be interested in "that social justice stuff," as one "apostolic" pastor put it at an evangelism conference I recently attended. The truth is, however, that they rarely show up at all.

All this is not to say that the reign of God is irrelevant to the felt needs of the secular individual narrated by modernity. But the important question is how it is related. When the need for self-esteem comes to be narrated as the need for prosperity, or the need for community as the need to have my white daughter date only white boys, or the need for peace narrated as the need for my country to win in its wars against other countries, or the need for freedom narrated as the need for convenient shopping options, then the good news of God's reign is certainly relevant, but subversively so. Hunter is undoubtedly correct that evangelistic contextualization is always in some sense an adaptation of the good news to the lives, concerns, and, indeed, "needs" of "secular" persons. But while this contextualization certainly contradicts the cultural inflexibility of what he calls "traditional" congregations, the accommodation of the church to the corporate ethos, marketing orientation, and consumer culture of its surroundings represents a failure to embody the strangeness of God's reign in such a way that it can be taken seriously as a new and alternative, yet habitable, way of life—as salvation. Evangelism may be deemed by some external measures to have "worked," but it will not have been practiced well.

Where "apostolic" evangelism is right, of course, is its insistence that the strangeness of Christianity should not be the strangeness of Bach in a hip-hop culture. But the presumption that one can remove the "culture barrier" between the church and secular people without challenging the intrinsically individualist, consumerist, and ultimately violent presuppositions of secular culture represents a blindness to the subversive, cultural, and corporately embodied dimensions of Christian faith itself.

Perhaps the primary reason that the end of evangelistic practice as narrated by modernity can be altered and externalized from its means is that both means and end have been disconnected from the ecclesial *habitus* that, as Pierre Bourdieu reminds us, "gives practices their relative autonomy with respect to external determinations of the immediate present" (1990:56). Apart from the coherence and continuity across time and from situation to situation that is provided by the church as *habitus*, evangelism cannot help but be subject to external determinations. "Apostolic" evangelism does focus on the church, of course, in the name of countering "ecclesiocentrism" for the sake of "cultural relevancy." But here the church is externalized in relation to salvation. Its worship and indeed its very existence are now converted into an evangelistic "tool" or "resource" that serves the end of reaching individuals along with informing, influencing, convincing, and inviting them to enter the faith through, as Hunter, says, "an act of will" (1992:35).

Operating within the social imagination(s) of modernity, the church is unable to grasp the extent to which modernity has shaped its existence. The church is able to survive and thrive, but largely insofar as it is transformed into an aggregate of "free" individuals who have contracted together for their mutual benefit—"tourists who happen to find ourselves on the same bus," as Hauerwas and Willimon put it (1992:6). Evangelism can now be focused wholly on "effectively" leading the individual into an experience of salvation as a matter of personal freedom by appealing to his or her self-interest, whether that be construed materially in terms of social belonging, assimilation, uplift, prosperity, and security or spiritually in terms of inner peace or the hope of eternal salvation. Rather than the church's serving as a new peoplehood, a sacramental body that is a mode of participation in the life of God, and a community of virtue into which persons are formed, disciplined, and educated, the church is itself disciplined by the formative practices of modernity. In this way, far from being practiced as a form of resistance and subversion, the type of evangelism celebrated today as having achieved "results" comes to complement the (pseudo-salvific) work of both the market and the state in providing individuals economic prosperity, security from outsiders, and "peace" among other competing selves.

The Challenge of Religious Pluralism

Christians have always known that there were other religions in the world whose adherents lived and thought differently from the way they did. But a mere awareness of plurality is not the same as the robust pluralism we are likely to find under the conditions of late modernity—the widespread advocacy of a "live and let live" attitude in matters religious, of plurality as something to be embraced and nourished. Not only are we more likely to encounter a greater variety of cultural, ethnic, and religious diversity, but our attitudes toward diversity have become more open and tolerant, leaving evangelism, when understood as a violation of this embrace and acceptance, in a state of disrepute.

Central, then, to the challenge of practicing evangelism in a postmodern context where any overarching and unifying "metanarrative" is distrusted is the question of how the church is to take account of this pluralism, its accompanying relativism, and its rejection of the modern conviction that truth rests upon a universally available foundation.[19] If, on the one hand, we accept the relativity of the Christian faith among a plurality of religious options, what could possibly serve as the motivation for and aim of inviting other persons to become Christians? If, on the other hand, we insist that the Christian story is the truth about all peoples and about all history, thereby affirming its standing as a "metanarrative," what is to be the evangelist's attitude toward adherents of other religions and toward interfaith dialogue?

In his book *So You Can't Stand Evangelism? A Thinking Person's Guide to Church Growth*, James Adams responds to such questions by arguing for a transformation of evangelism in a more liberal direction that accepts pluralism and refuses to allow conservative evangelicals proprietary ownership of both the term and the practice: "If we are going to use the word 'evangelism,'" says Adams, "we will need a new definition that will convey an open attitude toward religious doubt and intellectual curiosity. We will need to qualify the term to avoid the stance of spiritual superiority that conventional evangelism suggests. We will need a concept of evangelism that accepts the validity of other religious traditions" (1994:22).

Adams's approach to evangelism is not unconcerned with the irrelevance of the church to secular people more generally, but unlike the pastors of the congregations studied by Hunter, his concern has more to do with the offensiveness of Christianity's exclusive and absolute truth claims to those he describes as "open-minded, thinking" persons. As Adams says,

> Perceptive people cannot help but notice that Muslims, Jews, Buddhists, Hindus, and adherents of Native American religions also seem to have access to God. If the churches insist on their claim that Christianity is "truer" than other religions, they will automatically exclude not only half the people who have left the church but the vast majority of those who never have belonged. (ibid. 12)

19. It is worth noting, however, that precisely the secularization of society and the accompanying condition of moral and religious pluralism provide "the breeding ground for the attempt to develop foundationalist epistemologies and for the correlative fear that if we surrender the assumption that our beliefs can be grounded, then 'anything goes'" (Hauerwas 2001b:27–28). Hauerwas is here drawing on the work of Nicholas Wolterstorff.

One of the reasons that "thinking persons" reject evangelism, according to Adams, is its association with fundamentalists or those who work vocally on behalf of right-wing political causes. In addition, popular evangelists tend to be anti-intellectual in a way that "has convinced many college-educated Christians that evangelism is a lower class phenomenon" (ibid. 14). This class bias against evangelism is especially prominent among the mainline churches to which Adams is deliberately addressing himself and is based to some degree on different educational backgrounds, geographic locations, and political preferences. But as Adams notes, it is also attributable to what may be described as "snobbishness" and to the perception that "evangelism is a tasteless business" (ibid. 15). For this and other reasons, reclaiming evangelism in mainline churches is extraordinarily difficult. Too often the only enthusiasm for evangelism that can be generated in mainline congregations comes "not out of a concern for human beings who live without hope, but out of an anxiety about dwindling numbers. . . . Unless they are facing the question of actual survival, most of the members do not want their churches to grow" (ibid. 16).

Adams, like his conservative evangelical counterparts, ends up implicitly identifying evangelism with church growth not only in the above quotation but throughout his book (indeed, within the very title of his book). His position on pluralism may be miles apart from that of conservative Christians who more willingly embrace evangelism, but when it comes to the fundamental logic governing the practice there is little difference between the two. What matters most is what "works" in regard to the growth of the church. For Adams, what isn't working—at least for growing numbers of "thinking people"—are the strategies of conventional evangelism with its arrogant claims to possess exclusive truth, its emphasis on what is "wrong" with people (thereby adopting a posture of superiority toward others), and its requirement that persons sacrifice their intellect in order to take matters "on faith."

Adams, an Episcopal priest, begins his reconstruction of evangelism by criticizing a definition produced by the Episcopal Church during its recent "Decade of Evangelism": "the presentation of Jesus Christ, in the power of the Holy Spirit, in such ways that persons may be led to believe in Him as Savior and follow Him as Lord within the fellowship of His Church" (quoted in Adams 1994:11). Adams rejects the emphasis on "believing" that has come to be associated with such definitions of evangelism because it "suggests that the purpose of the enterprise is to convert people from one set of beliefs, which are wrong or misguided, to a belief in Jesus, which is the only correct form of believing" (ibid. 12). Christians should instead be willing to exist modestly as one option among a plurality of options and be careful not to overstep the bounds of what is intellectually warranted by our pluralistic context. Attempting to convince others to leave behind one set of beliefs and adopt another would, of course, count as overstepping those bounds, because this would clearly imply an attitude of superiority. Adams also thinks that his church's emphasis on doing evangelism "in the power of the Holy Spirit" assigns to Christians "an air of superiority that outsiders experience as arrogant and unattractive," because it suggests that the power of the Spirit "backs Jesus in the competition for religious affiliation" (ibid.). Such claims imply "a unique and exclusive revelation" on the part of the church. No wonder that "thinking people" who have doubts about such audacious claims end up leaving the church. Adams cites research done on mainline Protestant baby boomers which shows that more than two-thirds of those who have left disagree with the notion that "the absolute truth for humankind is in Jesus Christ'" (ibid.).

It is not "belief" in the sense of mental assent to propositions or creeds, then, that is required for acceptance into the life of the church, argues Adams. Neither is evangelism a matter of giving people the "right" answers to their questions. Rather, Christian identity is a matter of behavior, how we treat one another in love. This love, expressed through kindness, mutual support, and care, is the standard for inclusion sought by evangelism. Faith is a matter of "loyalty" to Christ rather than the blind acceptance of doctrine. As Adams says, "Switching the emphasis from belief to behavior for the sake of evangelism, far from watering down the faith, might help a congregation find the true meaning of faith" (ibid. 35). Skepticism and doubt, therefore, can be understood as consistent with Christian faith and, indeed, as dispositions to be encouraged as healthy and natural rather than sinful.

Though Adams refuses to equate faith with belief, this should not be thought of as leading to a diminishment in the church's commitment to invitation and outreach. For Adams, if conventional evangelism produces "exclusive congregations," so also does *no* evangelism (1994:24). But he is convinced that the larger public would be more tolerant of evangelism if the church began to think of it in terms of "generosity" rather than "stinginess and exclusivity." He suggests an option called "progressive Christianity," a movement to reclaim evangelism "by defining it as *church members letting outsiders in on what they have found of value in Christianity*" (ibid. 22). Whereas Hunter's "apostolic" congregations claim to be holding to a constant message over time but transmitting it in new cultural forms, for Adams we must not be afraid to "adjust the message for the sake of the mission" and to "adapt Christianity to popular ways of thinking" (ibid. 83). People will be lured to the neighborly contribution of Christianity to their lives once the church becomes a "spiritually generous" place where people can feel free to ask questions and explore doubts. The adjustment of the message that leads to "effective evange-lism," says Adams,

> involves a three-step process that begins with helping prospective members put into words the philosophy they have used in trying to make sense out of their lives. The second step involves showing them how they can un-derstand Christianity in terms of their personal philosophy and how the church can support them in what they are already doing. In the third step, the church encourages people to question the assumptions and conclusions they arrived at in step two. By emphasizing the importance of the questions, the church can help people understand that any philosophy, any way of thinking, can be a false savior, a substitute for God. (ibid. 88)

The problem with step three's critical questioning of the prospective member's views, however, is that Adams can point to no normative source outside one's own experience by which any particular way of thinking would be judged false. Indeed, the meaning of Scripture and the church's teachings are systematically reinterpreted and reconstructed in terms of that experience.

On the basis of Isaiah 25:6, Adams argues for a universalistic under-standing of salvation in which all people are included at God's table and no particular people is to be understood as having a special relationship with God. As Isaiah says,

> On this mountain the LORD of hosts will make for all peoples
> a feast of rich food, a feast of well-aged wines,
> of rich food filled with marrow, of well-aged wines strained
> clear.

God neither makes demands on those who are invited to this feast, argues Adams, nor sets standards by which one would qualify for an invitation (1994:26). The practice of evangelism should likewise be modeled after such generosity and graciousness:

> The fewer barriers to the Lord's table that congregations erect, based on their opinion of what constitutes proper belief or unacceptable disbelief, the closer their gatherings will approach the prophetic vision of God's feast for all peoples. This gathering can be a potent symbol of [a] congregation's commitment to tell the world about Jesus and his message. The table to which all are invited stands as a reminder that members of the congrega-tion have accepted a responsibility to amend their common life in order to welcome all people to God's feast. (ibid. 186)

Adams's position has much to commend it. Christian evangelism must be dialogical, open, and inviting—on the grounds of the very nature of the gospel, I should add, and not because it might otherwise offend postmodern sensibilities. As with "apostolic" evangelism, there is also something intrinsically correct about Adams' insistence that the church should make room for doubters and skeptics, welcoming them rather than alienating them simply because "they are not like us" and letting them know, as Hunter says, "that it is okay to become a Christian before all of one's doubts are resolved" (1992:58). Belief in the narrow sense of mental assent to propositions or creeds can never be a prerequisite for being included in the life of the church or the focus of the church's invitation; indeed, as I shall argue in chapter 9, belief is impossible apart from incorporation into the church as the *habitus* in which belief is acquired as a way of life and over time from within a community that embraces nonbelievers not out of scarcity, as Adams rightly notes, but out of generosity and abundance. It is only by inhabiting this ecclesial *habitus*, this alternative way of living and seeing, that beliefs become intelligible and can come to be understood as true.

At the same time, it is highly doubtful that any religious faith, Christian or otherwise, can bracket or relativize the cognitive dimensions of belief and commitment as easily as Adams does. While faith is certainly a matter of loyalty rather than mere belief (in the sense of assent to propositions), the comprehensive way of life to which evangelism stands as an invitation necessarily implies claims about the nature of God, human beings, and the cosmos, about who Jesus is and the nature of the salvation that is discovered in and through the church. Adams is quite right that the church must be a place where people can express their doubts, where preaching is interactive, and where honest inquiry can take place. For Adams, however, the permission to doubt requires that the church alter its story to conform to what doubters find it possible to believe. On this view, in order to hold that other religions are not inferior and that agnostics or skeptics are not misguided, Christians are required also to hold the position that Jesus is not "the only way to God" but rather "the way to God that they have chosen" (Adams 1994:36). By extension, the evangelistic responsibility of Christians is "to make the way of Jesus open to people who are unable to have beliefs like theirs" (ibid. 66). A good example of this principle is the resurrection of Jesus, which, for Adams, is the primary intellectual scandal for "thinking people," so that "any congregation dedicated to open-minded evangelism must find an approach to resurrection for doubters" (ibid. 135). This means treating resurrection as a "metaphor" to describe "what happens to people when they encounter Jesus. They discover the capacity to get themselves together, to get up and get going" (ibid. 69).

Adams' transparent liberalism proves that one need not be committed either to a Constantinian Christianization of the social order or to a modern rationalist apologetics in order to refuse the world the option of disbelief. If the Christian message can no longer be believed, then that message must be changed to what can be believed and, indeed, to what is already believed (again, for the sake of church growth). In fact, it could even be said that for Adams "belief" is still very much the essence of Christian faith (notice his emphasis on "thinking")—only now Christian beliefs, if true, must be shown to be "symbols," "metaphors," or "expressions" for what intelligent people already believe, even if only implicitly. Eliminated, no less than in the case of Hunter's "apostolic" evangelism, is the strangeness of the gospel and the distinctiveness of the church and its story. It is the good news that must change, not us. Adams appeals to Isaiah's prophetic vision of an eschatological feast for all peoples, but absent here is the particularity of that people through whom, according to Isaiah, this eschatological universalism is accomplished by God and through whom the whole world stands invited. For Isaiah, Israel is imagined as a "light to the nations" so that by coming to Israel ("on this mountain"), adopting its ways, and worshiping its God, the nations will find salvation.

Adams is a textbook example of what George Lindbeck refers to as a liberal "experiential-expressive" approach to religious truth and doctrine. Lindbeck's well-known typology, developed in *The Nature of Doctrine: Religion and Theology in a Postliberal Age* (1984), distinguishes between three such approaches. A *preliberal* approach (referred to by Lindbeck as "cognitive-propositionalist") emphasizes the cognitive content of religious claims and holds that such claims are propositional references to "objective" reality. Faith, accordingly, is mental assent to these objective, referential propositions and depends upon establishing the correspondence of those propositions to "facts." A *liberal* approach, by contrast, understands the truth of a religious doctrine or claim as giving expression to the inner feelings, attitudes, or experience of human beings. For the preliberal position, the real meaning of biblical stories or Christian truth claims is the "objective" history or reality recorded in those stories or referred to in those claims, whereas for the liberal, it is "the way of being in the world which the story symbolizes or the liberating actions and attitudes it expresses or the ethical ideals it instantiates or the metaphysical truths about God and humanity it illustrates or the gospel promises it embodies" (Lindbeck 1984:179).

In contrast to both of these, a *postliberal* (what Lindbeck refers to as "cultural-linguistic") approach rejects the appeal to all foundations outside a religion, emphasizing instead the way a religion is a communal form of life (and thus like a culture) in which truth is embedded within the practices and social patterns of that community. In this way, a religion is not unlike a language, and in order to understand its truth one has to understand its internal grammar.[20] As an "identity" document, Scripture, read and interpreted in the context of the church and its worship, is the starting point or lens through which postliberals view the world and judge experience, rather than locating the foundation for the truth of Scripture outside of Scripture either in "facts" or in "experience." This does not mean that a postliberal approach to evangelism takes a precritical approach to Scripture or is unconcerned with the relevance of the gospel to human experience. What we can learn about the social and historical context, literary forms, and transmission of Scripture along with what we can learn about human experience (for example, culture, sexuality, politics, economics) will all shape and inform our reading of Scripture. But if Scripture does not offer us a "world" wide enough and ultimate enough to encompass, interpret, and "reveal" the world we find outside of Scripture, it will inevitably be the latter that encompasses, interprets, and reveals the former.

In a number of ways, the approach to evangelism and religious pluralism for which I am advocating in this book may be deemed "postliberal." If that is so, however, it is because it understands itself as having neither a metaphysical "high ground" nor a historical or experiential "foundation" on the basis of which it might argue for the universal superiority of Christianity and thereby persuade persons to become Christian. It has only the story it has been given and the community formed by the God to whom both the community and its story bear witness. But there is no avoiding the fact that it is the very nature of this story to make or imply fully comprehensive claims about history and the cosmos. In engaging persons with the gospel, a postliberal approach to evangelism follows the interpretive direction described by Lindbeck as "intratextual" and as classically employed in the case of typology:

> Typology does not make scriptural contents into metaphors for extrascriptural realities, but the other way around. It does not suggest, as is often said in our day, that believers find their stories in the Bible, but rather that they make the story of the Bible their story. The cross is not to be viewed as a figurative representation of suffering nor the messianic kingdom as a symbol for hope in the future; rather, suffering should be cruciform, and hopes for the future messianic. More generally stated, it is the religion instantiated in Scripture which defines being, truth, goodness, and beauty, and the nonscriptural exemplification of these realities need to be transformed into figures (or types or antitypes) of the scriptural ones.

20. As William Willimon says, "I cannot know Christian discipleship by having Jesus translated into the language of psychological self-esteem any more than I can know French by reading *Madame Bovary* in an English translation" (Hauerwas and Willimon 1992:140).

> Intratextual theology redescribes reality within the scriptural framework
> rather than translating Scripture into extrascriptural categories. It is the
> text, so to speak, which absorbs the world, rather than the world the text.
> (1984:118)

In a world where religions have become "foreign texts," it will always be tempting to translate them into extrascriptural frameworks and popular categories rather than reading them "in terms of their intrinsic sense" (Lindbeck 2002:184). But postliberals are dedicated to the latter and thereby hope to preserve the distinctiveness of Scripture as that which points to what Karl Barth called "the strange new world, the world of God" (1935:33). Thus, says Lindbeck, "liberals start with experience, with an account of the present, and then adjust their vision of the kingdom of God accordingly, while postliberals are in principle committed to doing the reverse" (1984:185).

I will have more to say about the "intratextuality" of Lindbeck's post-liberal approach as it concerns the question of conversion, but clearly James Adams's way of relating evangelism to religious pluralism fits well within the liberal approach rejected by postliberals. In resisting what he rightly sees as the arrogance and exclusiveness of conventional approaches to evangelism, Adams argues that Christian witness can be validated only if it can achieve a universality that offends no one (except, of course, those who are arrogant) and can be embraced by everyone. Narrated by the story of liberal modernity, interfaith dialogue likewise is imagined as possible only from within some supposedly wider, neutral, universal, and all-encompassing horizon greater than any one religion and on the basis of which they may all be compared.

By contrast, the relationship between evangelism and religious pluralism that I am advocating presupposes the historicity and the particularity of each religion in every meeting of their respective positions. This approach is not unlike what James McClendon refers to as "the practical theory of religion," for which "a religion is a set of powerful *practices* that embody the life-forming convictions of its practitioners" (1986:2:421). In coming to know a religion—and all the more in coming to adopt it as one's own—we are required to do something quite other than isolate and abstract its "beliefs," on the one hand (here Adams is correct), or validate its meaning in terms of our own knowledge and experience, on the other hand (here Adams is mistaken). If we are to avoid faulty generalizations about religions that reduce them to some common "essence," we must attend closely and sympathetically to the rich particularity of a religion's stories, its practices, and the comprehensive way of life that makes it a community-embodied tradition. Only then can we begin to understand a religion in such a way that it can be taken seriously enough to reject or adopt. But then this means that the church's practice of evangelism is nothing less than an opening up to others of the "strange new world of God" that it has discovered and an embodied invitation *to live into it*. It also means that salvation is more a matter of enculturation or "language acquisition" than an act of mental assent, the sheer exercise of individual will, or the adjustment of one's attitude.

On this view, the Christian has no grounds for rejecting other religions as intrinsically sinful, idolatrous, or in error. The first and most important thing to be said about them is not that they are deficient but that they are different. As McClendon says,

> What Christians call "salvation" is *not simply another word for* what Hindus call deliverance (*moksha*), or simply another word for what Buddhists call release (*nirvana*). This is so because the contents of religion are not typical experiences to which the religions just happen to have given different names. "Salvation" in Christian terms is not just any experience of success or religious attainment, but is having a share in the liberation and healing associated with the rule of God Jesus proclaimed. Salvation is exactly the "success" that comes when in faith one shares the practices and convictions of that new rule, and to intelligent outsiders, that may seem more like failure than success! (1986:2:422)

The particular narrative determines the meaning of salvation; the meaning of the narrative is not determined by a prior and abstract existential understanding of salvation. From within this particular narrative and the "strange new world" to which it points, Christians will, of course, make judgments about other religions, their practices and convictions, and indeed about all other institutions, powers, narratives, and practices it encounters. The church cannot avoid this if it is obedient, for it has no neutral, storyless place to stand. The particularity of the story from within which it stands, moreover, does not reduce the One whom Christians claim is the God of the universe to, in the words of Rodney Clapp, "a (private) household idol" (2000:112). But this does not mean that Christianity must therefore assume itself to be superior to or the fulfillment of other religions. To hold that a congregation is acting arrogantly or exclusively because it invites persons into a distinctive, even odd, way of living and thinking that is unlike other religions or that is found offensive by "thinking persons" is to deny the unavoidably storied and community-formed nature of all religious witness and conviction and, in fact, arrogantly to presume the superiority of another tradition—namely, modern liberalism.

The concrete difference of Christianity from other religions does not prevent us from finding God at work in the lives of non-Christians. In fact, given the comprehensiveness of the Christian story, we should expect this. Within a postliberal approach to religious pluralism, comprehensiveness is a matter of inclusion rather than exclusion. But this postliberal inclusivism is not at all like its liberal counterpart, for which other religions are essentially saying and doing the same thing as Christianity, albeit anonymously or implicitly.[21] It is by fully admitting rather than attempting to deny or disguise the material difference of Christianity from other religions that dialogue becomes possible. Indeed, it becomes more than merely possible, but, as Newbigin says, "a part of obedient witness to Jesus Christ":

> But this does not mean that the purpose of dialogue is to persuade the non-Christian partner to accept the Christianity of the Christian partner. Its purpose is not that Christianity should acquire one more recruit. On the contrary, *obedient* witness to Christ means that whenever we come with another person (Christian or not) into the presence of the cross, we are prepared to receive judgment and correction, to find that our Christianity hides within its appearance of obedience the reality of disobedience. Each meeting with a non-Christian partner in dialogue therefore puts my own Christianity at risk. (1995:182)

The risk, of course, is that my Christianity may have to change. Interreligious dialogue is, consequently, a spiritual discipline by which evangelizing Christians seek the mutual transformation of their partners and of themselves in repentance and hope.

> The church, therefore, as it is *in via*, does not face the world as the exclusive possessor of salvation, nor as the fullness of what others have in part, the answer to the questions they ask, or the open revelation of what they are anonymously. The church faces the world, rather, as *arrabon* of that salvation—as sign, firstfruit, token, witness of that salvation which God purposes for the whole. It can do so only because it lives by the Word and sacraments of the gospel by which it is again and again brought to judgment at the foot of the cross. And the bearer of that judgment may well be and often is a man or woman of another faith. (ibid. 180)

This openness to the judgment of the dialogue partner of which Newbigin speaks is especially critical for the post-Christendom practice of evangelism. For the sake of faithful and obedient witness, the Christian is called to repent of the specific abuses and unfaithfulness of the church in its wrongheaded attempt to Christianize the world. To thus

21. Like McClendon, Lindbeck sees religions "not as expressions of the depth or transcendental heights of human experience, but as systems of ritual, myth, belief and conduct which constitute, rather than being constituted by, that which is profound in [humanity], e.g. [our] existential self-understanding" (2002:86).

repent, moreover, is not to merely offer explanations or admit the faults of those who have come before us; rather it means "taking responsibility for the past, naming the errors and correcting them" (Yoder 1998:251). Repentance, it must be admitted, has generally not been understood as a form of evangelism—and certainly not as a part of Christian apologetics understood as the defense of Christianity against all objections. But if, as Yoder rightly notes, repentance is a central feature of the salvation to which Christians bear witness, then it is difficult to see how one can be fully faithful as a witness to the gospel apart from repentance. The point is not that repentance "works" in converting others to Christianity; the point is that the logic of evangelism is not, in the first place, a matter of what "works" but rather a matter of faithfulness and obedience.

The argument for a postliberal evangelism takes seriously both the historical relativity of the gospel and its intrinsic claims to comprehensiveness; it seeks obediently to bear witness to that gospel but also repentantly to receive correction from others. It is not the case, therefore, that evangelistic invitation and genuine interfaith dialogue are mutually exclusive practices. Indeed, it is doubtful that dialogue has fully taken place apart from the possibility of and openness to mutual transformation and conversion. Yoder, drawing upon insights from Islamicist Kenneth Cragg, says, "I have only really understood another faith if I begin to feel I could be at home in it, if its tug at me questions my own prior (Christian) allegiance anew. Likewise, I am only validly expositing my own faith if I can imagine my interlocutor's coming to share it" (1998:255).

While a postliberal approach to interfaith dialogue does not shrink from commending its faith, hope, and love to others as truth, it will at the same time refuse any practice of evangelism that has as its inner *telos* its own "triumph" or acceptance. It likewise rejects any attempt to shore up the validity of its witness by diminishing the particularity of the story of Israel, Jesus, and the church so as to establish its irrefutability and universality. In that case, as Yoder puts it, "Jesus then matters less and agreement more. Universality will be sought at the price of specificity. Dialogue will mean the uncovering of commonality. One will speak of common denominators, of anthropological constants, of several paths up the same mountain" (ibid. 257). If, however, consensus is the aim neither of interfaith dialogue nor of evangelism, it is no part of either practice to apologize for, mitigate, or abandon the distinctiveness of its confession. For confession need not be identified with triumphalism, disrespect, or intolerance. Indeed, given the centrality to Christianity of the way of the cross, the love of both neighbor and enemy, and the dignity of the "other," such triumphalism must be understood as a negation of the very heart of its confession. Thus, "the error in the age of triumphalism was not that it was tied to Jesus but that it denied him, precisely in its power and its disrespect for the neighbor. . . . Its error was not that it propagated Christianity around the world but that what it propagated was not Christian enough" (ibid.).

Free Market Evangelism

While secularization and religious pluralism provide important challenges for evangelism, they are not developments against which the church must somehow "fight." At the same time, the church must resolutely refuse to meet those challenges solely on their own terms and from within the resources of a modern narration of the self, its rights, desires, decisions, and agency. That narration locates individual human beings as autonomous egos whose political and economic relationships serve no substantive common good but merely the procedural good of coordinating individual self-interest (and inevitably the self-interest of the powerful). The "peace" of modernity, then, can never be the material wholeness, justice, and reconciliation envisioned in the prophetic imagination of shalom but only the ever-volatile contract between essentially competitive selves. This means that the value of all objects, persons, and relationships is their exchange value as commodities—their profit or loss to the individual as calculated from within a social order constructed on the basis of scarcity and competition. The individual of modernity is thereby narrated as essentially a consumer.

One of the common denominators in the two forms of evangelism surveyed in this chapter is that to the extent they have adopted the modern story as their own (even when in the form of late modern reactions to that story), they find themselves also adopting the modern story's individualist consumer orientation, along with its commodification of salvation as a possession to be acquired or consumed within marketplace laws of supply and demand. The practice of evangelism is overtaken by and reconstructed from within a capitalist "free market" *habitus*, where the story, agenda, culture, needs, and desires of the individual as consumer provide the starting point for determining the value, meaning, truth, and beauty of the gospel.

One of the crucial challenges of the church's evangelism today is whether it is able to resist and indeed to pose a challenge to the powerful and formative processes of capitalism. For if the modern nation-state has succeeded in subordinating the church to its own ends in order to maintain its monopoly on power and its control over the bodies of the individuals whose rights and freedoms it professes to secure, then capitalism has succeeded in subordinating both the state and the church to its own ends.[22] Time after time, a capitalist economics has proved its ability to adapt to and operate within diverse technologies of power and formation and through "freedom" itself, in order that capital might overcome all obstacles to its realization.[23] Daniel Bell describes the development of this "savage" capitalism as one in which culture, art, science, spirituality, and persons themselves come to be objectified and commodified:

> Whereas early liberalism was characterized by what might be called a passive *laissez-faire* attitude, with government striving to minimize intervention in and interference with the naturally occurring patterns and processes of the economy, neoliberal governmentality displays a much more active attitude. Neoliberal government aggressively encourages and advocates the extension of economic reason into every fiber and cell of human life. Economic or market rationale controls all conduct. Capitalism has enveloped society, absorbing all the conditions of production and reproduction. . . . It is the golden age of capitalism, a time when capitalism can set aside its ill-fitting human mask. . . . Capitalism has prevailed. It has subsumed society; it has become social. No longer is it sufficient for modern economic individuals to accept their place beside their machines, in their cubicles, in the lines at the malls as producers and consumers; now they must submit every aspect of their lives to the logic of the economy; they must be entrepreneurs of themselves. . . . Churches are now run like businesses, with ministers proclaiming themselves "CEOs" and corporations offering contributions in exchange for advertising space. Schools are corporate-sponsored training camps for producers and consumers. Athletic events are saturated with corporate logos and viewed by the participants as merely a means to financial gain in the form of endorsements. Public media and public libraries face extinction. Capitalism has taken control. (2001:31)

It is not human desire that is the problem here, nor is *eros* itself sinful. As Bell argues, the success of capitalism is its ability effectively to

22. As Sarah Coakley warns, "Whilst academics have been announcing the advent of 'post-modernity,' and professedly sounding the death knell of all hegemonic 'grand narratives,' global capitalism has insidiously established its power as perhaps the most rapacious grand narrative in the history of the West" (2002:xiv).

23. Daniel Bell says:

> Liberalism does not juxtapose government and freedom. Rather, liberal government is government *through* freedom. . . . It recognizes that some government is more effective and efficient when left in private hands. This illumines the state/civil society distinction as well as the public/private split that emerged with liberalism. Such distinctions do not establish boundaries between government and freedom; rather, they demarcate modes of government. . . . Civil society and the realm of the "private" designate areas of the social field where, in the name of efficiency, government is the responsibility of apparatuses other than the state. By establishing civil society, liberalism does not dismantle government; it only ends the narrow identification of government with the state. (2001:29)

discipline desire, which always flows through social or cultural channels that organize and regulate it. Capitalism finds ways to overtake those channels so as to release and redirect desire (to "deterritorialize" and "reterritorialize" desire) for the sake of the market (ibid. 19).

As the church is itself overtaken by capitalism and its practices taken hostage by the social imagination that sustains this formation of desire, it is not unusual to find the church hostile to desire even as it is being given over to an economics that has perverted desire by directing it to destructive ends. But the church's resistance to capitalism in a postmodern world can never be a simple opposition to desire. Only its embodied offer of a set of practices and disciplines is able to redirect desire to its proper end in God. Thus, Bell is correct when he claims that "the conflict between capitalism and Christianity is nothing less than a clash of opposing technologies of desire" (ibid. 2).

The redirection of desire toward God requires of evangelism a substantive account of what is true, good, and beautiful—an account that is exemplified in the lives of its saints. This account must, by its very nature, run contrary to the merely formal and utilitarian logic of the market, which recognizes nothing as holding intrinsic value beyond its value for the market. What is further required of evangelism, as I shall suggest in the next chapter, is that it reject modernity's false boundaries between spirituality and economics and reclaim the church as a fully material and economic "household" (as opposed to a dispenser of piety that is only subsequently and derivatively economic). Within God's commonwealth, or household, the church's offer of good news is premised on abundance, giftedness, sharing, and peace rather than scarcity, acquisition, competition, and exchange.

But we must have no illusions. There are numerous ways that capitalism disciplines us into rejecting any and all formations but its own. One of the most important ways is capitalism's intrinsic commitment to the modern liberal conviction that all discipline is itself to be rejected in favor of something called "freedom" (which, of course, turns out to be the freedom to be disciplined by formations other than those we rejected). Because religion is by definition a binding together of persons within a substantive common good, any formative processes that would look like "religion" now become disgusting and repulsive—any formative processes, that is, that would attempt to tell us what to do with the realm of the "private" and "individual," that would attempt to redirect our desires materially, politically, and economically, or that would locate authority other than within the subject herself. We desire something less "particularistic, dogmatic, exclusionary" and instead more "universal, accommodating, inclusive, and personally empowering"—something called "spirituality" (Budde and Brimlow 2002:32).

Of course, what passes for "spirituality" in modernity is a far cry from the intensely material and economic, even bodily, formative processes of historic Christian spirituality. As modernity becomes postmodernity (though it may be better to call this "hypermodernity"), resistance to any overtly religious discipline (but openness to the covert disciplines of capitalism) yields spiritual eclecticism—one may take a little from this religion and a little from that, whatever works for the individual, providing that one not experience herself or himself as being overly formed or disciplined by any one community or tradition outside oneself. Robert Bellah has drawn attention to this as "Sheila-ism," the name of the particular religion constructed by a woman named Sheila out of bits and pieces from various philosophies, worldviews, and religious traditions (see Bellah et al. 1985). But this eclecticism can itself be viewed as the product of a capitalist discipline that molds us into consumers and organizes every aspect of our lives in service of the economy.

Sheer "choice" is now understood as freedom and accordingly becomes the highest good and measure of human life. As Christian Smith puts it:

> For moderns—perhaps especially modern Americans—the ultimate criteria of identity and lifestyle validity is individual choice. It is by choosing a product, a mate, a lifestyle, or an identity that one makes it one's very own, personal, special, and meaningful—not "merely" something one inherits or assumes. In the value-epistemology of modern American culture, to believe, to want, or to do something simply because that is what one's parents believe, or what one's friends want, or what somebody else does is considered inferior and unauthentic. It is not enough simply to assume mindlessly the religion of one's family, to absorb uncritically the outlook of one's neighborhood, to follow by default the career path that somebody else has laid out. That is parochial, acquiescent, and artificial. Rather, every such thing must be personalized and substantiated through individual choice. And even if (as is often the case) one chooses what one was already inheriting or assuming, it is only through the observance of individual choice—whether actual or ritualized—that it becomes "real" and personally meaningful. If the primary socially normative basis of modern identity-legitimation is individual choice, then we should find that moderns having to choose their religion makes the religion they choose no less real or authentic to them. For, according to the cultural epistemology, personal choice is the fundamental basis of identity validity. (1998:103)[24]

24. My thanks to Tyron Inbody, *The Many Faces of Christology* (Nashville: Abingdon, 2002), through whom I first discovered Smith's work. Inbody quite rightly argues that evangelicalism, despite its relatively premodern focus on the authority of Scripture and tradition, is in its epistemology "modern liberalism at its core" insofar as authority is ultimately located in the subject and its "free" choices (82).

Evangelism in such a context is a deeply subversive activity, for it holds out the offer of a substantive hope expressed in terms of a divine "reign" that is bound to clash with the prevailing construction of freedom and its corresponding rejection of the notion that humans have any intrinsic *telos* other than that of their own choosing. As David Yeago says, "We no longer readily believe that it could be *good* news that we have a Lord and King. . . . Never before in Christian history has the notion of salvation been so completely divorced from the notion of a hopeful discipline of life" (1999:112–13). From within this modern construction of freedom as essentially empty and as little more than "choice," evangelism is inevitably reduced to "church marketing," a project that in our time has become more than a merely useful tool for reaching unchurched people: it has the status of a rival ecclesiology in which "exchange" rather than "gift" has come to characterize the relationship between evangelist and evangelized.

As argued by Philip Kenneson and James Street in their book *Selling Out the Church*, the past two centuries have witnessed dramatic shifts in the economic life of developed nations, from a production orientation to a sales orientation and now to a marketing orientation. The church has itself been advised also to take on a marketing orientation if it wants to succeed in getting its message out. Whether we like it or not, most Westerners have come to understand themselves fundamentally as consumers. The "successful" church therefore will have to ask, What will attract the consumer and meet her or his needs? And what turns off consumers? What turns them away?

Church marketing is pervasive in evangelistic strategies today. Disciplined by a capitalist formation in which choice has become a value in and of itself, fast-growing churches understand and acquiesce to the fact that in a post-Constantinian world the church is of an order little different from clothing, diapers, and green beans—we can even speak of ourselves as "church shopping." In order to appeal to a designer-conscious public that knows it has many options, the evangelistic church must focus its energies on providing multiple programming and ministry choices ("hooks").

This marketing orientation becomes deadly dangerous for the church that is tempted toward either of the two primary buyer's market strategies: price reduction or sugarcoating. As Kenneson and Street point out, "The 'good news' has been filtered through a rather fine marketing sieve, the result being that many of the less marketable claims that God has on our lives have been removed, leaving for the consumer those aspects of the Christian faith most readily translated into terms of self-interest" (1997:62). This exchange relationship between the church and those it intends to reach is reinforced to the extent the church benefits from treating persons like customers. For what the church learns through repeated experience and the testimony of its evangelistic "experts" is that "if you treat people like customers, they will act like customers. Or the flip side: When people come expecting to be treated like customers, you will likely benefit if you so treat them" (ibid. 67).

In a marketing or consumer orientation, the "strangeness" of the church is perceived as the problem, and the task of evangelism is to rid the church of this strangeness (ibid. 141). Gone is the possibility that evangelism is an invitation to be strange, to become a member of a prototypical but inevitably deviant community intended by God for the whole world. In this eccentric community, it is not competition for scarce resources or our common identity as consumers that binds us together, but rather Christ himself made present through the Spirit who enables us to participate in the life and shalom of God. Evangelism then does not seek "customer satisfaction" but is carried out as a response to the new world that in Jesus of Nazareth has broken in and because of which things can never be the same.

Yet another way of saying this is that the church is called to reach out to the world not out of a desire to offer "help" but as a response to and participation in the salvation it has been given. As Schmemann observes,

> If "help" were the criterion, one would have to admit that life-centered secularism *helps* actually more than religion. To compete with it, religion has to present itself as "adjustment to life," "counselling," "enrichment," it has to be publicized in subways and buses as a valuable addition to "your friendly bank" and all other "friendly dealers": try it, it *helps*! For Christianity *help* is not the criterion. Truth is the criterion. The purpose of Christianity is not to help people by reconciling them with death, but to reveal the Truth about life and death in order that people may be saved by this Truth. Salvation, however, is not only not identical with help, but is, in fact, opposed to it.[25] (1997:99)

The primary issue here is, again, ecclesiology. The question we must ask is whether the church is the eschatological sign and living demonstration that the end of time has come or whether it is to be viewed in strictly functional terms so that our primary concern is, as George Barna puts it, "how—in the midst of a sophisticated, technological, fast-paced, affluent society—you can position your church as a relevant, valuable, and desirable institution for modern man" (quoted in Kenneson and

25. It is true, of course, that "help" is a term often used positively in Scripture, especially by the Psalmist who cries out for "help" and exults in God who has been his "help." This, however, is to be distinguished from help in achieving our own ends.

Street 1997:80). The church that allows itself to be narrated by modernity may for some time be an attractive option insofar as its members will be able "spiritually" to follow Jesus while giving over their bodies, their loyalties, and their money to the twin powers of state and market. But thus narrated, the church can only be but a private association of like-minded individuals who do not so much embody the truth as wear a brand name. By contrast, a postmodern and postliberal church may yet recover an evangelical and uncivil resistance to capitalism that originates in its worship and following of a crucified and risen Lord; is sustained by disciplines and practices such as the breaking of bread, the revolutionary love of enemies, and the welcoming of strangers; and is energized by the transforming, egalitarian, and reconciling power of the Holy Spirit.

It cannot be denied, of course, that modernity's focus on the individual abstracted from and set over against any necessary social identity, substantive common good, or shared *telos* has motivated the quest for liberation and equality in many forms and accomplished much in securing the dignity of persons against injustice and discrimination. By insisting that all social order and all individual functions within that order are contingent and historical rather than fixed and necessary, modernity has proved successful in dismantling authoritarian hierarchies that had been written into the fabric of existence by religious and philosophical ontologies. It must also be admitted that the modern notion of the individual understood as naturally free and functionally equal with respect to all other autonomous selves bears important similarities to the relativization of social, gender, and ethnic identities embodied in Christian baptism, intrinsic to the gospel demand to leave family and property in order to follow Christ, and the body politics of *ecclesia* in which the differences in function among the members of Christ's body are premised on giftedness rather than on inherent or genealogical differences in dignity or worth.

But sheer autonomy and unqualified detachment from or relativization of former allegiances and identities can never, in and of itself, approximate the Christian vision of liberation and equality apart from the new solidarity and fellowship of love for which they ultimately exist. In fact, the distinctively modern mode of narrating the quest for liberation, equality, and justice as "maturity" and "progress," as Charles Taylor points out, while standing in contrast to premodern modes of narration based on a transcendent or founding order (in their more Platonic form) or the natural evolution of what is intrinsic to the world (in their more Aristotelian form), are still capable of being "interwoven with apocalyptic and messianic modes drawn from religious understandings of *Heilsgeschichte* (history of salvation)" (2004:177) in such a way as to sustain the empire

170 Rival Narratives, Subverted Evangelism

building, conquering, and scapegoating violence of powerful nations that come to see themselves as instruments of a "peaceful universalism" in the fulfillment of their "manifest destiny."

If resistance is to be offered to the formative disciplines of the state or the market, that resistance will come not from an individual with rights, or even from an aggregate of such individuals, but from a communion of persons in which the goods of human life are embodied and the practices and disciplines necessary for attaining those goods are nurtured and sustained, along with the virtues required for excellence in those practices and disciplines. Ecclesial existence, and the practice of evangelism inhabiting such existence, provides a unity that transcends the separation and division intrinsic to individual existence. In so doing, ecclesial existence is at the same time an affirmation of *personal* existence, albeit in the mode of communion with others. As John Zizioulas says, "Communion which does not come from . . . a concrete and free person, and which does not lead to . . . concrete and free persons, is not an 'image' of the being of God. The person cannot exist without communion; but every form of communion which denies or suppresses the person, is inadmissible" (1997:18).

Only insofar as the church is itself a visible communion, a material culture, a form of life, an embodied social imagination, a public, a politics and economics in its own right, will it pose a threat to the individualization and subsequent massification of persons inherent in the modern invention of sociality and its institutional offspring. The faithful practice of evangelism cannot avoid posing a threat to modernity, for in bearing public and embodied witness to the peace of God by inviting persons into a social body that must of necessity come between the individual and the state, and by offering an economic formation that is rival to that of capitalism, it can only be viewed as traitorous, sectarian, and extremist.

Evangelism, therefore, is not a Christian scratching of the world's itches. In fact, evangelism does not even lie primarily in the offering of Christian answers to the world's questions. Evangelism is just as likely, if not more likely, to insist that the gospel poses new questions. As McClendon says, "Scripture confronts its readers with another world and asks if it will not become our world; with another hope than our own hope, and thus teaches us to ask, 'What wait I for?'" (Psalm 39:7) (1986:1:38).

Part 4

The Evangelizing Community

The political novelty that God brings into the world is a community of those who serve instead of ruling, who suffer instead of inflicting suffering, whose fellowship crosses social lines instead of reinforcing them. This new Christian community in which the walls are broken down not by human idealism or democratic legalism but by the work of Christ is not only a vehicle of the gospel or only a fruit of the gospel; it is the good news. It is not merely the agent of mission or the constituency of a mission agency. This is the mission.

John Howard Yoder (1998:91)

In part 1, I drew attention to Alasdair MacIntyre's argument for how it is that stories narrate the unity, meaning, and direction of our practices, thereby specifying the internal goods they embody and toward which they are aimed. A narrative helps us to see in ways we otherwise could not. It specifies the beginning, journey, and end from within which a practice makes sense and from within which the convictions and intentions of that practice are framed as causally related and historically ordered. In parts 2 and 3, I tried to show the importance of the particular story that narrates the practice of evangelism by contrasting the story of the people of God with two rival narrations that have wrenched the practice of evangelism from its ecclesial *habitus*, cutting it off from the cultivation of virtues that would orient it toward God's peace and instead orienting it toward other, ultimately violent ends. The story of the people of God shapes the evangelistic offer of good news by imagining God's reign of shalom as the *telos* of all human life, by giving that reign a distinctively

171

christological form, and by casting the Spirit's invitation to participate in that reign in the form of a people who, through its worship and obedience, is a witness and foretaste of that reign.

This narrative, like all such formative narratives, is not free floating. It is told by a people but also embedded in and constitutive of that people, even while being retold, embellished, and reconstructed by them. MacIntyre's way of talking about this is to speak of *tradition*, of the traditioned nature of practices, and of the community that both forms and is formed by that tradition. A tradition, as MacIntyre reminds us, is a "historically extended, socially embodied argument"; and for Christians, that socially embodied argument is the church. To the subject of the church as evangelizing community, therefore, I turn in this fourth part of the book.

In the case of evangelism, specifying the nature of the church is especially important, because as a community of practice, the church not only provides a historical and embodied argument about the proper ends of evangelism, but is, in several important respects, that to which evangelism is an invitation. As I mentioned in chapter 1, one of the important features of evangelism is its critical role in defining the relationship of the church as a tradition-formed community with other tradition-formed communities and, indeed, with the world itself. Evangelism is a practice that is performed at boundaries and along the edges of difference. Because of that, nothing could be more important to a theology of evangelism than clarifying the nature of that difference and how the Christian community's posture toward the world along those boundaries is always one of both invitation and subversion.

The relationship of the church's story to the church itself and to its institutional forms and practices is neither simple nor straightforward. The church's story is not a *theory* that can be applied in some direct way to practice. That relationship is instead a dynamic, historical, and intertextual process of community formation: the narrative is engaged imaginatively and assigned meaning by the community while at the same time overflowing into the community (Paul Ricouer talks about "narrative extravagance"), often displacing and dislocating prior meaning. The church, moreover, does not merely interpret or apply a narrative but also finds itself interpreted by the narrative and formed into it. If the church is a form of life, or *habitus*, then it may neither exist without institutional forms, on the one hand, nor idealize any one institutional form as the exclusive form of the church in any and every context, on the other hand.[1]

---

1. On this point, see Haight 2004:137–39, who also borrows the notion of *habitus* from Bourdieu in his historical study of the church. According to Haight, because Christian identity is a *habitus*, attempting to figure out what it would mean to be faithful is "possible but not easy, and never free from pluralism that involves some level of conflict" (ibid. 138).

Yet the church's story does nourish and legitimate a social imagination, a cluster of common assumptions about the way things are and the way things ought to be. This social imagination, as Charles Taylor describes it, is an "ensemble of imaginings that enable our practices by making sense of them" (2004:165). It is embodied in a complex set of social habits, relations, and patterns that habituate us (often unconsciously) into ways of living and acting that come to be understood as not only possible but natural and right. Among the important features of a social imaginary are its distinctive ways of forming us into a "public" and its provision of a creative framework within which we construe space and time, our relation to others, our sense of common agency, and our relation to power.

I am convinced that if social imaginations "enable our practices by making sense of them," this is especially true of the practice of evangelism, which in our time has increasingly ceased to make sense as an ecclesial practice, having been deformed by the social imaginations both of Constantinianism and of modernity. The following three chapters, therefore, attempt to unpack this social imagination a bit more by looking at the way the church provides the corporate *habitus* of Christian faith and practice in which the practice of evangelism is normatively and substantively guided toward its ultimate *telos* as well as to those intermediate ends that serve that *telos*. In chapter 7, I describe the distinctive patterns of the ecclesial community inhabited by the practice of evangelism, examining ways that the "politics" and "economics" of that community both *shape* that practice and *are* that practice. Practices such as baptism, Eucharist, worship, proclamation, hospitality, and forgiveness embody this politics and this economics, thereby "locating" evangelism and forming the context in which it may be performed as a core ecclesial practice. Chapter 8 relates the ecclesiality of evangelistic practice to the Holy Spirit and argues for evangelism as a practice of the Holy Spirit and for the church as the "public" of the Holy Spirit. At

---

In order to access normativity in a credible way, the church "must focus on the generative principle of the church itself, namely, the message, ministry, and person of Jesus of Nazareth" (ibid.). While Haight is right, I believe, in holding that "normativity does not and cannot function by literal appropriation," he unfortunately decides that it "must be found in the spirit or 'communitas' within the forms, the primitive logic of experience that generated the structures in the first place" (ibid.). This idea that *communitas* generates structures and then resists and transcends them or, as with Max Weber, that the charisma is reforming and progressive while institutions represent the conservative routinization of charisma, creates a faulty dichotomy (as I hope to show in the next chapter). I do agree with Haight that "one cannot take one institutional form from the early church and make it exclusive of other early church forms. It is rather the point or the deeper *telos* of the function that has to be appreciated and drawn forward in yet another new form for a new context" (ibid. 138–39).

the same time, this pneumatological constitution of evangelism points to Christ and is the offer of Christ to the world through incorporation into his body. Chapter 9 looks more explicitly at the ecclesial nature of the conversion for which evangelism hopes and toward which it seeks to open up a way. It seeks to imagine Christian conversion as something like gaining a new citizenship, learning a new trade, or acquiring a new language; thus evangelism requires corporate embodiment and exemplification before it requires apologetic argument or the transmission of "information."

7

Evangelism and *Ecclesia*

Let not the church's mission of evangelizing and working for justice be confused with subversive activities. It is very different—unless the gospel is to be called subversive, because it does indeed touch the foundations of an order that should not exist, because it is unjust.

Oscar Romero (2004:151–52)

The church is not the world. With this "humble fact," says James Mc-Clendon, the struggle called "theology" begins (1986:1:17). But this "fact" is, of course, far from self-evident. Indeed, it could be argued that the greater part of Christian theology and church practice has not only refused this fact but very often considered it a matter of theological and evangelistic priority that church and world be harmonized by demonstrating either that the church's witness is credible on the world's terms or that any distinction between church and world ought to be abandoned in favor of an integrated narrative in which the church's story is at best a "sign" or "sacrament" of the world's story. In a postmodern world, moreover, identities are increasingly blurred and the boundaries between them under constant renegotiation. Cultures and communities seem less and less like unified, self-contained, and internally coherent wholes and more like uncentered sites of ongoing conflict, adaptation, crosspollinization, and improvisation.[1] Is not any stark disjunction between church and world bound to strike us as presumptuous rather than "humble"?

McClendon, however, is not making a descriptive claim, nor is he offering a sociological observation or a historical account; rather he is providing a theological premise, a convictional starting point—and one that is not arbitrary, as I trust can be seen from the previous chapters. In like manner, the ecclesiology of evangelism outlined in the following pages operates on the premise that the church is not the world. It argues that the church's story is an alternative—indeed, a radical alternative—to the world's story, and it asks what evangelistic significance it would make for the church to take this "humble fact" seriously. In other words, it argues that evangelism is centrally (though never entirely) about *difference* and the difference that difference makes.

In modern Western cultures, the church's difference from the world is often viewed (by both church and world) as an obstacle to the church's ability to offer a "plausible," "relevant," and "effective" witness in the world. The church's primary evangelistic task is to reduce or eliminate difference by demonstrating that the church is every bit as smart, entertaining, or useful as other institutions. In contrast to that position, this chapter argues that the church's difference from the world, far from diminishing its ability to offer a credible witness to the world, is a necessary condition of that witness and is intrinsic to the church's invitation to the world to accept that witness as truth. Of course, historically this difference has frequently meant the church's marginalization and rejection by the world as irrelevant, sectarian, dangerous, or treasonous. To the extent that the church's difference from the world is constituted by the latter's acceptance of domination, exclusion, hatred, greed, and violence as normal, Christian evangelism is inevitably a subversive activity. Evangelism need not *try* to be subversive, nor does it employ subversion as one of its "strategies." As is clear from the ambivalence in Archbishop Oscar Romero's words that begin this chapter, insofar as the gospel addresses the very foundations of "an order that should not exist," the subversive nature of evangelism is inescapable. For this reason, the practice of evangelism is not exempt from struggle and conflict. A church that has ceased to be different from the world, however, is able to neither invite nor subvert.

1. Cf. Kathryn Tanner's discussion of cultures in *Theories of Culture* and her analysis of the shift from a modern anthropological understanding of cultures as "self-contained and clearly bounded units" to a postmodern understanding, in which, if cultures are to be considered wholes, they are "contradictory and internally fissured wholes" (1997:38, 57). Tanner asks whether Christianity itself can be considered a "culture" or a "society" and concludes that at best we can talk about Christian identity as a "style" (ibid. 144–45).

What sort of difference, then, is entailed in the claim that "the church is not the world"? A number of contemporary philosophers interpret difference as necessarily requiring exclusion and separation, as inevitably grounded in an act of violence. The story of the people of God, however, narrates the possibility of a difference *from* the world as a difference *for* the world. This evangelistic difference seeks neither separation nor exclusion but is instead a cruciform difference—a generosity toward and openness to the world that both witnesses to a new creation and invites other persons into that new creation. Moreover, because this difference is cruciform, it is willing to suffer vulnerability, rejection, and defeat while seeking neither to grasp nor to possess. In making space for itself, this difference need edge out no one, triumph over no one. Its foothold in the world is in places of abandonment and suffering.

By refusing domination, exclusion, and violence, a cruciform (and therefore pacifist) evangelism is far from invisible or inactive. Nor is its "difference" any less social, visible, or material. The new creation to which evangelism witnesses is God's peaceable reign—a work of prophetic imagination that both demands and makes possible a distinctive reordering of loyalties, priorities, and relationships and of the way power and resources are shared and distributed. The practice of evangelism announces and embodies this imaginary even as it seeks to invite and initiate persons into it through a fully material formation into a people, a Spirit-created social option in space and time.

The first Christians called this new social option *ecclesia* and in so doing took over a Greek political term used to refer to "the coming together of all those with citizen rights in a given city" (Lohfink 1999:218). The term was likely adopted, at least in part, because it referred to a gathering of the whole city, or *polis* (rather than this or that guild, club, faction, or natural affinity group), by literally calling out citizens from their private homes into a public assembly. Equally important was the way the term linked early Christians with the public assembly at Sinai that constituted Israel as a nation and as the people of God (ibid. 219–20). To speak of *ecclesia* is to speak of a calling to be the people of God in public,[2] a new and transnational nation gathered and assembled as a visible politics in and for the world.

Though the notion of *ecclesia* had its origins in a political context, its lived reality in the first centuries of Christianity was based in and patterned after the household (*oikos*) more than other civic structures or voluntary associations. These early household communities were

2. The phrase *in public* here is simply a convention for referring to the material visibility, availability, and openness of the church in the world. I do not otherwise believe there is anything in reality that corresponds to a single, monolithic "public," as will become clearer throughout the following chapters.

comprehensive in their socialization of members, and even though they retained much of the ancient household hierarchies and could even be considered in some sense "exclusive and totalistic," they were also far more inclusive than other voluntary clubs, guilds, or cultic associations in terms of bringing together persons from diverse social strata and social networks (Meeks 1983:77–80). It is not surprising, then, to find household language and metaphors (*family, brother, sister, children*) figuring prominently in the New Testament to describe the *ecclesia* alongside political language (*city, nation*), religious language (*temple*), and biological language (*body*).

In this chapter, while I will discuss the *ecclesia* in its political (and therefore *polis*like) dimensions, I will also examine its economic (and therefore *oikos*like) dimensions in an attempt to depict the form of life and social context (*habitus*) in which Christian evangelism is grounded and in which it makes sense as a practice. The evangelistic difference of the church both from and for the world is, I shall argue, both a political and an economic difference. The politics of evangelism stands in contrast to (and offers a salvation from) a politics of domination, exclusion, national idolatry, and individualistic rights, while its economics stands in contrast to (and offers a salvation from) an economics of scarcity, consumption, greed, utility, and competition. In fact, it would be entirely appropriate to construe the conversion to which evangelism is an invitation as centrally a political and economic conversion. There are, of course, aspects of the church's life that cannot be fully expressed in the language of politics and economics, so plural and rich is the language used to describe the people of God throughout the Bible. But while vigilance is required in remaining alert to the limitations of such language, we may with confidence follow the author of the Epistle to the Ephesians in using both political and economic language to describe Christians as "no longer strangers and aliens" but "citizens with the saints and also members of the household of God" (2:19).

The Politics of Evangelism

To speak of the church as a *polis* or to talk about the "politics" of evangelism may sound strange at first. Most of us are familiar with the word *politics* in the context of the public life of a nation, where it refers to options such as Democrat or Republican, liberal or conservative. As with that usage, *politics* here refers to the processes, rules, and skills that help us as a people to understand, order, and form our involvements and relations. It likewise has everything to do with power, conflict, change, and authority. *Politics* originally referred to the shape and organization of the *polis* and thus to the particular grammar of a people's common story and life together. As Yoder says, "Anything is political which deals with how people live together in organized ways: how decisions are made and how they are implemented; how work is organized and its products shared; who controls space, land, freedom of movement; how people are ranked; how offenses are handled" (1997:223).

That being the case, it should come as no surprise that the church as a social body has frequently imagined itself as very much like an alternative city or nation (Matt. 5:14; Heb. 11:9–16; 1 Peter 2:9; Rev. 21). For to live together as a body is to exercise precisely those functions that constitute that body as a politics. Although we are commanded to seek the shalom of the city in which God has placed us (Jer. 29:7), the church is inevitably a counterpolitics insofar as it is shaped by the politics of God's reign rather than the politics of the city or nation in which it finds itself. Again, the church is not the world. As Dietrich Bonhoeffer wrote in *The Cost of Discipleship*:

> Now the Church is the city set on the hill and founded on earth by the direct act of God, it is the "polis" of Matthew 5.14, and as such it is God's own sealed possession. Hence there is a certain "political" character involved in the idea of sanctification and it is this character which provides the only basis for the Church's political ethic. The world is the world and the Church is the Church, and yet the Word of God must go forth from the Church into all the world, proclaiming that the earth is the Lord's and all that therein is. Herein lies the "political" character of the Church. (1959:280)

Much of the confusion regarding Christianity and politics swirls around whether (and if so, how) the church should be *involved* in politics, or which political options a Christian should choose within a particular society or nation. But this typically cedes far too much to a secular politics, construing it as the only game in town and failing to recognize that living together as the people of God is itself already a politics. It presumes politics as an autonomous sphere of the social order having a fixed boundary that separates it from the realm of faith, so that faith can only ever be related to politics as a subsequent application or engagement. By contrast, to speak of the politics of evangelism in the way I intend it here is to begin with the church as itself a politics and to point to the visible, bodily, and corporate way that persons are invited to be formed into that alternative *polis*. The church then is not called merely to be political but to be a new and unprecedented politics; not merely in public but as a new and alternative public; not merely in society but as a new and distinct society, a new and extraordinary social existence where enemies are loved, sins are forgiven, the poor are valued, and violence is rejected. Yet if evangelism is political or if, for that matter, the church is itself a politics, this politics is no utopian ideal, nor is it a lofty set of "causes" that we are merely summoned to stand in favor of. Evangelism is a summons to take the reign of God seriously, and it is an invitation to allow our lives, commitments, and relations to be ordered within that deviant politics called the church.

I have already cited John Howard Yoder (1926–1997), and it is now time to bring his contribution to thinking about the politics of *ecclesia* into the present discussion more explicitly, especially as it bears upon the practice of evangelism. Yoder's thought is more than merely incidental to these matters; indeed, anyone who has read Yoder's work—for example, *The Politics of Jesus* (1972) or *Body Politics* (1992a)—will already recognize that my use of the word *politics* and the association I make between it and *ecclesia* are deeply dependent upon him. While Yoder mentions the word *evangelism* only infrequently in his writings, the thrust of his work stresses the way core practices of the church embody a politics that is the church's evangelistic witness in the world.

For Yoder, the very existence of the people of God is political, not by extension, application, or implication but inherently and inescapably as a paradigmatic, alternative social order in the world. For Yoder,

> No "bridge" or "translation" is needed to make the Bible a book about politics. The new order, the new humanity, does not replace or destroy the old, but that does not make the new order apolitical. Its very existence is subversive at the points where the old order is repressive, and creative where the old is without vision. The transcendence of the new consists not in escaping the realm where the old order rules, but in its subverting and transforming that realm. It does that by virtue of being an alternative story. (1997:84)

The people of God do not have to sit around and think of ways to "become political"—just as they need not strategize how to be revolutionary or subversive. The calling and formation of a people by God is, as Yoder says, the "original revolution," and the very existence of a people whose lives are marked by such practices as forgiveness, enemy-love, inclusive table fellowship, and sharing of material possessions is intrinsically subversive of an old order that since Jesus is passing away.

What is true of the Bible and the people of God with regard to politics is no less true of Jesus himself, and in *The Politics of Jesus* Yoder argues against the view, held in a number of forms, that Jesus' life, ministry, and teachings are irrelevant to politics and to social ethics. Yoder demonstrates that the interpretation of Jesus' life and ministry as apolitical is itself a political option, albeit with disastrous consequences for the Christian life, which is then free (however unwittingly) to be pressed into the service of lords other than Jesus and sovereigns other than God:

> The choice or tension which the Bible is concerned with is not between politics and something else which is not politics, but between right politics and wrong politics. Not between "spirit" and something else which is not spiritual, but between true and false spirits. Not between God and something else unrelated to God, but between the true God and false gods. Not between the politics of "men" and something else that would not be "of men," but between men and women under God and men and women in rebellion against God's rule. (1997:222)

The question then is not whether the Christian should be political or not. The question is rather to what sort of politics the Christian is called. Yoder's ongoing project was to clarify the sense in which the church is itself a politics and to show how the church's missionary engagement with the world intersects with and *is* in fact its obedience to the politics of the cross. One of the important lessons we learn from Yoder is that the church's evangelism exhibits the same cruciform politics as its social ethics.

What may we identify as the central features of the ecclesial politics shared by the practice of evangelism? For Yoder, the place to begin is not with conceptual abstractions but with the actual practices, or patterns of social process, in which that politics are visibly embodied and exemplified. Yoder mentions five in particular: (1) the eucharistic practice of sharing economic and material goods within a community in which members no longer claim possessions to be their own; (2) the baptismal formation of a new people that is inclusive of diversity while relativizing prior social and ethnic boundaries; (3) the social process of "binding and loosing," in which sins are forgiven and a process of reconciliation and restoration is carried out by the community; (4) the public meeting as an open assembly in the freedom of the Spirit, in which the floor is open to all as the Spirit leads and in which decisions are made on the basis of consensus arising from open conversation and spiritual discernment rather than hierarchical coercion, manipulation, or the rule of the majority; and (5) the ordering of the community as a body on the basis of the universal giftedness of the Spirit in which all are called, gifted, and empowered to play a role (1992a).

These five practices are not meant to be an exhaustive list. We might very well identify others that should be added to their number. For our purposes, what is important about them is threefold. First, these practices constitute to some degree the way of life into which Christian evangelism is an invitation. Second, these practices exhibit normative social patterns that guide and characterize the intentional practice of evangelism and apart from which evangelism lacks appropriate ecclesiality. Third, these practices are themselves to be understood as evangelism (even if not the whole of it). They bear witness to the gospel so that, as Yoder says, "the very shape of the people of God in the world is a public witness, or is 'good news,' for the world" (1997:6). As we know from communication theorists, the most important messages we send to one another are not delivered in the form of propositions or bits of data but are communicated through "pattern recognition" (ibid. 43). The church's politics is its public witness to, participation in, and offer of the salvation it has received from Christ. Nothing speaks more convincingly to the world than the habits, disciplines, patterns, and processes by which our lives are lived and ordered together.

For the moment bracketing eucharistic practice, which I will treat below as part of the church's economics, let us look at each of the practices mentioned by Yoder, beginning with baptism. When baptism is treated in theologies of evangelism, it typically assumes a place as the hoped-for *telos* of evangelistic practice—and in many respects it is, if not ultimately, at least proximately. But here I want to think of the way baptism embodies vital social patterns that both shape and are the practice of evangelism itself. For a number of reasons, baptism may be said to be the central ritual of a Christian politics.[3] Baptism marks the induction of persons into a new and distinct people and is thus an expression of Paul's claim that "when anyone is united to Christ, there is a new world; the old order has gone, and a new order has already begun" (2 Cor. 5:17 NEB). No wonder that among early Christians, persons who were baptized by the church were given new names. Baptism intentionally relativizes (without denying or abolishing) all prior social differences, whether given or chosen, "rejecting their discriminatory impact" (Yoder 1998:369). Jew and Gentile, male and female, slave and free are reconciled in baptism, not through a process of homogenization but through reconciliation and acceptance. What baptism accomplishes through a ritual of initiation, therefore, it also proclaims and offers to the world as a ritual of invitation. As Yoder puts it, "Just being, just being there as an unprecedented social phenomenon in which persons from two contrasting, even conflicting histories rejoice in their being reconciled, is the necessary but also sufficient condition of being able to invite the rest of the world into the new history" (ibid. 41).

At the heart of the church's identity, practice, and outreach is a politics of gender, racial, and interethnic acceptance and inclusion. For Yoder, this acceptance is grounded not on an allegedly "self-evident" confidence that all persons have been created equal, the product of Enlightenment

3. Hauerwas says quite rightly that baptism and Eucharist are "the essential rituals of our politics. Through them we learn who we are. . . . It is in baptism and eucharist that we see most clearly the marks of God's kingdom in the world. They set our standard, as we try to bring every aspect of our lives under their sway" (1983:99).

humanism, but rather on the work of Christ on the cross in which all barriers to acceptance have been broken down. The political nature of the church, then, is a public and visible union of Jew and Gentile into "a new humanity": "Neither ethnic isolation nor cosmopolitan chaos, neither melting pot nor confederation, the new humanity is called elsewhere a citizenship, a city, a new creation. Jew remains Jew, Gentile remains Gentile, but they eat at the same table (which blows the Jews' rules) and they pray to the same God of Abraham, father of them both (which blows the Gentiles' minds)" (Yoder 1998:87).

Baptism initiates us into *ecclesia* through our narrative identification with the history of Jesus and our incorporation by grace into the life-death-resurrection pattern of Christ himself, a pattern within which the entire Christian life is to be lived. Through baptism, the believer is raised to new life "in Christ," united not primarily in a mystical or pietistic sense (though this may certainly be experienced by some, however wrongly it is then insisted upon as the essence of that union) but practically through a shared fellowship, worship, ministry, obedience, and body life. By uniting us to Christ's history, pattern of life, and body, baptism also functions as the translation of believers from the rule of the powers of sin and death to the rule of the Spirit, a rule of freedom and of peace.[4]

This translation to a new rule is, to be sure, only a foretaste, and in no way is the church to be identified simply or exclusively with the Spirit of God. But participation in the life of the Spirit affirms that Jesus was not wrong about the arrival of God's reign. The new age has begun, and the church is the embodied and corporate witness to that new age and the sign of what is to come. To live as a Christian therefore is to live as if this new world of the Spirit is real. It is to trust that the meaning of history is found in the way of Jesus, the way of the cross, a way that rejects violence and coercion. The end of the world has entered into history in the person of Christ, making a way for us. But it is still a "way"—a victorious way, but one that is characterized by an overlapping of this new age with an old age that is dying, so that we nonetheless live in the tension between already and not yet.

The primary significance of baptism is not to be found in some other or deeper meaning that is *symbolized* or *signified* by it (a cleansing of original sin, for example) and stands beyond the egalitarian politics of the practice itself. It is not that such interpretations of sacramental practice are wrong as that they become possible only in later Christian theological reflection, when what really counts about Christian

4. As Newbigin says, commenting on Romans 8, "All 'liberation' is a change of government" (1995:63).

salvation is no longer visible, political, and countercultural. They arise within a context where church and world have been effectively fused by imperial edict, so that, by definition, there no longer stands a world outside the church to evangelize. The "Liturgy of the Catechumens," for example, which always preceded baptism and recapitulated the demanding and rather lengthy process of evangelization and initiation in the early church (baptism was, after all, the central content of religious education), would eventually become a rather meaningless ritual in need of explanation when the egalitarian and countercultural dimensions of baptismal practice were diminished. Then, as Yoder notes, baptism became "a celebration of birth, reinforcing in-group identity rather than transcending it" (1992a:32).[5]

Baptism enacts, proclaims, and celebrates a visible change in identity for those who have now become part of a social order in which something new is possible, such that recourse to esoteric doctrines of what "really" happens in baptism are largely beside the point. Moreover, the "new world" Paul talks of in 2 Corinthians 5 is not simply an aggregate of individual conversions, so that the newness of holiness is primarily individual and only derivatively "social." Rather, the newness created in baptism "is that now within history there is a group of people whom it is not exaggerating to call a 'new world' or a 'new humanity'" (Yoder 1992a:37).[6] Although this group of people represents a variety of callings and giftedness, in baptism we are constituted as one by the Holy Spirit and given a common calling by the Spirit to mutual accountability and to the ministry of reconciliation (2 Cor. 5:18). Clearly, baptism represents a very different "politics of identity" from that which pertains in late modernity with its emphasis on entitlements and rights. To be baptized is not an assertion of one's new identity over and against other persons but is a receiving of new identity that allows our lives to be opened up to others. In this way, a baptismal politics of inclusion is, as we shall see, inseparable from a eucharistic economics of hospitality. Each is the premise of the other, and together both contribute decisively to the *habitus* apart from which Christian evangelistic practice is inevitably distorted and deformed.

5. While I will not attempt to develop this here, the question of infant baptism certainly needs to be rethought in a post-Christendom world, given the challenges and opportunities of practicing evangelism in such a world. Much of the debate over infant baptism has not been conducted in the context of missiological and evangelistic considerations but in terms of abstract considerations of the relationship between grace and freedom and between salvation and sacrament. Indeed, the very notion of sacramentality itself has often been taken up largely independently of missiological and evangelistic considerations.

6. This parallels the exilic notion of Israel's initial formation out of a "gathering" of different ethnic groups (cf. Lohfink 1999:58).

The notion that baptism marks our common calling to a ministry of reconciliation should remind us that despite our incorporation into a new and egalitarian social order, reconciliation is in some sense not a once-for-all, accomplished fact. As Yoder says, "To be human is to be in conflict, to offend and to be offended" (1992a:13). Yet one of the distinctive characteristics of an ecclesial politics is that conflict is faced from within a social process of redemptive dialogue rather than by building up competing power claims or by abandoning one another to the discipline of an impersonal and fixed moral code. We learn from Matthew 18:15–20 that this process begins at the point of concrete offense ("if another member of the church sins against you . . .") rather than at the point where church leaders reckon that "a big enough sin" has been committed. Acts of "binding," or moral discernment, as well as acts of "loosing," or forgiveness—the remitting of the offense—are then required. This process of "binding and loosing" is, for Yoder, a second practice embodying an ecclesial politics.[7]

The authority to forgive sins—and indeed the *charge* to forgive sins (since the church never stands in a position *not* to forgive)—is, needless to say, a sobering responsibility. Jesus is recorded in Matthew 18:18 as saying, "Whatever you bind on earth will be bound in heaven." The point is made just as powerfully in John 20:23, in the context of the disciples' receiving the Holy Spirit from Jesus: "If you forgive the sins of any, they are forgiven them; if you retain the sins of any, they are retained." It is not necessary to reconstruct here the process of binding and loosing in detail, including the role of the various participants in the conflict; but Matthew understands Jesus to have mandated a relatively clear and detailed social process for how Christians are to carry out this activity. It must also be stressed that the aim of this process is the same as that of our common calling in baptism—namely, reconciliation and restoration rather than punishment or exclusion.

Forgiveness is not simply the discarding or absolving of the past, it is the establishing of something new. Thus, rather than being characterized solely as a matter of forgetting, "it might be more truly said of forgiveness that it is a special kind of remembrance" (McClendon 1986:1:225)—and this is at least one reason that confession and forgiveness go together. For confession is but a way of remembering. It is a re-creation of the past but with an invitation to open our lives toward a new future. As Daniel Bell writes,

> When situated within the gift of forgiveness, confession becomes a way of remembering that ironically, and in contrast with a forgetting that closes

---

7. Cf. the discussion of binding and loosing in Yoder 1992a and also his essay entitled "Binding and Loosing" (Yoder 1998:323–58).

off the future precisely by its inability to let go of the past, sets both the offender and victim free from the past for the sake of the future. As part of the judgment of grace that is forgiveness, the confession of truth does not exacerbate either the wound of sin or the cycle of violence that is the wound's effect. This is to say, confession of sin involves the recollection of sin in such a way that such recollection does not appear as a threat. . . . Confession is an invitation to renarrate our lives, to renegotiate our identities under the impact of a truer story than the story of our sin. (2001:176–77)

To be a Christian—and thus to live one's existence within the politics of *ecclesia*—is to participate in this process of confession, binding, and loosing. Forgiveness is neither a once-for-all experience at conversion nor the ongoing prerogative of a minority priestly class within the body of Christ. It is the continuous responsibility of all who are forgiven by God. Indeed, the practice of both forgiving and receiving forgiveness—and so our priestly vocation—is constitutive of Christian existence.

A third practice addressed by Yoder has to do with the meeting practices of the people of God—again, in the context of the activity of the Holy Spirit and specifically premised upon the freedom of the Spirit in the meeting. We know that the first Christians practiced a common table, but they also practiced an open assembly in which the floor was open to all as the Holy Spirit should lead and within the constraints of good order. Yoder speaks of this open dialogue as "the rule of Paul," developed at length in the fourteenth chapter of 1 Corinthians. Ecclesial dialogue is ordered procedurally in keeping with the liberty of the Spirit (the more talkative are told to listen, the more timid are encouraged to speak out, etc.). So intrinsic to the politics of *ecclesia* is this social process of making decisions on the basis of consensus arising from open conversation, rather than hierarchical coercion or the rule of the majority through voting, that Yoder can even refer to it as "the hermeneutics of peoplehood."

As with the practice of binding and loosing, Christian meeting habits are at the core of our politics and embody a trust in the Holy Spirit that is central to all practices, including evangelism. The politics of evangelism is marked by social processes of discernment, openness, and inclusion rather than a capitulation to coercive, hierarchical forms of decision making that on the surface appear to be far more "expedient" and "effective." Within the *ecclesia*, both our individual and our communal vocations are decided within the open dialogue of the people of God (rather than privately) and on the basis of confidence that the Spirit speaks to us within that body. We may therefore speak of the Holy Spirit's "calling" but also of the church's "sending," and this we see throughout the book of Acts as the missionary enterprise of the church unfolds.

If each of us is called by the Spirit within the body that is the church, we are also each gifted and enabled by the Spirit within that body. A fourth practice embodying the politics of *ecclesia*, for Yoder, is premised upon the characteristically Pauline emphasis on the church as a body and focuses on the way the church orders its life and ministry with the universality and diversity of enablements given by the Spirit to each member of that body. As Yoder says, "The same Spirit which gives every individual the right to the floor also qualifies every individual for his or her own role or service in the body" (1997:33). Within Paul's theology of ministry, one's "calling" may never be viewed as a possession but always as a gift and indeed a debt. Likewise, we must speak of the call to ministry as being charismatically authorized and of ministry itself as being charismatically ordered within the body. Politically speaking, here is "a new mode of group relationships, in which each member of a body has a distinctly identifiable, divinely validated and empowered role" (Yoder 1992a:47); in which more honor is given to weaker and less esteemed members; in which all gifts are of equal dignity; and in which hierarchy is undercut in favor of a richly textured equality built on differentiation, complementarity, and mutuality.[8]

As Yoder cautions, this politics of charismatically empowered roles (apostle, prophet, evangelist, pastor, teacher, etc.) characterizes the gathered *ecclesia* and cannot properly be made to serve or to justify the various social roles, professions, or "stations" in which we might find ourselves—for example, "butcher, baker, candlestick maker" or "rich man, poor man, beggar man, thief, doctor, lawyer, merchant, chief" (1992a:51–60). How to establish the honor of secular or "lay" vocation arises as an ecclesial problem when a few of the charismatic gifts are wrongly made more central to the life of the church than others, then professionalized and institutionalized in such a way as to undercut the validity of every member's calling to ministry. We are then forced to look outside the church, in the sphere of work, to find some meaningful way of talking about the vocation of the vast majority of the members of the church. For Yoder, however much we may feel the need to talk about an occupation as carpenter, farmer, or journalist in terms of Christian "vocation," it surely cannot be on the basis of Paul's vision of ecclesia.[9]

8. Protestants may well claim the doctrine of the priesthood of believers to be among the most important insights of the Reformation, but Yoder stresses that this doctrine has yet to fully shape the theology of Christian vocation in Protestant churches except in the rarest instances. It remains, as Yoder says, "the reformation that has yet to happen" and, of the various practices thus far mentioned, "the first that has not yet had its reformation . . . the first whose adequate concrete form has still to be retrieved" (1992a:59).

9. At this point I find especially helpful Stanley Hauerwas's discussion of work in "Work as Co-creation" (1995:109–24).

It is a distinguishing mark of the politics of *ecclesia* that each of its core practices is inherently social. The individual is not lost or reduced to a cog in the machine within the body of Christ. Yet the individual is not the pivotal point for changing the world either through her "changed 'insights' or 'insides'" (Yoder 1992a:76; cf. 1998:371). One can readily begin to see at work here a soteriology that is fully incarnational, practical, ecclesial, and political. The salvation to which evangelism is an invitation and into which baptism stands as an initiation is not to be distinguished from the church's practices, patterns, and politics; salvation does not somehow stand behind the latter as the end through which they are the means. Neither are the church's practices, patterns, and politics the social application of a prior and individual, saving faith. Rather, Christian salvation is our being made a part of a people and incorporated into the practices, politics, and economics of that people.

It is with this meaning of both *ecclesia* and salvation in mind that we may insist with ancient Cyprian that *extra ecclesiam nulla salus*, "apart from the church there is no salvation." This formula is wrong within the social imagination of Constantinianism, where it comes to refer to an exclusive institution bearing an already attained perfection (Cyprian's static images for the church—an ark, a walled garden, a sealed fountain, etc.—do not help matters).[10] It is also wrong within the social imagination of modernity, in which the church is taken to be a consumer-oriented vendor of a salvation that is intrinsically private and egocentric. But it is quite right as a post-Constantinian expression of the ecclesiological shape of salvation and Christian practice. Salvation is impossible apart from the church, not because the church has received salvation as a possession and is now in a position to dispense it to or withhold it from others. It is instead because salvation is, in the first place, a distinct form of social existence. To be saved is to be made part of a new people and a new politics, the body of Christ.[11]

10. See John H. Erickson's critique of the Cyprianic position at this point. Erickson advocates quite rightly that we should look to images of the church other than those of Cyprian, such as temple, vine, paradise, body: "We find in the Bible and the fathers not just images of achieved perfection, which might incline us to hold a triumphalist and exclusive view of the church, but also images of repentance, conversion, and striving" (56).

11. Dietrich Bonhoeffer says something like this in his discussion of Paul's image of putting on "the new self": "In baptism a [person] puts on Christ, and that means the same as being incorporated into the body, into the one [self], in whom there is neither Greek nor Jew, neither bond nor free. No one can become a new [self] except by entering the Church, and becoming a member of the Body of Christ. It is impossible to become a new [self] as a solitary individual. The new [self] means more than the individual believer after [he or she] has been justified and sanctified. It means the Church, the Body of Christ, in fact it means Christ himself" (1959:242). Barth puts it this way: "[The Christian] is not in [the church] in the sense that he might first be a more or less good Christian by his personal

To assign the church this sort of centrality is not, however, to reduce God's reign to the church or to make it identical with the church. It is rather to construe the church as a people whose confession of God as sovereign is embodied in its politics. For a reign without a politics would be no reign at all, just as "a sovereign without a people would be no sovereign at all" (Lohfink 1999:42). The relationship of the church to God's reign is not that of practice to theory, means to end, or form to content. It is instead the relationship of a people to the government it confesses to be true and by which it attempts to order its life in the world.

There is much talk today of the "missional church,"[12] and I do not disagree entirely with those theologies of evangelism and mission that urge a shift away from what is disparagingly called "ecclesiocentrism" to a focus instead on *God's* mission in the world, a mission in which the church is an instrument and agent and so exists for the world rather than for itself. Any evangelism divorced from the *missio Dei* can easily degenerate into little more than a form of ecclesiastical narcissism that neglects, among other things, vital matters such as justice, peacemaking, or the well-being of the ecosphere. But if God's calling out of a people is, in fact, the *missio Dei*, then pitting a mission-centered evangelism over against a church-centered evangelism is setting up a false dichotomy. Another way of saying this is that the Christian "*way of being*" is an event of communion such that it can only be realized "as an *ecclesial fact*" (Zizioulas 1997:15).

The oft-cited report from the 1961 New Delhi Assembly of the World Council of Churches would have us shift the church's missional thinking from a "God-church-world" paradigm to a "God-world-church" paradigm, because "it is the world and not the Church that is the focus of God's plan" (WCC 1967:17). But while that shift might prove to be a healthy corrective to the ingrown, patriarchal, and Constantinian tendencies of the church over the centuries, it forces a trade-off that too easily loses the eschatological and not merely functional nature of the people of God in God's economy of salvation. While it may be important to talk about the "missional church," perhaps we also need a renewed sense of "ecclesial mission."[13] As the papal document *Evangelii Nuntiandi* puts it:

---

choice and calling and on his own responsibility as a lonely hearer of God's Word, and only later, perhaps optionally and only at his own pleasure, he might take into account his membership in the church. If he were not in the church, he would not be in Christ. He is elected and called, not to the being and action of a private person with a Christian interest, but to be a living member of the living community of the living Lord Jesus" (1981:188).

12. See, for example, Darrell L. Guder, ed., *Missional Church: A Vision for the Sending of the Church in North America* (Grand Rapids: Eerdmans, 1998).

13. Or as Yoder says, in contrast to a study of "the missionary structure of the congregation," we ought to seek "the congregational structure of the mission" (1998:253–54).

Evangelization is for no one an individual and isolated act; it is one that is deeply ecclesial. When the most obscure preacher, catechist or pastor in the most distant land preaches the Gospel, gathers his little community together or administers a sacrament, even alone, he is carrying out an ecclesial act, and his action is certainly attached to the evangelizing activity of the whole Church by institutional relationships, but also by profound invisible links in the order of grace. This presupposes that he acts not in virtue of a mission which he attributes to himself or by a personal inspiration, but in union with the mission of the Church and in her name.

Church and World

Yoder's way of affirming the fundamentally political nature of Christianity has affinities with as well as important differences from liberation theologians like Gustavo Gutiérrez, who reject antitheses such as political-apolitical, temporal-spiritual, or profane-sacred, which are perceived as being built on an unwarranted and unbiblical distinction between the natural and supernatural (Gutiérrez 1988:43). For Gutiérrez, the processes of secularization have "matured" us, thereby enabling us to refuse a "distinction of planes" that makes the priest more important than the layperson and that constructs the church as the sole locus of salvation within the world. Instead, the world in which we are related to one another and to God is "entirely worldly" (ibid. 41–42). Moreover, it is thoroughly political precisely because, in a world that has become increasingly autonomous and secular, the political has become the "sphere for the exercise of a critical freedom which is won down through history" and "the collective arena for human fulfillment"—our aspiration to direct our own lives and forge our own destinies. For Gutiérrez,

> Nothing lies outside the political sphere understood in this way. Everything has a political color. It is always in the political fabric—and never outside of it—that a person emerges as a free and responsible being, as a person in relationship with other persons, as someone who takes on a historical task. Personal relationships themselves acquire an ever-increasing political dimension. Persons enter into relationships among themselves through political means. (ibid. 30–31)

There are not two histories, therefore, but only "one call to salvation" that unifies the sacred and the profane and one redemptive work that "embraces all the dimensions of existence and brings them to their fullness" (ibid. 86). Salvation for Gutiérrez is "not something otherworldly, in regard to which the present life is merely a test. Salvation—the communion of human beings with God and among themselves—is something which embraces all human reality, transforms it, and leads it to its fullness in Christ" (ibid. 85).

The implications of this position for evangelism are, as one might guess, profound. Because the one call to salvation is both personal and political, evangelism necessarily includes prophetic denunciation of unjust social structures and should be understood as a "conscienticizing" practice that aims, said the bishops at Medellín, "to educate the Christian conscience, to inspire, stimulate, and help orient all of the initiatives that contribute to the formation of [humanity]" (quoted in Gutiérrez 1988:69).

Following Vatican II in stressing a call to salvation that is "integral" and "unitary," Gutiérrez believes that any lines we might draw between faith and works or between the church and the world must be held very loosely. He can thus quote approvingly Johann Metz: "Is not the Church also world? . . . The Church is of the world: in a certain sense the Church is the world: the Church is not Non-World" (ibid. 46). Gutiérrez believes that it is through the church that "the Lord reveals the world to itself" and thereby "rescues it from anonymity and enables it to know the ultimate meaning of its historical future and the value of every human act"; but a fully autonomous and secular world is the location of salvation rather than the church. In fact, "the Church must turn to the world, in which Christ and his Spirit are present and active; the Church must allow itself to be inhabited and evangelized by the world" (ibid. 147).

It is not difficult to embrace much of what Gutiérrez says about the thoroughly political nature of human existence, salvation, and evangelism, especially if one takes seriously the social, material, and economic dimensions of the story of the people of God. To agree with Gutiérrez on these points, however, is not necessarily to agree with his positive assessment of secularization,[14] nor is it to agree with his way of construing the relationship between church and world (or, for that matter, between the natural and the supernatural). The problem I see here is not the integralism for which Vatican II rightly issues a call or Gutiérrez's denunciation of "two planes of existence" in favor of a unity of the political and spiritual, of faith and works. It is, rather, the way this unity is achieved on the world's terms and on the basis of secularist presuppositions.[15]

14. Secularization, for Gutiérrez "is a process which not only coincides perfectly with a Christian vision of human nature, of history, and of the cosmos; it also favors a more complete fulfillment of the Christian life insofar as it offers human beings the possibility of being more fully human" (1988:42).

15. For a telling critique of liberation theology at this point, see Milbank 1990:206–55, the chapter entitled "Founding the Supernatural: Political and Liberation Theology in the Context of Modern Catholic Thought." Milbank argues that we must distinguish between two versions of Catholic integralism following Vatican II—a French version that

Gutiérrez accepts the arena of the "political" as defined and located by the world and then politicizes the Christian faith and the church accordingly. He is thus prevented from entertaining a third possibility beyond the "distinction of planes" (which he rightly rejects), on the one hand, and a unity of the sacred and profane constructed on the basis of profane intellectual resources (which he unfortunately adopts), on the other hand. For this third possibility, the church remains the locus of salvation and not merely a sign that points to the politics that presents itself to us within history. This is not because the church is or ought to be at the controlling center of the world's political order. Indeed, that is precisely the flaw in the logic of Constantinianism. Neither is it because God's mission is to the church first and only secondarily to the world. Rather, God's mission to the world is the creation of a people begun in Israel and extended to include the Gentiles through Christ.

The politics of *ecclesia* is an alternative politics, one that is not to be found in the world, even anonymously—though that is not to say that the practices that embody this politics may not be borrowed and emulated by the world (cf. Yoder 1992a:75). The politics of *ecclesia* is instead *sui generis* because it is premised on confession and worship of the triune God. It is, to be sure, a politics that is in its own way "entirely worldly," but its worldliness is to be found in a visible body created by the Holy Spirit, liturgically enacted, and materialized in the social patterns and practices of that body. Here there is no refusal of politics, nor is the work of the priest prioritized over the work of the layperson. Moreover, there is no denial of the fact that the Spirit does indeed work in all of human history, not just in the church. But this politics refuses to blur the distinction between church and world and thereby opens itself to the possibility that the very purpose of God's rule in the world is the creation and formation by grace of a people that is different both from and for the world.

Of course, the nature of the church's difference from and for the world requires considerable explanation. For one thing, both *church* and *world* are complex terms, frequently inviting rather than resolving ambiguities in this discussion. *World* can simply mean the earth, the universe, nature, or creation. In both Judaism and Christianity, this use of the word is more than merely neutral; it is positive and at times reverent. So, for

---

"supernaturalizes the natural" and a German version that "naturalizes the supernatural." Liberation theologians unfortunately follow the latter, with the consequence that "theirs has been simply another effort to reinterpret Christianity in terms of a dominant secular discourse of our day" (ibid. 208). The former, however, to be found especially in the work of Maurice Blondel, grounds its unitary vision of a just social order not on some autonomous or allegedly universal secular reason but on the possibilities of grace that we can speak about only from within the Christian tradition.

example, Paul says that through the world we are able to discover God's "eternal power and divine nature" (Rom. 1:20). And, of course, in the creation narratives, God refers to the world as "good."

At the same time, and indeed much more frequently, the New Testament uses *world* as shorthand for a refusal to worship God or to follow Jesus as Lord. It is in this sense of the word that the world is, as Yoder puts it, "structured unbelief" and "a demonic blend of order and revolt"; it is not the creation but rather "the fallen form of the same, no longer conformed to the creative intent" (1998:62, 56, 55). The Epistle of James, for example, instructs us to keep ourselves "unstained by the world" (1:27). In fact, "friendship with the world is hostility toward God" (James 4:4). Paul also bids us not to be "conformed to this world" (Rom. 12:2). The wisdom of the world is foolishness to God (1 Cor. 1:20), and we have been given the Spirit of God, not the Spirit of the world (1 Cor. 2:12). According to Paul, we no longer walk according to "the course of this world" (Eph. 2:2), nor ought we to love this present world (2 Tim. 4:10).

Nowhere do we see the church and world in conflict as much as in the Johannine literature, where usage of the term *world* is especially prominent. It is clear from John that God loves the world (John 3:16), that Jesus is the light of the world (John 8:12), and that Jesus gives himself for the life of the world (John 6:51). At the same time, Jesus is not "of this world" (John 8:23), nor is his kingdom of this world (John 18:36). The world hates Jesus because he exposes its evil deeds (John 7:7), and it will also hate the disciples, who have been "chosen out of the world" and no longer "belong to the world" (John 15:19). The Spirit that Jesus gives cannot be received by the world, because it does not know Jesus (John 14:17). The peace Jesus gives is not at all like the peace the world gives (John 14:27). Moreover, Jesus has "conquered the world" (John 16:33). Thus, the Christian's attitude toward the world may be summed up as follows:

> Do not love the world or the things in the world. The love of the Father is not in those who love the world; for all that is in the world—the desire of the flesh, the desire of the eyes, the pride in riches—comes not from the Father but from the world. And the world and its desires are passing away, but those who do the will of God live forever. (1 John 2:15–17)

This excursus into the Johannine literature should not lead us to believe that the politics of *ecclesia* may be construed only negatively as over against the world. We do not start with "world" in order to understand what we mean by "church." However subversive this politics may be, it is so precisely because it embodies the good news of God's reign in a situation where hostility to that reign passes for normalcy. Nor may we absolutize the difference between church and world. For one thing, there is a good deal of "world" in all of us, including the church.[16] But more than that, while it is true that the church's story is not the world's story, Christian evangelism operates out of an unyielding trust that it *can* be, the audacious confidence that it *should* be, and the outrageous hope that it *will* be. As Yoder puts the matter, the world "really is" estranged from what it "really is" (1998:56–57). While the narration of history that the church offers is not the same as the history narrated by the world, evangelism is the church's way of affirming that this distinction is not ultimately or ontologically a dualism: "To confess Jesus as Lord makes it inconceivable that there should be any realm where his writ would not run. That authority, however, is not coercive but nonviolent; it cannot be imposed, only offered. It cannot be excluded by being declared to be alien, or 'private' or 'personal' or 'sectarian,' but only not (i.e., not yet) being heard" (Yoder 1997:25).

The practice of evangelism then is premised on what Christians take to be an ontological unity of church and world and on a single true history in which confession of the lordship of Jesus is not, in the first place, a matter of private Christian belief or subjective experience but rather a claim about the nature of the cosmos (Yoder 1998:131). The peace to which the church is called is the same peace to which the world is called, just as the God of Jesus is the God of all. Another way of saying this is that the new world into which Christians invite other people "is not an 'other' world, different from the one God has created and given to us. It is our same world, already perfected in Christ but not yet in us" (Schmemann 1997:42). For that reason, the patterns of social process that Yoder calls practices are not only that to which the body of Christ is called but also that to which the world is called: "Church and world are not two compartments under separate legislation or two institutions with contradictory assignments, but two levels of pertinence of the same Lordship. The people of God is called to be today what the world is called to be ultimately" (1992a:ix).

It should be clear by now then that Christian evangelism requires as a condition of its very possibility the presence in the world, though distinct from the world, of a visible people, a new society, into which persons may be invited and formed. Apart from such a people, the good news will inevitably be privatized, individualized, interiorized, or turned into a utility for ends other than peace and holiness. This evangelistic peoplehood

16. "The line between the church and the world still passes through the heart of every believer, and . . . through the heart of every churchly practice as well" (McClendon 1986:1:230).

to which the church is called is not unlike the distinctive particularity of Israel—indeed it is a derivative of Jewish particularity—though, like Israel itself, the church stands ever in need of prophetic self-criticism when that particularity tends toward nationalism and ethnocentrism. In our time, however, the church has largely lost a sense of Israel-like peoplehood, a fact that is more frequently celebrated than repented by Christians, given our dual inheritance in Constantinian and Enlightenment universalism (cf. Lindbeck 2002:246). This neglect of peoplehood may well be the central challenge facing Christian evangelism. If the error of Constantinian Christianity is its belief that evangelism is possible without a church that is visibly different from the world, the error of a Christianity formed within the social imagination of modernity is its belief that evangelism is possible without any church at all.

It is not the lordship of Jesus that distinguishes the church from the world but the *confession* of that lordship in baptism, worship, discipline, and obedience. The recovery of evangelism as a practice in "good working order" today, therefore, requires that we find a way to maintain two fundamental convictions simultaneously: (1) the unity of the church and the world in a common calling and a common destiny, and under the common lordship of Jesus, and (2) the church's visible difference from the world that results from its confession of Jesus as Lord.[17] In other words, as Yoder puts it, "for the people of God to be over against the world at those points where 'the world' is defined by its rebellion against God and for us to be in, with, and for the world, as anticipation of the shape of redemption, are not alternative strategies" (1992a:78).

As a way of unpacking how we are to hold these theological convictions simultaneously, I offer the following six suggestions.

First, this does not mean that the church *is* the reign of God or that Christians are sinless. The difference between church and world is not the difference between good and evil or between perfection and sinfulness. The difference between church and world is a difference of confession. The shape of that confession, however, must be visible and nonconformist.

Second, Christian difference implies neither passivity nor a withdrawal and detachment from the world. Holiness is never a way out of the world but ever and always a way into the world. It is *for* the world that the church is called to be both in the world and visibly different from the world.

Third, to insist that both the church and the world have a common Lord (though not commonly confessed) does not entail an expectation

---

17. One of the best articulations of these two convictions together is Yoder's "The Otherness of the Church" (1998:53–64).

that the world should live and act as the church is called to live and act without its first believing in Jesus as Lord. The politics of *ecclesia* is not a design for nonbelieving communities, however much the practices that embody this politics are parabolic and "lend themselves to being observed, imitated, and extrapolated" by the world (Yoder 1992a:75).

Fourth, the fact that the peace to which the body of Christ is called is the same peace to which the world is called in no way justifies any Christian attempt to impose its peace or "the things that make for peace" upon the world. While throughout history one can certainly link the rise of totalitarian violence with metanarratives that seek to embrace all of reality and to explain all of history from within a single story that projects a universal goal for all humanity,[18] the church's story narrates a peace that is vulnerable and cruciform—the "peace of Christ." It is, moreover, a story that can never identify its word as the "final word" nor its peace as the *Pax Christi*—both because of its openness to the narrative interruptions of the "other" (the stranger, the poor, the outsider) and because of its "eschatological reserve" grounded in the hope of Christ's parousia, which judges and corrects every present claim to ultimacy and comprehensiveness of vision. The church's narration of peace is the critique of all violent and idolatrous metanarratives rather than one more among them.

Fifth, the church need not overstate its difference from the world and should value and seek whatever advances may be achieved in the world in terms of peace, human dignity, justice for the poor and marginalized, and religious liberty. Part of what it means to be different *for* the world is an empowerment "to speak to the world in God's name, not only in evangelism, but in ethical judgment as well" (Yoder 1998:56).[19]

Sixth, an evangelistic confidence that church and world have a common Lord does not provide a warrant for the church to condone or adjust itself to the world's violence and rebellion, "to posit or to broker some wider or thinner vision, some lower common denominator or some halfway meeting point, in order to make the world's divine destination more acceptable or more accessible" (Yoder 1997:24). Exemplification rather than accommodation is the church's primary evangelistic strategy.

The politics of evangelism, then, is the church's "otherness" in worship, fellowship, baptism, discipline, morality, and martyrdom (cf. Yoder

18. Cf. Hannah Arendt, *The Origins of Totalitarianism* (New York: Harcourt, Brace, 1951).

19. The church is able "to take on a prophetic responsibility for civil ethics without baptizing the state or the statesman. The justice the church demanded of the state was not Christian righteousness but human iustitia; this it could demand from pagans, not because of any belief in a universal, innate moral sense, but because of its faith in the Lord" (Yoder 1998:56). See also Yoder 1964.

1998:56, 360–73). To practice this politics is to bear embodied witness to the good news of God's reign in a way that both invites and subverts. Consequently, there can never be an apolitical evangelism that is only or even primarily about "spiritual" sorts of things. In the first place, our lives are much more whole than that. If evangelism is primarily about spiritual matters, then the word *spiritual* must refer not to some single dimension of our lives but to the way our lives are formed meaningfully into a pattern or whole, or directed toward a particular end—and to the way this formation takes place through intentional relationships, habits, and practices. I earlier said that it is possible to construe the conversion to which evangelism is an invitation as a political and economic conversion. In no sense, however, does this make that conversion any less "spiritual."

The Economics of Evangelism

> The community does not speak with words alone. It speaks by the very fact of its existence in the world; by its characteristic attitude to world problems; and, moreover and especially, by its silent service to all the handicapped, weak, and needy in the world. It speaks, finally, by the simple fact that it prays for the world. It does all this because this is the purpose of its summons by the Word of God.
>
> Karl Barth (1963:38)

However much the early church could imagine itself as a *polis* and employ political language and images to describe itself (*ecclesia*, nation, country, citizens, etc.), this *polis* was clearly not like others of the ancient world and was understood by Christians as standing in contrast to them. One way this contrast came to be developed was in relation to the *oikos*, or household. According to Hannah Arendt, the *polis* of antiquity was circumscribed as a distinct "public" in contrast to and over against the *oikos* (1958:28–29).[20] While the *polis* was a sphere of freedom and equality constructed on the basis of the interactions among plural and "free" men, the *oikos* was the sphere of fixed and irreversible relations, the realm of uncontested rule by the single *paterfamilias*; it was the place of marginalized persons (women, children, slaves) who were excluded from the "public" of the *polis*. As Milbank says, the ancient *polis* was "partly constituted as a machine for minimizing the *oikos*, or as a kind

20. In addition to Arendt's *The Human Condition*, see also Reinhard Hütter's fine summary of her work in *Suffering Divine Things* (2000:159–64) and Mary Doak's analysis of Arendt in *Reclaiming Narrative for Public Theology* (2004).

of cultural bypass operation to disassociate continuity and succession from wombs and domestic nurture" (1990:364).

Arendt has no interest in returning to or supporting a patriarchal *oikos*, but this distinction between *polis* and *oikos* is to her mind essential if the *polis* is to be a place where human beings can distinguish themselves *as* humans in freedom. The public of the *polis* must not exist *for* something, lest it be instrumentalized in the service of some predetermined goal or project and thus be restricted as a place of plurality and freedom. Economic concerns such as labor (of the sort necessary to keep ourselves alive) must not intrude into or come to dominate the public life of the *polis*—not because such concerns are unimportant but just the opposite, because of their urgency. It is only in a public that is set apart from the private realm of the *oikos* that humans can experience other humans in their full uniqueness, freedom, and plurality without subjecting that freedom to the pressing concerns of the *oikos*. While Arendt's distinctions here may strike one as a denigration of the private, or of the *oikos*, that is not at all her intent. She is instead offering a critique of modern societies that have become so preoccupied with processes of production and consumption in the name of expanding "freedom" that they end up incapable of freedom (and in her time this would have characterized the Marxist as well as the capitalist preoccupation with such material concerns).

For Arendt, the church can never be a true public (or *polis*) in the proper sense of nurturing human plurality and freedom (and so must necessarily belong to the realm of the private, lest it insinuate its particular vision on others coercively in public). Reinhard Hütter argues, in contrast, that the New Testament church, rather than understanding the *oikos* as the "other" over against which the Christian *polis* was defined, saw itself as both *polis* and *oikos* (2000:162–63). It is true that the church is not a *polis* in the classically Greek sense of the word to which Arendt is drawn, but one can make a case (I will discuss this more in chapter 8) that the church is a public in its own right and that as "the public of the Holy Spirit" it is wider and more inclusive than other publics precisely because (rather than *despite the fact that*) it is united by a common love and a substantive *telos*. The church is a part of God's economy (*oikonomia*) and is thus a *polis* that, "rather than being conceived in radical antithesis to the *oikos*, transcends both polis and *oikos* in a revolutionary way and precisely therein also fundamentally transforms the *oikos* of antiquity" (ibid. 163). If the church is a *polis*, says Hütter, it a "polis sui generis."

In this section I will consider what it means for *ecclesia* to be characterized as a transformed *oikos* and the significance of this for the practice of evangelism. Given the unique synthesis of *polis* and *oikos* that characterizes *ecclesia*, however, we would do well not to make too rigid a distinction between the two or between the church's politics and its economics. As in most societies, the church's economic and political factors do not disentangle easily. How we order our relationships, make decisions, share power, handle conflict, and construe authority has everything to do with how people are ranked, how work is organized, and how material resources are shared. To apply either of the terms *politics* or *economics* to the church is, then, already to stretch those terms beyond their customary usage. *Ecclesia* shares features of a *polis* and an *oikos* but is, at the same time, an alternative to them both. Yet I believe that much is gained for the practice of evangelism when we emphasize the political and economic dimensions of ecclesial life. For while specifying those dimensions makes clear how new and different from the world is the form of life into which persons are called by the gospel, it also makes clear that the church is not just an empty, critical protest in its difference but rather a visible and social embodiment of and journeying toward a substantive good for which God has created us.

In the previous discussion on the "politics" of *ecclesia*, I began with four of Yoder's five practices in order to highlight the particular social patterns that characterize the common life of a people created and formed by the Spirit of God as witnesses to God's peaceable reign in the world. Baptism, I suggested, is the central ritual of that politics, for it both enacts and proclaims the acceptance, inclusion, liberation, and reconciliation (the "new world") that is begun when persons are united with Christ, incorporated into his history, and formed into his body by participating in his death and resurrection. The other three practices mentioned by Yoder—binding and loosing, the public meeting as an open assembly in the freedom of the Spirit, and the ordering of the body on the basis of the universal giftedness of the Spirit—likewise enact and embody a distinctive peoplehood that is inherently social and in which the Holy Spirit is trusted through corporate discernment rather than more expedient, coercive, and hierarchical forms of decision making. In turning to the economics of *ecclesia*, I will now focus on a fifth social practice: eucharistic fellowship and sharing.

If baptism is something like the central ritual of the church's politics, one could argue on solid theological and historical grounds that eucharistic practice is the central ritual of the church's economics (though, again, the distinction between a "politics" and an "economics" should not be overdrawn). This is not to diminish an entire constellation of other economic practices and patterns that are essential to Christian identity and witness including hospitality, debt forgiveness, Sabbath keeping, simplicity, gratitude, compassion, and justice, each of which surfaces in the discussion to follow. But eucharistic practice is so central in defin-

ing and positioning the economic dimensions of ecclesial life that it is
no exaggeration to call Christian economics a "eucharistic economics."
Likewise, insofar as evangelism is a core church practice, it is essential
to understand it as a eucharistic practice through and through.

Whatever else we may say about the Eucharist, it is essentially a
shared meal. The early Christian practice of breaking bread together is
presented throughout the New Testament as paradigmatic of social relations within the *ecclesia* and should be understood in the first place as
the daily practice it was rather than as a commemorative ceremony or
a mystical ritual symbolizing some other spiritual reality. The centrality
of a common meal in the apostolic age, as Yoder reminds us, was not an
innovation but rather a continuation of the way the disciples had been
living with Jesus throughout his ministry. By the time the first narrative
accounts of Jesus were being written, around forty years' worth of common meals among the early Christians had transpired, thereby shaping
and lifting to importance such stories as the feeding of the multitudes,
the meeting with the resurrected Jesus on the Emmaus road, and of
course the story of the Last Supper itself (Haight 2004:98).

The sharing of bread, therefore, is not in the first place a "sign," nor
does it "stand for" daily sustenance, hospitality, or community formation; rather, "bread *is* daily sustenance. Bread eaten together *is* economic
sharing. Not merely symbolically, but also in fact" (Yoder 1992a:20). No
translation or interpretation is needed to make the Eucharist economically "relevant," for it is the daily sharing of material resources within a
community in which members no longer claim possessions to be their
own. The breaking of bread around a common table creates a solidarity and a unity that may be organically extended to every area of life
and that further reinforces the leveling of rank and status established
in baptism. As Yoder says, "The Eucharist is an economic act. To do
rightly the practice of breaking bread together is a matter of economic
ethics" (ibid. 21).

Here again Christian ethics and evangelism are inseparable—and to
some extent indistinguishable. Both are rooted in concrete practices of
thanksgiving, sharing, and hospitality that keep alive the memory of
Jesus while forming us into his story and into his body. We have already
seen that one of the distinctive (and disruptive) features of Jesus' life
was the eating habits he practiced and cultivated in his disciples, who
had left the security of homes and jobs to form a new family in which
Jesus functioned as something like the head of the household. But Jesus'
way of eating was also centrally an invitation, especially to the poor and
excluded, to take a seat at a banquet prepared for them and now made
ready with the dawning of a new age. There may be no more important
link between ecclesiology and evangelism than the table fellowship that

Christians believe both constitutes them as a distinctive people and at the same time stands as an invitation to the rest of the world. Here is an instance where the strong assertion of a group's identity need not be understood as excluding others but may instead be understood as a posture of openness and invitation along the margins of difference.

The centrality of this distinctive table fellowship is what draws feminist theologian Letty Russell in her book *Church in the Round* to God's household as the most appropriate image for any understanding of the church that takes seriously Christ's "table principle" and the shape of his preaching—an invitation to those on the margins of society to come share in the feasting of this new *oikos* (Luke 19:1–10; cf. Russell 1993:25). Russell prefers the domestic imagery of the household to more patriarchal images such as kingship or kingdom and the hierarchical language implied by such images. But this preference for the domestic over the patriarchal should not be understood as a preference for the domestic over the political (and thus a reversal of Arendt).

On the contrary, Russell finds in domestic imagery of households, kitchens, and table fellowship the resources for articulating a politics of Christian leadership, power, justice, and community, thereby demonstrating that not all politics must be patriarchal. In fact, if we recall that our word *economics* is derived from the Greek words for both "household" and "rule, law, or order," we are justified in claiming that for the church, our economics *is* our politics. How God's household is ordered, who is welcome at the table, and, in fact, at what sort of table we gather (round or hierarchical)—all of these "economic" considerations display our politics. Russell's own vision of a "church in the round," gathered in God's household and around God's table of justice, equality, and inclusion, suggests a particular way of configuring and sharing power, making decisions, organizing work, and welcoming those into the family who are strangers or who once were excluded. Her work, I believe, constitutes the closest thing to a feminist theology of evangelism I know of, despite the fact that she is like most feminists, who, for reasons worth considering, do not talk much about evangelism.[21]

21. See also Russell 1978. Feminists have not had much to say about the practice of evangelism, nor have very many of those who have written about evangelism been women (much less feminists). There are likely multiple reasons for this, but insofar as the practice of evangelism is taken necessarily to be tied to soteriological paradigms that are individualistic, hierarchical, and even militaristic (relying on the language of "campaigns," "winning," and "conquering"), it is necessarily incompatible with feminist principles and insights. That evangelism need not be tied to such paradigms and imagery is, of course, central to the argument of this book. Feminist reticence to talk about evangelism explicitly does not mean, however, that most evangelism has been carried out by males rather than females.

While it is unlikely that a feminist like Russell would find acceptable any talk of God as the "head" of the household (thereby projecting a hierarchical divine order onto the church), one could also make the case, as does Hütter, that the very fact that God is the head of the household prevents us from the temptation of inscribing our own hierarchical and oppressive social relationships (our own "household codes") into God's household. The economy of God's household does, to be sure, imply a trinitarian set of relationships that are "irreversible" and "rather than being freely disposed, are fixed." But this economic logic does not perpetuate the kind of hierarchy and exclusion we see in the *oikos* of antiquity; instead it "radically calls into question the *oikos* of antiquity itself, since those who by definition were excluded from the polis of antiquity and imprisoned in the *oikos*, namely, women, children, and slaves, all similarly become through baptism 'fellow citizens' (*sympolitai*) of that particular public that is entirely determined by God's own economy, God's own 'household rule'" (Hütter 2000:164).

Hütter's argument makes sense, though it is not clear that over the centuries it has proved to have the effect he envisions—in fact, quite the opposite. That does not mean, of course, that household imagery is inadequate for thinking about *ecclesia* and evangelism or that we ought to give up on the language of God as head of the household. But it may mean that we would do well to express that headship in more inclusive language and "round" images if it is to convey what we intend and if it is to sustain a Christian economics in our time (Russell, for example, rather than using "head of household" language, can speak of the table as "prepared by" God and of Jesus as the "host").

This much I believe must be said, however: the way Christians eat together, keep time, celebrate, forgive debts, express thanks, show hospitality, demonstrate compassion, live simply, and share their material resources with one another is an actual participation in the life of the triune God through whose Spirit we have been incorporated into a body whose head is Christ. Likewise, it is in practices such as these that the church shares this divine life with the world thereby living out its mission as a model "family of believers" (1 Peter 2:17). Christian evangelism, as I hope to show, is thoroughly economic in nature, and this economics has to do not only with money but with all of our household practices as they are lived out in the world. The economic patterns displayed and enacted in such practices are a necessary condition for inviting the world into a new *oikos* that by its very existence subverts rival ideological claims about family, gender, race, sexuality, or class.

The entirety of the Christian's economic life is premised on what we have received from God as a gift and as a participation. In contrast to the economics of modernity premised on scarcity and competition, a eucharistic economics is an economics of abundance, generosity, and overflowing. We see this abundance narrated in God's feeding of Israel in the wilderness with manna and quail, in the prophetic vision of shalom, and in Israel's provisions for the poor and the sojourner. We see it in Jesus' feeding of the multitudes, the filling of fishnets, the "wasted" perfume poured out on Jesus, and the parables of banqueting and feasting. And we see it in the story of Pentecost, where the pouring out of the Spirit brings into existence a community so united that "there was not a needy person among them" (Acts 4:34) and for whom energy, creativity, and possibilities now exist that were never imagined before. In fact, the entire story of the trinitarian God is the story of a divine overflowing and surplus that creates, reaches out, redeems, gifts, sanctifies, and guides. It is only in the context of such abundance that the virtues of charity, hope, and faith can be cultivated (because they are essentially gifts) and that the economic commands we encounter in the Bible come to make sense as *for* us rather than *against* us (Long 2000:237–38). When abundance rather than scarcity defines our situation, we need not steal or covet; we are able to lend "expecting nothing in return" (Luke 6:35). Likewise, trading practices can be carried out honestly and without exploitation.

The logic of God's reign is a logic of extravagance and superfluity premised on God's victory over death in Christ, which releases us from fear and liberates us for hope and love. Thus, while the premise of modern economics is that "all is insufficient and must be struggled for through an antagonistic competition for scarce resources" (Long 2000:92), eucharistic economics is grounded in the confidence that "God is able to provide you with every blessing in abundance, so that by always having enough of everything, you may share abundantly in every good work" (2 Cor. 9:8). As Jürgen Moltmann puts it,

> Whenever God, the fountain and source of life and all goodly powers, ceases to be a God far away in heaven and becomes present among us, then there is no longer any want, there is no longer any struggle for power either, and no more rivalry. And where there is no struggle for power and no rivalry, the age-old fears of one another we have built up simply fall away, and so do our desperately bottled-up aggressions. We step out into free life. Our fears and our aggressions simply become ludicrous, because there is enough for everyone there. God himself is there. He lives among us and invites us through his Spirit of fellowship to become "of one heart and soul." (1983:131)

"There is enough for everyone." In the church's Pentecostal experience of abundance, where fear and rivalry are canceled, we find the origin not only of a new economic ethic but of the practice of evangelism, which is itself premised on abundance rather than scarcity. For the gospel, to put it simply, is a gift. It cannot be commodified, bought, sold, bartered, or traded. Its value is not dependent upon its utility within a market of "helpful" and "satisfying" options. Rather, the gospel is life. And the desire to share that life with others finds its wellspring in thanksgiving (*eucharistia*) for our having received it abundantly and gratuitously.

How then does the practice of evangelism inhabit this ecclesial household in which an abundant, eucharistic fellowship is central and defining? In what ways does this fellowship determine evangelism by shaping the *habitus* in which it makes sense and is rightly ordered as a practice? In what follows I suggest four ways this takes place: liturgically, bodily, eschatologically, and heterologically (that is, in relation to alterity, to "the other").

Eucharistic Economics and the Liturgical Formation of Evangelism

If the first thing to be said about Christian eucharistic practice is that it is a daily practice of economic and material sharing rather than primarily a ceremonial or ritual act performed in weekly worship and symbolizing something else, it is also true that this economic sharing was early on correlated with and deeply connected to liturgical practices in which celebration of the Lord's Supper was central. From the very beginning, the disciples' common meals would naturally have been accompanied by prayer and, like all Jewish meals, were considered acts of worship (Yoder 1992a:19). This undoubtedly would have been the case even while Jesus was alive and presiding over meals with his followers. But while what we now call "the Lord's Supper" was certainly not the first time Jesus and his disciples would have taken a meal together, the reenactment of that meal quickly became a way of interpreting, positioning, and shaping all other meals so that the Eucharist would become "the meal of meals."

While it is impossible to know how the original relationship between liturgical practice and economic practice developed among Christians, that they implied one another can be assumed not only from Luke's account of the church's beginning in Acts but from Paul's instructions in 1 Corinthians 11, where economic division and social ranking are understood to be incompatible with correct eucharistic practice. The church's celebration of the Lord's Supper need not therefore be seen as a removal of Christian table fellowship from its original context of daily economic life, but rather the proper posturing—physically, imaginatively, narratively, doxologically, and christologically—of the church and its economic life toward God and world, in and through the rhythms and movements, assembling and sending forth (in other words, the liturgy), enacted in the Eucharist.

This liturgical patterning and positioning of Christian economics is critical for the practice of evangelism, for in the double movement to and from the Lord's table a community of witnesses is created and made competent to be for the world something it otherwise would not and could not be. This "something" we may call salvation, or, as in John's Gospel, we may refer to it simply as "life," but it takes many forms—bread, housing, solidarity, hope, justice, mercy, and healing. The Eucharist is a gift and a blessing that, by *making the church what it is* (Schmemann 1997:26), makes the church what it is *for the world*, an entirely new configuring of relationships in which we come to live "as a member of a body which transcends every exclusiveness of a biological or social kind" (Zizioulas 1997:60). Thus, eucharistic practice fixes the balance between Christian identity and witness by removing the difference between the two. The Eucharist is "the *moment of truth*" in which we can now see the world "in Christ, as it really is, and not from our particular and therefore limited and partial points of view" (ibid. 44). Far from an escape from the world, it is only from this vantage point that we can begin to be a people *for* the world.

It is true, of course, that the liturgical celebration of Eucharist has often become detached from the real world of hunger and thirst and been subjected to intricate and often futile debates about what it "symbolizes" rather than a public offer to the world of a new table fellowship embodied in simple daily household practices such as economic sharing and eating together. But this represents a faulty liturgical theology rather than a fault with the liturgical ordering of economic practice. Apart from having our material and economic life formed rightly through worship in relation to the life we have received from God in Christ, the church cannot be life for the world. As Nicolas Berdyaev once said, "The question of bread for myself is a material question, but the question of bread for my neighbours, for everybody, is a spiritual and a religious question. . . . Christians ought to be permeated with a sense of the religious importance of the elementary daily needs of [people], the vast masses of [people], and not to despise these needs from the point of view of an exalted spirituality" (1937:225–26).

Because of this eucharistic positioning of evangelism, we might be tempted to treat the Eucharist as something "useful." Some of the language in the preceding paragraphs might even seem to open itself to this distortion ("the Eucharist makes us competent," "it helps us to see rightly," etc.). But the liturgical positioning of Christian economic life shapes evangelism by reinforcing the utter difference, extravagance, and "useless beauty" of worship and eucharistic practice. Thus, the hijacking of worship in the name of marketing the church to unbelievers can never be reconciled with eucharistic beauty. In contrast to a modern economics in which value is determined by utility, the logic of Eucharist is the logic of donation and thanksgiving. A eucharistic evangelism removes the church's practice of sharing its life with the world from the context of production, commodification, consumption, and accumulation. What the church has to give it never possessed, and so it cannot subject its gift to a calculus of utility and exchange. Its invitation and offer arises out of a charity that overflows into the world rather than out of a calculation of effectiveness or the likelihood of receptivity.

Eucharistic beauty shapes evangelism liturgically by inviting the world to Christ's table and into Christ's household, not in such a way as to diminish the difference of that household from the world but rather by starting with that difference. As Schmemann says,

> The liturgy begins then as a real separation from the world. In our attempt to make Christianity appeal to the [person] on the street, we have often minimized, or even completely forgotten, this necessary separation. We always want to make Christianity "understandable" and "acceptable" to this mythical "modern" [person] on the street. And we forget that the Christ of whom we speak is "not of this world," and that after his resurrection He was not recognized even by His own disciples. (1997:27)

Difference from the world is not, however, distance from the world. In the "ascension to heaven" that is the church's worship, the church is made a witnessing body in and for the world. We should not be surprised, therefore, when the world is attracted by our worship of the God whom we serve. Arguments over whether high worship or low worship is better for reaching the unchurched usually turn on the question of the utility of worship. But the truth and the beauty of which the church is made witnesses in worship is never merely "functional" or "useful."

It is helpful to recall that the original meaning of the Greek word *leitourgia* is "an action by which a group of people become something corporately which they had not been as a mere collection of individuals—a whole greater than the sum of its parts" (Schmemann 1997:25). If this is true, then evangelism is inescapably liturgical just as worship must always be evangelistic. This is not, however, because worship resituates the gospel in terms of our lives in an existentially compelling way but rather because it resituates our lives in terms of the gospel in a doxologically truthful way. Worship is "a way of seeing; a grasp of which end is up, which way is forward" (Yoder 1998:129). It is therefore a way of re-creating our world by allowing it to be confronted with a new one, a world that in worship we are invited to make our own.

Eucharistic Economics and the Bodily Formation of Evangelism

One of the distinctively modern deformations of evangelism is its restriction to the realm of the private, the interior, and the individual, a realm that comes to be known as the "spiritual." Evangelism imagined from within a eucharistic economics, by contrast, is social and incarnate. This bodiliness makes it no less "personal" (or "spiritual," as Berdyaev might affirm), for a eucharistic economics is not an impersonal law or abstract system but a communion of persons. As the church gathers around a common table in remembrance, confession, reconciliation, and thanksgiving, a new space is created where bodies once separated and placed in opposition to one another (Jew and Gentile, male and female, slave and free) are now united.[22] This it does by enacting a participation in one another that contradicts social relations based on contract and exchange. Thus, the politics of inclusion proclaimed and enacted in baptism, whereby natural and social divisions are reconciled rather than being homogenized or erased, is reenacted in every celebration of the Eucharist. The church is made capable of witnessing, because it now *is* a witness. It has become something different from and for the world. Of course, if salvation is shifted from everyday practices of eating, sharing, and reconciliation to the individual's personal and private relationship with God, a visible social body is largely irrelevant to Christian witness, and our economics must be "applied" or "interpreted" in order to be offered. The church then can be at best only a means for initiating and conserving the private relationships of individuals with God.

Eucharistic life positions the practice of evangelism from within an imagining of space and time that is literally a "re-membering" of Christ's body (Cavanaugh 1998:229). In this way, the truth that the church has to offer and into which it invites persons is not merely a set of creeds, doctrines, or propositions to be heard and believed or to whose authority persons are asked to consent. Rather, that truth is Christ himself, who is present to the world not as a private experience or as a theological abstraction but in and through a community of material sharing, discipline, and reconciliation.[23] God's love is not an abstraction. It has a body.

22. I find useful here Michel de Certeau's distinction between *place* and *space* in his *The Practice of Everyday Life*. While the former is proper, stable, definable, and limited (as, for example, a street defined by urban planners), the latter comes into existence through actual use and movement: "In short, *space is a practiced place*. Thus the street geometrically defined by urban planning is transformed into a space by walkers" (1984:117). Indeed, as Cavanaugh suggests, the storied performance of space may very well be "an act of resistance to the dominant overcoding of the map" (2002:117).

23. On this point see especially John Zizioulas, according to whom "all separation between Christology and ecclesiology vanishes in the Spirit" (1997:111). In the Eucharist, "Christ Himself becomes revealed as truth not *in* a community, but *as* a community. So

Jesus is the "bread of life," and his ecclesial body becomes bread for
the world by being offered as a way of life in which bread is physically
shared, strangers are tangibly welcomed, and debts are actually canceled.
In this way, eucharistic practice creates the imaginative time and space
in which a new body can be present in the world and for the world.

Following William Cavanaugh's analysis in *Torture and Eucharist*, I am
here deliberately working against an ecclesiology in which the church,
if it is a body at all, is a "mystical" body that functions as the soul of the
larger society and in which it is allowed to exercise only a "spiritual"[24]
influence on the world, usually in indirect ways through the inspiration
of the individual consciences of its members.[25] Evangelism, in such an
ecclesiology, is restricted to saving persons' souls, while their bodies are
handed over to society or the state and the institutions of society and
state (the mall or the military, for example). As Cavanaugh explains, for
patristic and early medieval theology, the ecclesial body of Christ (the
church) was the *corpus verum*, the true body of Christ, while the sacramental body of Christ (the bread and the wine) was the *corpus mysticum*,
Christ's mystical body.[26] But in this later ecclesiology, just the opposite is
the case. The true body of Christ came to be identified with the visible,
sacramental body, while the ecclesial body was made mystical, invisible.
This, as Cavanaugh interestingly suggests, "would be slight comfort to

truth is not just something 'expressed' or 'heard,' a propositional or a logical truth; but
something which *is*, i.e. an ontological truth: the community itself becoming the truth"
(ibid. 115). Zizioulas goes on to say, "*Christ without His body is not Christ but an individual
of the worst type*" (ibid. 182). Christ is not, for Christians, simply a historical personage.
We live "in Christ" and become part of his body. Christ, who exists in the Spirit today,
exists in and through communion.

24. I use the words *mystical* and *spiritual* in quotation marks here because the way
they are cast in opposition to the real, the material, or the visible in this context I take to
be a tragically false dualism.

25. This does not mean, by the way, that the church is any less "institutional"; in fact, a
deeply institutionalized and overly bureaucratic church, as Cavanaugh points out, turns out
to be perfectly compatible with a "mystical body" ecclesiology. See Cavanaugh's discussion
at this point, especially his tracing of "mystical body" or New Christendom ecclesiologies
in chapter 4 of *Torture and Eucharist*. As Cavanaugh says, "The church must see that its
own disciplinary resources—Eucharist, penance, virtue, works of mercy, martyrdom—are
not matters of the soul which may somehow 'animate' the 'real world' of bodies, but are
rather body/soul disciplines meant to produce actions, practices, habits that are visible
in the world" (1998:197).

26. According to Schmemann, "What 'happens' to bread and wine happens because
something has, first of all, happened to us, to the Church. It is because we have 'constituted'
the Church, and this means we have followed Christ in His ascension; because He has
accepted us at His table in His kingdom; because, in terms of theology, we have entered
the Eschaton, and are now standing beyond time and space; it is because all this has first
happened to us that something will happen to bread and wine" (1997:37).

the Christian on the battlefield who finds that a fellow member of the mystical body of Christ is trying to blow his legs off" (1998:212).

The identification of sin with that which is visible and bodily, on the one hand, and salvation (or the "true church") with that which is invisible and incorporeal, on the other hand, is, to be sure, not a distinctively modern phenomenon but has plagued Christianity from its beginnings. But as Schmemann rightly points out, human "fallenness" did not originate in a love of the world, a preference of the material over the spiritual; it was instead our having made the world "material" in the first place when we were to have "transformed it into 'life in God,' filled with meaning and spirit" (1997:18). The fallenness of humanity, therefore, is "noneucharistic life in a noneucharistic world," while salvation is eucharistic life that overcomes the dichotomies of soul and body, spiritual and material, private and public. It is "life in all its totality" that is returned to humans, "given again as sacrament and communion" (ibid. 20). In a world where Christianity is no longer the driving cultural force, nothing could be more vital to the church's ability to bear faithful witness to "life in all its totality" than its visibility—not by way of a return to the Constantinian *corpus Christianum* but as a eucharistic "contrast-society."[27] Other social bodies are likely to be offended and threatened by such visible and economic corporeality and will try to find ways to make the church invisible—by relegating it to the sphere of the "private," for example. That is why, while evangelism is always an invitation, it is bound to be somewhat repulsive precisely to the extent that it is shaped by a fully embodied ecclesial economics. As Schleiermacher once remarked, the world can tolerate Christianity "so long as it only infects individuals here and there," but "the common danger is increased and everything put in jeopardy by too close association among the patients" (ibid. 147). Evangelism is the bodily (and therefore subversive) announcement to the world that God desires whole persons in communion rather than disembodied souls.

Given this visible, bodily nature of the church and its witness, one might be tempted toward the ecclesial triumphalism that has often plagued evangelism, especially when practiced within a Constantinian social imagination. This, however, would be a failure to recognize that

27. "The early Church's theological disputes about the real bodiliness of the Risen One [e.g., Lk 24:39] also touch on the bodiliness of the Church. It is visible, palpable, tangible. It is socially organized. Anyone who locates it only in the word of proclamation or in the hearts of the faithful, and pretends that invisibility is its true nature, takes seriously neither its existence as the beginning of the eschatological Israel nor its origins in the Risen One and his bodiliness. Because the Church is a sacrament of salvation it must be as physical as its sacraments" (Lohfink 1999:207). On the church as a "contrast-society," see also Lohfink 1984:122–32, 157–63.

it is not just any body into which the church is made in the Eucharist but *Christ's* body, a body that suffered and was crucified. In fact, the first evangelists interpreted this death through the symbol of the paschal lamb that, having been killed, becomes food for the world. An evangelism patterned eucharistically will likewise affirm that our incorporation into Christ means that "we then become food for the world, to be broken, given away, and consumed" (Schmemann 1997:232). To be made part of Christ's body is to be made part of Christ's cross; hence, there is no way to avoid the fact that evangelistic witness will always be rooted in disciplines of self-emptying and dispossession that are risky, costly, and, to all outward appearances, unhealthy and unnatural. This is one reason that for the early Christians, evangelistic exemplars were "martyrs"—those who, as Cavanaugh reminds us, "keep alive the subversive memory of Christ through their *public* witness, and thus make the body of Christ visible" (1998:58).

It is essential at this point to underscore that the emphasis on sacrifice and martyrdom within a eucharistic economics is not meant as a commendation of sacrifice itself, nor is it to advocate in any way for a satisfaction theory of the atonement.[28] To be sure, to offer Christ is to offer a form of life that entails the cross. But there is nothing in itself redemptive about a violent death at the hands of the world's powers. The death of Christ is not a glorification of violence but an affirmation of the utterly nonviolent nature of God's reign and the costliness of a discipleship that refuses to strike back or take matters into its own hands. Christ's torture and death must always be spoken of in the context of his life as "the price of his social nonconformity" and in the context of his resurrection as a victory that signals not the delay but the arrival of God's reign (Yoder 1972:97).[29] In no way should evangelism as martyrdom mean that violence is being praised or cast as redemptive (contrast Tertullian's claim in the second century that "the blood of Christians is seed"[30] with Thomas Jefferson's "The tree of liberty must be refreshed from time to time with the blood

28. This is also the position of Hauerwas, who agrees with the feminist critique of the idea of sacrifice: based on an abstract account of sacrifice separated from the cross, self-sacrifice is made into a "norm in and of itself," and this is "inherently destructive to women." Rather, "Christ got put to death for reminding the world that God is our ruler. What is at stake here is to call into question certain satisfaction theories of the atonement that are correlative to a church that is socially accommodated" (Hauerwas and Willimon 1992:39).

29. The fullness of the church's evangelistic offer can be maintained only insofar as we are able to keep the life, death, and resurrection of Jesus together in that offer. This is, I take it, not unlike John Wesley's insistence that Christ be proclaimed in "all his offices"—prophet, priest, and king. Cf. Sermon 36, "The Law Established through Faith: Discourse II," §1.6, 1975:2:37–38.

30. *Apology* 50, in Roberts and Donaldson 1931:3:55.

of patriots and tyrants"[31]). The only sacrifice celebrated and memorialized in the Eucharist is that of Christ on the cross, and his sacrifice is, as the author of Hebrews argues, the end of all sacrificial systems and scapegoating.

Eucharistic evangelism does not prey on weakness, nor does it victimize those in need by trading its help for their "conversions." It does not ask for sacrifice from those who have already been sacrificed by the world. Rather, by standing in solidarity with them (often at a "sacrificial" cost to the evangelist), it is a witness and protest against all sacrificial violence, "for its aim is not to create new victims but rather martyrs, witnesses to the end of victimization" (Cavanaugh 1998:232).

The gospel the church offers the world is always public because it is, to put it bluntly, a body. The gospel is not a set of beliefs or doctrines that first need to be decoded and then reencoded so as to be intelligible in this or that context. The gospel is Christ himself; and Christ has a body. But bodies are public precisely because they are present. This is why it is so important that the church, which is Christ's body, be made holy in bodily ways through the worship, habits, and service it has been given by God, for as the body of Christ it is a public sign of God's glory, not its own. Another way of saying this is that the salvation offered by God to the world through the church is not a set of ideas it presents to the world to be judged as credible or incredible and then "decided upon." It is quite literally an *oikonomia* to be patiently "shared" and into which persons are invited to be incorporated by the power of the Spirit. There is no greater barrier to evangelism than a church that lacks this *oikonomia* and in which the marks of the body of Christ such as worship, interethnic inclusion, forgiveness, reconciliation and peacemaking, enemy-love, and suffering are absent or distorted. Sanctification does not happen *first* behind the closed doors of the church and prior to its bodily social engagement with the world. Rather, the church's eucharistic engagement with the world *is* its sanctification as a visible and public body that glorifies God.

To reject a "mystical body" ecclesiology and to affirm instead with Martin Luther that the church is "recognized" externally by various "marks" is not a denial of the fact that there is yet a hiddenness to the church, in the sense that the church as the body of Christ is not fully revealed, not fully here yet.[32] But this hiddenness is not best understood with the categories of visibility and invisibility, given that they typically presuppose a dualism in which *visibility* refers to materiality and *invis-*

---

31. Letter to William Stephens Smith, November 13, 1787, in *The Papers of Thomas Jefferson*, ed. Julian P. Boyd (Princeton, NJ: Princeton University Press, 1955), 12:356.

32. On this point, see Luther, "On the Councils and the Church," in 1955–76:41:148–68.

ibility refers to immateriality. The hiddenness of the church lies not in its invisibility but in its being an eschatological anticipation and foretaste of that which is yet to come (Forde 1999:1).

Eucharistic Economics and the Eschatological Formation of Evangelism

As hinted at in the last sentence of the previous paragraph, if evangelism is to be practiced from within a eucharistic reimagining of space in which the church is constituted as the body of Christ for the world, it is also to be practiced from within a eucharistic reimagining of *time*. In fact, the gift we receive in the Eucharist is a gift of time (Schmemann 1997:47). In proclaiming Christ's death, confessing his resurrection, and anticipating his return, the Eucharist provides a passage or transformation of our time into Christ's time. Because of this, even though the Eucharist enacts the church as a visible and social body that has "presence" and creates "space," that body is not so much a bounded or enclosed place as a pilgrimage toward an end that, while it has already broken into history, awaits its future consummation and makes of life a sojourn, a restless seeking, even a homelessness.

To live eucharistically is to live at the intersection of "dangerous memory" (Metz 1980) and restless hope in a way that is at odds with a secular imagination of history. The former is "a uniform sequence of cause and effect, measured not by the divine plan, but by clock and calendar" in which persons "move linearly out of the past, through the present and into an endless future" (Cavanaugh 1998:223). A eucharistic and eschatological imagination of history, by contrast, narrates the origin of the world in plenitude (God creates not *ex nihilo*, out of nothing, but *ex amore*, out of an overflow of love)[33] and toward a peaceful future that is both already and not yet. Not yet, because the church's sinfulness (rather than its materiality) thwarts it from becoming in the present what it eschatologically is. Already, because "now is the day of salvation" (2 Cor. 6:2). History is pregnant with God's time, with God's end, which irrupts into the present as a *kairos* ("the right time"). Thus we can speak of the church as always and already "a communion of saints," a present communion of an eternal gathering across space and time. To be saved is to become a fellow citizen with those who have gone before us, to be made part of a new world and a new time, heaven's time.

33. See Michael E. Lodahl, "Creation out of Nothing? Or Is *Next* to Nothing Enough?" in *Thy Nature and Thy Name Is Love: Wesleyan and Process Theologies in Dialogue*, ed. Bryan P. Stone and Thomas Jay Oord (Nashville: Kingswood, 2002), 217–38.

Evangelism, when configured within eucharistic time, is essential to the life of every believer, because that life can never be one of only receiving, much less of hoarding God's blessings (recall again the story of the manna in the wilderness). The Christian life is one of day-to-day trust that by sharing what we have received we are not diminished but enriched. Yet even this way of putting it is still not quite right, for in the eucharistic gift of time, what we have received is in fact a way of sharing. The salvation offered by the church to the world is not something it first receives and then offers to others. It is received only and insofar as it is offered to others.[34] To live "between the times," or on a different clock, so to speak, is to operate within a different logic of cause and effect, a transformed sense of agency that is communal, creative, hopeful, and open to surprise. I will have more to say about the significance of this eschatological orientation for how we construe evangelistic agency and effectiveness in chapter 9. But two things should be stressed at this point. First, from within eucharistic timefulness, the church will always see its mission in the world as urgent and will take seriously its calling to read the signs of the times and to treat each moment as if it were "ripe" time. Yet, second, in no way does this mean the church has grounds for narrating its own history or interpreting its own growth in size or influence as part of a steady progress, maturity, and evolution toward God's reign. While we must speak of our participation in God's reign, Christians have no scriptural warrant for understanding themselves as "building" the kingdom of God. Through participation, however, we are called to bear living and embodied witness to it.

The journeying made possible by a eucharistic timefulness reminds us that the church is more like an "event" than a "thing." It is not of course free floating; we inherit from the past the wisdom, structures, institutions, patterns, and exemplars that make a "new world" imaginable. At the same time, the church is eschatological, *in via*. "The eucharistic community," says Zizioulas, "frees it from the causality of natural and historical events, from limitations which are the results of the individualism implied in our natural biological existence," and "manifests the Church not simply as something instituted, that is historically *given*, but also as something *con-stituted*, that is constantly realized as an event of free communion, prefiguring the divine life and the Kingdom to come" (1997:22). "Constantly realized as an event of free communion" is precisely what it means to live as if on a pilgrimage, to live as if we are sojourners in a

34. As Newbigin says, "The corporate nature of the salvation that God purposes is a necessary part of the divine purpose of salvation according to the biblical view that no one could receive it as a direct revelation from above but only through the neighbor, only as part of an action in which one opens one's door and invites one's neighbor to come in" (1995:76).

foreign land. The journey cannot be undertaken if we make ourselves at home in the world or in the world's time. Neither can we undertake the journey if we believe we have already arrived at the journey's end. To evangelize the world while on such a pilgrimage turns out to be a very strange practice, for sojourners are typically the ones who seek welcome, acceptance, and hospitality from those through whose land they journey. But in evangelistic practice, Christian sojourners invite their hosts into their journey and bid them welcome at their table (which is of necessity a "movable feast"), at which there is enough for everyone.

Evangelism is an eschatological activity, but not because it holds out a future reward (or punishment) as a carrot to get people to convert; rather it is because the church knows that "then is now" and that life can no longer be lived on present terms, with present vision, and according to present expectations. Something new has been made possible. Evangelism as an eschatological practice is the offer of a new way of seeing made possible through eucharistic memory, presence, and expectation narrated in the three temporalizations implicit in 1 Corinthians 11:26: "For as often as you eat this bread and drink the cup, you proclaim the Lord's death until he comes" (Cavanaugh 1998:227).

Eucharistic Economics and the Heterological Formation of Evangelism

In the discussion thus far I have been attempting to emphasize the extent to which eucharistic practice forms the church into a distinctive economics in and for the world. It locates the church's social, bodily, and temporal identity relative to the economy of the triune God, gathers a communion of saints from across the ages, and configures Christian life and practice within a social imagination premised on abundance, inclusion, and gratitude. But the language of incorporation, inclusion, gathering, and communion so essential to the significance of Eucharist can be misleading if it is taken as legitimating a totalizing mission in which "otherness" is masked, trivialized, or removed, whether through absorption or elimination. Distinctiveness does not require homogeneity, and while eucharistic practice is indeed a gathering, invitation, and communion, it is also a rupture in every attempt by the church to constitute a totality based on sameness by extending itself indefinitely in space and time.

In this sense the Eucharist as a *gift to* the church is also a *judgment on* the church. Eucharistic evangelism encounters the other *as other* without attempting to eliminate that alterity by dominating, annihilating, or assimilating the other through a unilateral absorption, while at the same time demonstrating hospitality, receptivity, and openness. The embrace of otherness required in evangelism is confident, inviting, and joyous but also vulnerable, humble, and open to refusal.

I cannot do justice here to every form of alterity that might be envisioned as shaping Christian evangelism, but otherness is encountered in at least four perennial forms in the ongoing story of the people of God, each of which makes vital claims upon the church's worship, witness, and obedience: (1) the otherness of the poor, oppressed, orphaned, and widowed; (2) the otherness of strangers, aliens, and sojourners; (3) the otherness of the dead in Christ; and (4) the otherness of nature itself, including all plant and animal life ("otherkind"). In none of these cases is the "other" merely a foil for establishing that which is "not other." Rather, in each encounter with otherness it can also be said that the people of God encounters God as Other and so rediscovers its essential dependence upon God.

To welcome the other is in many respects the essence of evangelistic practice. This is one of the reasons the Eucharist is central to the practice of evangelism, for the Lord's table is a place of welcome and hospitality, an anticipation of the "heavenly banquet of the Lord." Yet how easy and natural it is to welcome only those who are like us. The story of the people of God, however, is a story of hospitality to strangers, to immigrants and refugees, to persons with disabilities, and to those who cannot return our hospitality. We find this hospitality narrated in the story of Abraham and Sarah, whom the writer of Hebrews says entertained angels; we find it in the Levitical gleaning laws that ensured a periphery of cut grain was not harvested but left for the poor to gather; we find it in the story of the woman in the house of Simon who poured expensive perfume on Jesus; and we find it in Jesus' own openness to eating with tax collectors and sinners, thereby incurring the disapproval of the Pharisees and their scribes (Luke 5:30). We also find it in Jesus' claim that whoever shows hospitality to strangers is showing hospitality to him.

But hospitality is exercised inappropriately when employed as a program or strategy for some external end such as adding to the church's numbers. Hospitality is an overflowing embodiment of good news offered without expectation of something in return, not as a utility for something more important or ultimate (in which case hospitality would cease to be hospitality). As Jesus instructs us, "When you give a banquet, invite the poor, the crippled, the lame, and the blind. And you will be blessed, because they cannot repay you" (Luke 14:13–14).

Christine Pohl has shown in her comprehensive study of the topic (1999)[35] that the practice of hospitality is not just about being friendly

---

35. See also Amy G. Oden, ed., *And You Welcomed Me: A Sourcebook on Hospitality in Early Christianity* (Nashville: Abingdon, 2001).

or nice but instead about dignity, respect, care, justice, and empowerment: "Although we often think of hospitality as a tame and pleasant
practice, Christian hospitality has always had a subversive countercultural dimension. . . . Hospitality that welcomes 'the least' and recognizes
their equal value can be an act of resistance and defiance, a challenge
to the values and expectations of the larger community" (1999:61–62).
Hospitality, like the Eucharist itself, has a christological shape and re-
flects the priorities and allegiances embodied in the birth, life, death,
and resurrection of Jesus: solidarity with the poor, identification with
the marginalized, and compassionate suffering with the downtrodden.
In eucharistic liturgy and practice, we are reminded that salvation is not
abstract or immaterial. It has to do with everyday things like hunger and
thirst. It is true, of course, that we may never reduce the hunger of the
world to physical hunger; for eating has always been what Schmemann
calls "the last 'natural sacrament' of family and friendship, of life that
is more than 'eating' and 'drinking'" (1997:16). But precisely because
eating a meal together does more than satiate our hunger, creating and
expressing also a sense of community and solidarity, the presence in our
midst of persons who are hungry or lonely is a double scandal for the
church's witness. It is impossible to eat together joyously at the Lord's
table when those around us go hungry. The church may retreat into affluent ghettoes where it can attempt to avoid contact with hunger and
poverty, but then this can only be understood as a failure to discern the
body of Christ, and so the Lord's table becomes not a place of nourishment but, as Paul insists, a place of judgment (1 Cor. 11:27–30).

Poverty is, in the biblical vision, never something to be put up with
or to be adjusted to as normal.[36] It is, as Arendt says, "a political, not a
natural phenomenon, the result of violence and violation rather than of
scarcity" (1958:56). For this reason, the poor, the hungry, the stranger,
and the oppressed are interpreted as bearers of salvation in the life and
ministry of Jesus. "Besides being human beings," as Archbishop Romero
said, they "are also divine beings, since Jesus said that whatever is done
to them he takes as done to him" (2004:200; Matt. 25:31–46). The point
is not that those who are crucified daily by the economics of our world
are identical to Christ (any similar romanticization of poverty has no
support in Scripture), but they reveal to us the conditions under which
participation in God's reign and incorporation into Christ's body become
for us a possibility. They likewise "interrupt" any disincarnate evangelism that is insulated and isolated from the real world of poverty and

36. Jesus' words "You always have the poor with you" (Matt. 26:11) are to be interpreted
as implying not resignation but rather a commission. This is true also in the original context
of Deuteronomy: "Since there will never cease to be some in need on the earth, I therefore
command you, 'Open your hand to the poor and needy neighbor in your land'" (15:11).

marginalization; they contextualize the very meaning of "good news" so that, as with Jesus, it is always "good news for the poor."

To accept the call to Christian discipleship is to accept responsibility for a situation in which many in the world have no bread on the table and to be empowered through a Spirit-created community to be that bread. To be an evangelizing church is to be more than "willing" to invite to our table the poor and the hungry who might stray by our door. It is to go out into the streets and seek those for whom the table of the Lord has been prepared. It is to alter the way we spend and store our money such that resources will be freed up for the relief of the poor. It is to make sure that our buildings, sanctuaries, and meeting houses are places that cry out welcome to the poor. Any evangelistic strategy designed to make the rich and powerful comfortable can find no home in the story of the people of God and in a world where wealth and poverty do not exist in a vacuum but are related to one another as cause and effect.

The basis for such radical hospitality in the practice of evangelism is, from the standpoint of the Bible, the fact that we the evangelizers, the people of God, were also once strangers and aliens (Eph. 2:19). The experience of being a stranger is consistently presented in the Hebrew Scriptures as the normative foundation for the treatment of other strangers. So, for example, in Exodus 23:9 we find the instructions "You shall not oppress a resident alien; you know the heart of an alien, for you were aliens in the land of Egypt." Anyone who has ministered with the poor and the disenfranchised will recognize immediately the truth of this identification—the seemingly infinite capacity of the poor to show hospitality as compared to those who live in affluence and abundance. Perhaps that is why, as Pohl claims, "the periods in church history when hospitality has been most vibrantly practiced have been times when the hosts were themselves marginal to their larger society" (1999:106).

The evangelistic "interruption" of the poor and the stranger who are invited to the Lord's table must be construed, therefore, not as a negation but as a donation. The divine excess and abundance encountered in the poor and the sojourner interrupt our witness and our invitation and subvert our paternalism and condescension, but always in the mode of gift. Evangelistic hospitality, accordingly, is never to be understood merely as an act of *offering* or *helping* but as a willingness to *receive* and *discover*. The stranger, the poor, and the powerless can be treated as "other" in a proper and eucharistic sense only when we come to understand our own otherness at the table of the Lord and our utter dependence upon and thankfulness to God.[37] Again, exile and margin-

---

37. Indeed, as John Wesley once said, "Religion must not go from the greatest to the least, or the power would appear to be of [humans]" (1979:3:178).

ality are not the exception but the normative condition of the people of God in the world.[38]

While the Eucharist is a practice that creates a space and time for the people of God as a body, we must also conclude that it is a practice that makes space and time for the other—both in our hearts and outwardly and concretely (cf. Pohl 1999:39, 152). For this reason, the eucharistic practice of hospitality can at times be experienced as a displacement: we are called from our *other* tables—tables where not all are welcome and where only those who have money can afford to gather—to a new, "round" table not of our creation, prepared by Christ himself, where all are welcome and equal. This is not to suggest that the people of God require no firm sense of identity, for as Russell rightly cautions, "if a Christian community has no sense of its identity in Christ as the center of its life, it will not have a great deal of generosity and compassion to share with others" (1993:178). That identity is always to be found in Christ at the center of the church's life, worship, and practice rather than in carefully maintained boundaries out at the edge.[39] The unity sought by the body of Christ is demanding, requires discipline, and may even entail "excommunication" of members who violate that body (hospitality is not an unqualified inclusion).[40] But it does not seek a unanimity

38. Hauerwas puts this just right when he says,

Christians know no "barbarians," but only strangers whom we hope to make our friends. We extend hospitality to God's kingdom by inviting the stranger to share our story. Of course we know that the stranger does not come to us as a cipher, but the stranger also has a story to tell us. Through the stranger's reception of the story of Jesus (which may often take the form of rejection), we too learn more fully to hear the story of God. Without the constant challenge of the stranger—who often, interestingly enough, is but one side of ourselves—we are tempted to lose the power of Jesus' story because we have so conventionalized it. (1983:109)

39. Or perhaps it would be better to say, as Russell suggests, that we do need to "tend" our boundaries and margins, but in order to *connect* with the other rather than to *protect* ourselves from the other (1993:176).

40. As Cavanaugh explains,

Excommunication, therefore, is not the expulsion of the sinner from the church, but a recognition that the sinner has *already excluded himself* from communion in the body of Christ by his own actions. Excommunication by the community clarifies for the sinner the seriousness of the offense, and, if accompanied by a proper penitential discipline, shows the sinner the way to reconciliation with the body of Christ while shielding the sinner from the adverse effects of continued participation in the Eucharist in the absence of true reconciliation. As an invitation to reconciliation, then, excommunication done well is an act of *hospitality*, in which the church does not expel the sinner, but says to her, "You are already outside our communion. Here is what you need to do to come back in." Excommunication does not abandon the sinner to her fate; in fact, precisely the opposite is the case. It is *failure* to excommunicate the notorious sinner that leaves her to eat and drink her own condemnation. (1998:243)

where everyone is asked or expected to look, act, and think alike. The practice of eucharistic hospitality is therefore always unsettling, because it is rooted in an identity that is essentially a letting go, a release of all grasping, utilizing, and control.

Like the poor and the stranger, the dead have little place in modern societies because they have no "utility." Only that which bears an exchange value is allowed to make a claim on us, and so the dead, who can do nothing for us, are either forgotten or fetishized (and thereby turned into a commodity). Our medical, bereavement, and funerary practices keep the bodies of the dead at a distance and diminish any contact with them that is not entirely antiseptic and pumped full of formaldehyde. In the Christian household, however, both the living and the dead belong.[41] The dead in Christ commune with and make a claim on the living. This "communication" with the dead is not morbid, and though it is unsupported in modern cultures, it is quite common in cultures around the globe that have not yet been given over wholly to an instrumental rationality in which value is defined by usefulness (indeed, these cultures frequently include the dead in a ritual meal). For Christians, death does not have the last word, and the table of the Lord, in its reconstitution of time and in its re-membering of the body of Christ, is literally a gathering of saints from across the ages within a local assembly. To evangelize the world, therefore, is to invite persons into a concrete local fellowship that is at the same time made truly *catholic* ("according to the whole") around that table.

Memory, according to J. B. Metz, is a form of solidarity with the dead, the suffering, and the conquered that is "dangerous" because it "breaks the grip of history as a history of triumph and conquest interpreted dialectically or as evolution" (1980:184). The dead are part of our story, and through a eucharistic solidarity with the dead, we are saved both from resignation and from narcissism and thus freed to be life for the world. The "great cloud of witnesses" (for they are, indeed, evangelists) will not let us forget; and neither will they let us reduce hope to that which our own rationalities and technologies might produce in the world. Evangelism carried out eucharistically is both faithful and hopeful, because it is a telling and a sharing that is essentially a "remembering forward."

Among the "others" we might consider as shaping evangelism, animal and plant life might seem like rather unusual candidates. It does not make much sense initially to think of "otherkind" as potentially

---

41. As Thomas Long says of Christian funeral rituals historically, "The dead body was neither a mere shell to be discarded as rubbish nor the totality of the person to be clutched and preserved in desperation, but a tangible sign, like the eucharistic bread, of God's gift of life" (quoted in Budde and Brimlow 2002:106).

members of the body of Christ or as invited to the Lord's table. But let us recall that throughout the story of the people of God, any notion of a purely individualistic, private, or even anthropocentric shalom is self-contradictory nonsense. Shalom is by its very nature a communal reality and one, moreover, that extends to plant and animal life, requiring our just social relations with them and stewardship of them.[42] A eucharistic economics does not idolize or fetishize nature, but it affirms that salvation is cosmic in scope, and it enacts a participation in Christ in which the sacramentality of all nature is affirmed as proclaiming God's glory. The question is not so much whether we are to evangelize nature as whether we will allow ourselves to evangelize *with* nature and to be evangelized *by* nature.

Evangelism, when practiced from within an economics of the household of God, must always be practiced in such a way as to celebrate God's love for the entire world and to mediate that love without reducing it to its utility for humans. In this way, we can speak of humans as having a priestly function not only relative to one another but relative to nature, a priestly relationship that reconnects it to God and "liberates it from slavery to necessity by letting it develop its potentialities to the maximum" (Zizioulas 1997:119). Our task then is to make of nature a "eucharistic reality," to free nature from its subjection to our technological enslavements so that, like us, it may be "capable of communion" (ibid.). In a world where our banqueting is frequently at the expense not only of the poor but also of the ecosphere, eucharistic fellowship at the Lord's table forms us into a people who are learning how to eat properly at other tables (see Lodahl 2003).

If the *telos* of all Christian practice, including especially the practice of evangelism, is the eschatological city of God—the city of shalom—we also know that within this renewed and redeemed city is a renewed and redeemed nature. And so that city is narrated as an everlasting fellowship of the people of God with nature and with God:

> Then the angel showed me the river of the water of life, bright as crystal, flowing from the throne of God and of the Lamb through the middle of the street of the city. On either side of the river is the tree of life with its twelve kinds of fruit, producing its fruit each month; and the leaves of

42. Remember that the commandment to keep the sabbath includes not only people but livestock (Exod. 20:8-11). It is also worth noting that once the people of Nineveh had been called to repentance by the prophet Jonah, they put sackcloth, a symbol of repentance, not only on themselves but on their animals (Jonah 3:5-8). Indeed, God's own self-revelation to Jonah includes compassion specifically for animals: "And should I not be concerned about Nineveh, that great city, in which there are more than a hundred and twenty thousand persons who do not know their right hand from their left, and also many animals?" (4:11).

the tree are for the healing of the nations. Nothing accursed will be found there any more. But the throne of God and of the Lamb will be in it, and his servants will worship him; they will see his face, and his name will be on their foreheads. And there will be no more night; they need no light of lamp or sun, for the Lord God will be their light, and they will reign forever and ever. (Rev. 22:1–5)

8

Evangelism as a Practice
of the Holy Spirit

In chapter 1, I argued on the basis of MacIntyre's thought that to construe evangelism as an exercise in the "production" of converts would be to misunderstand its nature as a practice embodying ends internal to itself. Evangelism does not necessarily produce anything, nor is it a means to some other end; rather, faithfulness in witnessing to God's peaceable reign is its end, even if that witness is rejected. MacIntyre argues for a notion of practice that moves beyond the more conservative aspects of an Aristotelian teleology tied to the social structures of the ancient *polis* by reconceiving the good of a life from within a historically situated and community-traditioned narrative that specifies the movement, telos, continuity, and unity of a human life. For MacIntyre, of course, *narrative*, *community*, and *tradition* are essential but strictly formal philosophical categories. For Christians, however, that community is particular and identifiable, the *ecclesia*, and its story is the story of the people of God, a people created in God's calling and formation of Israel and extended messianically in Christ to include Gentiles. The *telos*, or "end," of the story (and therefore the eschatology of that community), moreover, is vastly different from the ends of other stories (and likewise from the eschatologies of other communities), especially those that prevail in modern Western cultures.

How evangelism is practiced has everything to do, or so I have been arguing, with the story with which it begins and the community in which it holds together and makes sense. Only as eschatologically ordered toward the end narrated by the story of the people of God and from within the context of a new *polis* and a new *oikos* created by the Holy Spirit can the practice of evangelism escape the expedient, conquering, and short-sighted pragmatism of modern politics as well as the productive and consumerist logic of modern capitalist economies (both of which provide the platform for much of church growth theory). MacIntyre's work is certainly open to such an eschatology (indeed, he actively resists the prevailing eschatology of modern liberalism), but he does not develop this theologically. In this chapter, I attempt to take up the task.

As a way of doing this, I will build upon the significance of eschatology, developed in the previous chapter's discussion of the Eucharist, for how we understand the relationship between means and ends. Eschatology is not simply about the ends toward which our lives and our actions are aimed but also about the means internal to those ends. In this way, the church's eschatology has everything to do with how we understand agency within the logic of Christian practice. While in the previous chapter I attempted to show how eucharistic practice positions evangelism from within an eschatology that is both peaceful and cruciform, thereby challenging any simple correspondence between obedience and "results," in this chapter I attempt to say more about the role of the Holy Spirit in evangelism and to draw out the connections between the pneumatological and christological dimensions of that practice.

The Pacifist Logic of Evangelism

> The standard by which we measure our obedience is therefore Jesus Christ himself; from him we learn that brokenness, not success, is the normal path of faithfulness to the servanthood of God. This is not to glorify failure or some sort of heroic uselessness, but to claim, as a confession that can be only made in faith, that true "success" in Christian obedience is not to be measured by changing the world in a given direction within a given length of time, but by the congruence between our path and the triumph of Christ.
>
> John Howard Yoder (1997:109)

One of the more helpful ways of thinking about the practical eschatology embodied in evangelistic practice is to be found in Reinhard Hütter's distinction between a "utopian" and a "pneumatological" eschatology.

While the first "follows the logic of modern politics, where the implementation of the end defines the success of the political agents and thereby justifies both them and the means employed," the second follows the logic of the Holy Spirit, in which "the ends are embodied in the means, and 'success' is defined only by the specific nature of particular ends" (1993:435). Hütter's point is something like a theological version of the point made by MacIntyre that a practice in good working order must focus primarily not on the realization of external goods but on its internal goods and thus on the nature of the practice itself, along with the virtues required for and cultivated by that practice. In the case of a pneumatological eschatology, these virtues are to be considered "gifts" infused by the Spirit (however much they require a disciplined life for their reception and cultivation), and the practices that embody these virtues are never simply "productive" but are always oriented toward the future in a hope that is cruciform. To claim that evangelism is an eschatological practice that follows the logic of the Spirit, then, is to claim that it is possible only in hope. As Hütter puts it,

> The success of the church's faithful witness might be hidden in a twofold way: under the form of the cross and in the future of God's reign. Therefore, in a pneumatological ecclesiology, the church's "success" can never be made intelligible independent of Jesus Christ's crucifixion and resurrection and God's eschatological activity in the Holy Spirit. While utopian eschatology trusts in the transforming power of revolutionary human activity and its respective "success," pneumatological eschatology trusts in the transforming power of God's salvific and redeeming activity—and God's respective "success." (1993:435)

To follow Hütter at this point is not to deny that Christian practice requires faithful obedience, resolute confidence, and a sure direction (not to mention a lot of hard work). It is instead to insist that constitutive Christian practices such as evangelism are first and foremost works of the Holy Spirit and must, in fact, be seen as God's own activity. We saw this to be the case already with the five "political" practices mentioned by Yoder, for whom one of the marks of a core church practice is that "it is formally said in the New Testament that when humans do it, God is doing it" and therefore "each is a way God acts" (1992a:44, 71). This does not mean that Christian practices are any less the actions or "works" of human beings. Within a pneumatological eschatology, however, they must now also be understood as in some sense also "consequences"[1] and therefore as works of obedience in openness to the Spirit. Along

1. As John Milbank says, "Every action begins to be a consequence. In aiming for a goal, it also emanates" (1990:228).

with every other Christian practice, evangelism is fundamentally a mode of reception. It is the Spirit who makes the future present, who brings it into history; it is the Spirit who "confronts the process of history with its consummation, with its transformation and transfiguration" (Zizioulas 1997:180).

As we construe evangelism as a Christian practice, then, MacIntyre's more formal definition of a practice as the action of humans ordered virtuously toward a *telos* narrated by and embodied in a tradition will need to be qualified theologically as the action of the Spirit ordered toward the Spirit's own *telos*, peace, and as embodied in a community that does not exist prior to the Spirit but which is instead "constantly re-enacted and re-received in the Spirit" (Zizioulas 1997:207). This means that MacIntyre's category of narrative will also need to undergo a pneumatological qualification, for history can no longer be simply about "the past," nor can historical causality be understood as moving from past to present to future. Instead, "the sequence of 'yesterday-today-tomorrow' is transcended" in a Christian eschatology, for "the Spirit is 'the Lord' who transcends linear history and turns historical continuity into a presence" (ibid. 180).[2] To evangelize, therefore, is not only to transmit a story but to invite persons into that story by inviting them into a future that has been made present in the Spirit. In this respect, Christians never cease to be "seekers." Rather, they continue "looking for the city which is to come" (Heb. 13:14). Likewise, to evangelize is not simply to offer Christ as a historical person about whom things are supposed to be believed but to offer Christ as a Spirit-constituted form of social existence, *ecclesia*. To be "in Christ" is a real participation in what is yet to come, an anticipation of the end of history, an embodying forward toward the future that enacts the possibilities of that future here and now.[3]

The church's practices, as Hütter notes, are therefore characterized by a pathos or "suffering," so that, without being merely passive, these practices have the form of obedience, reception, and active surrender. Another way of saying this is that the church receives the Spirit—and therefore its future—through *epiclesis*, or "invocation." As Hütter says,

> Although they do indeed refer to human activities, through them the human being "undergoes" or "is subject to" the actions of the Holy Spirit. . . . The Holy Spirit is now to be understood as the real subject of these practices;

2. Zizioulas describes the church's memory as a *"memory of the future"* and cites a wonderful anaphora from the Liturgy of St. John Chrysostom: "Remembering the cross, the resurrection, the ascension *and the second coming*, Thine own of Thine own we offer Thee" (1997:180).

3. See "The Eschatological Body: Gender, Transformation, and God," Coakley 2002: 153–67.

their teleological focus is soteriological, and the "excellence" in question involves a person's growth in faith or sanctification. Although the human being is always *present* in these activities, and is always and especially *actively present*, listening, receiving, responding, praising, and rendering obedience, still this human activity does *not* constitute these practices. . . . The disposition . . . is rather such that in them the human being is always the *recipient*, that is always remains in the mode of pathos. The human being remains the one who *through* these works of the Holy Spirit is qualified and receives a new "form," the one who thus is modeled through the Spirit of Christ, the *forma fidei*. (2000:131–32)

Here again it is important to emphasize the way evangelism is not only a distinct and necessary practice in its own right but also a quality of the comprehensive praxis of Christian faith in and through which the Holy Spirit is at work bearing embodied witness. Christians practicing evangelism throughout the centuries have frequently resisted this "pathic" dimension of witness in an effort to reach the world effectively and expediently and to secure victory in producing conversions. Whether that has taken the form of political arrangements that attempted to guarantee Christian success, emotional manipulations such as those associated with modern revivalism, or the intellectual gymnastics of Christian apologetics, a common denominator of many Christian evangelistic strategies has been their basic distrust of the Holy Spirit to work through the simplicity of Christian obedience lived out in daily practices, habits, and gestures. Instead, evangelism gets carried out as if it were either a sales campaign or a military operation, both of which, by their very nature, follow a practical logic other than that of the Spirit.

Of course, no Christian evangelist would ever argue against faithfulness, simplicity, worship, and virtue as essential to evangelistic practice. But to the extent that salvation is construed individualistically and privately as the result of one's personal "decision" (as it clearly is within the prevailing coordinates of modern evangelicalism), aggressive efforts to win converts will always end up trumping the simple daily obedience of a consistent Christian witness because the former will always be deemed more evangelistically efficient. It is a recurring feature of modern evangelicalism that it must ever find ways to make visible, public, urgent, and inviting a salvation that remains essentially invisible, private, and innocuous. Faithful witness in the form of simple and daily obedience can never rise to the level of adequate evangelistic strategy, for it can never attain the "results" of a utopian eschatology. What is largely missing is a visible, material, and subversive faith that is intrinsically practical and ecclesial and therefore already and unmistakably public.

The pneumatological constitution of Christian witness to which persons like Hütter, Yoder, and Zizioulas point is, in one sense, always "hidden" in that the Spirit's activity in the church is an article of faith for which we have no historical guarantees. But the work of the evangelist is not to render public what is essentially private. Evangelism is an invitation to "come and see" (John 1:46). It is, moreover, the cultivation of a *way* of seeing and sensing that is nothing less than the nurturing of a basic aesthetic sensibility. This is one more reason why evangelism is an inherently ecclesial practice. For however "personal" may be the evangelistic invitation, it requires incorporating persons into the church as "a school of attention."[4]

The evangelizing work of the church is spiritual, therefore, but also sensual and worldly. That is because the "real" to which evangelism directs and invites persons is not that which invisibly transcends the visible but rather that which is donated by God as both the inheritance and ultimate *telos* of the visible. As mentioned in the previous chapter, all of nature stands as an evangelistic witness, for "the heavens are telling the glory of God, and the firmament proclaims [God's] handiwork" (Psalm 19:1). But if there is no social body called church, no communion of saints, no daily practices of forgiveness, material sharing, or inclusive table fellowship, then evangelism remains quite impossible. For it is in and through the concrete form of life called *ecclesia* that we are educated into the patterns and rhythms of the Spirit and so learn to see.[5]

If evangelism is a practice, it is a strange sort of practice—as, indeed, are all constitutive Christian practices. For it is both a "doing" and a "be it done unto me." The *martyria* at the heart of evangelistic practice is fundamentally a *pathos*, a formation, or, if you will, a determination (though that word will always be resisted by those of us who fear that others, especially God, may do something to us over which we have no control). This pathic determination is incredibly important for any understanding of evangelism grounded in ecclesial existence, for the church is not something we do, or have, or make, but is a creation and a gift of the Holy Spirit. To practice an evangelism that is constituted pathically by the Spirit is to refuse to objectify the gospel in a way that would turn it into a product to be controlled and manipulated in order somehow to achieve "success."

The evangelist, then, does not stand at the beginning of the practice of evangelism as giver or revealer or provocateur but is instead pathically determined by the practices of the church. Thus, the only certainty that

4. This is Timothy Gorringe's fitting description of art. As Gorringe says, "All great art helps us to see, attend to, sense, the depth, mystery and glory of God's creation" (2001:2). On the basis of this, one could rightly claim that evangelism is an "art."

5. "To flee into invisibility is to deny the call. Any community of Jesus which wants to be invisible is no longer a community that follows him" (Bonhoeffer, quoted in Hauerwas 2004:44).

justifies Christian witness is not its effectiveness in winning others to Christ but a hope that cannot be measured by external appearances and that defies apparent success or failure. In Jesus of Nazareth we have been given a new *practical logic*. Success may just as likely appear cruciform while failure wears a crown. And lest we glory in our ability to secure results, we know that the "calculating link between our obedience and ultimate efficacy has been broken," as Yoder says, "since the triumph of God comes through resurrection" (1972:246). Therefore only an unseen hope can give meaning and purpose to evangelism.

What is more, since the church follows a poor, naked, and crucified Christ, there is no reason to believe that the church's faithful witness will result in masses of wealthy suburban consumers lining up around the block on a Sunday just to be a part of our worn-down storefront church. As Gustavo Gutiérrez observes,

> Evangelization, the proclamation of the gospel, will be genuinely liberating when the poor themselves become its messengers. That is when we shall see the preaching of the gospel become a stumbling block and a scandal. For then we shall have a gospel that is no longer "presentable" in society. It will not sound nice and it will not smell good. The Lord who scarcely looks like a human at all (cf. the songs of the Servant of Yahweh in Isaiah) will speak to us then, and only at the sound of his voice will we recognize him as our liberator. That voice will convoke the *ek-klesia*, the assembly of those "called apart," in a new and different way. (1983:22)

Given the particular relationship between obedience and effectiveness narrated by the story of the people of God and, decisively, by the life, death, and resurrection of Jesus, and given the fact that within a pneumatological eschatology the practice of evangelism is characterized by *witness* rather than by *effectiveness* determined by criteria outside the content of that witness, we may affirm that the politics of evangelism is, from beginning to end, pacifist. Pacifism, as I mean it here, is not merely an ethical position one takes toward war, nor is it in any sense sheer passivity. It is rather a fundamental orientation that arises, first, from trust that the Spirit goes before us so that we need not be anxious, manipulative, or controlling in our evangelism. In the words of Jesus to his disciples, "It is not you who speak, but the Holy Spirit" (Mark 13:11). This pacifist orientation arises, second, from the conviction that Jesus alone is normative for the Christian's action in the world, not some other criterion (generated from either reason or experience) or some other calculus of effectiveness or potential receptivity. As Yoder says, the

> link between our obedience and the accomplishments of God's purposes
> . . . is more cognancy than causation. We see it when we find life by way

230 The Evangelizing Community

of the cross, power by means of weakness, wisdom by means of foolishness. We see it when we find wealth by throwing our bread on the waters, when we find brothers and sisters and houses and lands by giving them up, when we save our life by losing it. This is the evangelical norm of social efficacy. (1998:207)

Here I think we find ourselves back on MacIntyre's doorstep with respect to his notion of the relationship of means and ends in a practice and what is meant by speaking of "success" in that relationship. It is simply not possible to measure the efficacy of a practice such as evangelism apart from consideration of the ends internal to that practice and apart from the community that provides the context or *habitus* in which the logic of that practice is rendered intelligible. In the case of a *habitus* that is pneumatologically constituted toward the future and eucharistically shaped into a cruciform body, it is obedient witness that represents "right practice" rather than apparent and immediate effectiveness or results. This, of course, does not mean that obedience itself is somehow "the best way" of arriving at the proper ends of evangelistic practice but rather that obedience *is* the proper end of evangelistic practice. In this sense the evangelism for which I am advocating, to put it bluntly, does not "work." As the above quotation from Yoder points out, we do not control the world, nor can we predict or calculate the effect or consequences of our actions. Obedience, therefore, is a hopeful response to the work of Christ and an openness to the Holy Spirit. If we may speak of accountability in the practice of evangelism, this accountability is a matter of fidelity and obedience, a matter of performance rather than results. At times this obedience will attract non-Christians, and it may even result in their conversion. At other times it will turn them away and prove to be a scandal. Ultimately, however, obedience signifies and is a response to the lordship of Christ rather than being a course of life designed to secure a set of desired ends.

The Beauty of Holiness: Apologetics as Aesthetics

Beauty will save the world.

Fyodor Dostoyevski, *The Idiot* (374)

In reflecting upon the political and economic dimensions of *ecclesia* in the previous chapter, I tried to emphasize ways the church's core practices are both particular and traditioned, on the one hand, and open, available, and accessible to those who stand outside the tradition, on the other hand. They are, as Yoder says, *"both* the internal activities of the gathered Christian congregation *and* the ways the church interfaces with the world" (1998:361). They originate from within a narrative that is Jewish; they derive from the life and teachings of a first-century rabbi from Galilee; and they are formed from within a distinct community in space and time called *ecclesia*. Yet their particularity makes them neither obscure nor private; it renders them no less *public*. In fact, precisely this dialectic between the particular and the public nature of Christian practices renders them "evangelical" and therefore "good news" for the world:

> For a practice to qualify as "evangelical" in the functional sense means first of all that it communicates *news*. It says something particular that would not be known and could not be believed were it not said. Second, it must mean functionally that this "news" is attested as *good*; it comes across to those whom it addresses as helping, as saving, as *shalom*. It must be public, not esoteric, but the way for it to be public is not an a priori logical move that subtracts the particular. It is an a posteriori political practice that tells the world something it did not know and could not believe before. It tells the world what is the world's own calling and destiny, not by announcing either a utopian or a realistic goal to be imposed on the whole society, but by pioneering a paradigmatic demonstration of both the power and the practices that define the shape of restored humanity. The confessing people of God is the new world on its way. (Yoder 1998:373)

Because the social, political, and economic shape of the Christian community is itself evangelical, the "real meaning" of its practices does not need to be explained to the world, for there is no "deeper" or "real" meaning behind them. There are of course "beliefs" that support these practices which may or may not be readily apparent, but the mediation, or bridge, between the church and the world "is not a mental or verbal operation of translation or conceptual bridging, but rather the concrete presences, among their neighbors, of believers who for Jesus' sake do ordinary social things differently" (Yoder 1992a:75). Practices such as forgiveness, interethnic inclusion, the sharing of material goods, and the recognition of all as equally gifted and valuable may be "odd," but they are not mysterious, esoteric, or difficult to understand. They are "publicly accessible behaviors" (ibid. 73), something the surrounding world can see plainly and comprehend readily (whatever the reaction and response of the world might be to those behaviors). Though Yoder has primarily in mind an ethical bridging or mediation, his principle is intrinsically missiological and has, I believe, substantial consequences for evangelism; for it means that the first task of evangelism is not apologet-ics—an intellectual defense of the Christian gospel or its translation into non-Christian categories. Nor does evangelism require an alteration and adjustment of Christian practices for the sake of a wider acceptance by the world. Confession, proclamation, and public exemplification of the gospel are the first and primary tasks of Christian evangelism.

What Milbank says of theology, therefore, I hold to be true also for the practice of evangelism: its task is "not apologetic, nor even argument. Rather it is to tell again the Christian *mythos*, pronounce again the Christian *logos*, and call again for Christian *praxis* in a manner that restores their freshness and originality. It must articulate Christian difference in such a fashion as to make it strange" (1990:381). In this task, evangelism may certainly form ad hoc alliances with any and all forms of human inquiry, culture, science, art, and the imagination. The fact that the visible shape of the Christian community is itself the church's public witness does not release us from the enormous responsibility of contextualization and of making explicit the invitation to strangeness that is often only implicit in our economic and political practices and patterns. It likewise does not release us from the need to break down old walls that inappropriately divide the church from the world and from the need to provide ever new paths and doorways so that persons can journey toward a new citizenship. On the contrary, the practice of evangelism requires that the church offer not only itself as embodied witness but also an account of why it does "ordinary social things differently"—that is, "for Jesus' sake." There is, then, an apologetic dimension to evangelism, however secondary and ad hoc it remains in relation to the primary evangelistic logic of witness and incarnation.

An evangelizing church will make room for skeptics and doubters, encouraging them to ask questions, learning what it can from them, and refusing to give condescending or flip answers. But it is impossible for the church to offer an account of its faith or to correct misunderstandings and respond to objections where the church is no different from the world. Moreover, none of the apologetic alliances we might form for the sake of communication may become foundational for the evangelistic enterprise as a way of securing the plausibility of Christian truth claims or providing "objective" and "universal" grounds for belief. The good news must always be expressed in such a way that its being understood by hearers is balanced with the possibility of its rejection. Of course, the church never desires the refusal of its news. But when a hearer's acceptance of the Christian message becomes obligatory, when witness is no longer surprising but coercive because it is presented as undeniable, then the good news is neither news nor good. Weakness, vulnerability, incarnation, and refusability are all markers of faithful Christian witness.

In a situation that is increasingly pluralistic and secular, little could be more critically important for a theology of evangelism than how we understand the relationship between the particularity of our Christian faith stance, on the one hand, and public accountability to and relationship with other stances, convictions, and communities. Too often we are tempted to believe there must be a "null-sum trade-off" between faithfulness and relevance, between maintaining the particularity of our faith identity and trusting that this faith will make sense to others and serve others. But more of one does not mean less of the other. The particularity of faith need not be proved universally valid in order for it to be universally open, shared, and available. "In fact," says Yoder, "there is no reason to want to make sense to your neighbors if you have no identity worth sharing with them" (1997:28, 41). Even to the extent that Christian evangelism engages in defense or persuasion, it need not accept the seductive and pervasive notion that "there is 'out there' an objective or agreed account of reality and that faith perspectives must come to terms with that wider picture by fitting into it, as a subset of the generally unbelieving worldview" (Yoder 1992a:74). Every way of viewing the world and reading history arises from some particular set of convictions we might call "faith" and from within some particular narrative. To believe that the "real world" is something other (or larger) than the world of the gospel is to deform Christian evangelism from the beginning.

The theology of evangelism I am here espousing, therefore, begins by rejecting the notion that there is out there a single monolithic "public" that an evangelizing church must engage or in terms of which the gospel must be translated or rendered credible in order to "come across to those whom it addresses as helping, as saving, as *shalom*." Instead, evangelism presupposes the church as a public in its own right, or as Hütter says, "the public of the Holy Spirit" (2000:158). On this view, the world of the gospel is wider and more public than the provincial world of unbelief.[6] Moreover, this Spirit-constituted "publicity" enables the church to relate itself politically, ethically, and evangelistically to other publics.[7]

<hr />

6. Likewise, there is no single "history" that is the starting point or horizon for thinking about the church. The church's story is the horizon against which we read all histories. See Hütter 2000:201.

7. For Hütter, "As long as the church is not understood *as* a public, any reference to the 'public church' is merely an external perspective on the church from the perspective of the normative public of modern, differentiated liberal society that promptly effects the church's eclipse *as* a public. If by contrast one understands the church first of all ecclesiologically as a public itself, one can then also consider its complex relationships with a multiplicity of other, different publics, including that of a democratically constituted modern society" (2000:169). Hutter even goes so far as to insist that the church is not only *not* the "church of society," but that it also is *not* the "church as contrast community." While this latter

While the early Christians did not hesitate to share their faith in ways that engaged the practices, thought forms, and beliefs of the Greco-Roman world, they early on discovered that the universalism of the Greco-Roman world was too small for the particularity of a church made alive and sent forth by the Spirit of God. The apostle Paul in front of the Areopagus in Athens, therefore, sets the "provincial" religiosity and "sectarian" worship of an unknown god within the larger context of the activity of the "God who made the world and everything in it," the "Lord of heaven and earth" who "gives to all mortals life and breath and all things" (Acts 17:24–25). Paul's apologetic here consists not in arguing that what Christians believe and practice is just another version of or name for what others have been doing all along whether they know it or not, or that Christianity is a particular species of a more basic existential faith. His point is a very different one: the Athenian worship is a more tentative "groping" for this one true God, who, though "not far from each of us" (Acts 17:27) has been made known in the life, death, and resurrection of Jesus of Nazareth.[8]

In similar fashion, Christian "apologists" of the second century took up a missionary strategy that built upon parallels and commonalities they found between their faith and pagan culture. For someone like Justin Martyr, for instance, the *logos* incarnate in Christ is the same as the *logos* that is the rational principle of the universe and the sources

---

point would seem to contradict my argument about the church thus far, what Hütter is emphasizing is that the church is not to be defined in the first place as over against the world. To do that would be to make the world the wider "public" within which we think about the church's publicity and thus fail to begin with the church *as* a public. That being said, Hütter admits that "under certain circumstances the church as public can indeed or even must assume the form of a 'contrast community'," though this is "a question of ecclesial *judgment*, that is an answer—to be determined in each given case—to the question of how under changing circumstances the church can itself remain a public, and not to the question of how within a single normatively understood public the church acquires a 'public character' from the perspective of that public" (171).

8. Yoder puts the matter this way:

The one thing that never would have occurred to the Jews in Babylon was to try to bridge the distance between their language world and that of their hosts by a foundationalist mental or linguistic move, trying to rise to a higher level or dig to a deeper one, so that the difference could be engulfed in some *tertium quid*, which would convince the Babylonians of moral monotheism without making them Jews, and to which the Jews could yield without sacrificing their local color. They did not look for or seek to construct common ground. Jews knew that there was no larger world than the one their Lord had made and their prophets knew the most about. Its compatibility with kinds of "wisdom" that the Gentiles could understand seemed to them to validate their holy history rather than to relativize it. When Hellenism penetrated their world, they did not hesitate to affirm that whatever truth there was in Plato or Aristotle was derived from Moses. (1997:73)

of all human knowledge. Yet it must be noted that these apologists took the church and its tradition as their starting point in relating to those outside the faith: "Apologetic theology was a secondary endeavor because the premodern apologist would never allow questions of unbelief to order the theological agenda" (Hauerwas 2001a:53).[9] In our time, by contrast, the notion that God's grace is pervasive in creation is understood as implying the autonomy of the world or (as in the case of Gutiérrez) the subordination of *ecclesia* to the politics of secular history. In this way, modern apologetics reverses the premodern approach by justifying Christianity insofar as it confirms what humans already know and underwrites what humans already desire. As Hauerwas says,

> There is, of course, a proper sense in which . . . the conviction that the kingdom wrought in Christ is meant to fulfill our deepest and strongest desires is at the heart of Christianity. Insofar as we are God's creatures his redemption is certainly the fulfillment of the natural. But unfortunately we quickly trivialize this insight by seeking fulfillment without recognizing that in order to know and worship God rightly we must have our desires transformed. They must be transformed—we must be trained to desire rightly—because, bent by sin, we have little sense of what it is that we should rightly want. (1983:13–14)

Whatever legitimate "bridging" can be accomplished by apologetic arguments that attempt to demonstrate the common ground between Christian and non-Christian worldviews or that seek to answer objections and correct misunderstandings, it is rarely true that persons come to faith or decide between different faith traditions on the basis of rational "evidence" or logical argument. As I shall attempt to show later in my discussion of conversion, embracing religious beliefs is, as Sarah Coakley suggests, "more like the adopting of a whole new way of life, or 'picturing' differently, or making a particular narrative central to one's existence, than coolly adjudicating on their likelihood with the 'specula-

9. Yoder does not quite share Hauerwas's more positive assessment of the Greek apologists and finds instead that something new and distorting has already begun to happen in the second century. "It is with the beginning of an apologetic approach to the wisdom of the Gentile world, that the meaning of the Christian mission had been radically shifted. . . . The apologetes are missionary in that they try to show the Gentiles that they can have the God of the Jews without the Jews. That shift, somewhere between the New Testament canon and the middle of the next century is the real change in character in the Christian community, the sell-out to Greek or Roman provincialism instead of Hebrew universality. This is then what we would have to call the Fall of the Church." "Tertium Datur: Refocusing the Jewish-Christian Schism," paper presented at the Notre Dame Graduate Union, October 13, 1977, 3, quoted by Gayle Gerber Koontz, "Confessional Theology in a Pluralistic Context: A Study of the Theological Ethics of H. Richard Niebuhr and John H. Yoder," Ph.D. diss., Boston University, 1985, 218.

tive intelligence'" (2002:143).[10] For just this reason, if we may speak of apologetics as central to the practice of evangelism, we should perhaps speak of that apologetics as primarily an aesthetics.

To speak of apologetics as aesthetics does not mean that evangelism is merely about "presentation" or the projection of an "image" (though the category of image, or icon, is historically a rich resource for grasping the truth that beauty is essentially transparency to God). So also, to claim that the apologetics of evangelism is primarily aesthetic is in no way to imply that either witnessing to faith or coming to faith is a noncognitive process. It is to affirm rather that both evangelism and conversion have to do not with one aspect of human existence but rather a comprehensive way of life that cannot, in the final analysis, be rationally "explained" or "understood" but rather confessed, narrated, and embodied in the rhythms, patterns, practices, and allegiances of Christian fellowship. Evangelism is a way of living openly, engagingly, virtuously—and therefore *beautifully* before a watching world.

The evangelistic appeal to beauty, however, cannot be reduced merely to what the world finds "beautiful" or "desirable." As Gregory of Nyssa says, "Now beauty itself can either be really beautiful or can be decked out with the semblance of beauty. The power to distinguish between the two is the mind that resides within us" (in Meredith 1999:78). Gregory goes on to illustrate his point with the fable of the dog that, when it sees its reflection in water, drops its food in order to snatch what it sees, thereby remaining hungry. According to Gregory, "In a similar fashion, the mind, being cheated of its desire for that which is really good, was carried away to what is unreal . . . by having been persuaded that that truly is beautiful, which is the opposite of beautiful" (ibid.).

Those who have read Dostoyevski's novel *The Idiot* will know that when the words "Beauty will save the world" appear, they are not so much a claim as a question. For Christian evangelism, the question must be answered in the affirmative, for it is indeed "beauty" that saves us by captivating our hearts, minds, and imaginations. But Christian beauty is fixed

10. Coakley, building on the work of Wittgenstein, describes this coming to faith as "a patient moral transformation" similar to what may be termed a "virtue epistemology" (2002:146). This is "a view of faith profoundly sensitive to its differing 'levels' of intensity, perceptual/tactile response, and spiritual and moral maturity. Here is a view of faith rooted in 'practice,' involving *particular* forms of vision and a 'layered' understanding of doctrine's possible 'meanings.' Here is a view of faith that involves 'turning around' and coming to perceive ('picture') *differently*" (ibid. 148). Coakley goes on to make a good case that this epistemology has much in common with feminist epistemology, "which has incisively challenged the hegemony of the 'recognition-of-hard-objects-at-five-paces' model for normative epistemological discussion, a challenge that draws attention instead to the *contextual* significance of any 'S-knowing-p,' and to the varieties of types of possible 'knowing,' personal as well as cognitive" (ibid. 149–50).

in Christ and is therefore cruciform and so, in some sense, grotesque. To be sure, the good news we have to share with the world is that resurrection, not crucifixion, has the last word in human existence—hope is not swallowed up in tragedy. But the cross is not thereby negated or eclipsed; its nonviolence and vulnerability remain the Christian "way"—not in the sense of chastening our hopes or making us more "realistic" about what we can expect from ourselves but in teaching us patiently to love and to serve, even if church growth experts find that uninspiring or fruitless.

There is an intrinsic violence to an evangelism that fears vulnerability and will do whatever it takes to ensure the "public" validation (and therefore "power") of its claims.[11] As Yoder says,

> We want what we say not only to be understandable, credible, meaningful. . . . We want people to *have* to believe us. We hanker for patterns of argument which will not be subject to reasonable doubt. We are impressed by the power to convince which we see exercised by demonstrations in mathematics and logic, in the natural sciences, and in documented history . . . and we want our claims about God or morality to be similarly coercive. We think that truth must somehow be made irresistible, because that is the way in which the small world in which we grew up taught us what the rules are, and that is how the larger world we since moved into imposed itself on us. We become "apologetic," ready to decrease the vigor of our claims, if that will decrease their vulnerability to rejection. (1992b:287)

Such an evangelism can never be beautiful, for beauty can never be proved or imposed. It can only be offered.

Christ's purpose for the church is to call forth from it beauty, to present it to himself "in splendor, without a spot or wrinkle or anything of the kind—yes, so that she may be holy and without blemish" (Eph. 5:27). This beautiful holiness is not an achievement on our part or a possession or a perfection to be associated with our sinlessness.[12] It is a participation, or "dwelling," in the Truth that has come to "dwell" with us (John 1:14) and that thereby makes of our lives something beautiful, though always as a gift to be obediently received. Because obedience

11. As Hauerwas argues, the attempt to justify Christian belief on the basis of rationality "or some other 'inherent' human characteristic, ironically underwrites coercion. If others refuse to accept my account of 'rationality,' it seems within my bounds to force them to be true to their 'true' selves" (1983:12).

12. The church can never wait to evangelize until it becomes "holy." On the priority of first being the church, Yoder says, "The sense in which this calling to be first of all the believing community is primary is not a chronological sequence whereby one task must be achieved before there is leisure to turn to the other. The church's being the church is primordial rather in the sense of orientation. . . . We speak of a priority or primordiality in terms of identity and not of sequence" (1998:119).

is required, truth is not something we merely tell but something we practice (1 John 1:6). We are able to offer the truth only by receiving it, that is, by being re-created by it, "taken into it, and defined anew by it" (Zizioulas 1997:156).

The Church as the "Public" of the Holy Spirit

If it can be said that the church is called to be a "public" in its own right rather than having its witness determined by an allegedly wider public outside the church, it must also be said that virtually everything in modern liberal society stands as a refusal of the church thus understood, thereby creating a serious challenge for an evangelism that is intrinsically committed to the gospel's publicity. This refusal usually takes one of two forms: either the church is restricted to the realm of the private or sectarian (and therefore not public at all), or it is allowed to "engage" what is taken to be the wider public of modern liberal society, but only on that public's own terms. But this, as Hütter rightly notes, invariably includes the church's own "subtle political discipline and domestication" and, finally, its "eclipse *as* a public" altogether (2000:169). The church that would evangelize by "going public" ends up instead proselytized into a comprehensive process called "civil religion," whereby its "helpfulness" in the service of modern liberal social orders and the institutions of those social orders may now be measured.

What might it mean, then, for evangelism to be carried out as a practice from within an understanding of the church as itself a public, the body of Christ, constituted by the Holy Spirit in loving openness to the world? To begin with, as I tried to demonstrate in chapter 7, the church as a public is marked (and to that extent, bounded) by the particularity of its own politics. In this formal respect it is no different from any other public, whether that is the public of the Greek *polis*, to which Arendt was attracted as a realm of human freedom (though necessarily excluding the *oikos* with its urgent, restrictive, material concerns), or whether that is the empty and purposeless public of modernity, which does little more than mediate between the competing private projects of individuals. The type of publicity marked by the politics of *ecclesia*, however, is an openness (and thus a universality or catholicity) that invites us to move beyond the spatial, temporal, economic, and sociopolitical boundaries created by other publics. Indeed, it could even be said that the church appears in the world as a public not by virtue of boundaries but by virtue of the presence of the Spirit, who, according to the book of Acts, seems to be interested in nothing so much as shattering boundaries.

Yet this boundary-shattering openness is not an undifferentiating and purposeless inclusion along the lines narrated by modernity, which, as Miroslav Volf has brilliantly shown, ends up imploding on itself, first, by generating new patterns of exclusion in the form of binary oppositions between those of us who are "civilized includers" and others who are "barbaric excluders" and, second, by removing any sort of established identity or criteria by which we could say what should or should not be excluded.[13] The church as a public, therefore, can be neither a walled-up fortress nor an "endless plain." In the case of the Christian *ecclesia*, that which renders the church an identifiable public and at the same time distinguishes its politics from all other publics is its pneumatological constitution and its soteriological *telos* (cf. Hütter 2000:158–59). The church exists in the power of the Holy Spirit as the offer of Christ to the world. This constitution and *telos* can never be transcended, thereby forming something like a distinguishing "boundary" (though, as Hütter notes, the word *center* would be better than *boundary*). Yet the church's difference from the world is its evangelical openness to the world. Again, it is not scarcity but abundance that defines the church's normative relationship to the world.

Because the church is the public of the Holy Spirit, the logic of its growth and expansion is vastly different from that of a public constructed within the spatial logic of a Constantinian imagination (exemplified in the notion of "empire") or within the spatial logic of a modern imagination (exemplified in the notion of "market"). Both are premised on a scarcity that must always hold Israel, Jesus, and the church as finite and therefore partial and fragmentary disclosures of a fuller and more fundamental universalism that is to be achieved through conquest and expansion.[14] Both, as Hütter notes, are preoccupied with boundaries and on overcoming them. The church, by way of contrast, "is constituted not through 'boundaries' but through a 'center' . . . of an utterly christological nature" (Hütter 2000:165). The church expands not by extending itself through fragmented "parts" or through "branch outlets, a kind of ecclesiastical McDonalds's Incorporated" (McClendon 1986:2:364), but through the establishing of local, concrete assemblies, each united with Christ and gathered around his table and together united in one faith, one baptism, and one Spirit. The eucharistic creation of the "local" is therefore a "'concentration' of the whole" that turns out to be far more

13. As Volf asks, should every act of ethnic cleansing, violence, rape, and destruction be "included" and "embraced" (cf. 1996:58–64)?

14. See Stephen Long's critique of the "metaphysics of scarcity" at this point and, in particular, his critique of Rosemary Radford Ruether, from whom the phrase "partial and fragmentary" in reference to Israel, Jesus, and the church is taken, because they are "circumscribed in time, culture, and gender" (Long 2000:148).

universal than the globalism of modernity built on fragmentation, the reproduction of competition and divisions between the rich and the poor, and an aggressive detachment from the local in the name of free-flowing "capital."[15]

The emphasis on the Holy Spirit here in construing the unique sense in which the church is a public is far from accidental or tangential. Evangelism is a participation in the work of the Holy Spirit, for it is only through the Spirit that Christ is made present and available in the world or, as Hütter puts it, that "Christ becomes 'public' in the world" (2000:145). The Holy Spirit, consequently, is a reference not to Christ's absence but to Christ's presence. The Spirit's purpose in making Christ public, moreover, is to draw persons into communion. This double movement of the Spirit—what James McClendon refers to as the twin gifts of the Spirit, "ecstasy" and "fellowship" (1986:2:418)—constitutes the church's very existence as "public" and also makes of evangelism a practice intrinsic to the nature of the church as church. Evangelism is "ecstatic" in that we are led out, made "public," by the Spirit. But evangelism is also an invitation to communion as through it the Spirit draws persons into its fellowship and into its bonds of love and freedom. Neither the sending nor the drawing takes place by compulsion but by excess, overflowing, and donation, as revealed in the story of Pentecost, which is a defining narrative for evangelism. In and through the Pentecostal gathering of a new people from among all tribes and nations, "the church is disclosed as the locus of the Spirit's missionary action, the place where ecstasy and fellowship converge" (ibid. 2:419).

This construal of the church as the public of the Spirit is not meant to deny, however, that the Spirit goes before the church as the witness who is already there. A failure to humbly confess this is to make that which is derivative original, to lapse into the sort of practical illogic that confuses obedience with results and leading with being led. Yet however much the Spirit goes before the church and however much the church as Christ's body is itself "on its way" and thus provisional, the Spirit's calling out and creation of a people are not provisional, as the author of Ephesians affirms, but intrinsically connected to God's eternal purpose of "gathering up all things in Christ." By the Spirit, Christ is present in the church's proclamation and in its meal, worship, hospitality, doctrines, and order. The church as a work of the Spirit constitutes the material form, gestures, language, habits, and practices that are the means by which we are sanctified, drawn into the trinitarian life of God, and sent out into the world as participants in the *missio Dei*.

15. See the engaging article "The Myth of Globalization as Catholicity" in Cavanaugh 2002:97–122.

When we consider the practice of evangelism from within a pneu-matologically grounded ecclesiology, the "institutional" dimensions of the church need not be played off negatively against the "charismatic" dimensions (or to use Victor Turner's categories, *structure* against *communitas*),[16] for all practices require institutions in order to be sustained over time. It is true, of course, that institutions have what MacIntyre calls a "corrupting power" that tends to distort the very practices they were formed to foster and tends to subvert the virtues they were initially created to cultivate. This is because institutions by their very nature are acquisitive and seek external goods (money, material goods, power) to "sustain not only themselves, but also the practices of which they are the bearers" (MacIntyre 1984:194). The institutional dimensions of *ecclesia* are not wholly corrupting, however, and can render core practices such as evangelism "powerful" (cf. McClendon 1986:1:173–77), so that they are capable of resisting the deformative influence of other institutions and powers in our world. But clearly the competitive and corruptive tendency of institutions will require the centrality of Spirit-formed virtues within the church that nourish a single-minded commitment to the ends for which the church exists and an obedience that is compatible with the power we see manifest in the manger and on the cross rather than in the boardroom and the battlefield.

Offering Christ in the Power of the Spirit

The pneumatological and ecclesiological constitution of evangelistic practice establishes rather than displaces the centrality of Christ in that practice. Indeed, this is true of all ministry, as Zizioulas reminds us: "Instead of *first* establishing in our minds the scheme 'Christ-ministry' and *then* trying to fill this with the work of the Holy Spirit," the Spirit is instead *"constitutive of the very relation between Christ and the ministry"* (1997:212). Thus, even though evangelism may be understood quite simply as the offer of Christ to the world, when understood within a trinitarian logic, that offer is part of "one motion" wrought by God through the Spirit and from within the fellowship created in history by the Spirit.[17] The Spirit is unbounded and "blows where it chooses"

16. See Starkloff 1997 for a thoughtful ecclesiological appropriation of Turner's work.
17. Thus says Gregory of Nyssa in his *On "Not Three Gods" (To Ablabius)*,

When we inquire, then, whence this good gift came to us, we find by the guidance of the Scriptures that it was from the Father, Son, and Holy Spirit. Yet although we set forth Three Persons and three names, we do not consider that we have had bestowed upon us three lives, one from each Person separately but the same life is wrought in us by the Father and prepared by the Son, and depends on the will

(John 3:8), but it is nonetheless the Spirit *of Christ* and testifies *to Christ*, so that in its freedom the Spirit always retains a christological particularity.

In creating the church as an embodied witness to Christ, the Spirit does more than "point." It empowers us to participate in the reign of God announced by Jesus and embodied in his person. We have already seen that the early church did not separate the proclamation of Jesus from the person of Jesus. Even where we noticed a shift in language from a preoccupation with "God's reign" characteristic of Jesus' evangelism to the apostolic preoccupation with Jesus *as the Christ*, the actual daily practices and patterns of the first Christian communities (which, as we know, often speak louder than words) presuppose and are characterized by the economics and politics of that reign. In fact, the very transmission of Jesus' pre-Easter message of God's reign by the four Gospels is a form of post-Easter evangelism and laden, even if only implicitly, with christological claims for Jesus. In portraying Jesus and in telling his story, the very structure of the Gospels is an invitation to make his story one's own. Clearly, one does not have to abandon the message to believe in the messenger or to believe that God has acted decisively in and through him. But if the early Christians were unable or unwilling to divorce the proclaimer from the proclamation, contemporary evangelism has not fared so well, being prone instead to favor either the message or the messenger (each to the neglect of the other), resulting in an entire spectrum of evangelistic distortions.

On one end of the spectrum, the significance of Jesus is reduced to that of a prophet whose moral example and teachings stimulate the creation of an ethical community that promotes "the fatherhood of God and the brotherhood of man," as the liberal theologians of the nineteenth and early twentieth century put it. And while the use of such sexist language to describe the reign of God would today be largely rejected as a way of characterizing the aim of this evangelism, its driving concern is very much alive in those quarters of Christianity that, unable to make high christological claims for Jesus, can yet admire him for his liberating social potential. The message of God's reign remains central in this form of evangelism, even if that reign tends to become, in the words of Hauerwas, a "cipher that we can fill in with our ideas about what a good society ought to look like" (1983:82). The significance of Jesus as the Messiah of Israel, Lord of history, Savior of the world, or Son of God is then banished to the margins of evangelistic practice.

---

of the Holy Spirit. . . . The Holy Trinity fulfils every operation . . . not by separate action according to the number of the Persons, but so that there is one motion and disposition of the good will which is communicated from the Father through the Son to the Spirit. (in Schaff and Wace 5:334)

On the other end of the spectrum, evangelism is oriented entirely toward the end goal of leading persons to "accept Jesus as their personal Savior"—a twentieth-century neologism that has gained almost canonical status within Protestant evangelical churches, is used increasingly within mainline denominations, and has even made its presence felt among Roman Catholics. If the reign of God is mentioned at all in this form of evangelism (and it rarely is), it is the reign of God in one's heart. This "personal relationship with Jesus" is fed and nourished by the narcissism and individualism of Western culture, so that just as I might employ a personal trainer, a personal assistant, or a personal masseuse, I can also enjoy Jesus as my personal Savior. In thus locating the meaning of salvation within the individual and in terms of a private and interior decision aimed typically at otherworldly and eternal consequences, conversion is emptied of the public, visible, and communal allegiances that participation in God's reign demands. What finally matters is not God's reign "on earth as it is in heaven" but God's reign in my heart or in heaven after earth is gone. The ethical and ecclesiological dimensions of the gospel have now been reduced to mere "implications"—afterthoughts to be worked out later—rather than the very reality to which an acceptance of Christ's lordship is intrinsically a conversion.

In contrast to both extremes on this spectrum, there is a way forward that, as I suggested in chapter 4, is narrativist in its logic and ecclesial in its form. To offer Christ is to offer the reign of God proclaimed by Christ, present in him, and offered to the world in his life, death, and resurrection. The church offers Christ by telling his story and also by embodying that story in its worship, ministry, and obedience. But while this offer has experiential and cognitive dimensions, it is not in the first place the offer of an experience of Christ or a set of beliefs about Christ—at least not as those are configured within the modern logic of desire, production, and exchange, as commodities to be possessed or consumed. The offer of Christ is instead the offer of a peoplehood, of participation in a body. It is the offer of a "way" and of a formation by the Spirit into that way.

Evangelism is, to be sure, the offer to the world of Jesus *as* the Christ; and thus the invitation to follow Jesus and to be formed into the narrative of his life, death, and resurrection does not preclude but rather entails the highest claims for his identity as the *logos* (Word) and *sophia* (Wisdom) of God, the One in whom God was present reconciling the world. But disconnected from the story of the people of God and abstracted from the actual course of Jesus' life, lofty claims about Jesus become sentimental ideologies in the service of the status quo by robbing him of any public, material, or political significance. Jesus then becomes little more than the Christ of inner piety, the haloed and gold-ensconced

figure of devotion, or the abstract referent of fundamentalist propositions and historical-critical questing (both of which are the product of
the same objectifying mindset). His "way" vanishes into the mist, as
do the historical and social conditions of the salvation offered by God
through him and the necessity of any sort of visible community that
would provide an embodied witness to that way in the world. Evangelism is then aimed at securing a "personal" experience, decision, or
belief rather than a multilayered and communally embodied invitation
to a journey.

To offer Jesus as the Christ is to offer him not merely as a theological
proposition to be believed but as Lord, as the One to whom obedience is
due. Christ is not then introduced merely as a fellow pilgrim to be imitated
on the way. He himself is "the way." Of course there is and will always
be a dimension of imitation in the discipleship to which evangelism is
an invitation. To offer Christ is to offer the cup out of which Jesus drank
and the baptism with which he was baptized (Mark 10:38). This means
that the imitation to which evangelism is an invitation is essentially
cruciform. To follow Jesus the crucified Lord is to be formed into the
way of the cross.[18] So Dietrich Bonhoeffer could say, "The cross is not
the terrible end to an otherwise godfearing and happy life, but it meets
us at the beginning of our communion with Christ. When Christ calls [a
person], he bids [that person] come and die" (1959:89).

There is no avoiding this evangelistic scandal. To offer Christ is to
offer the way of the cross—not as a path to self-negation but as the path
toward a recentering of ourselves in Christ. We are invited to be crucified with Christ and to be buried with him in baptism, yet raised again
to new life and freed from all former enslavements, dominations, and
subjugations. But this means that the offer of crucifixion at the center
of evangelistic practice is a call to subordinate all other forms of obedience and all other lords to Christ, who, as Barth reminds us, is not
only mediator but lawgiver—Savior precisely because he is also judge
(1936–77:4/1:217). Evangelism, therefore, has an inescapably moral dimension, the neglect of which entitles us to the same criticism that John
Wesley leveled against the "gospel preachers" of his day who preached
promise, consolation, and forgiveness without an accompanying exhortation to moral transformation:

18. Yoder's caution about, but affirmation of, cruciform discipleship is worth repeating:
"There is thus but one realm in which the concept of imitation holds—but there it holds
in every strand of the New Testament literature and all the more strikingly by virtue of
the absence of parallels in other realms: this is at the point of the concrete social meaning
of the cross in its relation to enmity and power. Servanthood replaces dominion, forgiveness absorbs hostility. Thus—and only thus—are we bound by the New Testament to 'be
like Jesus'" (1972:134).

The "gospel preachers" so called corrupt their hearers; they vitiate their taste, so that they cannot relish sound doctrine; and spoil their appetite, so that they cannot turn it into nourishment; they, as it were, feed them with sweetmeats, till the genuine wine of the kingdom seems quite insipid to them. They give them cordial upon cordial, which make them all life and spirit for the present; but meantime their appetite is destroyed, so that they can neither retain nor digest the pure milk of the Word. (1931:3:84)

Here we encounter an important challenge in the evangelistic offer of Christ as Lord. For given what we know about the peaceable nature of God's rule, the language of "lordship" and "obedience" might strike us as wholly inadequate to the good news, perhaps even legitimating practices of violence, domination, and victimization that stand in opposition to that news. How can the offer of Jesus as Lord (an invitation to subordination) be made today to women, for example, without requiring that they consent to their own oppression at the hands of patriarchal structures in both church and society?

The confession of Jesus as Lord was originally a way of confessing the end of longstanding patterns of domination and subordination. Jesus was Lord, we should remember, before Christ became Pantokrater within the imperial imagination of Constantinianism. It is also true, as Kathryn Tanner suggests, that while the confession of Jesus as Lord could be taken as implying that "the emperor is a lord to be obeyed like Jesus," it could also "permit the anti-imperial interpretation favored by the poor audience for them [in, for example, the sermons of some church officials]—the emperor must obey the Lord Jesus who is the loving servant of the people" (1997:90). But in our contemporary context, is not the invitation to obey Jesus as Lord bound not only to "sound" oppressive (thus failing to come across to persons as helping, as saving, as shalom) but also to *be* oppressive—that is, to legitimate existing structures of domination and subordination?

One potential answer to this question comes from Coakley, who reminds us that not all forms of dependence, submission, and subordination are the same, nor are they all oppressive. Indeed, it is impossible to eliminate every form of dependence from the Christian faith without doing great violence to it. What can be eliminated, however, is a mode of Christian dependence configured wholly in terms of traditionally male processes of individuation, in which obedience to Jesus as Lord is always construed as the subordination of one's will to his (and, by extension, to the church). For many women, as Coakley notes, pride and will to power are not as likely to characterize the sinful condition from which they need saving but rather overdependence and self-hatred (2002:66–67).

One of our root problems in thinking about the lordship of Jesus is connected to a more fundamental problem in how we relate the sovereignty of God to human freedom generally. Especially in the West, both God's sovereignty and human freedom have been imagined largely in terms of an individualistic model for which the freedom of one person is incompatible or in competition with the freedom of others, producing a contest of wills. God is then "a magnified version of the *human* 'unmoved mover' . . . of incompatibilist freedom, an 'individual' of unrivaled power and autonomy who takes on the traditional attributes of classical theism, but more revealingly mirrors a (masculinist) vision of self specific to the Enlightenment" (Coakley 2002:101). Within this conception of freedom, there are really only two courses of action available: domination and absorption of the other or "withdrawal to make space for the other's autonomy." What is missing, Coakley argues, is more focused attention to "the nurturing and all-encompassing dimensions of divine love" and to "gendered metaphors that have well-known instantiations in the history of Christian theology and spirituality" (ibid.).

One way of following up on Coakley's suggestion, though focused more on how Christ is offered evangelistically than on the relationship of God to humans generally, is to construe Christ's lordship as implying a *participation in* Christ rather than, in the first place, a *subordination to* Christ. Again, the point is not to eliminate every form of obedience and dependence from the Christian account of salvation. Nor is it to refocus salvation on humans rather than on Christ in order to meet the modern demand for the preservation of human subjectivity, freedom, and autonomy in the process of salvation.

At its best, the feminist critique of masculinist models of freedom and sovereignty is not just a reversal of masculinism in the name of the human subject but a way of moving beyond the characteristically modern assertion of freedom as autonomy toward freedom as mutuality, participation, solidarity, and communion. On this account, salvation is narrated less from within the juridical framework of Western theologies, as the forgiveness of past acts of disobedience and the resolution of guilt, and more from within the therapeutic framework of Eastern theologies, as a participation in the life and character of the triune God (often characterized as *theosis* or divinization). Because salvation here is less about the subordination of one's will and more about a lived participation, what it means to follow Jesus as Lord implies a distinctive sort of obedience—one that cannot be co-opted by any other form of obedience because it is entirely unlike any other. This obedience requires an end to the entire scheme of domination and subordination that, since Adam and Eve, is the curse of sin. In other words, what is subordinated in our surrender to the lordship of Jesus (and thereby nailed to the cross) is every form of worldly domination whereby one person's freedom, dignity, or regard is achieved at the expense of another.

There is a mutual dependence at the heart of Christian *ecclesia* as every member of the body seeking to be formed into "the mind of Christ" is empowered to look to the interests of others over their own and, as Paul instructs, in humility to regard others more highly than themselves (Phil. 2:3–4). But while the evangelistic offer of Christ is always an invitation to discipleship, obedience, dependency, and cruciformity, these are always to be configured wholly within the bonds of love that characterize our friendship with God through participation in Christ. Thus, even if the lordship of Jesus can be described as a political and economic government into which we are initiated with something like citizenship or family membership, it must also be described (as in the Gospel of John) using more organic and intimate metaphors like a vine into which we are engrafted, bread by which we are nourished, and living water by which our thirst is quenched.

The intimacy of this incorporation into Christ and the organic nature of this union with Christ is, however, deeply misunderstood when construed as a wholly private and interior incorporation of the individual into an ethereal and disembodied Christ. Incorporation into Christ is incorporation into Christ's body; as Paul says, "In the one Spirit we were all baptized into one body . . . and we were all made to drink of one Spirit" (1 Cor. 12:13). That is why the evangelistic offer of Christ is at the same time the offer of Christ's body, the church. Strictly speaking, of course, Christ cannot be equated with the church. But we are able nonetheless to speak of Christ *as* the church, for there is an intrinsic continuity between the risen Jesus and the church's proclamation, worship, and prayer, its solidarity with those who suffer, its forgiveness, and its prophetic witness. The church is the visible body where one meets Christ, or as Bonhoeffer puts it so powerfully:

> Just as Christ is present as Word and in the Word, as sacrament and in the sacrament, so he is also present as Church and in the Church. His presence in Word and sacrament is related to his presence in the Church as reality is related to form. Christ is the Church by virtue of his *pro me* being. Between his ascension and his coming again the Church is his form and indeed his only form. . . . The Church is the body of Christ. Here body is not only a symbol. The Church *is* the body of Christ, it does not *signify* the body of Christ. When applied to the Church, the concept of body is not only a concept of function, which refers only to the members of this body. It is a comprehensive and central concept of the mode of existence of the one who is present in his exaltation and humiliation. (1960:58–59)

To offer Christ is to invite persons to share in the life, death, and resurrection of Jesus, and this offer is made by proclaiming and living out his story together in such a way that new believers can make this story *their* own. Indeed, to offer the story of Jesus is itself to extend that story, on the part of both the one making the invitation and the one accepting the invitation to become a new character in the story. Christ's existence does not end with the resurrection or with his ascension into heaven. The offer of participation in the resurrected body of Christ is the offer both of a story and a social body, a message and a person, a lordship and a life, an obedience and a liberation.

Public Proclamation

> Since we are not the lord of history there will be times when the only thing we can do is to speak and the only word we can speak is the word clothed in a deed, a word that can command attention from no one and that can coerce no one. But even in this situation the word must be spoken in the deed in confidence that it is the Lord of history and God's Holy Spirit, not our eloquence or artistic creativity, which will make of our sign a message.
>
> John Howard Yoder (1998:204)

We are now in a position to ask more pointedly about the role of public proclamation in evangelism. This is hardly an insignificant question, for the practice of evangelism is often equated with the activity of proclamation, and because of this it is frequently reduced to verbal exchanges, especially those that are initiated and carried out by professional evangelists, preachers, and pastors.[19] *The Oxford English Diction-*

---

19. William Abraham has provided a thorough account of the arguments for and against identifying evangelism with proclamation, arguing persuasively that the reduction of evangelism to proclamation is artificial and incompatible with the practices of the earliest Christian communities. It also renders evangelism susceptible to individualistic, privatizing, and anthropocentric tendencies already rife in Western Christianity. One of the benefits of defining evangelism as verbal proclamation of the gospel is that it "provides a clear, manageable concept that is rooted in the early history of the word and that calls the church to excellence in communicating the Christian gospel to those who are prepared to listen" (1989:44–45). This restriction helps us to see how evangelism is a distinct practice in its own right rather than merely "everything" the Christian does. At the same time, the restriction tends toward making evangelism the responsibility of just a few—those who exercise pastoral leadership or who are gifted public speakers—rather than of every Christian. The strict identification of evangelism with public proclamation, moreover, fails to take into account the full range of activities that characterized the early evangelists of the church, who often bore evangelistic witness through conversation, teaching, healing, discipling, and, of course, the very form of their lives and their communities.

ary, for example, defines *evangelism* as "the preaching or promulgation of the Gospel"; likewise, to *evangelize* is "to bring or tell good tidings; to preach, proclaim the gospel." By contrast, I have tried to argue that evangelism is an intrinsically material and social practice. The offer of Christ is a visible and embodied offer made by a Christ-shaped social body in and through the form of its daily habits and social patterns, its baptismal "politics" and its eucharistic "economics." Because of this, the character of the evangelistic summons is as aesthetic and material as it is cognitive and verbal, inviting participation in a community rather than mere assent to a set of ideas. The case I have been trying to build thus far is that our present context requires a more robust contextualization of Christian witness in a particular form of life called *ecclesia*. It also requires a clearer grasp of how the embodied witness of the church in its care for the poor, its forgiveness of enemies, and its hospitality to strangers serves in many circumstances not only as a prerequisite for the credibility of proclamation but as the very act of proclamation (cf. Yoder 1998:81). If this is the case, the practice of evangelism cannot be wholly concentrated in the activity of verbal proclamation.

But this does not mean that verbal proclamation has no place in evangelism or that its place is not central. It is impossible to attend faithfully to the witness of the Hebrew prophets, Jesus, and the apostles and to miss the commanding importance for them of the public proclamation of God's reign and of a verbal summons to take that reign seriously. My emphasis on embodiment in evangelistic witness is not intended as an argument for diminishing the importance of verbal witness but should instead be taken as affirming the visibility of the church as its necessary condition. I am aware, however, that an emphasis on the visibility of the church may be employed, even if unconsciously, as a justification for public silence with regard to questions of faith, especially in contexts characterized by what Jerome Burce terms "spiritual agnosticism." According to Burce, "The fundamental truth claim of our culture with respect to matters spiritual is that we cannot know about them with anything approaching sufficient certainty to command the allegiance or shape the conduct or, least of all, correct the spiritual and/or moral opinions of another" (2000:55). We confuse certainty with conviction and become something like the "unscripted anxious stutterers" mentioned earlier, deprived not only of conviction but also of a story. While it is undoubtedly true that Christians have often been noisy when they needed to be listening and while the world rightly becomes weary of our words when clothed in hypocrisy, Christians do indeed have a message to announce and a story to tell.

Words, then, are not necessarily inferior to deeds in evangelism. In fact, the proclamation of the gospel whether in the form of preaching, confession, or testimony is a type of deed—and an incredibly powerful one at that. Words create the worlds we inhabit. They may at times become for us the length and breadth of our prison cells (Paul's "dead letter"), but they may also become life-giving pathways to ever new worlds, vehicles of imagination and transcendence. The book of Genesis can even claim that it is by God's word that the heavens and earth were created. Words create and make alive; they grant permission and offer absolution. But of course words can also kill and destroy. "Language," as David Lose puts it so well, "colors our expectations, creates and limits possibilities for constructing meaning, and vastly determines not only how we see but what we are willing to look at" (2003:53).

At the same time, words do have their limits; Michael Polanyi was surely right when he said that "we can know more than we can tell" (1967:4). But perhaps Barth was no less right in claiming with regard to the Word of God that "cognizance becomes knowledge when [a person] becomes a responsible witness to its content" (1936–77:1/1:188). There is no reason to hold that proclamation must always be inadequate and reductive in the practice of evangelism. On the contrary, the twin activities of telling and hearing constitute an indispensable path toward inhabiting as one's own the stories of the people of God. Not only that, it is not entirely clear that we know our own stories without the act of telling them. As Stephen Webb says, "Christians do not know what they really believe until they publicly witness to their faith. In other words, faith is not something we possess and then hope we can express if and when the time comes to speak out. Faith is embodied when the confidence required to be a witness is experienced as a gift from God" (2004:17). It may be true, then, that words do not always express the fullness of what we know; they may even at times betray, reduce, or distort what we know. But it is also the case that words reveal what we might otherwise prefer to hide or neglect in a world that has taught us to fear our own convictions. Proclamation is one of the most important ways we become "witnesses."

Perhaps this is why the shape of conversation is so important within the people of God and why, as Yoder observes, it requires not only "agents of direction" (prophets), "agents of memory" (scribes), and "agents of order and due process" (pastors, elders, bishops) but also "agents of linguistic consciousness" (teachers; 1984:28–34):

> It is a significant anthropological insight to say that language can steer the community with a power disproportionate to other kinds of leadership. The demagogue, the poet, also the journalist, the novelist, the grammarian, all are engaged in steering society with the rudder of language. This applies to rhetoric as a skill and also to the place of any set of concepts in

predisposing what kinds of thoughts the members of a given community are capable of having. (ibid. 32)

While Yoder's comments are focused on the communal hermeneutic of the people of God by which it reasons together, resolves conflict, and makes decisions, one could also claim that the "shape of conversation" to which he refers is important not only *within* the people of God but *between* the people of God and their neighbors, between church and world, between believers and unbelievers (including all those who consider themselves somewhere in between!). In other words, the practice of evangelism requires the careful use of language, and thus the same "agents" (of direction, memory, order, and linguistic self-consciousness) will have critical roles to play here as well. All of this is complicated, however, by the fact that given contemporary patterns of church organization, these several roles tend to converge to some degree in the person of the pastor, who is not only the preacher but in many cases also the prophet, teacher, scribe, and overseer. Important dimensions of empowerment and accountability are eliminated within the congregation of the people of God, as the entire burden of evangelism too frequently is laid on the shoulders of the pastor.[20]

Of course, the pastor need not take full responsibility for the practice of evangelism if the congregation is enabled (very likely through the pastor's leadership) to recover more fully the ministry of the laity[21] or a multitextured understanding of the offices that once characterized the

20. Another reading of the situation would be to claim that under the conditions of modernity, the agents of communal memory and linguistic self-consciousness have been removed to the seminary and the agents of order to denominational headquarters, so that the pastor is left with the singular task of providing weekly "inspiration." This removal is a great loss for the congregation but also signals the ultimate debilitation and distortion of the tasks of communal memory (which now becomes the academic study of the Bible or of Christian history), linguistic self-consciousness (which now becomes the technical parsing out of theological language), and order (which is now reduced to the bureaucratic management of institutions) by removing the agents from their function within the community as servants of the community.

21. This is not the best place to develop an argument for restoring the practices of Christian ministry to the whole people of God instead of allowing them to become the sole responsibility (or prerogative) of a professional "clergy," but I agree with Yoder that while Protestants may well claim the doctrine of the priesthood of believers to be among the most important insights of the Reformation, that doctrine has yet to fully shape the theology of Christian vocation in Protestant churches except in the rarest of instances. It remains "the reformation that has yet to happen," and of the five patterns of social process identified by Yoder as characterizing the Christian "body politics," the "universality of charisma," or what Paul refers to as "the fullness of Christ," is "the first that has not yet had its reformation . . . the first whose adequate concrete form has still to be retrieved" (1992a:59).

early Christian communities (apostles, priests, deacons, bishops, doctors, evangelists, prophets, scribes, teachers, readers, doorkeepers, exorcists, etc.). But even where progress is made toward such a "reformation" and a greater discernment of gifts is cultivated within a community along with the empowerment and accountability appropriate to the employment of those gifts, in today's church the task of evangelism in the form of public proclamation is still likely to fall to the pastor. The ordination of clergy in many Christian communions still carries with it, and rightly so, the charge to "do the work of an evangelist" (2 Tim. 4:5). And regardless of how broadly we might understand the practice of evangelism, public proclamation in the form of the preached word is still critical to that practice, and so, therefore, is the role of the pastor as the member of the community who is both gifted and skilled at preaching.

Because proclamation is one of the primary ways a Christian becomes a witness, the preacher can never see her task as the mere handing over of a set of beliefs or an attempt to convince, persuade, or give advice, to evoke a decision, stir up the emotions, or meet a need.[22] Proclamation is performative speech—it does what it says. The very act of proclaiming not only makes the speaker into a witness but also transforms the words of the proclaimer into gospel and "carries the hearer beyond alternatives as it actually creates faith, bestows freedom, engenders joy, finally raises the dead . . . because of the Spirit who animates it" (Nestingen 2005). For this reason, proclamation is self-involving and sounds "less like 'Washington crossed the Delaware' and more like 'I love you'" (Michalson 2002:44). Thus, the *person* of the preacher has a unique and indispensable responsibility in Christian evangelism, even though proclamation is not "about" the preacher's ideas, personality, or experiences, nor is it an expression of the preacher's self-consciousness. Proclamation is self-involving speech, what we might describe as a particular type of confession (Lose 2003:3); but it is also self-emptying speech in which, by the Holy Spirit's work, Christ becomes incarnate. It is, as Bonhoeffer put it, "Christ himself walking through his congregation as the word" (1975:126).

But this is no magic act, no *ex opere operato* performance in which by merely mouthing certain words the preacher is able to guarantee a certain effect or outcome. As Hauerwas rightly insists, "Preaching is not just the telling; it is also the hearing. Just as great art creates an audience capable of hearing or seeing in new ways, so the church's preaching cre-

22. The decline of proclamation is, according to Webb, at least partly due to the increased adaptation of Christian ministry to psychology. "Private words of counsel came to sound more authentic than pronouncements from the pulpit, which contributed to the transformation of the ministry into a helping profession, making psychology and not the art of public speaking paramount for ministerial education" (2004:25–26).

ates an audience capable of being challenged by the story of Jesus and his kingdom" (1983:108). Whether proclamation is considered in relation to the community of believers as that which establishes and builds it up or whether it is considered in relation to nonbelievers in the mode of evangelistic summons and invitation, proclamation is always a communal action in which the preached word becomes God's word as the Holy Spirit makes us receptive and responsive listeners, capable of hearing the word rightly and being formed by it (cf. Hauerwas 2001a:159).[23] On the one hand, then, receptivity to the proclaimed word cannot be engineered or predicted, as when some might try to exploit loss, bereavement, or social marginalization as an open door for effective evangelization. On the other hand, as I shall attempt to develop further in the next chapter, the proclaimed word does presuppose a particular context—a visible church—in which the words of the proclaimer become the word of God and, thereby, life for the world.

While proclamation is self-involving and performative speech—its truth being bound up both with the teller of the good news as witness and the *ecclesia* as the visible context of that witness—the story that is proclaimed in evangelism remains of primary importance. Abraham puts the matter well:

> The gospel is constituted by the mighty acts of God in history for the liberation of the cosmos. It is not a set of rickety arguments about the divine order; it is not the expression of some sublime religious experience brought mysteriously to verbal form; it is not a romantic report about awareness of God in nature; it is not a speculative, philosophical theory about the nature of ultimate reality; it is not a set of pious or moral maxims designed to straighten out the world; it is not a legalistic lament about the meanness of human nature; it is not a sentimental journey down memory lane into ancient history. It is the unique narrative of what God has done to inaugurate [God's] kingdom in Jesus of Nazareth, crucified outside Jerusalem, risen from the dead, seated at the right hand of God, and now reigning eternally with the Father, through the activity of the Holy Spirit, in the church and in the world. Where this is not announced, it will not be known. (1989:170)

If that is true, then proclamation of the gospel is proclamation of a story. And while evangelism, as I have tried to argue, can never rest content with telling this story apart from an embodied and visible exemplification of it, the practice of evangelism depends from first to last for its inner coherence on rightly remembering the narrative by which

23. Karl Barth defined preaching as "the speech which obediently listens." As Webb remarks, "The preacher, in a way, is the church's chief listener. Barth expands this point by suggesting that the church should be understood as 'the listening Church'" (2004:25).

the church is called into existence and by which it lives, and then proclaiming it with confidence.

Naturally, how we construe verbal witness in relation to the visibility
of the church has significant practical implications for how worship and
preaching are carried out in relationship to evangelism. This is especially
true for those of us who stand in liturgical traditions that typically place
tremendous weight on the sermon and assign a special prominence to
the one who delivers the sermon. The Protestant reformers put public
proclamation of the Word of God at the center of Christian faith and
worship, and in the post–World War II era, "neo-orthodox" theologians
such as Karl Barth, Rudolf Bultmann, Gerhard Ebeling, and Dietrich
Bonhoeffer (as different as they are from one another) reinforced the
sense in which Christ is encountered in the moment of proclamation.

But without denying this emphasis on the centrality of the preached
word in evangelism and of the moment of existential encounter, crisis,
and decision occasioned by public proclamation, it is worth considering what it means to position the preached word ecclesiologically as a
practice of the Holy Spirit, a practice that does not merely contribute
more noise to an already noisy and "word-weary" world. In Protestant
theology, the proclamation of the word has often been contrasted with
(or even set in opposition to) the church's sacraments. Representing
the voice of Eastern Christianity, Alexander Schmemann observes that
Western Christians have difficulty thinking of the proclamation of the
word as sacramental, so dichotomous have word and sacrament become
for us over time. The path to overcoming this dichotomy, he suggests, is
in grasping that "the liturgy of the Word is as sacramental as the sacrament is 'evangelical'" (1997:32). Augustine taught that the sacraments
are "visible words"; but it is also the case that "the proclamation of the
Word is a sacramental act par excellence because it is a transforming
act. It transforms the human words of the Gospel into the Word of God
and the manifestation of the Kingdom. And it transforms the [person]
who hears the Word into a receptacle of the Word and a temple of the
Spirit" (ibid. 32–33).

What must be added to Schmemann's account is the importance both
of word to sacrament and sacrament to word. On the one hand, the
sacraments require words that specify their relationship to faith. Sacraments "do not work automatically, as Catholics and Protestants agree,
precisely because they do not work silently" (Webb 2004:44–45). On the
other hand, the Christ we proclaim in the sermon and who is incarnate
in the preached word is the host of a table that has been prepared for
the world—not an imaginary or figurative table but a material one that
is the site of Christian welcome, nourishment, and communion. In fact,
proclamation stands much to gain when practiced eucharistically, for

it now participates in and draws attention to the sharing, thanksgiving, and donation that characterize the Lord's table rather than being configured from within the alternative economics in which we are used to hearing public speech—typically, commercials, talk shows, and political discourse—as acts of production and consumption, contract and exchange. The Word of God is not for sale. It is inviting and appealing, yet also demanding and strange. It cannot be commodified or altered to become something either the proclaimer or the hearer thinks could be believed or might be of "help." Again, the task of proclamation is not, in the first place, an explanation of the Christian faith or an apologetic for the Christian life, nor is it a translation of the gospel into non-Christian categories. The aim of proclamation is not to achieve its own acceptance but rather to announce, offer, promise, and confess the Word of God, to "articulate Christian difference in such a fashion as to make it strange" (Milbank 1990:381).

9

Context and Conversion

Because the evangelistic invitation is intrinsically social, political, and economic, evangelism can never ultimately be the work of lone individuals. From the beginning, God has been calling forth a people that in its visible patterns and practices, in its worship and its obedience, and in its very existence as a people testifies to the good news of shalom and thereby serves as a light to the nations. While individuals certainly do practice evangelism by both living peacefully and offering that peace to others, it is ultimately the covenant community, called into being and empowered by God's Spirit, that bears embodied witness to God's redemptive purpose and in so doing evangelizes the world. That the faith community is itself evangelist then is not merely a pragmatic strategy for reaching the world; it is intrinsic to the good news that is being proclaimed and the invitation that is being offered.

In this chapter, I examine further the ecclesial context of evangelism and, in particular, the relationship between evangelism and conversion. Evangelism cannot be measured by the conversions it "produces." Its only measure is faithfulness to the gospel of Christ of which it is a witness and to which it is an invitation. Yet all Christian evangelism *calls* for a conversion that is nothing less than a complete "turning around" (*metanoia*). For resurrection bears the same relationship to death in every person's existence: new birth, new life, new peoplehood. By offering its witness and invitation, the church lives in hope and expectation that its offer will be accepted freely, its call heeded uncoercively. It does more than sit back waiting for that possibility. It seeks to nourish it by engaging in practices of outreach, proclamation, hospitality, formation, initiation, and discipleship that lead persons into a process of conversion to a life of holiness. Thus, while evangelism as a practice cannot be measured by whether it produces conversions, it most certainly is shaped by the kind of conversion for which it calls and for which it hopes. This chapter will attempt to clarify the nature of Christian conversion and the difference this makes for how evangelism is practiced.

A Culture of Conversion

To begin with, let us confess that we live in a "culture of conversion." The technologies of transformation assembled within our world and directed toward the endless formation of desire and the ongoing alteration of behavior are unrivaled by any other period in history. In every direction we turn, we are offered the promise of "makeover," whether of body, face, wardrobe, career, marriage, home, personality, or soul. Accompanying these makeovers is a pervasive ethos of confession and absolution—witness the proliferation of confessional autobiographies and the popularity of television talk shows, which, as Kathleen Lowney has shown, parallel the revivals of a bygone era complete with a "mourner's bench" where sinners can be brought forward to repent publicly and find salvation.[1]

To be converted is not something strange or out of the ordinary in our world. It is roughly equivalent to the air we breathe. In fact, part of what makes the call to Christian conversion strike us as so radical and invasive today is the level to which we have become acclimated to our ongoing conversion and formation by a staggering range of powers that contradict Christian faith and community and serve ends other than the shalom of God's reign.

While this ongoing conversion takes many different shapes, our primary formation from the day we are born is, as earlier noted, our for-

1. Lowney's *Baring Our Souls: TV Talk Shows and the Religion of Recovery* (1999) is a fascinating analysis of the "religion of recovery," which is fed by the basic tenets of the recovery movement and epitomized in the philosophy of various twelve-step programs (such as Alcoholics Anonymous). In her book, Lowney demonstrates how today's talk shows, with their endless parades of deviant behavior, combine elements of circuses and revivals, having become the "electronic tents" under which recovery religion provides at a popular level the basic assumptions for public moral discourse. The talk-show host is today the evangelist of the religion of recovery. Through a process of exposing the deviance of guests brought onto the show, followed by consulting with "exes" and "experts," television talk shows reinforce the notion that the sinful forces from which we must find liberation are the processes of socialization that have left us emotionally scarred and codependent (especially those that occur early in life at the hands of our families).

mation as consumers. We buy products not because we need them but because of the emotional and cultural bonds that have been formed between us and them through relentless and multiple forms of advertising that capitalize on (and create) cultural myths, narratives, and symbols into which we are socialized. Indeed, a growing, transnational sector of industry understands itself as manufacturing not merely products for consumption but culture itself.[2] This formation is so thorough, so seductive, and so pervasive that it is virtually impossible to resist apart from the power of the Holy Spirit and the disciplines of *ecclesia*. We are repeatedly invited to become different people—to adopt the mindset of those forming us and to imitate the referents placed before us. Given this formation, as Michael Budde and Robert Brimlow suggest, "the intellectual challenge is not in explaining why Christian formation loses out to that of capitalist culture, but why anyone would expect any other outcome" (2002:76). In modern cultures, marketing has become formation, and any Christian evangelism that does not subvert this arrangement by offering a rival formation (rather than attempting merely to mimic it in the form of a "marketing" of Christianity) will by necessity be made its accomplice if not its servant.

As Tertullian insisted, people are "made, not born, Christians,"[3] and we know that by at least the third century, the process of making Christians could take up to three years. Given the intense and ongoing culture of conversion within which we live today, there is no reason to believe that conversion to Christianity will take place any faster. Indeed, there is every reason to believe that the process will resemble an intensive and sustained process of detoxification. What is ultimately distinctive about Christian conversion, however, is not its timing but rather the holiness at which it is aimed. As Richard Heitzenrater has observed, "When holiness is your goal, you do evangelism differently."[4]

One of the reasons that conversion is a matter of formation over time is that it is not simply a decision or an experience but the acquisition of a way of life that is embodied and passed along in community. Though evangelism calls for conversion, the holiness toward which this conversion is oriented is, as we have seen, inherently ecclesial and therefore political and economic. Conversion and obedience cannot therefore be

2. As Budde and Brimlow put it, "Culture industries are increasingly combined in webs of cross-promotion and 'synergy' (for example, a Disney movie spawns a Disney-published book and a Disney-published soundtrack, all of which are hyped on Disney-owned television and radio networks, and which enjoy cross-promotions via Disney's long-term deal with McDonald's restaurants)" (2002:63).

3. *Apology* 18, in Roberts and Donaldson 1931:3:32.

4. Heitzenrater is here commenting on the evangelism of John Wesley and the beginnings of the Methodist movement; quoted in Gunter (1997:19).

separated in such a way that conversion has two stages, the first religious and the second ethical (Newbigin 1995:135–36). To "believe," in the sense most relevant to Christian conversion, may very well include a cognitive dimension, but "it would be quite strange," as Hauerwas observes, "to say that one 'believes,' for instance, in the resurrection and yet assume that some further decision or attitude needs to be taken in relation to such a belief. Even stranger would be the notion that believing any of these things as true could be abstracted from the kind of life commensurate with holding such beliefs" (1998:5).

The intrinsically ethical nature of Christian conversion naturally raises important questions about how much should be expected of conversion. Legalism is ever a danger, as is a cultural colonialism whereby the lifestyle of one group is foisted off onto converts as the essence of Christianity. If it is true that conversion is always a conversion to holiness as a way of life, it is also true that "the point of ethical crisis is often quite different from the one in the mind of the missionary" (Newbigin 1995:138). The evangelist is called to remember that the final end of evangelism is the glory of God, understood as God's own character and life imparted as a gift to human beings through participation—or, as Paul says in Galatians 4:19, the formation of Christ in believers. Because evangelism is the work of the Holy Spirit in imparting God's own Self to the human being through communion—thereby rendering the human "alive," as Irenaeus argued[5]—the church must continually allow the freedom for something new to take place in conversion. If evangelism is a practice oriented wholly toward holiness, it is also in every context an ecclesiogenesis by the Spirit.

This evangelistic flexibility and openness does not negate the truth that conversion is always a radical reorientation of the human person toward God embodied in new political and economic habits. Conversion is a change of *loves* that is a movement, as Augustine put it, from one city to another.[6] Yet apart from a clear focus on the new form of social existence (this "other city") that is the aim of conversion, any emphasis the practice of evangelism might place on conversion is bound to be distorting. If we think of the Christian life as a journey characterized by holiness as both its "way" and its "end," there is historically a tension between conversion-centered evangelism and holiness-centered evangelism. The problem is this: when the practice of evangelism becomes so preoccupied with entry that it loses sight of the journey itself, it is capable of being taken over by a logic foreign to the journey and even

5. *Against Heresies* 4.20.7, in Roberts and Donaldson 1931:1:490.
6. Or, as Augustine also says, *incipit exire qui incipit amare*, "the person who is beginning to go forth is the one who is beginning to love" ("Exposition of Psalm 64," in Augustine 1990:3/17:266–67).

antagonistic to it. Jesus recognizes this possibility when he censured those who "cross sea and land to make a single convert," while the convert ends up becoming "twice as much a child of hell" as the evangelists themselves (Matt. 23:15).

It is not the call to conversion that is at issue here. Jesus' proclamation of God's reign is unintelligible apart from such a call. The problem is that it is always possible to abstract conversion from that to which we are to be converted, to reify that abstraction into something like a "decision" or an "experience," and then to aim evangelism at this. While this process of abstraction has, throughout most of Christendom, been focused on the rite of infant baptism, it has increasingly been shaped in modernity by a voluntarist psychology in which the private decision of the autonomous self to "be saved" is determinative of one's salvation. In both cases, the point of entry into the Christian life is conceived as the goal of evangelism, with tragic consequences for the way evangelism is practiced, for now evangelism will take the form of any activity that is capable of securing this point of entry. Evangelism ceases to be a practice and becomes a mere "technology."

To the extent that Protestantism has proved susceptible to this distortion, this is largely because of its tendency to make justification more determinative of Christian salvation than sanctification. The danger here is that Protestant evangelism becomes more interested in leading persons into a conversion experience (understood as a new self-understanding) than in leading persons into a Christlike life (which typically gets worked out instead in the form of something called "ethical implications"). But even where sanctification has been emphasized in evangelism, a distorting preoccupation with the *experience* of holiness over the *life* of holiness can be detected, as for example with the American camp-meeting and holiness movement of the mid-nineteenth century. As Stephen Gunter remarks, "Eventually, conversion-centered evangelism rationalized becoming a Christian into steps and stages which are used to define the experience; and it is assumed that the experience is most often momentary, sudden, and completed within a few moments" (1997:19). Again, it is not an insistence on conversion that is the problem but rather the reduction of conversion to the moment of entrance and a fixation on that moment of entrance as the goal of evangelism.

Community and Conversion

Because of the intensive and comprehensive nature of Christian conversion, especially from a culture of conversion, we would be mistaken to think of faith as a simple act of individual will. Faith is instead a disposition formed over time and handed on in community. This does not mean that faith is passed along automatically from one generation to the next or that freedom is absent in the passing along of faith; but the freedom involved in coming to faith is not that of the individual autonomous self of modernity. In fact, it is only by being drawn into communion that individuals become "persons" in the first place and thereby transcend the modern constitution of the self as individualized being (cf. Zizioulas 1997:27–65). Hauerwas is exactly right, therefore, when he says, "The first words about the Christian life are about a life together, not about the individual" (2001a:372).

Conversion is much more than an individual's deciding to believe new pieces of information that she or he now possesses. It occurs at the level of one's *convictions*, which, as James McClendon and James Smith argue, are so central to one's character as a person that "a change in them would involve a change (would, indeed *be* a change) in that person's character" (1994:105). Moreover, convictions occur within convictional communities, so that a convictional conversion requires something more like changing communities. This does not mean that one merely decides to take the convictions of another community as true on the basis of the authority of that community; one will certainly test them against one's present knowledge of the world. But all knowledge is formed within communities of sense and experience that themselves embody convictional elements. In other words, no knowledge is conviction neutral or conviction free. McClendon and Smith are, I believe, therefore justified in the following conclusions:

> The acquiring of a conviction set and the justification of the set are often simultaneous and always interrelated—not to be understood apart from one another. To speak of choosing one's conviction set is not necessarily wrong, but it may be misleading unless we recognize that "choosing one's convictions" is a shorthand way of talking about many choices made over a period of time, reinforcing one another, accumulating, developing in more and more definite directions until we find ourselves with a conviction set that we acknowledge as our own, as being the way of life, the outlook, that we have chosen. . . . Dramatic conversions do indeed contain new convictional elements, but . . . (1) these are imbedded in a changing body of convictional material; (2) the previous convictional history of the convert contains the seeds of the new material that flowers in the conversion process; (3) in many cases, the conversion is a symbolic concentration representing changes that either precede or succeed it, as well as the changes of the luminous moment itself. (ibid. 168–70)

In conversion, the whole person is remade—heart, mind, body, relationships, allegiances, habits. In essence, a new identity is acquired—or rather learned—through the stories, practices, and traditions of the church. Becoming a Christian can therefore be likened to a process of apprenticeship associated with learning a trade or the discipline and competencies required in learning a foreign language. Conversion takes time, proceeds differently for different persons, and often includes periods of intense change when small changes over time can produce an entire shift in gestalt or worldview. By contrast, much of contemporary evangelism, disciplined as it is by modern social imaginations with the autonomous individual at its center, is oriented toward a model in which conversion is presented as preceding incorporation into the church and the result of conviction and persuasion sufficient to convince the individual to "decide" to convert.

I would not want to deny altogether the role of decision in conversion, but given the political and economic nature of the salvation God has given the world in the form of a Spirit-created *ecclesia*, and given the holistic nature of conversion aimed at a comprehensive socialization into a life of holiness, there is to my mind no avoiding Luther's dictum that the church is "the mother that begets and bears every Christian through the Word of God"[7] or his further claim that "[the one] who wants to find Christ must first find the church" (1955–76:52:39).

On this model, incorporation into the church precedes conversion—or rather is intrinsic to conversion—for it is only by being made part of a community of language and practice that we begin both to recognize the need for the kind of transformation that Christ has to offer and to discover the resources for moving toward it. It is for this reason that it may well be better to speak of the church as "birthing" Christians rather than "making" them.[8] Another way of saying this is that conversion is always contextualized by the politics and economics of *ecclesia*. Indeed, it is always susceptible to being destabilized and undercut by rival processes of formation that are themselves political and economic. What is required for conversion is the *ecclesia* as a subversive time and space in which other attachments, identities, and loyalties are reoriented if not abandoned altogether (and as Jesus makes clear, this may include not only one's ethnic identity and family loyalties but one's attachments to property and possessions).

7. Large Catechism of 1529 (Luther 1959:416).
8. "Therefore Sarah, or Jerusalem, our free mother, is the church, the bride of Christ who gives birth to all. She goes on giving birth to children without interruption until the end of the world, as long as she exercises the ministry of the Word, that is, as long as she preaches and propagates the Gospel; for this is what it means for her to give birth. . . . She teaches, cherishes, and carries us in her womb, her bosom, and her arms; she shapes and perfects us to the form of Christ, until we grow into perfect [adulthood] (Eph. 4:13). Thus everything happens through the ministry of the Word" (*Lectures on Galatians*, Luther 1955–76:26:441).

If becoming a Christian can be likened to learning a language, then in the beginning stages of conversion, new Christians will have very little to say about the syntax, vocabulary, and grammar of that language (and about the nature of their own conversion). Initial formation, as Lindbeck notes, "resembles ancient catechesis more than modern translation" (1982:132). In chapter 7 when contrasting the approach to evangelism of James Adams with a postliberal approach, I noted that the latter is "intratextual" in that it "redescribes reality within the scriptural framework rather than translating Scripture into extrascriptural categories." Again, to quote Lindbeck, "It is the text, so to speak, which absorbs the world, rather than the world the text" (ibid. 118).

Clearly an intratextual approach to evangelism and conversion goes very much against the grain of modernity, where the subjectivity, experience, or culture of the individual determines the meaning and truth of what is being learned. It may not, therefore, be as likely to attract the kind of church growth that today has become the measure of effective evangelism within the prevailing consensus.[9] While intratextual formation must always take into account the age, gender, and intellectual and sociocultural starting point of the new Christian (so that there is some element of extratextuality), these can only provide a "context of discovery" rather than a "context of justification" for that learning (cf. Hütter 2000:190–91). As Lindbeck observes, "Religions, like languages, can be understood only in their own terms, not by transposing them into an alien speech" (1982:129).

Lindbeck is not denying the possibility of translation in a very basic sense, such as the translation of Greek or Hebrew into English. Moreover, even if one agrees that evangelism is not so much a matter of translation as incarnation, it could also be said that incarnation is, in fact, a form of translation (cf. Walls 1990:25). What Lindbeck is arguing, however, is that Christianity—or any religion, for that matter—is a comprehensive way of living and thinking into which "every humanly conceivable reality can be translated (or redescribed) . . . with a gain rather than a loss of truth or significance" while at the same time being "untranslatable

---

9. Richard Lischer puts his finger on the standard evangelistic apologetic, expressed, as he notes, in modern liberal homiletic practice, which in recent decades

> has been uniformly critical of sermons that begin with the priority of the word of God, preferring instead to build the sermon on the authority of the needs, capacities, and experiences of the listener. . . . The common solution appears to be: Scratch deeply enough into the postmodern psyche and you will hit a vein of genuine spirituality. One way to tap into it is to tell stories whose religious dimension is recognizable and acceptable to all, and then to correlate the experience generated by these stories with the Christian message, e.g., "grace." When done successfully, the presence of Christ radiates as a spiritual dimension of everyday life. When the reliance on experience dominates the sermon, the gospel becomes an illustration of a greater truth. (1999:19–20)

. . . out of this idiom into some supposedly independent communica-
tive system without perversion, diminution or incoherence of meaning"
(2002:232). To come to an understanding of this "untranslatable" way of
life and thought, therefore, a non-Christian must acquire competence
in Christianity's "foreign language."

To avoid any misunderstanding, the untranslatability of the gospel
has nothing to do with its content being esoteric, abstract, or concep-
tually complex. Nor is conversion a matter of learning an obscure or
mysterious jargon. It has rather to do with the comprehensiveness of
a form of life to which a language or narrative is intrinsic and with the
irreducibly embodied and enpeopled nature of the faith as a context of
meaning and truth. While it is true, then, that Christian initiation is to
some degree the acquisition of a "language," this refers to gaining not
merely a new vocabulary but also a new grammar, so to speak, along
with its history, gestures, and conventions. Language in and of itself
is largely meaningless apart from the form of life or the practices[10] in
which it inheres (cf. Wittgenstein 1953:§30–33).

Of course, the process of learning the language of faith never ends in
the life of the believer and is always ongoing.[11] "The whole economy of
becoming a Christian," as Aidan Kavanagh says, "is thus the fundamental
paradigm for *remaining* a Christian" (1978:162). As the believer matures
in Christ, moreover, there is a natural movement from imitation to internalization to innovation (Budde and Brimlow 2002:60). But while
the convert is always to some degree an active participant in her or his
own conversion, argument in and with the tradition is possible only to
the extent that one has learned the language and grammar of that tradition (cf. Lindbeck 1982:132) and is now able, in MacIntyre's words, to
"contribute to" and "systematically extend" the tradition.

Modern revivalism dating from at least the nineteenth century (especially in America, epitomized in the evangelistic practices of Charles
Finney, Dwight Moody, Billy Sunday, and Billy Graham) overempha-
sized the responsibility of converts for their own salvation and made
conversion largely the consequence of the will, belief, or decision of the
converts themselves, thereby encouraging "the sanctification of choice"
at the center of the liberal consumerist paradigm (Clapp 2000:136). The

10. See also Kallenberg's helpful discussion of this point and of Wittgenstein in relation to evangelism (2002:20–24).

11. Hütter distinguishes between *catechetical learning,* which is "the initiatory learning
of the central configurations of language and traditional activities of the Christian faith,"
and *peregrinational learning,* or the ongoing learning that is central to the Christian journey
(peregrination) in which a person "develops the implications of the praxis of Christian
faith in various contexts; that is, the person interprets faith with regard to precisely these
contexts and maintains faith within them" (2000:50).

widespread result is that the faith community (frequently in the form of
the lone evangelist) became responsible only, or at least primarily, for
convincing unbelievers of their sin and offering them the possibility of
salvation in the form of a "decision for Christ."[12]

If the model of conversion I am advocating here is true, however, it
should be clear that this could never be the case, because both sin and
salvation (and therefore "conversion") are intelligible only from within
a form of life, a language, a fellowship, and a network of social practices
through which one is drawn into the economy of God's gift of salvation.
Especially given the culture of conversion in which we live, a high degree
of formation is required before we even begin to know what we need to
be saved *from*, much less *for*. Thus, while salvation may never be simply
equated with one's socialization into the community called *ecclesia*, it
can never be less than this (Kallenberg 2002:72).

Given the close relationship between conversion and ecclesial formation, the question naturally arises regarding the extent to which conversion is voluntary, if at all. Married persons, in looking back upon their
wedding, will often affirm that they did not—and could not—then know
what they were doing. Hauerwas is surely right when he observes that
"our lives are constituted by decisions we made when we did not know
what we were doing" (1998:102). Is the situation really all that different
in the case of conversion? Can persons fully know what they are doing
when they first become Christian? Or, to carry the question further, can
persons be converted without consciously willing it or "deciding" for it?
Can we be converted by association, so to speak?

The answers to these questions are complex, for they depend to some
degree on the existing social patterns and cognitive abilities of those
being evangelized. The preferential option for the individual that so
thoroughly shapes the evangelism of modernity can find little room
for anything but contempt for the conversion of entire communities in
which social cohesion and group identity are strong.[13] But while there
are numerous dangers with "mass conversions" associated especially
with the historic coerciveness of Constantinian Christianity, tribal patterns of social organization often provide the starting point through
which persons come to be formed by the church and led toward conversion (and not only in the remote jungles of the Amazon, it must be
added). They cannot be simply disregarded or discounted as evil or
sub-Christian. Neither, of course, need they be embraced by evangelism, any more than evangelism need embrace the distinctively modern

12. See especially McClendon's discussion of Finney's revivalism (1986:2:55–56, 110,
139).
13. On this point, see Newbigin's helpful discussion: 1995:141–43.

pattern of social organization premised on the contractual relations of autonomous individuals. In fact, a closer look at the way such communal conversions have historically taken place reveals the important truth that the process of coming to faith is far more "associative" than those of us raised in cultures that privilege Enlightenment-based forms of rationality have been led to believe.

Another important example of this principle is the conversion of those with developmental disabilities who lack the ability to "cognize" faith and for whom salvation is therefore largely a matter of association. Brad Kallenberg mentions, by way of illustrating this principle, the story recorded in Mark 2:5 of the paralytic whose sins Jesus forgives because of the faith of his companions, who, unable to get the man to Jesus through the front door, dug a hole in the roof and lowered him through it (2002:78–79). As Kallenberg says, "We sometimes think we are objective observers of the events that constitute our lives. It seems ridiculous to suggest that something might happen without our purview and we wouldn't immediately know both that something had happened and what it was that happened" (ibid. 81). But the experience of persons with developmental disabilities may teach us—especially if we cease to think of their experience as the exception in comparison to which ours is the rule—that conversion is just as much a transformation that happens to us as it is a transformation for which we have decided.

However much *ecclesia* provides the primary cultural and linguistic context for evangelism and conversion, there is in the initial process of invitation and formation always a work of extratextual imagination that must receive our attention. Just as the gospel is not more public and accessible when it merely says what the world already knows, so also it is not purer when kept hidden and closed off to outsiders. It is true that one can only ever be *drawn* to the reign of God by first encountering it in the world embodied in the life and work, patterns and practices of the church. One then goes about learning how to be a part of that world through the intratextual and catechetical acquisition of that world's language and practices. But in all this, we may still speak of persons being "drawn" and of our witnesses having "arrived" in such a way that persons upon encountering this other world are somehow enabled to begin to place themselves imaginatively and empathically within it, such that learning and formation can begin.[14] This does not diminish the necessity of a "conversion" to that world, nor does it mean that such a conversion could ever be the result of a simple act of will. But it does mean that coming to faith begins with an imaginative "drawing" of persons into a

14. On this point, see especially the final chapter of MacIntyre's *Whose Justice? Which Rationality?* (1988:389–403).

new world by the church that, as I earlier argued, if apologetic at all, is so in a chiefly aesthetic sense.[15]

This aesthetic arc between faithful witness and engaged reception requires a double contextualization that is at once "intratextual" and "extratextual." In the case of the latter, the church must attend carefully to the intellectual, sociocultural, and existential situation of those being evangelized (and, it must be added, of those of us doing the evangelizing, lest we assume our situation as normative), so that sufficient imaginative bridging can take place. This contextualization will, for example, take account of whether those being evangelized already stand inside or outside the household of faith (thereby presuming, as I do, that Christians need to be evangelized just as much as non-Christians).[16] It will also allow for the fact that most of us are not only sinners but also sinned against (cf. Arias 1984:79–80). As in the case of Jesus' own evangelism, it will give special attention to the relationship of the evangelized to unjust social conditions in regard to which the good news will be inevitably perceived as subversive (thus the good news may not at first "sound" like good news to one who benefits from an unjust social world). These extratextual considerations include any and all features of our existence, both personal and social, that are relevant to our capacity to see and hear the new world of the gospel and to respond to the church's invitation and embrace.

But even if we may identify important contextual features, even enduring ontological features of human existence, that shape the hearing and reception of the good news, these can never provide the context for establishing the normativity of Christ or the justification of the church's news as good. Even if the intellectual and sociocultural situation of persons being evangelized may itself be considered in some sense primary as a "context of discovery," it is never normative or absolute. Yet as Edward Farley cautions, "It is just this normativeness which unfaith would grant to the situation—the absolute status of what must be appeased, adapted to, satisfied. The self-oriented agendas, the principle of satisfaction, prompts the human being to grant not merely ontological but criteriological primacy to the situation" (1983:166).

The practice of evangelism begins with a contextual analysis of its situation and is concerned to find ways to relate the gospel to that situation

15. This is, I think, largely what Lindbeck is getting at when he says, "Reasonableness in religion and theology, as in other domains, has something of that aesthetic character, that quality of unformalizable skill, which we usually associate with the artist or the linguistically competent" (2002:190).

16. See Brueggemann 1993: here Brueggemann illustrates the breadth and wholeness of evangelism by contextualizing it as a process of helping (1) outsiders become insiders, (2) forgetters become remembers, and (3) beloved children become belief-ful adults.

with clarity and beauty, but it finally rejects every claim by the situation to be absolute. A failure to make this important distinction between an evangelistic "context of discovery" and an evangelistic "context of justification" has the potential to distort the practice of evangelism by co-opting it in service of the "felt needs" of the consumers it will inevitably seek to attract. It is only through a fully catholic ecclesial existence embodied in the worship, practices, disciplines, and saints of the church that evangelism is able to retain its integrity as a practice. Indeed, "without this rootage in ecclesiality," as Farley notes, the criteria by which evangelism would appraise both the situation and itself "coincide with the situation itself" (ibid. 184).[17]

Conversion cannot be a matter of being "convinced" of the truth, credibility, or utility of Christian claims within a non-Christian plausibility structure. Such a notion would be intrinsically self-contradictory. Conversion is a matter of being formed into a new world, a new way of life called *ecclesia* that is itself the plausibility structure from within which Christian claims begin to have meaning and truth. "In other words," as Kallenberg rightly says, "one doesn't move from apologetic answers to faith because the adoption of the form of life prerequisite to understanding the answers is the very conversion aimed at in the first place" (2002:100).

Culture is always the medium through which the gospel is communicated from one people to another. But given that the gospel is embodied in political and economic practices that must be understood as "cultural" in their own right (and indeed as also "linguistic," as Lindbeck has shown), the relationship between culture and gospel is complex and never simply that of cultural form to gospel content. The gospel is not a prior transcendent "meaning" that subsequently gets indigenized in various cultural forms, which can then be decoded in the mind of persons experiencing those forms. Such a dichotomy between form and content can only have the consequence of distancing conversion from formation into a life of holiness.

17. The starting point for contextualization is a theology of incarnation—one that is construed not abstractly but within the pattern of Abraham, Moses, and Jesus (cf. Yoder 1998:172).

When God came into human society God did not approve of and sanction *everything*, in "normal, healthy, human society"; God did not make of *all* human activity, not even of all well-intentioned human activity, a means of grace. There are some loyalties and practices in human community that God rejected when God came among us. When God came among us God was born in a migrant family and not in a palace. Abraham, the father of the faithful, forsook the great civilization of Chaldea to become a nomad; Israel escaped from Egypt. . . . When we then speak of incarnation it must not mean God sanctifying our society and our vocations as they are, but rather God's reaching into human reality to say what we must do and what we must leave behind. (ibid.)

Conversion and Church Growth

Given the ecclesial *habitus* of evangelism and of the conversion for which I have been arguing, it may seem natural to equate the practice of evangelism with efforts directed at the growth and expansion of the church. Walt Kallestad, pastor of one of the fastest-growing Lutheran congregations in the United States, argues explicitly for this identification:

> The basic conviction of most evangelical Christians is that the New Testament presumes the growth of the church. In the Gospels and in Acts, we see that Jesus and the early church want the church to grow, to reach the entire world with the news that Christ is risen and that Jesus is Lord. The claim that three thousand persons were baptized at Pentecost speaks more forcefully about the power of the Spirit to transform lives than if only three had been baptized. (1996:16–17)

The logic here is beguiling but ultimately perverse. It is sustained by a narrative (and its corresponding politics) of what counts as power that is ultimately violent and founded on the premise that "more is better" and "bigger is better." This is in no way the politics of God's reign, nor can its grammar be reconciled with that of the story of the people of God. In fact, if we follow the strict logic of the argument, we must inevitably conclude that the Holy Spirit was not as powerful at Pentecost as was possible. For example, if six thousand persons had been baptized instead of only three thousand, then this would have been an even more "forceful" example of the Holy Spirit's power. If ten thousand persons had been baptized, then we would know that we *really* serve a powerful Spirit! Once we adopt this logic, we will even need to conclude that Jesus' own evangelism was not as powerful as that of the apostles at Pentecost. After all, Jesus was able to gather around him only a relatively small band of committed followers. In fact, when measured by a worldly politics of success, we must finally conclude that Jesus was an abysmal failure.

Every aspect of Jesus' life and teaching stands in contradiction to this quantitative standard for measuring power and effectiveness. And though Christians believe that the Holy Spirit was powerfully at work at Pentecost, it is not the size but the social character of the early Christian community that speaks "forcefully" about the power of the Spirit. What is truly remarkable in the Pentecost story is the way lines of race, gender, and ethnicity were crossed so that "every nation under heaven" was able to hear the gospel in its own language (Acts 2:5–11) and the Spirit was poured out on men and women alike (2:18). What is remarkable is that those who believed "had all things in common" and would "sell their possessions and goods and distribute the proceeds to all, as any had need" (2:44–45). What is remarkable is that not one of them considered his or her belongings to be private property, but rather "everything they owned was held in common" and "there was not a needy person among them" (4:32–34). Whether there are twelve people or twelve hundred people, it is the embodied witness to the subversive values of God's reign that makes the church the church. Unfortunately, the fact that most of the largest churches in the United States are overwhelmingly segregated and affluent speaks far more convincingly about whether the Spirit is present than does their size. As Gideon discovered, an army of just three hundred people, equipped with no more than trumpets, torches, and the peace of God, is far more powerful than thousands of well-funded, high-tech, wall-building Midianites.

It is now a commonplace to note the fact that the Christendom framework within which the church has operated for hundreds of years has been steadily disintegrating for some time. Despite this fact, it is still possible to operate out of Christendom assumptions and toward Christendom aims—especially in the practice of evangelism and even by those churches who believe they have moved in post-Christendom directions by abandoning a "stained-glass culture" in their worship, preaching, and architecture. The most seductive of these assumptions remains the simple but ubiquitous identification of evangelism with the quantitative growth of the church. In both mainline and evangelical churches, the persistence of this identification is staggering. Larger churches are still presumed to have more successfully reached the world with the Christian message and more faithfully embodied the gospel of Jesus, while smaller churches, consequently, are presumed not to have done so well. And though within Protestantism evangelical churches have clearly been more successful than mainline churches in achieving church growth over the last half-century, that does not make the assumption any less universal in both camps.

It is important, therefore, to state and argue for the following premise as clearly and straightforwardly as possible so as to avoid any misunderstanding: while evangelism seeks to draw persons into the life of the church as a way of inviting them to a journey of conversion, the quantitative growth of the church *is no positive indication whatsoever* that God's intention of creating a new people is being fulfilled or that God's reign is breaking into history. It may in some cases be a negative indication, for even cancer may be characterized by rapid growth. It is quite possible to practice idolatry and to grow as a church at the same time. Likewise, the proliferation and growth of churches that perpetuate social divides can hardly be characterized as an extension of the *missio*

Dei. Simply put, the quantitative growth of the church can tell us only that people are attracted to what they find in the church or are having some perceived need or want met by the church. It tells us nothing about whether the politics of God's reign is being embodied or whether a conversion to that reign is taking place.

It is, of course, worth considering whether, if the latter are happening, the church will be growing; and we are never in the wrong to ask ourselves self-critically, if our churches are not growing, why that is the case. But it is not clear that rejection of the gospel implies a failure of evangelism or that fidelity to the gospel will naturally lead to church growth. Even if this were true, the logic flows in only one direction. Thus, even if it were true that the church's faithfulness to the gospel always leads to church growth (a questionable claim in itself), it is not true that church growth is always (or even regularly) a sign of the church's faithfulness to the gospel. What church growth advocates seem to miss with great regularity is the elementary theological point that it is never church growth that we are to seek but rather the reign of God (Matt. 6:33). The two do not amount to the same thing. Of course, we are also not justified in concluding that church decline or stagnation is a sign of the church's fidelity to the gospel![18]

If the identification of evangelism with church growth is premised upon a faulty practical logic, so also are the conclusions that flow from that logic. When the mission of the church becomes a mission of numerical growth, quantitative influence, and geographical spread, evangelism is easily reduced to whatever means, method, or gimmick will facilitate that mission. Conversion then becomes a lowest common denominator decision or experience that will allow a church, without too much embarrassment, to claim an individual as one of its own. Christianity is reduced, in Yoder's words, to "the general label for anyone's good intentions" (1997:112).

At the same time, if we reject quantitative measures such as numerical growth or geographical spread as legitimate indicators of evangelistic "success," we may well ask whether there are other measures by which the practice may still be held accountable. If evangelism cannot rightly be evaluated by an instrumental logic of production and achievement that externalizes the means from the end, are there ways of gauging whether or not we have practiced evangelism well? How do we go about

18. According to Hunter, 80 percent of the 360,000 churches in America are stagnant or in decline and only 1 percent of all churches experience substantial growth from new conversions to Christianity (2003:24, 26). I do not know where Hunter gets his figures, but I do not doubt them; neither would I attribute their cause to the church's faithfulness in offering a demanding and subversive gospel.

evaluating evangelism if the end of its practice is internal to it as a quality of faithful character and performance?

One of the reasons quantitative measures are so attractive and seductive to Christians is that we have been given a mandate by Christ to "go" and "make disciples of all nations" (Matt. 28:19). The temptation is enormous to translate this mandate into a results-oriented set of evaluations that measure the church's faithfulness by how many disciples have been made, how quickly, and in how many nations. Moreover, as the public of the Holy Spirit and as fully catholic, the Christian community is not allowed to characterize itself in terms of prevailing ethnic, geographic, political, and national boundaries, nor is it to rest content with remaining behind social and economic barriers created to exclude and marginalize others. A church that does not reflect adequately its nature and calling as *sent*—a church, in other words that is not characterized by eucharistic excess, overflowing, donation, and generosity in its community—cannot be called an evangelizing church. Thus, evangelism can be measured by how fully inclusive is our "reach" and how thoroughly we refuse to allow that "reach" to be domesticated by the political boundaries and economic disciplines of other publics. One way of answering the question of evaluation and accountability, then, is to distinguish evangelistic "reach" from "spread," the former indicating the measure to which Christians are open, inclusive, and engaged with their communities, thereby taking seriously what it means to be "sent," while the latter indicates the actual extent to which the Christian offer has been accepted and adopted in the world. We cannot judge the faithfulness of our witness by measuring the extent to which it is accepted or rejected; we can, however, judge our faithfulness by measuring the catholicity of our invitation—that is, whether it is offered to all or only to some.

Practically speaking, there are three qualifications to this that I would suggest. The first is that this reach must be intentional and proactive. Catholicity must characterize the invitation before it characterizes the response, for there is a very real sense in which the church exists for those who are "not there yet." By way of example, I recently consulted with a congregation that was struggling to find ways to become more open and inclusive in their community, more hospitable and less fortress-like. One of the suggestions voiced in the meeting was that because the physical infrastructure of the church building was difficult to negotiate for persons in wheelchairs, it might be a good idea to install an elevator. "But no one comes to our church in wheelchairs," exclaimed one of the members in exasperation. "Why would we focus on that?"

No sooner had the words come out of his mouth than he, along with everyone else in the room, realized the import of those words. "Perhaps that is the reason why," said another member.

If evangelism can be "measured" at all, perhaps it can best be measured by how well a community prepares a place at its table for those who are not there yet, for those who have not even heard, much less heeded, its invitation.

As noted in chapter 8 when describing the church as the public of the Spirit, a second qualification to measuring evangelical inclusivity is that while the church cannot be a walled-up fortress, neither can it be what has been described as an "endless plain" (Volf 1996:58–64). The church includes on the basis of the gospel's distinctive vision of the "common good" for which we have been created, not on the basis of a postmodern heterogeneity in which difference and diversity are valued in and of themselves as a substitute for any such common good and precisely because it is held that there can never be any substantive common good that is not at the same time violent and oppressive. For Christian evangelism, the measure of inclusivity is the distinctively upside-down set of priorities embodied in the life and ministry of Jesus and announced by him as characterizing God's reign. In particular, the measure of Christian evangelistic reach is its openness and hospitality to the poor, the stranger, and the socially ostracized. True, the church seeks to include all persons, but on very specific conditions—the just inclusion of those who are systematically excluded and trampled on because of their social position, gender, ability, or because they are in some way understood to be strange or "queer." As Rosemary Radford Ruether says, Jesus addressed his message particularly to the poor, "not in order to exclude the rich, but in order to make clear to them the conditions under which they will enter the kingdom" (1983:17). In other words, a particular social imagination and a reversal of customary vision and values characterizes the catholicity of evangelism, rightly described by liberation theologians as a "preferential option for the poor." Both the rich and the poor are included, but not on the same terms. No wonder that the book of Acts links the fact that the early church "held all possessions in common" with the fact that "there was not a needy person among them" (4:32–34). In the end, perhaps the church can do no better than to measure its evangelism by the same criterion Jesus applied to his own: "The poor have good news brought to them."

A third qualification to measuring the church's "reach" is the fact that it follows a crucified Lord. It is therefore committed to a pacifist embrace of others that seeks to remove all barriers to that embrace in its own midst, but always peaceably and always without forcing the embrace onto others. The fact that the Christian church can never allow itself to be identified with any ethnicity, geography, or nation and that it refuses to be bounded by any such borders or limits does not mean that the church has the responsibility (played out in the Christendom project) to abolish all such boundaries in the name of Christian empire building. Evangelistic reach is an offer, invitation, and even summons—but never an insinuation of the Christian community or its form of life (especially its worship and its obedience, or morality) onto others.

Because this third qualification raises the question of the character of the evangelists, it begins to turn our attention to what is, in many ways, the most important measure of evangelism done "well" and one that overlaps with all these others: whether evangelism is performed virtuously. So let us now consider what virtues are appropriate to evangelism and how we are to recognize and cultivate them.

Part 5

Evangelism
as a Virtuous Practice

If the primary logic of evangelism is *witness* rather than achievement, accomplishment, or production, then it is the character of the performance rather than the implementation of an assumed end that defines excellent practice. That is because the ends of the practice are internal to and embodied in the performance itself. Rejection of the Christian's invitation will now have to be judged as no less "successful" than acceptance, for it is faithfulness in offering the invitation that defines the practice. If, however, faithful performance defines the practice of evangelism, we do well to consider what kind of life is required by such performance and what sort of people we are called to be as practitioners. We will need to ask about the particular dispositions of character—the virtues—that are required for faithful performance, and we will need to seek out exemplars of those virtues. Evangelism is no single discrete action but a context of action, or course of action, emerging from a life patterned after the story of Christ through a lived participation in ecclesial fellowship. This last part of the book takes up the character of that life and the virtues that compose and sustain it.

In doing so, this final part asks about the particular lives that model evangelistic virtue—those whom the Christian tradition has called "saints" and "martyrs"—and the communities of virtue that form them. By learning from these saints as we work alongside them, we may perhaps find a new opening for thinking of evangelism in other than wholly pragmatic terms focused on winning, conquest, and production. The visibility of their witness affords us clues to how we might better share the beauty of holiness, which is the "apologetic" link between faithful witness and the imaginative, alluring, and captivating reception of that witness in the world.

10

Martyrdom and Virtue

The believer's cross must be, like his Lord's, the price of his social non-conformity. It is not, like sickness or catastrophe, an inexplicable, unpredictable suffering; it is the end of a path freely chosen after counting the cost . . . it is the social reality of representing in an unwilling world the Order to come.

John Howard Yoder (1972:97)

In considering the virtues required of faithful evangelistic practice, it is important at the outset to be clear that we are here not simply talking about what today are commonly called "personality traits," nor are we talking about the quality of a practitioner's inner motives or intentions. Following Thomas Aquinas, virtues might better be described as "habits"—or to be more precise, "good habits," developed over time and through repeated acts that dispose us toward good ends (1964–76:1-2.55). They are "enduring, defining, structural feature[s] of the human soul" (Farley 1983:35), exemplified in practices and, in fact, born of practice. Virtue, as Gregory of Nyssa says, "is hard to come by and demands much sweat and labour, and is achieved only with much seriousness and struggle" (in Meredith 1999:97). At the same time, as Aquinas makes clear, true Christian virtue is received as a gift from God. So while virtue requires our participation and consent, we must speak of virtues not as possessions but rather as responses, or as "dis-possessions drawing us into the life of God" (Long 2000:265).

Though *virtue* more accurately refers to inclination than to intention, it is nonetheless closely related to intention, for by inclining us toward the good, virtue molds and sustains our intentions, though never irresistibly. Christian virtues, then, are developed dispositions, habits that incline us toward good ends, born of practice yet received as gifts from God. They are not "ends" in themselves but order us toward good ends. This does not mean, however, that virtues are valuable only insofar as they attain "results." As MacIntyre says,

> It is of the character of a virtue that in order that it be effective in producing the internal goods which are the rewards of the virtues it should be exercised without regard to consequences. . . . Unless we practice them irrespective of whether in any particular set of contingent circumstances they will produce those goods or not, we cannot possess them at all. We cannot be genuinely courageous or truthful and be so only on occasion. (1984:198)

Virtuous practice may be said to be teleological, therefore, but not consequentialist (cf. ibid. 150). Yet for the Christian, even this way of putting the matter is not satisfactory, for it would be more accurate to say that virtue is *eschatological* rather than teleological. This is because virtue is not a matter of our own efforts as acting subjects to fulfill or bring about an incomplete *telos* but rather our participation in and witness to an end that has already been gifted to us by God in Christ (Fodor and Hauerwas 2004:96–97). The virtues form us into a people who see the world whole—not as it is but as it is promised to be. They are therefore part of a larger vision.

As noted in chapter 1, the cultivation and exercise of virtue requires a particular social structure in which the virtues are defined and in which the practices that exhibit and hold these virtues in place are properly ordered. For it is only in and through a comprehensive context of practice that our lives are given sufficient continuity and coherence such that the virtues can be formed and right intentions sustained. Every scheme of virtue, moreover, depends on how we understand the final end of life (by which I mean not so much a final terminus as that which is to be sought for the sake of itself and not something else) and therefore on a community-embodied tradition of what properly counts as that end and so makes life worth living. No single practice can, on its own, form in us the virtues appropriate to it simply by our engaging in that practice and apart from our having been nurtured in the all-embracing form of life in which that practice inheres. As McClendon reminds us, while practices can be "arenas of human excellence," they are also "foci of demonic and destructive energy. They can nurture our best but they necessarily risk

our worst" (1986:2:33). This is at least one of the reasons that it must
be said that virtues are located not within the individual but within a
community. There is no virtue-as-such, but always virtue as it is defined
and exercised in a particular tradition, community, or *polis*.

If virtue is always situated within a particular *polis*, then here again
it will be important to affirm that for the practice of evangelism the
polis that locates the evangelistic virtues is the *ecclesia*. Likewise, for the
Christian tradition, the final end of life toward which virtuous practice
is oriented is God's peaceable reign, and this end rather than some other
end (national security, economic growth, etc.) governs and defines the
character of the virtues. While Christian virtues might share much in
common with virtues as understood from within other traditions and
communities, it is ultimately the fellowship, practices, and stories of the
community called *ecclesia* that make Christian virtues what they are and
that constitute some dispositions as virtues while disqualifying others
(humility and patience, for example, were not virtues for Aristotle, while
they are for Christians). It would not be wrong to describe the church
as a community of virtue, or a "school" of virtue.

If, however, all virtues require a particular social context, they also
require a particular kind of person whose life is formed comprehensively
by that context—in Christian terms, a saint. Within such a life, and given
the narrative unity displayed in that life across time, we are able to see
that the virtues are interconnected. We may certainly distinguish among
them individually (patience, courage, justice, etc.), but no one virtue may
be cultivated rightly apart from the others. If we think of the practice of
evangelism as something like a craft learned in an apprenticeship (indeed,
the whole of the Christian life may profitably be viewed in these terms),
we can begin to see the importance of learning by working alongside
persons whose lives mark the path on which we are setting out. One of
the great problems in contemporary evangelism, however, is that too
often our models are not those who exemplify Christian virtue but those
who are effective in building, marketing, and filling churches. One of the
great losses of a church narrated by modernity is that it loses the ability
to recognize saints, having instead become enamored with experts.

In keeping with the logic of agency discussed in the previous chapter,
then, it is not the *accomplishments* of persons that make them our exemplars. Rather, exemplars are those who, as Hütter says, "allow God's
salvific actions to happen to them" and who are "defined as being primarily pathic, as those who let themselves be determined entirely by
God's actions, which from the opposite perspective means that they stand
fully within the praxis of Christian faith" (2000:49). This is, moreover,
the reason the entire church must be understood as a "communion
of saints." For both the sharing and the acquisition of faith begin in a

context of imitating models (however much it must proceed, as earlier noted, toward internalization and innovation). But if, as Hütter notes, "all saints are simultaneously both students and teachers of faith, are always oriented toward models as they are themselves models for others," it may also be affirmed that "there are paradigmatic models, whose concrete capacity for judgment provides a comprehensive point of orientation" (2000:50).

While the forgoing chapters have had much to say about the church as the context of evangelistic practice, in this final chapter I would like to look more closely at evangelistic virtue in relationship to one of these paradigmatic models, or "characters," produced by the church whose life displays evangelistic virtue—namely, the *martyr*. In fact, in the earliest tradition of the church, *saint* and *martyr* were practically synonymous, so much so that the church could be understood as a "church of martyrs."

That the martyr (rather than the revivalist or megachurch pastor) should be held up as an exemplar of evangelistic virtue does not mean that evangelism is best performed by those who are persecuted or who undergo violent death for the sake of the gospel. Persecution, in and of itself, does not produce martyrs but can only produce victims (cf. Cavanaugh 1998:58–71). It is the church that produces martyrs. And this it does by affirming in the martyr a pattern of life and death that exhibits a radical and paradigmatic loyalty to Jesus—in other words, by fixing the martyr's life and death within a larger web of practices and convictions (a "politics"). Because that loyalty is at the same time nonconformity to the world, it entails suffering, contradiction, and at times death—so much so that cruciformity may be claimed as one of the marks of the church and intrinsic to its nature as missionary.[1] But this does not mean that martyrdom is ever to be sought by the church as something desirable, nor does it mean that the violence that leads to a martyr's death is to be interpreted as "redemptive" (cf. Yoder 1972:243). It is the consistency of the martyr's character *even in death* rather than the martyr's death itself that is noteworthy.[2] Likewise, the martyr does not give herself over to others in order to "win" them or to prove to them the validity of her witness. Rather, the

1. See Luther's "On the Councils and the Church" (1955–76, vol. 41:3–178) or, as another example, Menno Simons's "Reply to Gellius Faber," in *The Complete Works of Menno Simons, c. 1496–1561*, trans. Leonard Verduin, ed. John Christian Wenger (Scottdale, PA: Herald, 1956), 739–44. See also Yoder 1998:77–89.

2. As Christopher Vogt notes in his discussion of dying well, "Virtues are not qualities that can be switched on instantly by sheer force of will. This implies that if you wish to be patient and hopeful at the hour of your death, you should have endeavored to become patient and hopeful during the more active stages of your life" (2004:4).

path of the martyr is entailed necessarily by the material convictions of the martyr.[3]

One of the challenges in appealing today to the martyr as evangelistic exemplar is that the concept of martyrdom we have inherited was formed decisively in the second and third centuries[4] and shaped largely by political and religious contexts far different from our own. The ancient martyrs were typically arrested, brought before a judicial authority or court, interrogated, and given a final chance to confess verbally their allegiance to a god or gods (often the emperor himself) and to seal that confession with a sacrifice to those gods. Refusing to do so, they were then sentenced to punishment, torture, or death, often in public displays, rituals, and games. In most modern cultures today, all of this takes a very different form. Yet it would not be wrong to claim that martyrdom still involves a political conflict between the martyr and "the powers" that is intrinsically a theological question about worship. Likewise, martyrdom is no less a matter of public confession and sacrifice that often leads to suffering, ostracization, and in some cases death.

The public and political nature of the martyr's witness, however, should not be understood as only or even primarily a matter of verbal confession, even though the road to martyrdom often hinges on such confession. As Theofried Baumeister has shown, what first made the martyr a martyr, thereby producing the association of that word with disciples who had been killed, was the way "word" and "deed" were understood to coincide in those disciples in order to produce *martyria*, "witness." "Dying because one is a Christian is the action *par excellence* in which the disciple who is called to this confirms his or her faith by following the example of Jesus' suffering and through action is able once again to become a word with power to speak to others" (1983:4). Here again, martyrdom is evangelistically exemplary not because suffering is commendable or violence redemptive but because the martyr's faith is confirmed in practice and proved by the martyr's character in such a way that it can be taken seriously by those who encounter it—so seriously, in fact, that others are willing to put a stop to that witness. The martyr is a model evangelist because the martyr practices and inhabits the faith with such

3. Hauerwas helpfully puts the matter this way: "In other words, that martyrs die for their faith does not *prove* that Jesus is risen; on the other hand, that some people have assented to a totality of belief that includes the belief that Jesus is risen surely means that martyrs will die for their faith. . . . Witnesses are not evidence; rather, they are people whose lives embody a totality of beliefs and, accordingly, make claims about 'how the world is arranged.' To understand what the church believes is to know what the world is like if these beliefs are true" (2001b:214).

4. Though also building on Jewish accounts from the Maccabean period (cf. Baumeister 1983:3).

clarity and concreteness that it can become habitable for others. This is what it means to speak of the martyr's life as a sign and sacrament of *gospel*. The pattern of life of the One to whom the martyr bears witness is exemplified courageously, patiently, and visibly before a watching world. In our time, by contrast, the popular view is that the public nature of our witness can be secured by wearing T-shirts with Christian slogans, holding up banners with Bible verses at football games, or affixing witty religious bumper stickers to our cars. If those around us take offense at our witness, however, it is not because they have taken seriously the import of our beliefs; they just find us annoying.

Both then and now, the martyr stakes out a path of public witness that is costly because it is *practiced*—in her refusal to render allegiance to powers other than Christ and to burn a pinch of incense to them. Clearly, martyrdom is not just about good intentions or about giving one's life for a "cause." It is an imitation of Christ,[5] a cruciformity, the acquisition of a set of daily habits that is "a highly skilled performance learned in a disciplined community of virtue by careful attention to the concrete contours of the Christian life and death as borne out by Jesus and the saints" (Cavanaugh 1998:61–62). The martyr's practice is, therefore, a display of virtue and is impossible without virtue.

While I will not here attempt to produce a complete catalog of the virtues required of Christian evangelistic practice, I will suggest four that I believe are especially important to the church given its present challenges and opportunities: presence, patience, courage, and humility. From the standpoint of the Christian virtue tradition originating in Aquinas, however, it is impossible to speak about any one of these apart from the primary theological virtues of faith, hope, and charity[6] that order and inform them. For while all virtues direct our lives toward good

5. Perhaps better than imitation is the word *patterning*. As Bonhoeffer says,

He is the only "pattern" we must follow. And because he really lives his life in us, we too can "walk even as he walked" (1 John 2:6), and "do as he has done" (John 13:15) and "love as he has loved" (Eph. 5:2; John 13:34; 15:12), "forgive as he forgave" (Col. 3:13), "have this mind, which was also in Christ Jesus" (Phil. 2:5), and therefore we are able to follow the example he has left us (1 Peter 2:21), lay down our lives for the brethren as he did (1 John 3:16). It is only because he became like us that we can become like him. It is only because we are identified with him that we can become like him. By being transformed into his image, we are enabled to model our lives on his. Now at last deeds are performed and life is lived in single-minded discipleship in the image of Christ and his words find unquestioning obedience. (1959:304)

6. "Charity" can at times prove an unfortunate translation of the Latin *caritas*, given its overtones of condescension and superiority in the context of modern Western societies and its function ideologically in debates about welfare, especially in the United States. That is unfortunate, but it would be tragic to lose this important word simply because of its contemporary distortions.

ends, they themselves must be rightly directed to their proper end by the theological virtues. So, for example, Christian patience is not an undifferentiated passivity or mere "waiting," but rather a quality of persevering formed by a hope that is narrated by a particular story, oriented toward a particular *telos*, and embodied in the life and practices of a particular community centered on Christ. As Aquinas insisted, the character of a virtue has everything to do with the end toward which it is ordered and in which it thereby directs us to participate (1964–76:1-2.62.1).

Presence

Simply to be present with and for others may not immediately come to mind as a virtue—it does not appear on the standard lists or in the usual textbooks that catalog the virtues, Christian or otherwise. Yet presence is surely one of the most basic and foundational of evangelistic virtues, and in several respects the prerequisite for all the others. As James Mc-Clendon notes in his *Ethics*,

> If we are members of a community one of whose practices is Christian witness or evangelism, it will be plain to us that the virtue of presence . . . is required by that practice—in MacIntyre's words, is "appropriate to, and partially definitive of, that form of activity," while the "perversions" of and vices contrary to presence (e.g., nosiness) will be condemned in part just because they defeat the practice of evangelism. For one who will not be present to and for the neighbor cannot effectively witness to that neighbor, even though witness consists in a good deal more than presence alone. (1986:1:169)

Presence understood as a virtue receives its original definition from the story of God's incarnate presence in Jesus and is further clarified both by our incorporation through baptism into the body of Christ and by the eucharistic repetition of Christ's presence in the Lord's Supper. In that story and in the sacraments we learn what it means to speak of God's presence with us and for us as the ground of our being with and for each other. Intrinsic to the virtue of presence, therefore, is a quality of *embodiment* that gives witness its visibility and tangibility and that communicates to others the habitability of the faith to which the witness points. That is why the gospel is not something that can be tossed at others at a distance, shouted out by megaphone, or beamed in by satellite; it must be made available in bodily form so that it can be tested and tried. The gospel is a gospel for bodies and not souls only. Thus while it is, of course, possible to be *bodily* present with others without truly "being there" for them, Mc-Clendon is surely right when he says, "It is only by metaphor or analogy that we can speak of a disembodied presence" (ibid. 1:106).

Though all Christian virtues owe their form and definition to the character of Christ, that character must be exemplified in each new generation and in each new context if it is to prove decisive in shaping virtue today. Our current challenges are such that we cannot duplicate the life of Jesus point by point; but we can live into his character by learning from virtuous exemplars who have enacted his life in their own situations. One of the more recent contexts in which we can see the enacted character of Christ's presence is the struggle against repression and violence in El Salvador during the late twentieth century, and particularly in the lives and witness of four churchwomen murdered by Salvadoran National Guardsmen on December 2, 1980. The martyrdom of these women stands alongside dozens of other such martyrdoms in El Salvador, including a number of priests, teachers, pastors, students, and laypersons and, notably, Archbishop Oscar Romero, who was murdered earlier in that same year. It also stands alongside the disappearance, torture, and brutal killings of thousands of unknown persons, most of them poor, whose stories will never be told and whose examples will never be celebrated, except perhaps anonymously.

Ursuline Sister Dorothy Kazel and lay missionary Jean Donovan had driven to the Comalapa International Airport outside San Salvador to pick up Maryknoll sisters Ita Ford and Maura Clarke, who were returning from a conference in Nicaragua.[7] The four women had been living and ministering in El Salvador in response to Archbishop Romero's call for international solidarity with the persecuted and the poor of El Salvador. Kazel and Donovan provided mission work with the poor in La Libertad, while Ford and Clarke served refugees in Chalatenango. On the way home from the airport, all four women were abducted at a roadblock by members of the National Guard and taken to another location, where they were raped, shot at close range, and buried in a shallow grave.

Attempts by the Salvadoran government and military to cover up the crimes and initial suggestions from U.S. officials that the women had been killed trying to run a roadblock or had been political activists eventually gave way to the truth as four of the five convicted guardsmen finally confessed to their actions. In addition, the 1993 report of the Commission on the Truth for El Salvador found that the guardsmen had obeyed orders from their superiors to execute the women and that high-ranking military officials had concealed the facts, thereby obstructing the investigation.[8]

7. I am here relying to a great deal on Swedish and Miller 1992.
8. "From Madness to Hope, the Twelve-Year War in El Salvador: Report of the Commission on the Truth for El Salvador," United Nations Document S/25500, April 1, 1993.

The four women were part of a church that not only served the poor and the persecuted but identified itself with them. By giving voice to the voiceless and by forming visible communities of hope in the midst of a regime bent on atomizing the population through terror and intimidation, the women would, as it turns out, share the same fate as those they served. As Archbishop Romero said in his funeral Mass for Father Rafael Palacios, the fourth of six priests murdered in his archdiocese, "How sad it would be, in a country where such horrible murders are being committed, if there were no priests among the victims! They are the testimony of a church incarnated in the problems of its people. . . . It is the glory of the church to have mixed its blood—the blood of its priests, catechists, and communities—with the massacres of the people, and ever to have borne the mark of persecution" (quoted in Dennis, Golden, and Wright 2000:86).

The story of these four churchwomen, however, is not in the first place a story of murder and victimization but of compassion, humility, and courage in the service of offering Christ to their world. That Dorothy, Jean, Ita, and Maura are considered martyrs today is a testament to the steadfastness of their evangelistic presence with the poor and their solidarity with political prisoners and refugees—an acquired disposition of "being there" learned across the months and years prior to their deaths in the context of a community whose perseverance in the face of opposition and persecution is remarkable. The virtue of presence exhibited in their lives, as their letters to friends and family attest, was very much the product of their own formation by the impoverished communities they served and demonstrates the importance of the capacity not only for giving but for receiving in the task of evangelization. As Ita Ford wrote during her seven years in Chile prior to moving to El Salvador, "Am I willing to suffer with the people here, the suffering of the powerless, the feeling impotent? Can I say to my neighbors—I have no solutions to this situation; I don't know the answers, but I will walk with you, search with you, be with you. Can I let myself be evangelized by this opportunity? Can I look at and accept my own poorness as I learn it from the poor ones?" (quoted in Swedish and Miller 1992:2).

During the closing liturgy at the conference she had attended with Maura on the day before their murders, Ita read the following words from a homily of Oscar Romero, whose words had brought them to El Salvador in the first place and would now come to characterize the costliness of their own evangelistic presence:

> Christ invites us not to fear persecution because, believe me, brothers
> and sisters, the one who is committed to the poor must run the same fate
> as the poor, and in El Salvador we know what the fate of the poor signi-

fies: to disappear, be tortured, to be held captive—and to be found dead.
(ibid. 4)

Each of the sisters had been active in serving the impoverished community where they lived by distributing food and medicine, providing
transportation, carrying out family education programs, working with
the homeless, and assisting in the training of catechists and the formation
of base Christian communities. Known not only for their generosity but
for their joy, the sisters stayed when others fled—and this because they
understood Christ to be present with them and with their community.

But as the story of these women reveals, the virtue of presence expressed in acts of service and compassion resists being sentimentalized,
and is not a mere catering to "felt needs." In them we see that evangelistic presence may just as likely prove to be scandalous and subversive,
perceived by the powers as dangerous and revolutionary (as indeed it
is, insofar as it represents a refusal to participate in a culture's practices
of consumption and violence). And thus their story is not unlike that of
the first Christians who learned to be present to their neighbors in acts
of mercy and service but who also learned to be present in their renunciation of pagan professions and military service. In fact, it is precisely
this "counterpresence" that makes of the martyr-witness such a threat
to the authorities and such an affront and challenge to the maintenance
of established social orders. If it were only a matter of holding private
beliefs, the martyr would find little opposition. But the material and
social nature of Christian truth and conviction, bodily present in the
martyr's life and actions, makes of her body a contested space, "the
battleground for a larger contest of rival imaginations, that of the state
and that of the church" (Cavanaugh 1998:65).

Dorothy, Jean, Ita, and Maura were the bodily presence of Christ to
their world. We claim them today as evangelistic saints because they
stake out for us a path of communicating God's peace and justice through
the integrity of their character and the constancy of their presence—by
keeping promises, loving enemies, standing with the victimized, and
telling the truth. That this sort of integrity "counts" in evangelism will
likely be lost, however, by those whose first question is whether they
made any converts and, if so, how many.

In reading the stories of these women's lives, it is clear that they, like
most every evangelist, had personal struggles and that the virtue of
presence does not come naturally. It is the product of formation, inten-
tionality, and a developed sense of how our "being with" others points
to the God we serve, so that presence becomes less and less a decision
that needs to be made in each new context and more and more a way of
life. For presence requires a disciplined formation and patterning into

Christ, a bodily process of unlearning old and inadequate ways of being with the world while learning new ways from within a community of witnesses who teach us that our bodies and, indeed, our lives are not our own but Christ's.

For this reason Tertullian can even compare martyrs to warriors and athletes. They must go through rigorous training, inconvenience, and struggle and must suffer the discipline of the body in order to attain their goal. In fact, Tertullian instructed martyrs to pay close attention to the integrity of their witness while in prison in order that, by dwelling together in peace and harmony, they might provide a faithful witness:

> Give [the devil] not the success in his own kingdom of setting you at vari-ance with each other, but let him find you armed and fortified with concord; for peace among you is battle with him. Some, not able to find this peace in the Church, have been used to seek it from the imprisoned martyrs. And so you ought to have it dwelling with you, and to cherish it, and to guard it, that you may be able perhaps to bestow it upon others.[9]

It is, of course, tempting to believe that, especially in the case of the poor, we may be able to accomplish more through coercion and manipu-lation, even violence, thereby serving what we imagine to be a greater justice. But the path of the martyr, formed as it is into the story of Christ crucified, is a reminder that the way God rules is not through coercion or manipulation but through a peaceful solidarity—a solidarity that for followers of Christ can be measured only by faithfulness. The aim of the martyr-evangelist is holiness itself. Says Tertullian, "We, with the crown eternal in our eye, look upon the prison as our training-ground, that at the goal of final judgment we may be brought forth well disciplined by many a trial; since virtue is built up by hardships, as by voluptuous indulgence it is overthrown."[10] The victory Tertullian has in mind is not having won over one's friends, neighbors, and enemies to Christianity (though he certainly believes the integrity of witness is capable of that, capable even of transforming one's captors). Such "winning," if it can be called that, will require the martyr's disciplined presence, but the truth of the matter is that the martyr's presence does not always triumph in this way.[11] Indeed, the martyr's presence may repel rather than attract

9. *Ad Martyras* 1, in Roberts and Donaldson 1931:3:693.
10. Ibid. 694.
11. Here is one of the stark differences of Christian virtue ordered by *caritas* toward peace from Greek heroic virtue ordered toward victory and achievement. Cf. Milbank 1990:352–64. Milbank demonstrates that the Greek notion of virtue presupposes an on-tological conflict from within which excellence (*arete*) is cast fundamentally as "effective-ness," while the Christian notion of virtue assigns an ontological priority of peace over conflict that grounds virtue in mutuality, friendship, and love.

and is no more likely to be interpreted as a gift than as an offense. It is possible to be virtuous and yet *lose*.

This is so precisely because the faith to which the martyr bears witness is not a set of ideas to which we are to give assent but rather a set of *habits*, a fully material set of political and economic practices that constitute an alternative peoplehood, a habituation that inclines us toward God as our final end and beatitude. *Martyria* always has as its end, therefore, the Christlike holiness with which the church is to be found before God rather than its success or effectiveness in facilitating conversions. But then this means that Christian presence as ordered by charity seeks an end that is, in an important sense, not *for* anything but is only the embodiment of a beauty that, while habitable, is unpredictable, useless, and excessive. As the lives of Dorothy, Jean, Ita, and Maura demonstrate, because Christian holiness is beautiful, it does indeed invite and allure, for there is something intrinsically attractive about righteousness. But as earlier noted, because the beauty of holiness bears an identification with the form of Christ crucified, it is also grotesque. And to persons whose lives are narrated by stories other than Christ's, the martyr's cruciform presence may well appear extremist, fanatical, and ugly.

It is important, however, that we locate the grotesque nature of Christian evangelistic presence rightly. If this presence is subversive, deviant, and contradictory, that is not because it seeks to impose itself on others, to conquer, win, or invade. Because the form of Christian presence is charity (as is the case with all Christian virtues), evangelistic presence will instead insist on "being there" under the conditions of a risky self-giving expressed through patient listening, sharing, learning, dialogue, and argument with no guarantee of success but only the promise of a participation in Christ's future.

Patience

Because evangelistic presence is often characterized by contradiction and rejection, it is costly and difficult to sustain across time and requires great patience. Unfortunately, the practice of evangelism has often been marked by impatience, manifest especially in the modern church's pervasive belief that it must always be "doing" something. I earlier noted an overemphasis in modernity on the responsibility of converts for their own salvation, so that conversion becomes largely the consequence of the will, belief, or decision of the converts themselves. This overemphasis has its counterpart in the church's belief that it is *responsible* for securing this assent along with a confidence that it is *able* to do so, thereby further molding the logic of evangelism into a logic of production rather than incarnation, accomplishment rather than exemplification.[12] In the early centuries of Christianity, the most revered evangelists were saints and martyrs whose patterns of living and dying exhibited a patience that was incomprehensible apart from the God they served as the ground of their hope. Sadly, one of the inevitable consequences of the modern evangelistic preoccupation with "results" and its shift from saints to experts is a corresponding loss of patience in the practice of evangelism.

It would be wrong to blame this shift on modernity, however, for at the very heart of the Constantinian synthesis is a rejection of patience, as suffering and vulnerability are also rejected in the name of triumphantly Christianizing the social order. The association of patience with suffering, by contrast, is unmistakable within the New Testament and the earliest writings of the Christian tradition (it is worth noting that the word *patience*, like the word *compassion*, is derived from the Latin *pati*, which means "suffering"). It is not that Christians should seek suffering as a good; indeed, to seek out harm to oneself is interpreted by early church thinkers as an act of *impatience* (cf. Hauerwas and Pinches 1997:173). For those who know their lives are lived on God's time and who follow Christ's example, however, patience is learned in suffering while impatience seeks always to find an escape from it. Newbigin says it this way: "Patience means suffering. It is in the measure that the church shares in the tribulation of the Messiah, in the conflict that occurs whenever the rule of God is challenged by other powers, that the church is also a bearer of hope. This suffering is not the passive acceptance of evil; it is the primary form of witness against it" (1995:107).

While suffering is not itself a virtue, the martyr's life and death teach us that suffering patterned after the life and death of Christ (rather than just any kind of suffering) is intrinsic to the cultivation of Christian virtue. As Paul says, "Suffering produces endurance, and endurance produces character, and character produces hope" (Rom. 5:3–4). It is not the martyr's suffering that constitutes her witness[13] (suffering

12. So, for example, Charles Finney can say in his *Lectures on Revivals of Religion*, "The connection between the right use of means for a revival and a revival is as philosophically sure as between the right use of means to raise grain and a crop of wheat" (xi).

13. Elizabeth A. Castelli offers the following conclusion about the relationship between violence and martyrdom in her fine study *Martyrdom and Memory: Early Christian Culture Making* (2004):

Suffering violence in and of itself is not enough. In order for martyrdom to emerge, both the violence and the suffering must be infused with particular meanings. Indeed, martyrdom can be understood as one form of refusing the *meaninglessness* of death itself, of insisting that suffering and death do not signify emptiness and nothingness, which they might otherwise seem to imply. Martyrdom always implies a broader narrative that invokes notions of justice and the right ordering of the cosmos. By turning the chaos and meaninglessness of violence into martyrdom,

is not, as Yoder says, "a tool to make people come around") but rather the virtues of patience, humility, and endurance, and ultimately the martyr's hope with regard to the very meaning of history. This hope is born out of a faith that Christ has defeated the powers in his life, death, and resurrection. Consequently, the martyr refuses to align herself with those powers and instead aligns herself with Christ's victory, even if this means accepting what to all outward appearances is defeat at their hands (Yoder 1972:245). From the standpoint of the church's faith in Christ, the entire performance of the martyr is interpreted in terms of an inverted theory of power: powerlessness is construed as a form of resistance and patience as fortitude. Because of this, the church is able to affirm with Tertullian that "Christ is in the martyr."[14]

It is true that physical, psychological, economic, and cultural violence has often been perpetuated in our world through an ideology that suffering is good, deserved, or a matter of fate. To insist, therefore, on an intrinsic connection between suffering and virtue is hazardous, to say the least, and easily given to misunderstanding or perversion. But in contexts such as modern Western cultures that are preoccupied with insulating ourselves from every discomfort in the quest to fulfill every desire, regardless of how trivial or superficial, it is crucial that we neither simply exempt suffering from a theological account of virtue, on the one hand, nor commend it without qualification, on the other hand. That qualification is a particular historical person named Jesus whom Christians believe provides a way of living that is to be followed regardless of the cost. That does not mean that Jesus himself is to be considered a martyr, nor is it Jesus to whom we look as an exemplar of virtue. Rather, he is the primal source of virtue; his story is the pattern that when followed produces virtue in the lives of those we call saints on the basis of that story.[15] Perhaps that is why the various *acta* of the

one reasserts the priority and superiority of an imagined or longed-for order and a privileged and idealized system of meaning. (2004:34)

14. *On Modesty* 22, in Roberts and Donaldson 1931:4:100.

15. This position stands in contrast to that of Leonardo Boff, for whom Jesus is the "martyr *par excellence*," the one who gives his life for the "cause" of the kingdom and "for those values that embody the Utopia of the kingdom, such as truth, justice, love of God and of the poor" (1983:12). But the relationship of the martyr to Christ is not that of witness to fellow-witness or of martyr to "the prototype martyr." Jesus is not merely the first in a chain of martyr-witnesses but rather the One to whom the martyr bears witness. For the Christian, Christ's life, death, and resurrection define the kingdom rather than merely serving as a witness to it. In other words, Christ is not Christ because he courageously works for love and justice; rather, we come to know what love and justice are by following Christ and by being patterned into his story and formed into his body.

Stanley Hauerwas and Charles Pinches make something like this same point in their treatment of the "magnanimous man," the paragon of virtue for Aristotle. While it is true that virtue does not stand on its own as an abstract concept but always requires

martyrs recorded through Christian history tend to interpret the patient suffering of the martyr not merely as an imitation of Christ's suffering but as an actual participation in it ("a share in the cup of Christ," as the martyred Polycarp put it)[16]—a participation in which the endurance of Christ is learned and the character of Christ produced. As a virtue that has to do with how we understand and experience time, therefore, patience is deeply formed by a joy and hope in what God will accomplish rather than in any achievement we might produce. Far from resignation, patience is an active confidence that we live in God's time and can therefore act without the need to control, manipulate, or predict the results of our acts.

If evangelism requires patience, multiple factors work against this patience. Not the least among these, as John Wesley taught, is wealth, for it accustoms us to getting what we want when we want it and insulates us from the vulnerability intrinsic to patience.[17] Patience, therefore, may be one of the most difficult of Christian virtues to cultivate in modern affluent cultures preoccupied with immediate gratification of deformed desire. But beyond this, there are also theological challenges that work against evangelistic patience, such as the pervasive construal of salvation as the guarantee of one's eternal future in heaven rather than hell, a notion that places on the evangelistic task a pressure to use "any means necessary" to ensure victory. For clearly, if a single decision made during one's lifetime determines one's eternal destiny in heaven or hell, there is no time for the evangelist to exercise patience. After all, the one being evangelized may die soon.

I will not attempt here to reiterate the understanding of salvation I earlier discussed—one that I would characterize as material, corporate, bodily, and ecclesial. Nor will I again attempt here to argue for that view over one that is otherworldly, interior, decisionistic, and testlike.[18]

---

narrative display in a particular life, Jesus is not Aristotle's magnanimous man. "As we see it, imagining Jesus as the person of highest virtue has been one of the most seductive temptations for Christians since the fourth century. . . . Rather, the moral life of Christians is determined by their allegiance to a historical person they believe is the decisive form of God's kingdom. After all, Jesus did not say if you are to be a follower of his you must develop those virtues that will make you a morally impressive person. Rather, he said, 'Come and follow me'" (1997:28–29).

16. "The Martyrdom of Polycarp," in Musurillo 1972:13.

17. Sermon 108, "On Riches," §1.7, in Wesley 1975:3:523.

18. To again cite Wesley: "By salvation I mean, not barely (according to the vulgar notion) deliverance from hell, or going to heaven, but a present deliverance from sin, a restoration of the soul to its primitive health, its original purity; a recovery of the divine nature; the renewal of our souls after the image of God in righteousness and true holiness, in justice, mercy, and truth. This implies all holy and heavenly tempers, and by consequence all holiness of conversation." *A Farther Appeal to Men of Reason and Religion* §1.3, 1975:11:106.

But I should like to stress that this latter view distorts the Christian's hope that we live in God's time rather than our own. In contrast to the evangelistic mania produced by an overindividualized and overly voluntaristic construal of both salvation and time, the evangelistic practice for which I have been arguing requires patience, because it is essentially a promissory activity shaped and grounded in a promissory gospel.[19] To evangelize is not to convince or convert; it is to share a promise that has been made by God, narrated in the story of God's people and embodied in the person of Jesus. In evangelistic practice, we are involved in speaking promises and indeed in living promissory lives, lives that witness to God's reign in such a way that they cannot be taken as other than a summons and an invitation.

The patience of evangelism, therefore, is similar to the patience required in the outstretching of one's arms to another as a gesture of invitation and embrace. As Miroslav Volf suggests, while an invitation is given in the form of open arms, room must be made for the rejection or acceptance of that invitation. We must be willing *not* to determine the outcome. Speaking of these outstretched arms, Volf says, "Like a door left opened for an expected friend, they are a call to come in. No knock is necessary, no question on the part of the other whether she can come in is needed, just the announcement of arrival and stepping over the threshold" (1996:142). But if these arms impatiently grasp the other, close around her prematurely, the offer turns to violent assimilation. The act of embrace becomes instead "a concealed power-act of exclusion" (ibid. 143). We must be patient and wait for the other. What is more, we must remember to *let go* if the embrace is not to become absorption and if the alterity of the other is to be preserved so that the new insights, perspectives, and contributions of the other may enrich and challenge our own.

Evangelism takes time. But for a people of hope, it is precisely time that we have been given. That is why hope is subversive in a world that is cynical and stoic about the way things are. That is also why an evangelism formed by hope will always stand fundamentally counter to an evangelism formed by that great impostor of hope, despair (even when it is thinly veiled as hope in Christian preaching). For despair, like hope, is oriented toward the future; indeed, it is preoccupied with the future. But where an eschatology of despair grants to the powers of this world a triumph that can be reversed only in a distant heaven, the virtue of hope is rooted in a confidence that Christ's victory has brought something

19. Not only is the nature of the offer of the gospel promissory; as Hütter says, "the nature of promissio also determines the mode of its reception; that is, it necessarily implies faith as the only proper, indeed, only possible mode of its adoption" (2000:79).

new into our place and time of which the church is an imperfect but real foretaste. The task of evangelism is to make that foretaste available to the world even while pointing forward to the full consummation of Christ's victory, the rule of peace. That martyrs have historically been understood by the church as demonstrating this patient and hopeful witness is due to the church's interpretation of their lives and deaths as a demonstration of God's power and as a compelling preview of the shalom that is the world's future.

Courage

Tertullian's images of the martyr as athlete and warrior emphasize the training, perseverance, and discipline required of patient witness. But those images can have unfortunate consequences when we think about the virtue of courage in evangelism without adequate qualification. As Stanley Hauerwas and Charles Pinches argue in their comparison of Aristotle and Aquinas, how we understand courage depends greatly on assumptions that derive from our starting paradigm and from the end toward which courage is directed (1997:149–65). For Aristotle, courage is a virtue best exemplified in the context of war by soldiers facing death in battle. For Aquinas, however, the starting paradigm for Christian courage is not war but martyrdom, and the exemplar of courage is for him not the soldier in battle but the martyr. Both Aristotle and Aquinas understand the virtue of courage as an acquired disposition that is the formation of our natural appetites and desires toward a proper mean somewhere between inordinate fear, on the one hand, and recklessness, on the other. Also, for both Aristotle and Aquinas, courage does not exempt a person from appropriate fear or from taking appropriate risks. But an important difference between Aristotle and Aquinas has to do with the end toward which courage is directed—the common good of the nation in the case of Aristotle, friendship with God in the case of Aquinas. It is this end that determines the kind of dangers we should properly fear while providing the ground of confidence in our risk taking. For Aquinas, moreover, courage must always be formed by the theological virtue of charity, for it is charity that directs virtuous action toward its proper end (1964–76:2-2.23.8). Courage exercised in the service of one's own gain, therefore, would not count as courage in Aquinas's scheme but only courage exercised as a form of self-giving for others or for God.

Theorizing the proper mean between inordinate fear and inordinate risk taking turns out to be difficult, however, because of the great variety of situations we encounter and in which we are called upon to display courage. There is no simple rule or set of principles we can follow.

Again, we are thrust back onto the importance of exemplars who provide concrete illustrations of how to do the right thing in the right way at the right time and in the right measure. One such exemplar, especially important in relation to evangelistic courage, is Oscar Arnulfo Romero, who became archbishop during El Salvador's twelve year-long civil war and was martyred on March 24, 1980, while preparing the Eucharist during Mass in the chapel of the Divina Providencia, a cancer hospital where he lived.

Romero was not always known for his courageous witness. He began his ministry as an intelligent, "safe," and conservative theologian and preacher who, though ever an advocate of social justice and reform, believed, as did many of his contemporaries, that the church should not overly involve itself in matters that would cause conflict and division among its members. Romero feared that those outside the church would perceive it as taking sides in secular political matters—a perception of critical importance when taking sides meant finding oneself on the same side as Marxists who were working to organize the poor in order to overthrow the totalitarian government and bring about land reform. By Romero's time, through a long history of legal manipulation and outright theft, a handful of elite and military-protected landowners had come to control well over half of the arable land in El Salvador (Dennis, Golden, and Wright 2000:9). To work for reform in such a situation was to earn the label "communist," and this label helped to justify government- and military-sponsored repression not only of all economic and land reform movements but also of the church itself insofar as it supported these movements. It also helped secure military and financial aid from the United States as a way of fighting the communism that was perceived to be infiltrating Central and Latin America. Romero, therefore, was critical of emerging theologies of liberation that advocated direct church involvement in the work of reform; he believed that the church should stay to the center and seek the ear of those in power to stop the escalating violence against anyone working for change.

By the time Romero was made archbishop in 1977, however, the torture, disappearance, or murder of virtually anyone who came out in favor of reform had grown to such proportions that he was moved to learn more about the suffering of his people and to find ways of entering into their struggle. The government continued to put pressure on the church by deporting foreign priests. Then, just three weeks after Romero's installation as archbishop, a Jesuit priest and friend Rutilio Grande, along with two parishioners, were ambushed and murdered. This event functioned as a catalyst in moving Romero beyond a neutrality that was, in any case, impossible. Grande had incited the wrath of the powerful landowners in his region by denouncing their monopoly on fertile land that consigned the poor to uninhabitable territory on the rocky sides of the mountains and by organizing sugarcane plantation workers in his parish (ibid. 26).

Romero's trip to rural Aguilares to view Grande's body and his experience with the throngs of poor campesinos there who held Grande in high esteem made a tremendous impact on him. After holding a commemorative Mass for Grande that evening, he called for a single Mass to be held in the national cathedral on the following Sunday as a public expression of the unity of the church—a unity built not on a feigned neutrality but on the church's Christly and therefore bodily identification with the poor and the persecuted. Both governmental and ecclesiastical leaders were distressed by this bold move and interpreted it as a political act, as indeed it was—as is any incursion of the church's politics into the space of an unjust politics.

Something happened to Romero during this period that would set the course of the next few years of his life up to his death. The transformation was deeply evangelical, pastoral, prophetic, and spiritual all at once. Indeed, we may, with Jon Sobrino, speak of it as nothing short of a "conversion" (2000:9–10). Romero became filled with a love for the poor that would increasingly translate into a courage to be present with them, to accompany them, and to take risks on their behalf, as his words over the body of Father Grande pledged: "I want to . . . ask for your prayers that I be faithful to this promise, that I will not abandon my people. Rather, I will run with them all the risks that my ministry demands" (quoted in Dennis, Golden, and Wright 2000:29).

This transformation in Romero is, I think, what Aquinas meant in speaking of charity as a gift of the Holy Spirit rather than an achievement on our part and also as the form of the virtues. That it was mediated to Romero through the poor makes it no less a gift of grace—indeed, all the more so. In Romero's self-understanding, this charity was not an abstract or sentimental notion but an actual participation in the life of the triune God, so that the church's mission must be understood as a Spirit-empowered participation in and extension of God's mission in Christ (Romero 2004:132).[20] For Romero, courage is the consequence—or, better, the requirement—of a life ordered from within the more fundamental movement of a love that in thankfulness to God seeks to extend friendship with God to one's neighbors. Romero was, in a word, an evangelist. Though he is often rightly thought of as a prophet, his courage must first be understood from within the context of his intention "to be an ordinary catechist, an evangelizer of the

---

20. On the importance of understanding charity not as a formal principle but as naming the relationship between the trinitarian persons, see Long 2000:233.

people, nothing else," to offer God's love to others, even and especially his enemies (ibid. 95).[21]

Of course, Romero's understanding of an evangelist is very different from that of modern purveyors of a "personal relationship with Jesus," a private and interior salvation that is just as likely to characterize the wealthy coffee plantation owner as the peasant worker on that plantation whose parents once owned the land on which he now labors. In Romero's understanding, an evangelist is one who tells the truth and who lives it in such a way that it is capable of calling forth faith in those who hear and see that truth. But that truth is not social or political merely by extension or implication; it is social and political because it is the visible and enpeopled presence of shalom in a violent and unjust world. It is intrinsically social and political because it is a form of communion that is characterized by a new government made present in Christ, a government that leads those who accept it not merely to become "involved in" politics but to *be* an alternative and new politics in and for the world.

> It is very easy to be servants of the word without disturbing the world: a very spiritualized word, a word without any commitment to history, a word that can sound in any part of the world because it belongs to no part of the world. A word like that creates no problems, starts no conflicts.
>
> What starts conflicts and persecutions, what marks the genuine church, is the word that, burning like the word of the prophets, proclaims and accuses: proclaims to the people God's wonders to be believed and venerated, and accuses of sin those who oppose God's reign, so that they may tear that sin out of their hearts, out of their societies, out of their laws—out of the structures that oppress, that imprison, that violate the rights of God and of humanity. (Romero 2004:18)

Romero's commitment to truth telling led him to recount specific abuses and violations each week and to challenge those who were responsible. These bold denunciations arose not from a desire to provoke and offend but from his pastoral love for the people and his identification with the powerless. Indeed, because charity rather than fear now ordered his courage, the fact that the church might end up on the "same side" as Marxists at various points would be defended rather than serving as a pretext for a depoliticized faith and an invisible, spiritualized church.[22] "The authentic church is one that does not mind conversing

21. As Romero goes on to say, "More important than all the chairs of all the sciences of the human race is the simple chair of evangelization, which teaches people the true meaning of life, their genuine relationship with God, their responsibilities in society. This is what we have tried to do" (2004:95).

22. Romero, however, criticized both Marxism and capitalism as equally atheistic at their very core:

with publicans and sinners, as Christ did—and with Marxists and those of various political movements—in order to bring them salvation's true message" (ibid. 102).

Romero also began to speak to the international community and to present to the world a different story of what was happening in El Salvador from the official versions coming from the Salvadoran government. He even took it upon himself to write U.S. president Jimmy Carter, urging him not to send further military or economic aid to El Salvador since it would only continue be used against the Salvadoran people by those in power (Brockman 1989:227).

Romero often spoke of not wishing to be perceived as subversive or to be understood as in conflict with the government. But for Romero, the church's mission was "a prolongation of Christ's"; therefore, "those that trample the people must be in conflict with the church" (2004:133). He did not seek to be "political," but insofar as the church is itself a politics expressed materially in such practices as solidarity with the poor, it is impossible that this politics should not be in conflict with a politics that sacrifices the poor in the name of economic growth and national security.[23] The church, for Romero, was not a place of safety but a place of risk.

All this does not mean that Romero's courage was a willful embrace of persecution or a self-destructive pursuit of opposition (what we today often characterize as a "martyr's complex").[24] As Romero saw it, how-

It is . . . absurd to say that the church has become Marxist. Since Marxist materialism destroys the church's transcendent meaning, a Marxist church would be not only self-destructive but senseless.

But there is an "atheism" that is closer at hand and more dangerous to our church. It is the atheism of capitalism, in which material possessions are set up as idols and take God's place. . . . Which is more serious: to deny God out of a false idea of human liberation, or to deny him out of selfishness raised to the level of idolatry? Who are the greater hypocrites: those who believe in this world to the point of denying openly what is transcendent, or those who use what is transcendent and religious as a tool and justification for their idolatry of the earth?

Both are atheism. Neither is the truth that the church of the gospel teaches so beautifully: "The sublimest reason for human dignity is human beings' call to communion with God." (2004:100–101)

23. It is in this sense that evangelism is indeed a "conflict practice," not because conflict is an ontological feature of creation (as Milbank has argued extensively) or because the modus operandi of evangelism is irritation, but because the practice of evangelism exposes the sinfulness of the world and God's judgment upon that sin while also disclosing God's offer of justification, the promise of "an alien righteousness" (cf. Hütter 2000:87). As Volf says so aptly, "Especially in a creation infested with sin, the proclamation and enactment of the kingdom of truth and justice is never an act of pure positing, but always already a transgression into spaces occupied by others" (1996:293).

24. "The Martyrdom of Polycarp" makes mention of a certain man named Quintus who appears to have sought martyrdom by giving himself up voluntarily to the authorities

ever, a greater presence and solidarity with the poor necessarily meant a greater distance from the powerful.

> In this situation of conflict and antagonism, in which just a few persons control economic and political power, the church has placed itself at the side of the poor and has undertaken their defense. The church cannot do otherwise. . . . But by defending the poor, it has entered into serious conflict with the powerful, who belong to the monied oligarchies, and with the political and military authorities of the state. This defense of the poor in a world so deep in conflict has occasioned something new in the recent history of our church: persecution. (1985:181)

If it is true that Romero believed an evangelist is one who tells the truth and offers it to others as a habitable form of life, it is also true that Romero was killed for doing just that. The truth, for him, was not a set of "ideas." It was, on the one hand, a profound embrace and affirmation of the dignity of the poor and, on the other hand, an exposing and denunciation of the violence of a totalitarian state. Romero's evangelism, therefore, was a mixture of bold truth telling along with humble entreaties and compassionate affirmations of solidarity with those whose lives had been touched by brutality and persecution. He consoled the powerless, urging them to "be not afraid" and to "have courage." But he also implored the powerful to "recover their lost human dignity," to receive forgiveness and "be converted." Both messages constituted his evangelism.

While the virtue of courage in Romero's life can become a model for our own, it is irreducible to a formula that can be simply or straightforwardly repeated in any context. One thing is certain: that courage was not so much a calculative, theoretical balancing of fear and risk as the quality of a life narrated by the cross and the resurrection of Jesus. On the one hand, the cross of Jesus was, for Romero, more than a past historical event. It was a revelation of the way God rules in history through love, humility, compassion, and solidarity. Every Christian, then, and indeed the church itself, is called to take up that cross and to follow Jesus.

> The church, entrusted with the earth's glory, believes that in each person is the Creator's image and that everyone who tramples it offends God. As holy defender of God's rights and of [God's] images, the church must cry out.
>
> It takes as spittle in its face, as lashes on its back, as the cross in its passion, all that human beings suffer, even though they be unbelievers.

---

and causing others to do so also. As the story goes, he turned cowardly upon seeing the wild animals and ended up denying the faith and offering sacrifice to the gods. The text is careful to offer the commentary that "we do not approve of those who come forward of themselves: this is not the teaching of the Gospel" (Musurillo 1972:5).

They suffer as God's images. There is no dichotomy between [humanity] and God's image.

Whoever tortures a human being, whoever abuses a human being, whoever outrages a human being abuses God's image, and the church takes as its own that cross, that martyrdom. (2004:26)

On the other hand, the resurrection of Jesus served as the ground of confidence for Romero's courage and directed it toward hope in the coming reign of God. Even when the situation was most desperate in El Salvador, Romero vocalized this courageous hope, which creates possibilities in the midst of impossibilities:

Let us not be afraid brothers and sisters. We are living through difficult and uncertain days. We do not know if this very evening we will be prisoners or murder victims. We do not know what the forces of evil will do with us. But one thing I do know: even those who have disappeared after arrest, even those who are mourned in the mystery of an abduction, are known and loved by God. He loves us. He keeps on loving. He loves our history too, and he knows where the ways of our land's redemption will lead. (ibid. 72)

The fact that Christians believe in and hope for resurrection, however, was not, for Romero, to be construed as an "acceptance of present injustice" (ibid. 14). That belief and hope point to a transcendent horizon of liberation that is never to be equated with our own solutions or reduced to strategies based on the short-term calculations of efficacy that typically lead to violence. In fact, it is because of a resurrection hope that Romero could find no room for violence in the church's mission: "We are a pilgrim church, exposed to misunderstanding, to persecution; but a church that walks peacefully because we carry within us the force of love" (Dennis, Golden, and Wright 2000:32). Romero's courage, therefore, is revealed as much in his direct denunciation of the powerful as in his unrelenting refusal of violence and retaliation against them. In this respect, Romero's example is consistent with the ancient martyrs, whose courage was expressed through nonviolence and the forsaking of their own claims to justice when all around them courage was being construed in terms of how bravely one committed violence and was able to defeat one's foes.

Here we can begin to see how it is that the virtues of presence, patience, courage, and humility intersect; for in the task of evangelism, the theological virtue of faith directs the virtues to forgo all coercive means that present themselves as potentially able to secure the truth of our convictions. Faith instead puts us in a position where we are able to rely only on the promises of God, so that what is required is a patient presence, unsure of how things will turn out, at least in the short term. For the martyr, therefore, to be courageous is to be pacifist. But because of this, the martyr is enabled to embody imaginative responses to violence and oppression that bear witness to the truth and have far-reaching consequences because they work "with the grain of the universe."[25]

Because of Romero's resurrection faith, he could both make promises and keep them; indeed, his courage was intrinsically related to the integrity of his promise keeping. Though he could confess to being shaken at times by the death threats he received, he was not preoccupied with a fear of death. He knew that there are worse things than dying and that, as sacred as life is, it is not an unqualified absolute value, nor is it more sacred than the good for which life exists.[26] Romero could even interpret his own potential death as an instrument of hope:

> I have often been threatened with death. I must tell you, as a Christian, I do not believe in death without resurrection. If I am killed, I shall arise in the Salvadoran people. I say so without boasting, with the greatest humility.
>
> As a shepherd, I am obliged by divine mandate to give my life for those I love—for all Salvadorans, even for those who may be going to kill me. If the threats are carried out, from this moment I offer my blood to God for the redemption and for the resurrection of El Salvador.
>
> Martyrdom is a grace of God that I do not believe I deserve. But if God accepts the sacrifice of my life, let my blood be a seed of freedom and the sign that hope will soon be reality. Let my death, if it is accepted by God, be for my people's liberation and as a witness of hope in the future. (quoted in Brockman 1989:248)

Romero's resurrection faith is the ground for the fact that his courage was incomprehensible apart from his humility. Because he had no need to secure the truth of his commitments in his own person, he was free to place his person courageously in total service to the God whom he took to be the source of truth. He was therefore free also to trust others and to surrender his fear for the future or of what might happen to his people if he were to be killed.

> A Christian community is evangelized in order to evangelize.
> A light is lit in order to give light.

25. A phrase from John Howard Yoder's essay "Armaments and Eschatology," *Studies in Christian Ethics* 1, no. 1 (1988): 58; quoted in Hauerwas 2001b. In "The Hermeneutics of Peoplehood," Yoder elaborates: "When it *seems* to me that my unjust deed is indispensable to prevent some much greater evil being done by another, I have narrowed my scope of time, or of space, or of global variety, or of history. I have ruled some people out of my Golden Rule, or have skewed the coefficients in my utility calculus" (1984:38).

26. For similar reasons, early Christians, as Hauerwas notes, would even take their children with them in martyrdom rather than have them raised pagan (1997:231).

A candle is not lit to be put under a bushel, said Christ.
It is lit and put up high in order to give light.
That is what a true community is like.
A community is a group of men and women who have found the
    truth in Christ and in his gospel, and who follow the truth and
    join together to follow it more strongly.
It is not just an individual conversion, but a community
    conversion.
It is a family that believes, a group that accepts God.
In the group, each one finds that the brother or sister is a source
    of strength and that in moments of weakness they help one an-
    other and, by loving one another and believing, they give light
    and example.
The preacher no longer needs to preach, for there are Christians
    who preach by their own lives.
I said once and I repeat today that if, unhappily, some day they
    silence our radio and don't let us write our newspaper, each of
    you who believe must become a microphone, a radio station, a
    loudspeaker, not to talk, but to call for faith.
I am not afraid that our faith may depend only on the archbishop's
    preaching; I don't think I'm that important.
I believe that this message, which is only a humble echo of God's
    word, enters your hearts, not because it is mine, but because it
    comes from God. (2004:98)

Humility

Much has already been said about humility in the preceding discussion of courage. As a virtue that sustains the practice of evangelism, humility qualifies the virtue of courage so that it does not become glamorous or arrogant self-confidence in the service of defeating one's enemies. But as we saw in the life of Archbishop Romero, courage also qualifies humility so that it is neither abstracted into an unqualified submission nor sentimentalized into a general civility, passivity, or tolerance. Hauerwas rightly notes that the only humility Christians are to embrace is "that determined by the cross of Christ" (1998:67).

The forgiveness extended by martyrs to others, especially their persecutors, is a good example of this cruciform humility (recalling Jesus' forgiveness from the cross) and one that surfaces as a recurrent pattern in the *acta* of the martyrs from the very earliest. Indeed, there may be no more important task before a church that would evangelize than the forgiveness by which it participates in extending God's salvation to others. Of course, in assuming the posture of forgiver, Christian humility is bound to appear arrogant.[27] But the reign of God does not become real, nor is it made visible and habitable in the world, to the extent that other reigns are dismantled and other sovereigns overthrown. It is made visible when, in the midst of violence and injustice, a people who confess God as their sovereign refuse to find the security and meaning of their lives in power and instead forgive others just as they understand themselves to have been forgiven. It is made visible when that people, by placing themselves into God's hands, become dispossessed of every pretense to gaining a foothold in the world for themselves or their cause.[28] Evangelistic humility is peaceableness; it is an acquired habit of counting for naught all those things we once figured for gain. It is a confidence that in the life, death, and resurrection of Jesus we discover that God rules the world through vulnerability, humility, and love.

This discovery, however, means that the church's evangelistic encounter with others can never rest on an arrogant or triumphalist sense of superiority and possession. What Lesslie Newbigin says about Christian dialogue with persons of other religious faiths is therefore true of every evangelistic encounter—there must be on the part of Christians "a *kenosis*, a 'self-emptying,'" a recognition that "Christians do not meet their partners in dialogue as those who possess the truth and the holiness of God but as those who bear witness to a truth and holiness that are God's judgment on them and who are ready to hear the judgment spoken through the lips and life of their partner of another faith" (1995:181–82).

If Newbigin is right, while evangelism has typically been associated with the activities of preaching, testifying, and persuading, it could be that

27. Hauerwas makes this point in his Gifford Lectures, *With the Grain of the Universe* (2001b:16).

28. Here I find Milbank's comments on Augustine's understanding of the relationship between virtue and forgiveness especially apropos:

Augustine asserts that, for us, the approach to divine perfection cannot be by any achieved excellence of virtue, but only through forgiveness. This does not, I think, imply a protestant resignation to sinfulness. Instead the assertion belongs with the social character of his thought: given the persistence of the sins of others (as well as our own sinfulness, which we cannot all at once overcome, but remains alien to our better desires) there is only one way to respond to them which would not itself be sinful and domineering, and that is to anticipate heaven, and act as if their sin was not there, by offering reconciliation. Augustine's real and astounding point is this: virtue cannot properly operate except when collectively possessed, when all are virtuous and all concur in the sequence of their differences; hence the actual, "possessed," realized virtues which we lay claim to, *least of all* resemble true, heavenly virtues. On the contrary, the only thing really like heavenly virtue is our constant attempt to compensate for, substitute for, even shortcut this total absence of virtue, by not taking offence, assuming the guilt of others, doing what they should have done, beyond the bounds of given "responsibility." Paradoxically, it is only in this exchange and sharing that any truly actual virtue is really present. (1990:411)

one of its most important activities is listening. Listening is, of course, a form of "receiving" and therefore requires presence, patience, and humility. Listening also leaves the evangelist open to the possibility of change and correction, as with the apostle Peter, who was instrumental in the conversion of the Gentile Cornelius (Acts 10) but who was himself also converted through his openness to the voice of God and the riches of the "other" (ibid. 182). Listening, therefore, requires the virtue of courage also—the courage to be changed, judged, and corrected.

But constituted by the movement of charity, listening may itself be understood as an embodied offer of good news, as the following words from William Stringfellow express:

> Listening is a rare happening among human beings. You cannot listen to the word another is speaking if you are preoccupied with your appearance or impressing the other, or if you are trying to decide what you are going to say when the other stops talking, or if you are debating about whether the word being spoken is true or relevant or agreeable. Such matters may have their place, but only after listening to the word as the word is being uttered. Listening, in other words, is a primitive act of love, in which a person gives self to another's word, making self accessible and vulnerable to that word. (1994:169)

While humility is a perennial virtue required of evangelistic practice, it has never been more important than now for those of us who live in societies where the church is still coping with the loss of Christendom privileges and our consignment to the fringes of cultural and political significance. The temptation is incredibly strong to disavow the church's politics, its distinctive worship and obedience, in favor of wider influence and acceptance. The antithesis of humility is not always arrogance and self-regard; sometimes it is an ingratiating servility that ever seeks the notice and admiration of others.

I think R. R. Reno is correct in suggesting that "the church is in ruins." But if so, then I think he may also be correct in claiming that "our vocation is to dwell within the ruins of the church," to bear that reality and "wear the fetters that our age has given us to wear: an increasingly inarticulate theological tradition, a capitulating and culturally captive church, a disintegrating spiritual discipline" (2002:15). It may even be the case that the church will need to shrink in order faithfully to evangelize the world, that it will need to die in order to live again. This need not imply the church's disengagement from the world or a retreat from its compassionate and prophetic service to the world. But it is rather to suggest that such service is evangelistic only when it is faithful to the One who has called us to that service, even if we must find our home among "the ruins."

Among the last words of Oscar Romero in his final homily were the following remarks, commenting on the Gospel reading from John 12:23–26:

> You have just heard in Christ's Gospel that one must not love oneself so much as to avoid getting involved in the risks of life that history demands of us, and that those who fend off the danger will lose their lives. But whoever out of love for Christ gives themselves to the service of others will live, like the grain of wheat that dies, but only apparently. If it did not die, it would remain alone. . . . Only in dying does it produce the harvest. (quoted in Brockman 1989:244)

Common Virtue

The account of virtuous evangelism I have provided up to this point is incomplete apart from further clarification regarding both its "ordinariness" and its communal nature. Maura Clarke, Ita Ford, Dorothy Kazel, Jean Donovan, and Archbishop Romero are beautiful examples of evangelistic presence, patience, courage, and humility, but it is not my intention to leave the impression that the exercise of evangelistic virtue is only the work of solitary individuals or, for that matter, "heroic" individuals in extraordinary situations. Most of us are not likely to find ourselves bearing witness under oppressive totalitarian regimes where hostility to the church is as overt and deadly as it was for Romero and the four churchwomen. Their examples are no less paradigmatic for that, but the truth of the matter is that for most Christians the price of *martyria* will not be a violent death. In the context of modern democracies, the public nonconformity at the heart of *martyria* is more likely to be met by trivialization, marginalization, or outright dismissal rather than persecution and murder.

There are, however, vivid signs of "common" evangelistic beauty in the North American church that stand as a witness to the distinctiveness of God's reign in the world while proclaiming and offering that reign to others and summoning them to a life together ordered by it. Christian virtue is likewise common in these communities, though their beauty and virtue is all the more striking and *un*common given the degree to which the North American church has accommodated itself to the surrounding culture. But such communities do exist, despite their imperfections and the flawed but saintly humanity of their members. One such community is the outdoor church I attend in Boston, Massachusetts, that reaches out especially to homeless persons and is known as "Common Cathedral." Common Cathedral began in 1994 when the Reverend Deborah Little, an Episcopal priest, began meeting daily on the streets of Boston with homeless persons, many of whom do not feel welcome in area churches and whose poverty often stands in stark contrast to the wealth and privilege on display in the historic downtown cathedrals and meetinghouses.

Deborah began by offering sandwiches and friendship and by referring those she met to appropriate service providers. But eventually the ministry evolved into a church community that invites both the homeless and the housed to weekly worship on Sunday afternoons. It is now characterized by shared leadership and a variety of ministries that bring together the resources of area service providers, clergy, churches, seminarians, and others in order to meet the physical, social, and spiritual needs of the homeless.[29]

When one talks with Rev. Little, it is clear that she does not see evangelism as some further step that needs to be taken beyond the distinctive presence of a community of believers in the midst of the city and the hospitality of a church that welcomes those whom others reject and invites them through worship and ministry to share in its corporate fellowship. As with many mainline Protestants, the word *evangelism* has a number of negative connotations that prevent church and staff members from using it very often as a way of describing either what they are or what they do. But evangelism as I have been describing it in this book is very much at the heart of this congregation's life and practice, and so also are the virtues of presence, patience, courage, and humility.

One of the defining characteristics of Common Cathedral that distinguishes it from area social service providers is the nature of its ecclesial fellowship, in which homeless persons are not "clients" but fellow saints who contribute to the life of the community, guide its worship, and share in its ministries. Central to this fellowship is the (very) public service of Holy Communion, offered each Sunday at 1:00 p.m. on historic Boston Common underneath a tree and next to the famous triple-tiered Brewer Fountain, a stone's throw from the Park Street subway station. A makeshift altar with a rugged cross is rolled into place, and a circle is formed while hundreds of tourists and other passersby walk around (and sometimes through) the circle, sometimes stopping to overhear what is going on. The very form of the community's fellowship is a distinctive combination of public boldness and simplicity. The community gathers each Sunday regardless of the weather or what other events might be taking place in the park or along the street that day; it is quite a feat, for example, to worship God when a parade is passing by! The connectedness of the congregation to nature as its sanctuary and to the noisy hustle-bustle of urban life is profound and deeply shapes the form and substance of its *presence*, which is simultaneously material and spiritual (any line between

29. I have developed my account of this church from personal experience, interviews, and the church's website at www.ecclesia-ministries.org.

the two disappears here). The connectedness of the congregation to the poor, who are people rather than an abstraction at Common Cathedral, also shapes the form and substance of that presence. In such a setting it is hard not to be reminded of the basics that make the church the church and of what it means for the church to make a space in the world peaceably yet publicly for bearing witness to God's reign.

The worship service is adapted from the Book of Common Prayer, with the reading and proclamation of the Word and the celebration of Eucharist as its twin centers of gravity. The weekly repetition of the same choruses ("Kumbaya," "Alleluia," "We Are Standing on Holy Ground") can be annoying to those who would advocate for depth, range, and complexity in the church's liturgical formation of its saints. But in this context, what might otherwise seem banal can be understood as contributing to the invitational quality of the gathered community by providing a high degree of familiarity, stability, and predictability that is often missing and proves to be critically important for people living on the streets. This invitational quality is marked further by the open participation of the community in the voicing of the Prayers of the People and responses to the proclamation of the Word. It is unusual to find a congregation that makes the time to include and value in worship the experiences, insights, and perceptions of all its saints, including those with serious mental illness,[30] a practice that is sustained by what might well be characterized as the corporate exercise of patience. One can never predict or control what someone might say or do in a worship service, and with such visibility, it is tempting for those concerned with the church's public "respectability" to be embarrassed by the quirky mannerisms, disheveled appearance, and sometimes shocking remarks of those who are made to feel welcome. But in the context of this congregational patience, the reflections on the sermon and the prayers offered by those who are gathered exhibit a refreshing concreteness that ranges from experience with addiction or immediate concerns about the weather to the status of soldiers in Iraq or the playoff hopes of the Boston Red Sox.

After an exchange of the peace, the service culminates in a celebration of the Lord's Supper, with a table that is open and extended bodily by the presiding ministers both to those in the circle of worshipers and to those sitting or standing in the immediate vicinity. The liturgical celebration then transitions into a shared meal, usually provided by one of numerous partnering churches that share in the work of Common Cathedral and often donate other material goods with those in the community with needs.

30. Some 20–25 percent of the homeless in the United States have serious mental illnesses, in contrast to the national average of about 4 percent. Up to 50 percent have co-occurring mental illnesses and substance abuse disorders (U.S. National Resource and Training Center on Homelessness and Mental Illness, www.nrchmi.samhsa.gov).

During the week, Common Cathedral offers recovery groups; pro bono legal aid and medical services; healing services; confirmation and baptism preparation; open gospel discussions focusing on the Sunday Gospel lesson in relation to everyday life; Common Art, a venue for the support and development of the artistic abilities of homeless members; and Common Cinema, an opportunity to watch films together as a community and to discuss them.

Most of us would not be inclined to describe any of these activities or worship opportunities as extraordinary, heroic, or earth-shaking. This is not the kind of congregation about which bestselling books get written or that brings together a convention of thousands of pastors eager to find out how to grow their churches and "maximize their effectiveness." But the vulnerability, accessibility, servanthood, and compassion that characterize this congregation's presence in its world are, I should like to argue, all defining marks of an evangelizing church that demonstrate its unity with a church of the martyrs throughout history. Precisely in the steady, even predictable, offer of witness such as this in the context of a social body that publicly and visibly worships God, welcomes the stranger, and values the poor we can rightly claim to find an example of *martyria* that is both beautiful and truthful.

The examples of congregations like Common Cathedral should remind us that however strange and foreign is the "difference" of Christian witness, it is not for that reason obscure or mysterious. It is instead a nonconformity that is "ordinary" insofar as it surfaces not in esoteric behaviors or arcane rituals but in everyday practices, such as those that Paul lists following his plea to the Romans (in chapter 12) not to be "conformed to this world":

- not thinking of ourselves more highly than we ought to think
- valuing the dignity and function of the diverse gifts in the body of Christ
- loving one another with mutual affection
- outdoing one another in showing honor
- being ardent in spirit and patient in suffering
- persevering in prayer
- contributing to the needs of the saints
- extending hospitality to strangers
- blessing rather than cursing those who persecute us
- sharing the joy and sorrow of others
- living in harmony with one another
- associating with the lowly

- refusing vengeance and retaliation
- living peaceably with all and overcoming evil with good

Not only in the witness and virtues of its ministers, Rev. Deb Little and Rev. Joan Murray, but also in the witness and virtues of the gathered community itself, one sees a glimpse of the "society" made possible by the Gospel. Because of differences in historical circumstance, the courage of the Christians who make up Common Cathedral is not put to the test in the same ways as it was for Archbishop Romero and the four churchwomen of El Salvador. But the way their courage intersects with humility and patience to form a distinctively Christlike presence in their particular context has striking resemblances to the Salvadoran martyrs. We can detect in these very different examples a common and identifiable pattern that is at the heart of Christian witness.

It is risky to cite contemporary examples like Common Cathedral, for the tendency will be to evaluate them as "proofs" rather than to learn from them as witnesses (this is especially dangerous since contemporary examples are still very much alive and "on the journey"). Likewise, our tendency with exemplars is to mimic them rather than to trace out the political and economic patterns in which evangelistic virtues are identified, learned, and cultivated. Not every feature of the lives of individual or congregational exemplars is replicable in other contexts, nor need it be. The beauty of evangelistic saints and martyrs is instead the alternative social imagination they embody and evoke.

What should be clear from all the examples I have mentioned in this chapter is that the practice of evangelism is not a simple or straightforward procedure like installing a door latch or repairing a faucet. It is more like a craft that is learned over time and requires the lived wisdom of others passed on from within a community of virtue. Aristotle referred to this practical wisdom as *phronesis*, and for him it was just as surely a virtue as courage, patience, or humility. At the same time, it is different from these other virtues insofar as it is a reflection on the right measure in which they are to be exercised.[31]

As previously noted, because of the endless variety of situations in which we find ourselves, we can never reduce virtuous performance of a practice to a finite set of techniques or rules ("ten easy steps"). In the words of MacIntyre, "The exercise of the virtues requires therefore a capacity to judge and to do the right thing in the right place at the right time in the right way" (1984:150). Practical wisdom is this capacity to judge. It is the internalization of a community-formed knowledge of how to act in various

---

31. Milbank can refer to *phronesis* as "the very heart of ethical *praxis*" for Aristotle (1990:349).

circumstances that has been built up over time and through attention to cases and examples along the way. It is handed on by lived participation in that community as it responds to ever new situations with reference to paradigm actions or people and by the telling of stories (Taylor 1989:28).[32] Normative among those paradigms and stories for Christians is, of course, the story and life pattern of Jesus. Insofar as the church does not merely proclaim the story of Jesus but extends it within history, however, the stories of the church and its saints also attain a certain normativity, even if that normativity is always derivative rather than originating.

The fact that the wisdom required for virtuous performance of evangelistic practice is historical and contextual, then, does not subject that practice to complete relativization and randomness. Rather, the traditions, stories, memories, exemplars, and patterns of the church provide a deep *habitus* from which that practice flows and through which the Holy Spirit guides the church from situation to situation. *Phronesis* requires the singularity of particular situations but at the same time draws upon human experience in a variety of situations. That is why we need not only the examples of individual saints and martyrs to illustrate the concrete, costly, and deeply personal nature of virtuous witness but also a "communion of saints" in which the virtues are defined and in which evangelism as a virtuous practice can be learned. As I have tried to argue throughout the book, evangelistic witness is impossible apart from a Spirit-created social body that can sustain that witness, form us into virtue, and order our lives (and indeed our bodies) toward God through worship, fellowship, and discipline.

All this does not mean that to be part of the community called *ecclesia* is to gain its wisdom by a process of osmosis or by simply deferring to its past experience and formulations. As Yoder points out, one of the fundamental patterns of social process that embodies the politics of *ecclesia* is the practice of open conversation and spiritual discernment within an inclusive, egalitarian fellowship in which the floor is open to all as the Spirit leads and in which decisions are made on the basis of consensus rather than more expedient forms of hierarchical coercion or rule of the majority. It was only in the context of such communities that Romero himself, otherwise very much a part of a traditionally hierarchical organization, could come to decide for the evangelistic approaches he eventually took, fleshed out in practices of pastoral solidarity on the one hand and prophetic denunciation on the other. As Stephen Fowl and Gregory Jones note, Romero's powerful readings both of Scripture

32. This, I think, is consistent with Pierre Bourdieu's statement that practices "have as their principle not a set of conscious, constant rules, but practical schemes, opaque to their possessors, varying according to the logic of the situation, the almost invariable partial viewpoint it imposes, etc." (1990:12).

and of the world were not developed in isolation; "they emerged from worshipping, conversing, and living among fellow Christians, particularly poor Salvadorans who gathered together for worship and study in 'base Christian communities'" (1997:130). Such communities, communities not unlike Common Cathedral, challenged—and continue to challenge—the customary and received practical wisdom of a church that for hundreds of years has acquiesced to the interests of the wealthy and powerful.

The virtue of *phronesis*, therefore, depends greatly on the *form of life* in which it is cultivated and on the particular notion of the "common good" toward which that form of life is ordered. Guided by the procedural notion of modernity, where the common good is simply a condition under which individuals may optimally pursue their own private good without the interference of others, the stories, memories, and traditions of the church (and *phronesis* itself) are discarded or pushed away in favor of rules, procedures, and bureaucratic technique. As Charles Taylor suggests, *phronesis* comes to be "mistrusted" because (1) it is "not fully reduced to reason" and (2) "as a consequence it could be the domain of blind parochial prejudice" (1989:29–30).

However, for an *ecclesia* in which through baptism we are reconciled into one body so that the common good is imagined economically as a community of abundance, joy, sharing, and hospitality, virtue is not subject to either ancient or modern bifurcations of public and private, *polis* and *oikos*, male and female (so that only males could exercise virtues such as courage, for example). Rather, the whole community is to exercise the Christian virtues in every aspect of their lives, and the whole community (not just free, propertied males) provides the common experiences, resources, and ongoing revitalization for an ecclesial *phronesis*.

Inscribed on the bottom of the Marine Corps War Memorial in Arlington, Virginia, are the words "Uncommon valor was a common virtue," a quotation from Admiral Chester W. Nimitz in tribute to the soldiers who fought on Iwo Jima during World War II. The context for identifying Christian courage, as previously noted, is that of the martyr rather than the soldier in battle. Yet the admiral's words could well apply to evangelistic virtues in the church, which are likewise both "common" and "uncommon." Uncommon, in that the dispositions of character required for the faithful practice of evangelism are formed from within an extraordinary social body called *ecclesia* whose politics and economics are not like those of other social bodies around it. The church is not the world. Yet those same virtues are also "common," both in the sense that they are shared by a community and therefore "held in common" and in the sense that even as nonconformist and countercultural, they are tempered in the stuff of the everyday and sustained and passed along in the lives of "ordinary saints."

Conclusion

Evangelism before a Watching World

By this everyone will know that you are my disciples, if you have love for one another.

John 13:35

You yourselves are our letter, written on our hearts, to be known and read by all; and you show that you are a letter of Christ, prepared by us, written not with ink, but with the Spirit of the living God, not on tablets of stone, but on tablets of human hearts.

2 Corinthians 3:2–3

In *Body Politics: Five Practices of the Christian Community Before the Watching World*, John Howard Yoder makes the case—a case upon which I have built extensively throughout this book—that the very shape of the church in the form of its ordinary practices and patterns of social process constitute its witness in the world by providing a visible and material foretaste of God's rule. As I tried to show in the last chapter, that ecclesial foretaste does not contradict but rather implies the visibility of the church in the form of individual saints and martyrs. But the church is often tempted to believe that the world is *not*, in fact, watching and that it may simply go unnoticed—or that it will be noticed but marginalized as uninteresting, useless, backward, or parochial. Because of this, the church eagerly accepts its toleration and domestication by the world, allowing itself to be relegated to a private realm of personal piety and belief or assuming a chaplaincy role by which it is allowed to trespass into the realm of the "public" as long as it is found useful in underwriting the economic and political orders of liberal modernity. In such a world, I would submit, the urgent task of an evangelizing church is to refuse to be thus tolerated.

What I have attempted to do in this book is to argue that the gospel can never be beauty or truth for the world apart from a beautiful and truthful witness that is inescapably public, though not on the world's own terms. The evangelistic invitation is, in the first place, a matter of living beautifully and truthfully before a watching world rather than first attempting to secure the attractiveness or credibility of the gospel on grounds that make its particular content secondary or irrelevant or that secure the necessity of Christianity by eliminating its refusability. I have tried to argue that the church is not accidental to this task. The church is not a social structuring of a prior salvation that is personal and interior or an institutional implication of a disembodied set of doctrines or ideas.[1] Instead, the existence of a distinctive people that finds itself called out of the world and living as an alternative to it is the necessary condition of the witness Christianity has to offer. This does not mean that the truth to which Christianity bears witness is a possession of the church or that it guarantees the church's superiority and dominance. But apart from a visible and enpeopled demonstration of the habitability of the truth—even if that demonstration must inevitably appear strange and foreign in the world—the truth of the gospel cannot be truth for the world.

Christian witness in the shape of an "ordinary nonconformity" is, as I have suggested throughout this book, the central and defining logic of evangelism. All attempts to sidestep that witness in an attempt to shore up the "success" of evangelism must inevitably prove to be violent to the extent that they seek to impose rather than offer the good news. This is true whether evangelism takes the form of a Constantinian elimination of the church's visible difference from the world by effectively fusing the two or the modern liberal attempt to bypass the church altogether and ground Christian truth on foundations in reason or experience. The truth of Christianity cannot be secured (however much it may be served) by an appeal to the authority of the church or of Scripture, on the one hand, or the authority of reason or experience, on the other. On the contrary, the authority of Christian truth is the authority of the cross,

---

1. Bonhoeffer says it this way: "A truth, a doctrine, or a religion need no space for themselves. They are disembodied entities. They are heard, learnt and apprehended, and that is all. But the incarnate son of God needs not only ears or hearts, but living [persons] who will follow him. That is why he called his disciples into a literal, bodily following, and thus made his fellowship with them a visible reality. . . . Having been called they could no longer remain in obscurity, for they were the light that must shine, the city on the hill which must be seen" (1959:248).

an authority that is vulnerable, peaceable, and refusable. It would not be an exaggeration to conclude that the whole of this book, in fact, has been an attempt to ask what difference it would make for evangelism if, as Yoder claims, "the relationship between the obedience of God's people and the triumph of God's cause is not a relationship of cause and effect but one of cross and resurrection" (1972:238).

If, however, the ordinary and peaceable nonconformity of the church *is* its evangelistic witness, then the "success" of evangelism is to be found in directions quite other than the marks of success that characterize the prevailing consensus among evangelistic practitioners today. Cruciformity rather than triumph, growth, and expansion will be among the primary marks of evangelism practiced well, and the virtuous evangelist will be identified not so much by her expertise as by her discipleship. The church's evangelistic effectiveness will have to be measured by the clarity, consistency, and inhabitability of its testimony rather than its toleration by a world where value is measured in terms of utility.

To refuse the world's toleration, however, is not to seek its rejection. It is but the exercise of a holy and evangelical eccentricity that by its very nature cannot and will not be tolerated, as the presence of martyrs throughout Christian history attests. For it is in and through a people that bears faithful witness to God's reign that the world comes to recognize what it truly is—and thereby stands invited and summoned but also exposed and judged. In that people's love of enemies and refusal of vengeance the world sees the circularity of its own violence. In its abundance, sharing, and joy the world sees the artificiality of its own scarcity and competition. In its care for the poor, the widow, and the orphan and in its welcome of the stranger, the world sees the arbitrariness of its own fears and suspicions. In the church's patterns of reconciliation and forgiveness the world sees the irrationality of its own hostility and divisions.

The church's invitation, just to the extent that it is embodied in the everyday and material practices of a people, is, by its very nature, subversive. In inviting the world to come and see the newness of which it is but a foretaste, the church calls attention not only to what it is but also to what the world is by contrast and thereby provokes the world's hatred and distrust. This, of course, comes as no surprise to those who have been called out of the world by Christ and told by him that they will be loved by the world if they belong to it and hated by it if they do not (John 15:18–19).

The world is, indeed, watching. The question is whether there is anything distinctive for the world to see. Whatever else evangelism may be, it is the practice of giving the world something to see—and to touch, and to try. There is no single best way to do this, no sure formula for effectively heralding or modeling the good news, no guaranteed method that persons will accept the church's invitation. Despite the many books and conferences that promote strategies for reaching the unchurched and making new Christians, it is the Holy Spirit that constitutes the church as Christ's body, not charismatic preachers, media-savvy youth workers, church boards, or denominational agencies. The entire evangelistic enterprise is, therefore, one before which we must stand with humility and awe. That fact does not diminish the importance of human beings in the practice of evangelism, but it accentuates the importance of an openness to the Spirit and the critical necessity of a community of discipline in which the Spirit can be discerned. If the church has learned anything about evangelism over time, it is that the Christians who evangelize are more important than the methods they use.

The practice of evangelism is a complex and multilayered process—a context of multiple activities that invite, herald, welcome, and provoke and that has as its end the peaceable reign of God and the social holiness by which persons are oriented toward that reign. As the end of evangelistic practice, the reign of God is not external to evangelistic practice but internal to it in the form of the politics by which that practice is carried out, a politics that is formed by a distinctive story and sustained by distinctive virtues such as presence, patience, courage, and humility. To practice evangelism faithfully and with excellence, then, is to practice it from within this politics, to play by the rules of this politics, so to speak. These rules, as McClendon reminds us, are not like "'no loitering in the hallways,' or 'be home by midnight at the latest.' Rather they are practice-constitutive rules: one who flouts them is to be thought of not as naughty or nasty, but simply as disengaged from the practice in question" (1986:2:38).

Practicing evangelism from within this politics does not eliminate our creativity and freedom. But that creativity will be the creativity of an imaginative remembering and communal reenactment of the story it has been gifted rather than an autonomous production by solitary, traditionless individuals (who may thus be described as "free" only in the negative sense of "privation"). If this sounds like an overly passive way of construing creativity, we may be helped by the comparison James Fodor and Stanley Hauerwas make between faithful Christian practice and artistic performance, especially the role of *improvisation* in that performance. The performer who improvises does not merely "make things up" but is absorbed in the work in such a way that, without diminishing the positive contribution of the performer, we may describe her or him as having been "given over" to it or even "taken over" by it.

> This ability to let go of oneself, to dispossess oneself in the very execution of the act, is a skill that is not learned quickly or easily and certainly not

on one's own. Indeed, if acquired at all, it is learned in communion and fellowship with others over the course of an entire Christian life. . . . Without the requisite alertness and respectful, disciplined attention to the creative rhythm of things, the performance falls flat; it fails to move or convince or enthrall performer and audience alike. In this sense, true performance takes us out of ourselves (*ekstasis*) only to return us to ourselves fuller, richer, more deeply challenged. . . .

Good performers of the Christian faith, like good musicians, are those who have refined the art of allowing themselves to be played by the work even as they perform it. The work plays them as much as, if not more than, they play the work. Christian performance is faithful, powerful, and compelling precisely inasmuch as its execution becomes a form of prayer. (2004:101–2)

The creativity of evangelistic practice, then, arises from within rather than standing over against the rich soil of a distinctive and ecclesial form of life, a *habitus* that stretches both the world's and the church's own imagination as to what is possible by enacting the story it has been given in continued receptiveness to God, the giver.

As I noted in the introduction to the book, the term *evangelism*, though of relatively recent origin, signifies the offer of "good news" or a "welcome message." That the term should be so closely associated with the art of communication may be a liability in modern Western cultures, given our predilection for thinking of communication as information delivery, especially in the form of sentences or bits of data. Evangelism may then be reduced to proclamation, and the gospel to a set of propositions. Characterizing evangelism in terms of "a message" or "news" may likewise disguise the fact that throughout history, as Scripture testifies, God calls and forms a people that, through its worship and obedience, is itself God's message and offer to the world—a living "letter," as Paul puts it.

From the earliest apostolic communities whose visible reconciliation of Jew and Gentile modeled a new social possibility to the martyr communities of the first centuries that refused to worship the emperor or fight his wars, to the base communities of Latin America or congregations like Common Cathedral in Boston in which the poor are valued and find voice, the Christian witness to the gospel is inseparable from the form of life in which the gospel is embodied. We need not denigrate proclamation, therefore, to insist that at the heart of evangelism is the Spirit's formation of a people into a distinctive set of habits, practices, disciplines, and loyalties that together constitute a visible and recognizable pattern before a watching world.

Before warning his disciples that the world would hate them if they belonged to it, Jesus charged them to love one another. "You did not choose me but I chose you," he said. "And I appointed you to go and bear fruit, fruit that will last" (John 15:16). But in thus sending and commissioning the disciples, he claimed that the obedience he sought from them was that of *friends* rather than *servants*. They were not merely to "follow orders" but had been made participants with Christ in the mission on which he had been sent. If the practice of evangelism can be understood as central to that mission, perhaps it would be for our good if we were reminded from time to time that the basis of that practice is friendship with Christ. "As his friends," so David Burrell points out, "we are liberated from having to prove ourselves by accomplishing great deeds. We are already accepted as intimates."[2] The practice of evangelism is thus grounded in patience, faithfulness, and trust rather than obligation and efficacy. Bearing fruit, likewise, is a matter of donation rather than compulsion. We are free to perform the practice with joy, making room for the unexpected, rather than with a tyrannizing sense that the results of that practice are ours to predict and control. At the same time, as Burrell continues, "we are not dispensed from the response characteristic of friendship: to become what the other's trust would call forth from us."

That this trust calls forth from us a cross-shaped way of life is clear from Jesus' observation that there is no greater love than "to lay down one's life for one's friends." So a triumphalistic evangelism is not more Christian but less, not more a reflection of Jesus but in fact a denial of him. Evangelism's cruciformity, however, is in no way to be understood as a celebration of suffering, tragedy, or death. On the contrary, as Paul affirms, we carry in our bodies the death of Jesus "so that the life of Jesus may also be made visible in our bodies" (2 Cor. 4:10). Evangelism practiced as a bodily response to the work of Christ cannot escape the fact that with materiality and visibility come weakness and imperfection. But even here, the visibility of the people of God may be understood as a sign and foretaste of what has already arrived and a promise of what is to come.

> For we do not proclaim ourselves; we proclaim Jesus Christ as Lord and ourselves as your slaves for Jesus' sake. For it is the God who said, "Let light shine out of darkness," who has shone in our hearts to give the light of the knowledge of the glory of God in the face of Jesus Christ.
>
> But we have this treasure in clay jars, so that it may be made clear that this extraordinary power belongs to God and does not come from us. (2 Cor. 4:5–7)

2. Quoted in Hauerwas 1983:151. Cf. David Burrell, "Contemplation and Action: Personal Spirituality/World Reality," in *Dimensions of Contemporary Spirituality*, ed. Francis A. Eigo (Philadelphia: Villanova University Press, 1982), 152.

Bibliography

Abraham, William
1989   *The Logic of Evangelism*. Grand Rapids: Eerdmans.
Adams, James R.
1994   *So You Can't Stand Evangelism? A Thinking Person's Guide to Church Growth*. Boston: Cowley.
Anderson, Benedict
1996   *Imagined Communities*. London: Verso.
Aquinas, Thomas
1964–76   *Summa Theologiae*. 60 vols. New York: Blackfriars.
Arendt, Hannah
1958   *The Human Condition*. 2nd ed. Chicago: University of Chicago Press.
Arias, Mortimer
1984   *Announcing the Reign of God: Evangelization and the Subversive Memory of Jesus*. Philadelphia: Fortress.
Augustine
1990   *Expositions of the Psalms*. Translated by Maria Boulding. The Works of Saint Augustine: A Translation for the Twenty-first Century. Hyde Park, NY: New City.
Barth, Karl
1935   *The Word of God and the Word of Man*. London: Hodder & Stoughton.
1936–77   *Church Dogmatics*. Trans. G. W. Bromiley. Edinburgh: T & T Clark.

1963 *Evangelical Theology*. New York: Holt, Rinehart, and
      Winston.

1981 *The Christian Life: Church Dogmatics 4/4, Lecture Frag-
      ments*. Grand Rapids: Eerdmans.

Bass, Dorothy, ed.

1998 *Practicing Our Faith: A Way of Life for a Searching People*.
      San Francisco: Jossey-Bass.

Baumeister, Theofried

1983 "Martyrdom and Persecution in Early Christianity."
      Concilium 3, no. 163: 3–8.

Bell, Daniel M., Jr.

2001 *Liberation Theology after the End of History*. London:
      Routledge.

Bellah, Robert, et al.

1985 *Habits of the Heart: Individualism and Commitment in
      American Life*. Berkeley: University of California Press.

Berdyaev, Nicolas

1937 *The Origin of Russian Communism*. London: Centenary.

Berger, Peter L.

1969 *The Sacred Canopy*. Garden City, NY: Doubleday.

Bettenson, Henry, ed.

1963 *Documents of the Christian Church*. 2nd ed. New York:
      Oxford University Press.

Boff, Leonardo

1978 *Jesus Christ Liberator: A Critical Christology for Our Time*.
      Translated by Patrick Hughes. Maryknoll, NY: Orbis.

1983 "Martyrdom: An Attempt at Systematic Reflection." In
      Martyrdom Today, edited by Johannes-Baptist Metz and
      Edward Schillebeeckx. New York: Seabury.

Bonhoeffer, Dietrich

1959 *The Cost of Discipleship*. New York: SCM Press.

1960 *Christ the Center*. San Francisco: Harper & Row.

1975 *Worldly Preaching*. Edited by Clyde E. Fant. Nashville:
      Thomas Nelson.

Bourdieu, Pierre

1990 *The Logic of Practice*. Stanford, CA: Stanford University
      Press.

Brockman, James R.

1989 *Romero: A Life*. Rev. ed. Maryknoll, NY: Orbis.

Brueggemann, Walter

  1978   *The Prophetic Imagination*. Philadelphia: Fortress.

  1993   *Biblical Perspectives on Evangelism: Living in a Three-Storied Universe*. Nashville: Abingdon.

Budde, Michael L., and Robert W. Brimlow

  2002   *Christianity Incorporated: How Big Business Is Buying the Church*. Grand Rapids: Brazos.

Bultmann, Rudolf

  1951   *Theology of the New Testament*. Translated by K. Grobel. New York: Charles Scribner's Sons.

  1961   *Kerygma and Myth: A Theological Debate*. New York: Harper & Brothers.

  1969   *Faith and Understanding*. Translated by Louise Pettibone Smith. Philadelphia: Fortress.

Burce, Jerome E.

  2000   *Proclaiming the Scandal: Reflections on Postmodern Ministry*. Harrisburg, PA: Trinity Press International.

Carnegie, Dale

  1936   *How to Win Friends and Influence People*. New York: Simon & Schuster.

Carter, Craig A.

  2001   *The Politics of the Cross*. Grand Rapids: Brazos.

Castelli, Elizabeth A.

  2004   *Martyrdom and Memory: Early Christian Culture Making*. New York: Columbia University Press.

Cavanaugh, William T.

  1998   *Torture and Eucharist: Theology, Politics, and the Body of Christ*. Oxford: Blackwell.

  2002   *Theopolitical Imagination*. London: T & T Clark.

Certeau, Michel de

  1984   *The Practice of Everyday Life*. Berkeley: University of California Press.

Clapp, Rodney

  2000   *Border Crossings*. Grand Rapids: Brazos.

Coakley, Sarah

  2002   *Powers and Submissions: Spirituality, Philosophy, and Gender*. Oxford: Blackwell.

Comby, Jean
    1982   *How to Read Church History*. Vol. 1. New York:
            Crossroad.

Dennis, Marie, Renny Golden, and Scott Wright
    2000   *Oscar Romero: Reflections on His Life and Writings*. Mary-
            knoll, NY: Orbis.

Doak, Mary
    2004   *Reclaiming Narrative for Public Theology*. Albany: State
            University of New York Press.

Dostoyevsky, Fyodor
    1913   *The Idiot*. Translated by Constance Garnett. London:
            William Heinemann.

Driver, John
    1988   *How Christians Made Peace With War*. Scottdale, PA:
            Herald.

Erickson, John H.
    1999   "Baptism and the Church's Faith." In *Marks of the Body
            of Christ*, edied by Carl E. Braaten and Robert W. Jenson,
            44–58. Grand Rapids: Eerdmans.

Fackre, Gabriel
    1978   *The Christian Story*. Grand Rapids: Eerdmans.

Farley, Edward
    1983   *Theologia: The Fragmentation and Unity of Theological
            Education*. Philadelphia: Fortress.

Finney, Charles G.
    1960   *Lectures on Revivals of Religion*. Cambridge, MA:
            Harvard University Press.

Fodor, James, and Stanley Hauerwas
    2004   "Performing Faith: The Peaceable Rhetoric of God's
            Church." In *Performing the Faith: Bonhoeffer and the
            Practice of Nonviolence*. Grand Rapids: Brazos.

Forde, Gerhard O.
    1999   "The Word That Kills and Makes Alive." In *Marks of the
            Body of Christ*, edited by Carl E. Braaten and Robert W.
            Jenson, 1–12. Grand Rapids: Eerdmans.

Fowl, Stephen E., and L. Gregory Jones
    1997   "Scripture, Exegesis, and Discernment in Christian Eth-
            ics." In *Virtues and Practices in the Christian Tradition:
            Christian Ethics after MacIntyre*, edited by Nancey Mur-

phy, Brad J. Kallenberg, and Mark Thiessen Nation, 111–31. Notre Dame, IN: University of Notre Dame Press.

Freire, Paulo

1983 *Pedagogy of the Oppressed*. New York: Crossroad.

Funk, Robert W.

1996 *Honest to Jesus: Jesus for a New Millenium*. San Francisco: Harper & Row.

Gorringe, Timothy J.

2001 *The Education of Desire*. London: SCM Press.

Grassow, Peter

1998 "John Wesley and Revolution: A South African Perspective." In *Rethinking John Wesley's Theology Today*, 183–96. Nashville: Kingswood.

Guder, Darrell L., ed.

1998 *Missional Church: A Vision for the Sending of the Church in North America*. Grand Rapids: Eerdmans.

Gunter, W. Stephen

1997 "Evangelism as the Heart of Mission: A Response to Dana L. Robert." Mission Evangelism Series 1. New York: General Board of Global Ministries, United Methodist Church.

Gutiérrez, Gustavo

1983 *The Power of the Poor in History: Selected Writings*. Maryknoll, NY: Orbis.

1988 *A Theology of Liberation: History, Politics, and Salvation*. Rev. ed. Maryknoll, NY: Orbis.

Haight, Roger

2004 *Christian Community in History*. Vol. 1. New York: Continuum.

Hanby, Michael

1999 "Augustine beyond Western Subjectivity." In *Radical Orthodoxy*. London: Routledge.

Hauerwas, Stanley

1983 *The Peaceable Kingdom: A Primer in Christian Ethics*. Notre Dame, IN: University of Notre Dame Press.

1991 *After Christendom? How the Church Is to Behave If Freedom, Justice, and a Christian Nation Are Bad Ideas*. Nashville: Abingdon.

1995 *In Good Company: The Church as Polis.* Notre Dame, IN: University of Notre Dame Press.

1998 *Sanctify Them in the Truth: Holiness Exemplified.* Nashville: Abingdon.

2000 *A Better Hope: Resources for a Church Confronting Capitalism, Democracy, and Postmodernity.* Grand Rapids: Brazos.

2001a *The Hauerwas Reader.* Edited by John Berkman and Michael Cartwright. Durham, NC: Duke University Press.

2001b *With the Grain of the Universe: The Church's Witness and Natural Theology.* Grand Rapids: Brazos.

2004 *Performing the Faith: Bonhoeffer and the Practice of Nonviolence.* Grand Rapids: Brazos.

Hauerwas, Stanley, and Charles Pinches

1997 *Christians among the Virtues: Theological Conversations with Ancient and Modern Ethics.* Notre Dame, IN: University of Notre Dame Press.

Hauerwas, Stanley, and William H. Willimon

1989 *Resident Aliens: Life in the Christian Colony.* Nashville: Abingdon.

1992 *Preaching to Strangers: Evangelism in Today's World.* Louisville, KY: Westminster John Knox Press.

Hunter, George G., III

1992 *How to Reach Secular People.* Nashville: Abingdon.

1996 *Church for the Unchurched.* Nashville: Abingdon.

2003 *Radical Outreach.* Nashville: Abingdon.

Hütter, Reinhard

1993 "Ecclesial Ethics, the Church's Vocation, and Paraclesis," *Pro Ecclesia* 2, no. 4 (Fall): 433–50.

2000 *Suffering Divine Things: Theology as Church Practice.* English translation by Doug Stott. Grand Rapids: Eerdmans.

2001 "The Church." In *Knowing the Triune God: The Work of the Spirit in the Practices of the Church*, edited by James J. Buckley and David S. Yeago. Grand Rapids: Eerdmans.

Hybels, Bill, and Mark Mittelberg

1994 *Becoming a Contagious Christian.* Grand Rapids: Zondervan.

Isasi-Díaz, Ada María, and Yolanda Tarango

1992 *Hispanic Women: Prophetic Voice in the Church*. Minneapolis: Augsburg Fortress.

Jewett, Robert

1993 *St. Paul Returns to the Movies*. Louisville, KY: Westminster John Knox Press.

Kallenberg, Brad

1997 "The Master Argument of MacIntyre's *After Virtue*." In *Virtues and Practices in the Christian Tradition: Christian Ethics after MacIntyre*, edited by Nancey Murphy, Brad J. Kallenberg, and Mark Thiessen Nation, 7–29. Notre Dame, IN: University of Notre Dame Press.

2002 *Live to Tell: Evangelism for a Postmodern Age*. Grand Rapids: Brazos.

Kallestad, Walt

1996 *Entertainment Evangelism: Taking the Church Public*. Nashville: Abingdon.

Kant, Immanuel

1993 "What Is Enlightenment?" In *Philosophical Writings*, edited by Ernst Behler. The German Library 13. New York: Crossroad.

Kavanagh, Aidan

1978 *The Shape of Baptism*. New York: Pueblo.

Kenneson, Philip D., and James L. Street

1997 *Selling Out the Church*. Nashville: Abingdon.

Kierkegaard, Søren

1956a *Attack upon "Christendom."* Translated by Walter Lowrie. Boston: Beacon.

1956b *The Prayers of Kierkegaard*. Edited by Perry D. LeFevre. Chicago: University of Chicago Press.

Klaiber, Walter

1997 *Call and Response: Biblical Foundations of a Theology of Evangelism*. Nashville: Abingdon.

Lessing, Gotthold

1956 "On the Proof of the Spirit and of Power." In *Lessing's Theological Writings*, translated by Henry Chadwick. Stanford, CA: Stanford University Press.

Lindbeck, George

1984 *The Nature of Doctrine: Religion and Theology in a Post-liberal Age*. Philadelphia: Westminster Press.

2002 *The Church in a Postliberal Age*. Edited by James J. Buckley. Grand Rapids: Eerdmans.

Lischer, Richard

1999 "Resurrection and Rhetoric." In *Marks of the Body of Christ*, edited by Carl E. Braaten and Robert W. Jenson, 13–24. Grand Rapids: Eerdmans.

Locke, John

1982 *Second Treatise of Government*. Edited by Richard H. Cox. Arlington Heights, IL: Harlan Davidson.

Lodahl, Michael E.

2002 "Creation out of Nothing? Or Is *Next* to Nothing Enough?" In *Thy Nature and Thy Name Is Love: Wesleyan and Process Theologies in Dialogue*, edited by Bryan P. Stone and Thomas Jay Oord, 217–38. Nashville: Kingswood.

2003 *God of Nature and of Grace: Reading the World in a Wesleyan Way*. Nashville: Abingdon.

Lohfink, Gerhard

1984 *Jesus and Community*. Philadelphia: Fortress.

1999 *Does God Need the Church? Toward a Theology of the People of God*. Collegeville, MN: Liturgical.

Long, D. Stephen

2000 *Divine Economy: Theology and the Market*. London: Routledge.

Lose, David J.

2003 *Confessing Jesus Christ: Preaching in a Postmodern World*. Grand Rapids: Eerdmans.

Lowney, Kathleen S.

1999 *Baring Our Souls: TV Talk Shows and the Religion of Recovery*. New York: Aldine de Gruyter.

Luther, Martin

1955–76 *Luther's Works*. Philadelphia: Fortress.

1959 *The Book of Concord*. Translated and edited by Theodore G. Tappert. Philadelphia: Fortress.

MacIntyre, Alasdair
> 1984 *After Virtue.* 2nd ed. Notre Dame, IN: University of Notre Dame Press.
> 1988 *Whose Justice? Which Rationality?* Notre Dame, IN: University of Notre Dame Press.
> 1990 *Three Rival Versions of Moral Enquiry: Encyclopaedia, Genealogy, and Tradition.* Notre Dame, IN: University of Notre Dame Press.
> 1994 "A Partial Response to My Critics." In *After MacIntyre: Critical Perspectives on the Work of Alasdair MacIntyre,* edited by John Horton and Susan Mendus. Notre Dame, IN: University of Notre Dame Press.

Maddox, Randy L.
> 1984 "Responsible Grace: The Systematic Perspective of Wesleyan Theology." *Wesleyan Theological Journal* 19, no. 2: 7–22.
> 1994 *Responsible Grace: John Wesley's Practical Theology.* Nashville: Abingdon.

Mark, Karl
> 1975 "Theses on Feuerbach." In Karl Marx and Frederick Engels, *On Religion,* 62–64. Moscow: Progress.

McClendon, James W., Jr.
> 1986 *Systematic Theology.* 3 vols. Nashville: Abingdon.

McClendon, James W., Jr., and James M. Smith
> 1994 *Convictions: Diffusing Religious Relativism.* Rev. ed. Harrisburg, PA: Trinity Press International.

Meeks, Wayne
> 1983 *The First Urban Christians: The Social World of the Apostle Paul.* New Haven, CT: Yale University Press.

Meredith, Anthony
> 1999 *Gregory of Nyssa.* London: Routledge.

Metz, Johann Baptiste
> 1980 *Faith in History and Society: Toward a Practical Fundamental Theology.* Translated by David Smith. New York: Seabury.

Michalson, Carl
> 2002 "Communicating the Gospel." In *The Company of Preachers: Wisdom on Preaching, Augustine to the Present,* edited by Richard Lischer, 38–45. Grand Rapids: Eerdmans.

Milbank, John

   1990   *Theology and Social Theory: Beyond Secular Reason*.
          Oxford: Blackwell.

Milbank, John, Catherine Pickstock, and Graham Ward

   1999   *Radical Orthodoxy*. London: Routledge.

Mittelberg, Mark

   1998   Interview in "Evangelism That Flows." *Leadership*,
          Summer, 22–30.

Moltmann, Jürgen

   1967   *Theology of Hope*. New York: Harper & Row.

   1983   *The Power of the Powerless*. San Francisco: Harper &
          Row.

Murphy, Nancey, Brad J. Kallenberg, and Mark Thiessen Nation,
eds.

   1997   *Virtues and Practices in the Christian Tradition: Christian
          Ethics after MacIntyre*. Notre Dame, IN: University of
          Notre Dame Press.

Musurillo, Herbert, ed. and trans.

   1972   *The Acts of the Christian Martyrs*. Oxford: Clarendon
          Press.

Nestingen, James

   2005   "Authority and Resistance in the ELCA." *Word Alone Net-
          work*, www.wordalone.org/docs/wa-authority-resistance-
          elca.htm.

Newbigin, Lesslie

   1995   *The Open Secret*. Rev. ed. Grand Rapids: Eerdmans.

Ogden, Schubert M.

   1961   *Christ without Myth: A Study Based on the Theology of
          Rudolf Bultmann*. Dallas: Southern Methodist University
          Press.

   1982   *The Point of Christology*. San Francisco: Harper & Row.

   1985   "Rudolf Bultmann and the Future of Revisionary Chris-
          tology." In *Bultmann: Retrospect and Prospect*, edited by
          Edward C. Hobbs, 35–58. Philadelphia: Fortress.

Outler, Albert C.

   1971   *Evangelism in the Wesleyan Spirit*. Nashville: Tidings.

Pannenberg, Wolfhart

   1968   *Jesus—God and Man*. Philadelphia: Westminster Press.

Park, Joon-Sik

2006 "John Howard Yoder as a Mission Theologian." *International Bulletin of Missionary Research* 30, no. 1: 14–17.

Pohl, Christine

1999 *Making Room: Recovering Hospitality as a Christian Tradition*. Grand Rapids: Eerdmans.

Polanyi, Michael

1967 *The Tacit Dimension*. New York: Anchor.

Pui-Lan, Kwok

2005 *Postcolonial Imagination and Feminist Theology*. Louisville, KY: Westminster John Knox.

Rahner, Karl

1981 *A Rahner Reader*. Edited by Gerald A. McCool. New York: Crossroad.

Reno, R. R.

2002 *In the Ruins of the Church: Sustaining Faith in an Age of Diminished Christianity*. Grand Rapids: Brazos.

Robert, Dana

1997 "Evangelism as the Heart of Mission." Mission Evangelism Series 1. New York: General Board of Global Ministries, United Methodist Church.

Roberts, Alexander, and James Donaldson, eds.

1931 *The Ante-Nicene Fathers*. Grand Rapids: Eerdmans.

Romero, Oscar

1985 *Voice of the Voiceless: The Four Pastoral Letters and Other Statements*. Maryknoll, NY: Orbis.

2004 *The Violence of Love*. Compiled and translated by James R. Brockman. Maryknoll, NY: Orbis.

Roxburgh, Alan J.

1997 *The Missionary Congregation, Leadership, and Liminality*. Harrisburg, PA: Trinity Press International.

Ruether, Rosemary Radford

1983 *To Change the World: Christology and Cultural Criticism*. New York: Crossroad.

Russell, Letty M.

1978 "Liberation and Evangelization—A Feminist Perspective," *Occasional Bulletin of Missionary Research* 2:128–30.

1993   *Church in the Round: Feminist Interpretation of the Church*. Louisville, KY: Westminster John Knox.

Schaff, Philip and Henry Wace, eds.

1955   *Nicene and Post-Nicene Fathers*. 2nd series. Grand Rapids: Eerdmans.

Schleiermacher, Friedrich

1958   *On Religion: Speeches to Its Cultured Despisers*. Translated by John Oman. New York: Harper & Row.

Schmemann, Alexander

1997   *For the Life of the World: Sacraments and Orthodoxy*. Revised ed. Crestwood, NY: St. Vladimir's Seminary Press.

Segundo, Juan Luis

1985   *The Historical Jesus of the Synoptics*. Vol. 2 of *Jesus of Nazareth: Yesterday and Today*. Edited and translated by John Drury. Maryknoll, NY: Orbis.

1987   *The Christ of the Ignatian Exercises*. Vol. 4 of *Jesus of Nazareth: Yesterday and Today*. Edited and translated by John Drury. Maryknoll, NY: Orbis.

1988   *An Evolutionary Approach to Jesus of Nazareth*. Vol. 5 of *Jesus of Nazareth: Yesterday and Today*. Edited and translated by John Drury. Maryknoll, NY: Orbis.

Smart, Barry

1993   *Post-modernity*. London: Routledge.

Smith, Christian

1998   *American Evangelicalism: Embattled and Thriving*. Chicago: University of Chicago Press.

Sobrino, Jon

2000   *Archbishop Romero: Memories and Reflections*. Maryknoll, NY: Orbis.

Starkloff, Carl F.

1997   "Church as Structure and Communitas: Victor Turner and Ecclesiology." *Theological Studies* 58:643–68.

Stone, Bryan

1994   *Effective Faith: A Critical Study of the Christology of Juan Luis Segundo*. Lanham, MD: University Press of America.

Stringfellow, William

1994   *A Keeper of the Word: Selected Writings of William Stringfellow*. Edited by Bill Wylie Kellerman. Grand Rapids: Eerdmans.

Swedish, Margaret, and Lee Miller

1992 *A Message Too Precious to Be Silenced*. Washington, DC: Religious Task Force on Central America and Mexico.

Tanner, Kathryn

1997 *Theories of Culture: A New Agenda for Theology*. Minneapolis: Augsburg Fortress.

Taylor, Charles

1989 *Sources of the Self: The Making of the Modern Identity*. Cambridge, MA: Harvard University Press.

2004 *Modern Social Imaginaries*. Durham, NC: Duke University Press.

Vogt, Christopher

2004 *Patience, Compassion, Hope, and the Christian Art of Dying Well*. Oxford: Rowman and Littlefield.

Volf, Miroslav

1996 *Exclusion and Embrace: A Theological Exploration of Identity, Otherness, and Reconciliation*. Nashville: Abingdon.

Walls, Andrew F.

1990 "The Translation Principle in Christian History." In *Bible Translation and the Spread of the Church: The Last Two Hundred Years*, edited by P. C. Stine, 24–39. New York: Brill.

Webb, Stephen H.

2004 *The Divine Voice: Christian Proclamation and the Theology of Sound*. Grand Rapids: Brazos.

Webb-Mitchell, Brent

2003 *Christly Gestures: Learning to Be Members of the Body of Christ*. Grand Rapids: Eerdmans.

Wesley, John

1931 *The Letters of the Rev. John Wesley, A.M.* Edited by John Telford. 8 vols. London: Epworth.

1979 *The Works of John Wesley*. Jackson ed. Kansas City, MO: Beach Hill.

1975– *The Works of John Wesley*. Begun as Oxford Edition of the Works of John Wesley. Oxford: Clarendon, 1975–83. Continued as Bicentennial Edition of the Works of John Wesley. Nashville: Abingdon.

Wittgenstein, Ludwig

> 1953 *Philosophical Investigations.* Translated by G. E. M. Anscombe. New York: Macmillan.

World Council of Churches (WCC)

> 1967 *The Church for Others: Two Reports on the Missionary Structure of the Congregation.* Geneva: World Council of Churches.

Yeago, David S.

> 1999 "The Office of the Keys." In *Marks of the Body of Christ,* edited by Carl E. Braaten and Robert W. Jenson, 95–122. Grand Rapids: Eerdmans.

Yoder, John Howard

> 1964 *The Christian Witness to the State.* Newton, KS: Faith and Life.

> 1972 *The Politics of Jesus.* Grand Rapids: Eerdmans.

> 1984 *The Priestly Kingdom.* Notre Dame, IN: University of Notre Dame Press.

> 1992a *Body Politics: Five Practices of the Christian Community before the Watching World.* Scottdale, PA: Herald.

> 1992b "On Not Being Ashamed of the Gospel: Particularity, Pluralism, and Validation." *Faith and Philosophy* 9, no. 3: 285–300.

> 1997 *For the Nations: Essays Public and Evangelical.* Grand Rapids: Eerdmans.

> 1998 *The Royal Priesthood: Essays Ecumenical and Ecclesiological.* Scottsdale, PA: Herald.

> 2003 *The Jewish-Christian Schism Revisited.* Edited by Michael G. Cartwright and Peter Ochs. Grand Rapids: Eerdmans.

Zizioulas, John

> 1997 *Being as Communion: Studies in Personhood and the Church.* Crestwood, NY: St. Vladimir's Seminary Press.

Index